EX LIBRIS
TSM

WALKING
ON THE WATER

To Tom.
With affection to the
honoured President
of the International
Editors' League of Hope

Hugh Cudlipp.
1976.

WALKING
ON THE WATER

HUGH CUDLIPP

THE BODLEY HEAD
LONDON SYDNEY
TORONTO

TO JODI AND EILEEN
and all the labourers in
the vineyard of Fleet Street,
including the Proprietors
and Lord Goodman

© Hugh Cudlipp 1976
ISBN 0 370 11313 6
Printed and bound in Great Britain for
The Bodley Head Ltd
9 Bow Street, London WC2E 7AL
by William Clowes & Sons Ltd
London, Beccles and Colchester
Set in Monophoto Plantin
First published 1976

CONTENTS

Introduction

PART I

DEATH BEFORE LIFE

1 Lloyd George Didn't Know My Father, 13
2 My Redeemer Liveth, 33

PART II

THE TURBULENT NEWSPAPERS

3 The Glorious Gamble, 49
4 A Noisy Conspiracy of Silence, 69
5 'Editor: Private', 81
6 The Change of Winds, 91
7 Lloyd George: Pétain in Waiting?, 104
8 Carpeted–by the War Cabinet, 114

PART III

THE QUILL BAYONET

9 'Get into that ——— truck!' 141
10 Newspapers, Always Bloody Newspapers, 147

PART IV

THE STORMS BEFORE THE STORM

11 Sword of Damocles, 171
12 The Demon Beaver, 186
13 Australia Rediscovered, 195
14 Fighting the Elections, 206
15 In Court. In Prison, 231
16 Wooing the Readers, 242
17 The Sun that Didn't Rise, 246

PART V

A MAN OF DESTINY

18 Chaste Minerva, 257
19 The Humble Seeker after Knowledge, 272
20 The Duel, 291
21 Coalition–or a New Regime?, 308
22 'Enough is Enough', 328
23 'Regicide in London', 348
24 Fascinating Myths, 371
25 The Tall Leprechaun, 383

PART VI

END STORY

26 'The Unpardonable Vanity', 401

Acknowledgements, 417

Index, 419

David Lloyd George was a neighbour of Lord Beaverbrook in the countryside of Surrey.

He called at Cherkley Court near Leatherhead, where Max Beaverbrook lived, to consult his friend about a current political conspiracy.

'Is the lord at home?' he asked the butler.

'No, sir, the lord is out walking.'

'Ah,' said Lloyd George, 'on the water, I presume.'

INTRODUCTION

This book, I can promise you, is not a portentous autobiography, still less an apologia. I believe that Editors and publishers should not take themselves or anybody else too seriously. Nor is it a history or, God forbid, a documentary. I am a reporter, an observer, a listener, a raconteur, not an historian.

What it is, I suppose, is one Editor's idiosyncratic view of our times and of some of the people, giants or gnomes, pompous or human, intelligent or silly, who tried and on the whole failed to dominate events.

It is at any rate a true story, and it is unembittered by some of the experiences, such as a salutary sacking to mention but one, which obliged me at times to move to fresh pastures through necessity rather than ambition or the need of new scenery.

Walking on the Water is about how newspaper publishers and other public performers behave behind the scenes. About balancing feats, not balance sheets. The standard literary reference work on union aggro, mergers, and management magic or madness will be written, and I trust read, by somebody else.

I have avoided cosmetics, and therefore any person mentioned in this book who appears to be fictional, like Harry Guy Bartholomew, did in fact–or does–exist.

There are many sightings in the early chapters of this story of the lonely, self-tortured soul of Cecil Harmsworth King. His status as Northcliffe's Nephew burdened him with enough problems, but he created others of his own, notably a reluctance to join the human race and an ambition in later years to direct its affairs. He has now retired from his ivory tower in Holborn Circus to a bungalow in the environs of Dublin, from whence he emerged. I write of him with affection and I miss him. I decided that the public fascination with this particular personality and his personal duels with Prime Ministers and other politicians, called for a clinical study in the final section, entitled 'A Man of Destiny'. Sir Harold Wilson's agreement to quotations from his personal record of *The Labour Government, 1964–70*, published by Weidenfeld & Nicolson and Michael Joseph, enables me to disclose at appropriate moments the thinking in No. 10 Downing Street.

I thank the friends who read the manuscript and helped me to keep the record straight and fair.

I am grateful to Times Newspapers Ltd for their permission to quote from two books by Cecil King in which they hold the copyright, *Strictly Personal*, published by Weidenfeld & Nicolson in 1969, and *With Malice Toward None*, published by Sidgwick & Jackson in 1970. The first of these books, in particular, contains the sole evidence of the inner thoughts of its author, notably of his early life and sterner struggles. Acknowledgements are also made to the author of *The Cecil King Diary, 1965–70* and *1970–74* and to his publishers Jonathan Cape for extracts from those books. The keepers of the *Daily Mirror* archives have been most helpful, and the research by Anthony Miles into that newspaper's performance in general elections, ranging from pro-Tory to pro-Labour, was a useful confirmation of my memories.

H. C.
1976

I

DEATH
BEFORE LIFE

----◆◆◆----

Lloyd George Didn't Know My Father

The problem is not life after death, a notion I still regard as absurd, but life before death. That is urgent, real and earnest. I shall follow the course charted by Graham Greene: 'There is a fashion today among many of my contemporaries to treat the events of their past with irony. It is a legitimate method of self-defence. "Look how absurd I was when I was young" forestalls cruel criticism, but it falsifies history . . . Those emotions were real when we felt them. Why should we be more ashamed of them than of the indifference of old age?'

The Order of the Bath at 118 Lisvane Street, Cathays, Cardiff was immutable when we were children. First our sister Phyllis, the youngest and therefore the cleanest and sweetest; then my elder brother Percy, the future Editor of Lord Beaverbrook's Tory *Evening Standard*, of the Labour *Daily Herald*, and finally of the *New Scientist*; then my brother Reg, Editor of the *News of the World* from 1953 to 1959; then me, by which time the water no longer resembled ass's milk. The mass baptism of the three Editors was in no sense unique because it took place every Saturday night before the coal fire in the kitchen. A pen-and-ink drawing of David Lloyd George framed in passe-partout surveyed the domestic scene.

Lloyd George did not know my father. Father did not know Lloyd George. Father's No. 3 son knew both. Readers who are not interested in people until they become a social menace, or a menace to a particular attitude to society, should skip the next 32 pages and begin at Chapter 3. They will, however, be missing significant clues.

It was in the kitchen that my inferiority complex first developed. In bathing order the kids were aged one, ten, six and three or thereabouts when the Saturday night ritual was abandoned, no doubt because of the cautious attitude in those innocent times to sexual awareness. The zinc bath was topped up during the ceremony by my mother, carrying a cast-iron kettle from the bubbling copper boiler in the scullery. Father, with sleeves rolled up and wearing braces, applied the red Lifebuoy soap ('Kills Germs'), with a flannel on the tender skin of baby sister, with his hands for my brothers and a scrubbing brush for me, neither the youngest nor the oldest but always last in the queue. If Napoleon or Wellington had been cut down to that size the world might never have heard of them.

During the breaks between topping up the bath, mother presided over the ceremony from her rocking chair, knitting, with a romantic novel on her lap. Her spectacles dawdled on the tip of her nose and her false teeth were 'at ease', and occasionally she looked up with approval at her children or affection at her husband, or both.

They called each other Bessie and Willie. He was a kindly soul, a big man with rosy cheeks without a whiff of envy or malevolence, forever optimistic and grateful for the mercies and pleasures life afforded him. He was a commercial traveller in eggs and bacon, journeying by train every day wet or fine from Taff Vale Station or Cardiff Central to the towns in the Welsh Valleys with his order book and umbrella, a new carnation in his button-hole. The flower nestled in a metal container which held a small amount of water to keep it fresh until Willie's return in the evening from Bridgend, Merthyr Tydfil, Llanelly, Caerphilly or Llanbradach, or wherever they were short of eggs and bacon and hopefully had the wherewithal to buy them.

The drawing of David Lloyd George was not the sole example of art at No. 118. There were photographs more expensively framed in bevelled mahogany of the Holy Sepulchre, the Mount of Olives, the Garden of Gethsemane, Nazareth and similar scenes of early Christian events and mythology which Willie had collected in the Middle East as an army canteen corporal. The other pious momentoes were a family Bible bound in olive wood, with the Cross ornately and deeply engraved, and a set of apostle teaspoons used only on Sundays. An Arab street vendor flogged them to him at the quayside in Port Said as he boarded the ship to go home. He polished them as heirlooms, unaware that they were available at a cheaper price and better quality in Woolworths in St Mary Street. At the end of World War Two, Cassandra and I took home from Italy a set of pottery mugs painted and kilned by the Franciscan friars in Assisi, but I suppose to others they were as tawdry as the apostle spoons.

The only time I recall my father in an angry mood was when I swopped the Bible for a ginger guinea-pig at Mr Cork's pet shop in City Road. 'It smells,' said Bessie, 'we don't want vermin here.' Mr Cork's doubts arose after I departed with my prize in a cardboard box with breathing holes bored in the top. He returned the book to the 'W. Cudlipp, 118 Lisvane Street, Cardiff' whose identity was written on the title page and took my guinea-pig back to the shop. I was playing in the street as this further barter was taking place and when I reported for tea was disturbed to see the Bible back in its place on the bookshelf. A visit to the outside WC confirmed that the ginger guinea-pig had vanished from its box. There was no clouting or bawling out, but my parents did not speak to me for several days. The punishment of the angry silence was unbearable, but my theft was never mentioned.

Bessie Amelia Kinsman was the daughter of a handsome bolt-upright docks policeman who later joined us to die in the middle room. She was volatile, impulsive, a tireless raconteur who could create an Othellian tragedy or a Ben Travers comedy from fragile over-the-wall gossip and routine family material. The bundle of nervous energy was packaged in a short trim figure, usually clothed in a skirt and satin blouse-and-bow meticulously laundered, topped with a perm renewed as frequently as the housekeeping money would run to, or more often. The message was coquettish, equably dispensed to the milkman and the baker who knocked on the door, and more than equably when bargaining with the bronzed French onion-men who parked their bicycles on the edge of the pavement. The only dialogue mutually understood was 'Too dear'.

To the delight of the neighbours or her brothers, dropping in on their cycles for a social call, she would mimic at some length Her Majesty Queen Mary, stately and stiff-backed but nonchalantly flapping her gloved hand in acknowledgement of the plaudits of the Cardiff crowd, having no doubt at all that she could play the role equally well or better. She specialised in the local scoop, acting each part. One of her stories, a throw-away merely to warm up the audience over the teacups, was of how she nursed me as a 'dying' baby back to health. 'And,' the story ended before she adjusted her mood and style for the next item in her repertoire, 'do you know what the doctor told me in the presence of Willie?' The pause was sustained with a theatrical effect which Edith Evans would not have scorned. 'He told me, and Willie was there, that if he had won the VC he would have pinned it on my breast:' breast, not blouse. The neighbours and relatives enjoyed her because she was the life and soul of the party without the aid of gin in a street where there were no parties. I heard people say that if she had been educated she would have been a formidable woman.

On Sunday mornings Bessie and Willie (there was never any doubt about the order of billing) ushered their brood on the trek to Roath Park lake, the boys in their pressed sailor suits heading the convoy. We were often overtaken on these walks by Mr Holloway, homing on the Conservative Club because the *Flora* like other pubs in Wales was bolted and barred on Sundays. Father doffed his grey trilby hat and said, 'Nice day, Mr Holloway' or 'Looks like rain, Mr Holloway,' but Bessie averted her eyes or tossed her head ostentatiously to express her distaste. On the return journey from Roath Park lake two hours later we often met up again with Mr Holloway, lurching from one side of the pavement to the other, muttering and spluttering and ignoring his neighbours, rolling home to vomit over his Sunday lunch, a journey he sometimes failed to complete in time. Our home was teetotal, not a drop in the house, even medicinal, so the brood were accelerated past the degrading spectacle of Mr H., our parents suddenly talking to us to divert our attention. Not that much escaped the three born reporters then or thereafter.

When we were children my older brothers excluded me from their confidences, trivial as they were, and conducted their dialogue in a conspiratorial gobbledegook beyond my comprehension: I was the fall guy but never certain why. I remember the simulated rows between them when they were breaking the economy maxims that applied in No. 118, in particular the order that we could have bread and butter, *or* bread and jam, but never bread and butter *and* jam. Reg was the *maître d'hôtel*. I heard the dialogue many times:

Percy: You fool, I said B and J not B, B and J. And you've
added cream as well.
Reg: Sorry.
Percy: Look, you ass, you've done it again, but don't for
heaven's sake add the cream. They might come back
before we've finished.

The end product was that while the Editor of the *Daily Herald* would be munching B B J and C, the Editor of the *News of the World* B B and J, I the future Editor of the *Sunday Pictorial*, would have to settle for B and B or B and J. The charade was presented as an elaborate mistake, but when it was my turn they always seemed to get it right. Boys have grown into bank robbers for less than that and it was greatly to my credit that I developed nothing worse than a suspicious nature–a useful weapon in the armoury of a journalist.

There was another refined form of torture imposed by Reginald: at difficult moments of the day like 4.26 or seventeen minutes to seven he asked me the time, which he knew was beyond my expertise. He denounced me as an oaf, to which my only reply was to race towards him, emitting a banshee wail, with the four legs of a chair pointed at his chest and often making savage contact. Mother was afraid I would turn out to be the violent one, but I suspected she was morally on my side.

The people who lived in our part of Cardiff would have resented the designation of working class but settled happily for lower middle class if the 'lower' were deleted. All human life was there (the boast of the *News of the World*) in Lisvane Street, pride and prejudice, energy and sloth, aspiration and defeatism, even–with the exception of Mr Holloway–sobriety, but not poverty. My first encounter with social taboos, with racial differences but not discrimination, with religion and politics and unemployment, took place in and around the terraced houses. Hundreds and hundreds of them of uniform design in rows facing each other, with garden patches at the back divided by a parallel three-yard lane from the garden patches at the back of the houses in Brithdir Street; upstairs three bedrooms, downstairs two rooms plus kitchen and scullery. With four kids you were playing to full capacity.

We were not in those days the orphans of the Permissive Age: sex was a rumour rather than a subject on the school curriculum with diagrams and coloured slides. The first tangible information came from my friend Bryn who surprised his sister in the bathroom and passed on to the gang a breathless and inarticulate report on pubic hair. His exit from the bathroom was so abrupt that he had no time to monitor any other information. I conducted my own initial studies among the Medical shelves of a second-hand bookshop in Duke Street, on the side which was later demolished so that the citizens could view the splendour of Cardiff Castle. When the bookseller passed by on his tour to look out for thieves I guiltily hopped over to Geography and History. The Grecian statues in the National Museum in the civic centre yielded a few more cold clues, but we were slow learners. When small girls wore a bandage on their leg (some first-aid treatment for an insect sting) I suspected it was something to do with menstruation, whatever that might be. We were able to confirm some of our theories by a clinical examination of Trevor Jones's cousin from Bridgend who came every year to spend a holiday with her Cardiff relatives. When we were surprised in our research by the unexpected arrival of Mr Osborne, a local busybody, the gang dispersed leaving the little girl on her own, crying. I did not sleep that night, dreading a knock on the front door from Mr Osborne with a report of the goings-on. We settled for the concept that though our parents didn't do it, other people's parents probably did but the Royal Family certainly did not. When the gang, observing two copulating horses on the Marquess of Bute's estate, were surprised by the sudden appearance of Willie, I was extracted from the scene and marched home shamefully six feet in front of him and on that occasion I was clouted and denounced as 'dirty-minded'.

Bessie was careless with her housekeeping money, leaving stacks of change on the sideboard or on the mantelpiece between two brass shells, souvenirs from World War One. Her sons were the best customers for everlasting liquorice sticks and gobstoppers at the corner shop. What astonished us years later, when we confessed over a drink in Fleet Street that as children we had been unilaterally raiding the same slender bank, was that the size of the massed haul passed undetected by our trusting parents. Nor did the pennies distributed to the two younger brothers before we set out for Sunday School at the Wesleyan Methodist Chapel often reach the collecting box: we were customers of some standing at the only sweet shop open on the Sabbath in Crwys Road. The moral question for us was Bassett's Liquorice All-sorts for the well-nourished Cudlipp kids, or aid for the unidentified little black boys of Zanzibar or, for that matter, Christian missions in China?

It was in Sunday School that I first found myself in conflict with the Establishment, or at any rate with the established notions of my elders. There was a hint of insolent disbelief about my questions, a lack of reverence towards the teachers, and the venerable Mr Francis– not the original Saint, but saintly none the less–expressed his concern to Willie at morning service more than once about my waywardness. The trouble was that I had read some parts of *The Origin of Species* and *The Descent of Man*, or as much of them as I could pretend to understand, and Charles Darwin's theory of the evolution of species by natural selection appealed to me as more credible than the fairy tale in *Genesis* about Adam and Eve and the Serpent. The distaste Mr Francis felt towards me began in the class when he said, 'Man from monkeys? What nonsense.' I smugly pointed out that Darwin had not suggested that man had descended from apes but that apes and man, including Mr Francis, had both evolved from a common anthropoid ancestor. I didn't really know what I was talking about; nor did Mr Francis.

He was a kindly man with a white beard and a quavering voice who told us stories with a high moral content. They always ended with, 'And the consequence was, that man (or boy) saw the light and came to the Lord.' I remember his blood-curdling tale of the experience of his nephew who foolishly went swimming in a river in Africa until his left leg was removed by a passing crocodile: the lad saw the light and came to the Lord. Our giggles offended Mr Francis and the consequence was that my friend Bob Williams and I were promoted to the class held by Mr Massey, a younger man of evangelical zeal but a stronger disciplinarian. Bob, who is now the Secretary and Solicitor of the South Wales Electricity Board (*Bwrdd Trydan de Cymru*), has recollections of our escapades and of my unaccountable rudeness in that Sunday School:

'The young Cudlipp stood clearly forth as a dangerous and subversive heretic. Mr Massey told us a story about a Birmingham chain-maker who lay dying, and in his extremity could think of nothing better than to send for Mr Massey. The man was gazing with feverish eyes at a picture of a racing pigeon he had once owned which had won many races. Mr Massey took in the scene at a glance. "I strode up to the wall and ripped down the picture of the pigeon and put up a picture of Our Lord," he said. Here he paused for effect, and I think we were all impressed–except Hugh. Taking advantage of the pause, he asked in a piping treble, "Mr Massey, what do you think of the Theory of Evolution?" At that time, in orthodox Methodist circles Darwin's theories were still held to be anathema. The question caused a wave of horror through the Sunday School.

'That he was a marked boy thereafter was proved a few Sundays later when in the temporary absence of Mr Massey we were attached to the class of Mr Hussey. He was a man with black hair, a black moustache, and bright black eyes. He taught the older boys in an eerie cavern beneath the main hall lit by a fantail gas burner. He was primed about the young heretic attached to his class, and Mr Hussey decided to strike first. We were hardly seated before he came up to Hugh and said in a deep voice, "I can see the devil in your face. Cast him out, my boy."

'It was impressive. The fantail burner flickered, Mr Hussey's black eyes gleamed and for ten minutes even Hugh was silenced, until Mr Hussey began to pray. He stood in the middle of the room and instead of closing his eyes, despatched the bright black pupils to an upper region of his head leaving only the whites visible and rolling–a fearsome sight.

'Hugh began to make some whispered and irreverent comments to me. Mr Hussey paused in his prayer, and then, without turning his head, raised his arm and pointed at Hugh and said, "There's a boy over there backsliding. Strike him, O Lord."

'Nothing happened, and so we decided after all that man was descended from the ape. At the time it seemed to be the answer to everything.'

The crunch came when I doubted the authenticity of the Miracles, an attitude which Mr Hussey regarded as the profoundest of heresies. Did he really believe that the tempest had been stilled? Was it conceivable that Lazarus was raised from the dead? And was the miracle of the loaves and fishes a likely story? And the casting out of the devil from the dumb demoniac? Water into wine at the wedding feast at Cana? The gift of sight to the man born blind? How was Mr Hussey or I to know that in 1947 I would be serialising in a national newspaper *The Rise of Christianity* by Bishop Barnes or in 1964 *Honest to God* by John Robinson, then Bishop of Woolwich, two books which proclaimed with theological erudition the same doubts which had impishly occurred to me in Sunday School?

A source of income arose which was less reprehensible than Bessie's handbag, the small change on the mantelpiece, and Sunday School collection. Mr Belman, patriarch of the Jewish family who lived opposite in Lisvane Street, asked me if I would perform a small service in his house on Saturday mornings, the day the Jew is forbidden to work. I said I would ask my mother: 'Oh, yes,' said Mr Belman, 'please do that, do ask your mother, of course.' He was in search of a *shabbus goy*, a Sabbath Christian.

On my first mission Bessie observed each step with mistrust from her observation post in the front room, a slit between the green venetian blind easily opened or closed at the flick of a finger. From this conning-tower she would announce to my father on Sundays that 'Alec and Mary are a nice couple, aren't they? I think they'll marry. Mrs Jenkins says they'll have to;' or, in a whisper, 'Mr Holloway is drunk again, can hardly walk. I hope he doesn't mistake our house for his again.' To her horror Mr Holloway had once crashed into our middle room late at night in the absence of Willie, who was commercially travelling.

I returned from Mr Belman's with an invitation to go back after sunset for my sixpence.

'What did he give you that for?'

'Turning on the gas stove and lighting it, and putting on the lights, that's all. He said the Jews can't do things like that on Saturdays.'

'Better ask your father if you can go again. What's it like inside the house? You must have kept your eyes open.'

'Mr Belman wears a funny hat on the back of his head. He gave me this packet of unleavened bread, too.'

Mr Belman was generous. He opened the bedroom window and threw a silver coin to the pavement whenever the unemployed miners strolled at a melancholy pace up the street singing *Sospan Fach* or *Guide me, O,* or *Men of Harlech,* carrying a board saying 'Wife and Children to Support', hollering in unison with their necks fully stretched and their heads close together like howling wolves: they had plenty to howl about and Mr Belman understood.

The unpopular wife in the district, solely because of her enterprise and ambition, was Mrs Price of Gelligaer Street, at right angles to Lisvane Street. You could see her front window from our back garden if you stood on a box, and it was from this vantage point that Bessie first observed an announcement pinned to Mrs Price's venetian blinds. I was despatched to see what was written on the board and ran back with the news.

'Faggots and peas.'

'Faggots and peas?'

'Yes, faggots and peas.'

'Well, I never. Faggots and peas. I must tell your father.' Then Mrs Jenkins of No. 120 and Mrs Lewis of No. 116 were consulted over the back garden wall: it was apparent even to the children that Mrs Price was letting down the neighbourhood and could not have caused more consternation if she had opened a brothel. Faggots and peas! It wasn't long before Mrs Price's tasty dish appeared weekly on the menu of No. 118, twice weekly when she added Pies. Within a few years Mrs Price had made enough pin-money to buy the corner shop on a mortgage from Mrs Beer, but the indolent wives who thrived on her industry and fed their families on her faggots never forgave Mrs Price for lowering the tone. Faggots and peas, whatever next? The

shop is now owned by Mr and Mrs Malik and their family of en-
trancing Pakistani children.

We were not confined to Lisvane Street. There were annual
holidays to the boarding-house at Barry Dock, a mile from the sand
at Barry Island but cheaper than the establishments claiming a sea
view, or to the farmhouse at Southerndown near Porthcawl in a
hired car laden to the Plimsoll line, usually delayed by tyre-bursts on
the way.

Once a year there was the Saturday trip to Weston-super-Mare or
Ilfracombe or Minehead in one of the P. & O. paddle-steamers, the
Cardiff Queen or the *Bristol Queen*. The singing of the Welsh miners
who had dug the coal to drive the ship could be heard from the bars
throughout the journey and I wandered as close as I dared to the scene
of revelry. The *Queens* are no longer with us: *Westward Ho* and
Balmoral have taken their place with diesel and propellers.

There was also the occasional Sunday treat in Uncle Theo's
Crossley to the beauty spots–the Wye Valley, Tintern Abbey, and
Symond's Yat from which they told us you could see five or six
counties. The climax of these special days was a picnic with cucumber
sandwiches and chocolate cake and cold ham and tongue and ice-
cream and raspberries and paper cups and forks and corned beef and
orangeade and salad and mayonnaise and Lea & Perrin's and paper
napkins and wasps and ants. We were warned by Bessie in advance
not to overpraise the feast or gobble it up as if we were starving. 'You
all make it look as if you never have anything at home.'

Gladstone Elementary School is a red-brick Victorian edifice overlooking the tombstones in Cardiff Cemetery: the pupils of successive
generations, contemplating the sombre view from the upper windows,
may not have known where they were going, or by what means and
with what result in material terms or happiness, but they could have
no reasonable doubt that they would end up eight feet below a bunch
of daffodils in an earthenware pot, a name on a marble slab. A number
of relatives were buried there. Some hatefully forgotten. Some
joyously remembered with tulips and anemones and hyacinths in
springtime. Others, with more dubious domestic records, acknowledged as gone for ever with a bunch of dahlias or chrysanthemums in
the autumn.

'The Elementary' was to me a formidable and soulless establishment. It was no blackboard jungle then, nor is it now. It has never been the sort of school where teachers are teased or cheeked or bullied or flick-knifed. But the regime of Mr Bill Barrett, the headmaster I met on a re-visit this year, is far more uninhibited than I endured. It is now a friendly building profusely decorated with the wild, fresh paintings and sketches by the children, with the black kids as happy as the rest. Mr Trewatha, who presided in my time, was an austere ramrod figure who was an expert at locating the tender spot with his cane. He would select the weapon with steely deliberation from his collection according to the enormity of the crime before he issued the command 'Bend down' to the rebel. Mr Trewatha was in charge.

I remember the day the histrionic Bessie, returning from a shopping spree in Crwys Road, waved and waved at me from the school railings until I reluctantly waved back from the third row during a solemn school parade in the playground before the headmaster; I was rebuked and mildly punished and had the greatest difficulty in restraining her from personally complaining to the school the next day. 'Why shouldn't you wave to your mother?'

There was the momentous day when the Elementary was visited by four professional musicians—two violins, viola and cello—to play Schubert's chamber music to those who volunteered to stay behind after school hours. I stayed and then I ran and leapt and gurgled the whole mile home without touching the pavement, up Gelligaer Street and into the back garden of 118. I said nothing all the evening and couldn't eat; they thought I was sickening for a fever. It was the first time I heard music 'live'. Until that day our experience of music, later a family malaise, was guided by multi-scratched HMV gramophone records borrowed by my brother Percy from Mrs Banwell of Gelligaer Street: *Roses of Picardy*, the *Peer Gynt Suite*, the first movement of Schubert's Unfinished, *The Laughing Vicar* and the Hallelujah Chorus. He was dismayed one day to find Mrs Banwell washing them with a brush and soap in hot water.

School for me was otherwise a joyless purgatory, but it was nobody's fault except my own that everything I learned I harvested outside the walls of 'Gladstone' and of Howard Gardens Secondary School. Life began at twelve, though there were two more years to serve in prison.

At twelve I frequently heard Pastor Jeffreys at the Big Tent Mission in the evenings. 'It is not I who am waiting,' he said, with his left hand on his heart and the Bible held aloft in his right, 'it is Christ who is waiting. Are there any more who want to give themselves to Him tonight? We shall sing another hymn while Jesus waits. Are there any more?' A cripple hobbled down the gangway followed by two old ladies. 'Any more? Jesus is patient. Do not come to Him tonight unless you have the faith and courage to make up your mind.' A pious drunk and a black man came forward. 'There is no colour bar, my friend, in the Kingdom of Heaven,' the evangelist intoned. I had seen the black man saved several times at previous meetings and wondered if he was in the touring cast or on the establishment, helping to erect and dismantle the Big Tent. My Sunday School suspicions were confirmed. And reconfirmed some years later when the Pastor was performing at Blackpool where I happened to be a reporter.

There were other things I learned at twelve.

The *Flora* was the public house on a corner of Cathays Terrace, opposite Mr Wah Kee's Chinese laundry. It then had swing doors like the cowboy bars in Hollywood films through which the chuckers-out despatched their victims. By jerking my head to and fro, like the man in the 'That's Shell, that was' advert, as the doors whizzed past each other, I could glimpse through the billowing smoke the Bacchanalian scenes inside. Tawdry women sitting at the bar, tipsy men laughing, a spectacle of luring and noisy Hogarthian vulgarity, just like the hell Mr Francis, Mr Massey and Mr Hussey had warned us about. What fun. Certainly Mr Holloway was among the revellers, or soon would be, or had just swayed out of another door to the Gents before he toppled home to taunt his sullen, crumpled spouse in Lisvane Street.

A visit this year to the *Flora* disillusioned me. It is now a respectable, newly-decorated public house where men take their wives for relaxation. How commendable it all is, the revolution in the pubs. But I prefer to remember it as it was.

On some Saturday mornings Percy took me to collect the laundry at Mr Wah Kee's. The bill was scribbled in Chinese with a brush on a piece of coarse yellow paper. Mr Wah Kee could speak hardly a word of English but there was *rapport* between them. My brother would entice Wah Kee to play on his *ku-ch'in* zither and sometimes his small daughter would sing in a high-pitched nervous voice until the next customer came in with his dirty shirts. Mr Wah Kee gave us lychees and showed us how he counted up the cost of our family laundry on his abacus. Even now, if I were blindfolded and asked to sniff a dozen test tubes filled with perfumes including Chanel *No. 5* and *L'Amour*, I could detect 'Chinese Laundry Shop'. Percy romantically told me the pong was opium and maybe he was right. Or was it merely the fragrance of China tea?

He also told me of Wah Kee's chilling experiences in Cathays, Cardiff during the First World War. The drunks emerging from the *Flora* at chucking-out time on Saturday night regularly smashed his windows with bricks, kicked in his door and denounced the 'warmongering Chinks'. The Chinese had played no part at all in that war as a nation and Mr Wah Kee himself was a patriotic British citizen of many years' standing. The family huddled together, terrified, in the back room praying for the arrival of the police. On Monday, the Saturday night pogrom forgotten, the wives of the tormentors would call for their laundry, complaining that a starched shirt was missing, a button gone astray, or deploring the late service. Percy gravely assured his audience of one small fascinated boy that was the reason why Wah Kee still shuttered his windows at night.

When my brother took me to a crummy but enchanting Chinese café in the docks area of Cardiff known as Tiger Bay–bird-nest soup, chow mien, sweet and sour pork, crispy noodles–I did not know that later on I would be able to compare the fare with the *Shanghai Restaurant* in Singapore, the *Mandarin Hotel* in Hong Kong, or the *Duck* in Peking. Percy fortified me with hair-curling stories, imaginary or true, of the goings-on in Cardiff's Chinatown. He identified the Indians, Arabs and fewer Africans (they don't like the sea) who had manned the freighters that came for coal from foreign parts, and pointed out the first whore I had seen: Percy was a lurid Baedeker and I was an eager tourist, for the foreigners rarely left the doss-houses and dingy hotels of the docks area to saunter through the city streets except to answer charges of malicious wounding or worse at the courts near the City Hall where I was to meet them frequently as a reporter in a few years' time. I entered into the conspiracy that we should not tell Bessie I had been to Tiger Bay or betray the promise that he would take me again.

I was twelve when I was invited by my father during the school holiday to accompany him on one of his journeys to the Welsh Valleys selling groceries to shopkeepers who couldn't afford at that time to buy them. It was commerce on the slate, survival on tick, or hope deferred, my first contact with industrial strife. Once a month, instead of setting off from Cardiff on the train, he would hire a driver and small car to go to places like Senghenydd, Dowlais, Merthyr, Ebbw Vale, and there was no extra charge for the nipper in the back. I suppose he was showing me the ropes, hoping I would follow him 'in the trade'. When he was exchanging Irish eggs and poultry and Danish bacon for post-dated cheques, or a promise or a smile, I sat waiting and watching in the car or turning down the window to over-hear the banter and the anger between the groups of men gathered at street corners. Their hands were stuffed in their pockets and they were wearing caps and mufflers.

It was May of 1926, the month and year of the General Strike. I did not know at the time that in my short pants, chewing wine gums, I was sitting in the front row of the most savage confrontation this country or any other has experienced between a government and the unions. This was my introduction to the wider world, or at any rate to the justification for Cardiff's existence and for the presence of our family in the locality. The schoolboy impressions were to be etched more deeply by my experience as a newspaperman, and by an early fascination with the political scene and the social conflict. I met other angry and frustrated men as life went on. Ebbw Vale and Dowlais and Merthyr Tydfil were the home towns of the miners singing *Sospan Fach* on the *Cardiff Queen* steamer, and of the unemployed men Mr Belman rewarded with his sixpences from the bedroom window on any morning except Saturday.

In 1926 miners were not on strike for *more* money, they were locked out for refusing to accept *less* money, a severe cut in the wage packet and an increase in the working hours. The national coal stop-page began at midnight on April 30 when the ultimatum of the owners expired, and the following day Ernest Bevin announced for the General Council of the TUC that they would support the miners by calling a strike of vital services on May 3. On May 4 the nine-day paralysis began: iron, steel, electricity, gas, building, all shut down, transport of every kind came to a standstill, the presses of the national newspapers stopped and the only avenue of communication between the Government and the 'ungovernable' was an official gazette.

My schoolboy's view of the catastrophe in Ebbw Vale took place during the Nine Days. I asked my father, 'Who is this A. J. Cook they keep talking about?' He replied, 'A shit.' It was the only bad word I remember him using in front of the family. 'He's a union bolshy. The men want to go back to work, you can take that from me.'

Willie was ignorant of the forces in conflict: it was beyond the capacity or the desire of a Dr Pangloss or a Mr Micawber to contem-plate the facts and come to the obvious conclusions. South Wales had been at the head of the world's coal-exporting league since 1891. The few who owned or bought or exploited the land which covered the black gold had prospered swiftly and lived in great country or seaside houses remote from the pitheads, or in the lusher parts of England even further afield from the source of their loot. Middlemen like my father had brought up their families in terraced houses in moderately well-heeled respectability when Cardiff, facing the Bristol Channel and close to the seams, became a bustling seaport. The hundreds of thousands of men who clawed the fuel from the bowels of Glamorgan in conditions of misery and danger, dust and damp and darkness and disease, were the source of the energy and wealth but had not fared so well. The region was in steep decline, eventually to be nominated by the Government of the day as a 'distressed area'. And trade unionism in South Wales had been a potent force for nearly a century.

After nine days the Government scared the General Council of the TUC into surrender at a meeting in Downing Street and the General Strike was called off, to the relief of millions of Willies. The miners, still locked out because they would not yield to the owners' terms, held on throughout the summer, loyal to each other and loyal to their union. In the autumn they did go back to work. They were starved into submission and the bitterness and suspicion and the sense of isolation—betrayal, they felt, by the other unions—remain to this day.

Willie had misguided me. A. J. Cook the Shit was in fact a militant leader of merit and courage with a majestic cause and public sympathy behind him until the country shuddered to a halt. Years later, as a reporter then working in Lancashire, I met up with Arthur Cook at a TUC annual conference in Blackpool. I was impressed by the miners' General Secretary. I was sympathetic to the miners.

I was barely twelve when Willie took the family on a brief visit to London, to stay with an old Army friend of his and to see the end of the British Empire Exhibition at Wembley. I remember the journey I hoped would never end on the top of the bus from Paddington Station to Forest Hill, rubbing the steamed windows with my sleeve and looking for the elephant and castle at Elephant and Castle. I remember the advertisements in flashing, coloured electric bulbs, and the crowds in the streets at night long after Cardiff had gone to bed. The wonders of the Empire Exhibition itself merely left me wide-eyed and silent. Who could forget London?

118 Lisvane Street was never visited by the Left-wing intellectuals who influenced Malcolm Muggeridge at an early age in his
father's house in Sanderstead: we only knew Lloyd George in passe-
partout. The source of the family culture was Arthur Mee's *Children's
Encyclopædia*, bought on easy terms. Willie was a soft sell for any
foot-in-the-door marauder: 'I come from the Educational . . . We all
want to do our best for our children, don't we? . . . I can tell you in
strict confidence what your neighbours, Mrs Jenkins and Mrs Lewis,
have decided . . . The Government would not want you to miss this
chance and the price will soon be going up . . . I'm sure you won't
want your children to have a worse start than the others . . . The
binding will last a lifetime: it smells like real leather. Smell it yourself.' There were also books of poetry and the Everyman classics,
especially Dickens, that Percy bought at market stalls in the city
from the shillings he picked up as Cardiff's Boy Poet from one of the
two local evening newspapers, the *South Wales Echo*:

> I cannot have been very old
>   When I began to write.
> The motive was not greed for gold,
>   Nor was it merely spite.
>
> I wrote in verse. Myself I saw
>   Performing wondrous feats
> As Wales's little Wordsworth, or
>   As Cardiff's pocket Keats.
>
> Yet though, at night, a hundred times,
>   I wrote till I was drowsy,
> The rhythms faltered and the rhymes
>   Were uniformly lousy.

The only occasion his appetite for reading caused any family
bother was at tea-time when the evening paper was used as a table-
cloth. The serial story continued from page to page to page with the
result that the meal was conducted on the principle of 'musical
chairs' in which we all finished up in a different seat from where we
began. The pages were torn to shreds when the serial happened to
continue on the reverse side.

Percy's choice of journalism as a career convinced his brothers,
who had no other thoughts of their own at the time, that it was the
natural thing to do. Hell, who wanted to be a commercial traveller
wearing a new carnation every day in his button-hole? Who would

opt for flogging bacon in the rain to grocers in the Valleys when the wicked city was beckoning? We heard his strange tales from the police courts, the inquests and the City Hall, the hints that a well-known Cardiff divine would shortly be resigning without disclosing the reason, the impending visit of the police to an alderman or councillor. All that—and free tickets to the *New Theatre*, the *Park Cinema*, the *Capitol*, and the dingy *Olympia* in Queen Street where they showed the repeats.

Percy had outstanding talent and, in his individual way, distinction. As a school kid I was able to boast that he played Shylock in *The Merchant of Venice* with the Wesleyan Dramatic Society at seventeen, learning the part on the tram going to work at the *Echo*. Because of the seven-year age gap Percy's influence upon me was limited, and I was the loser. When I was eleven, a member of the Cardiff Scottish Boy Scouts, spuriously wearing a Cameronian kilt, he was in Manchester writing funny features and theatre gossip. When I became a fledgling reporter at fourteen he was already working in London as a freelance journalist, writing lyrics for theatre revues based on news published an hour before the performance. One of his displays of originality was to interview A. P. Herbert in his riverside house at Hammersmith late at night and to produce by seven the next morning for the London *Evening Standard* a half-page version of the encounter in verse which A. P. himself would have been happy to sign: they became lifelong friends.

We did not know each other in any real sense until we were Editors in rival publishing houses in Fleet Street. My abrasive, crusading attitude to journalism did not fit easily into the mature, debunking, self-deprecating attitudes of his coterie on Lord Beaverbrook's London *Evening Standard*. The perfidy of politicians and the self-interest of newspaper proprietors were then merely matters I suspected. They knew. I did not even know that the most successful brothels in the Paddington Station area were conducted on property owned by the Commissioners of the Church of England (who also didn't know) and were allowed to pursue their business without interference by docile policemen. I mistook the urbanity of Percy's circle for cynicism, and to them I was no doubt tiresomely self-righteous and young. But he warmed to me cautiously a few months after my own arrival in London when I announced in the *Bell* in the presence of George Malcolm Thomson, Malcolm Muggeridge and Randolph Churchill that the mere coincidence of Percy and I being born from the same womb did not ordain that we should be bosom friends. But friends we were: unknown to others we discussed together over a drink in obscure hostelries the crises that engulfed one or other of us in the top echelons of the newspaper industry over the years. He became Editor of the *Evening Standard* at twenty-eight. When Cecil King appointed me Editor of a 'national', the *Sunday Pictorial*, at twenty-four, Percy's fraternal pride exceeded his irritation. Nikita Khrushchev would have felt the same if his younger brother had been made Emperor of Outer Mongolia. The appointment of Reg to the Editorship of the *News of the World* in 1953, completing the hat-trick, was celebrated with a suitably hilarious dinner.

The driving force when we were young was obviously maternal; we didn't know it and weren't grateful at the time. One of the reasons was Percy's devastating irreverence towards all institutions, including parents. He regarded the human race, including Bessie and Willie and the Lord Mayor and his first Editor, as material near at hand for caricature and parody. My contribution was to mimic Mr Davies, the Wesleyan parson, Mr Francis the Sunday School teacher, Mrs Price the Faggots and falling about like Mr Holloway on Sunday mornings.

To Bessie the publishing perils of libel and contempt of court or Parliament were remote, and when we ran newspapers ourselves we occasionally telephoned her in advance from Fleet Street if one of us was about to be involved in some newsworthy libel suit by a famous or notorious person. There is no story more succulent for the provincial Press than Local Boy Makes Bad, and we knew that the Cardiff papers would report the cases generously. We told Bessie to ignore the spleen of the complainant's counsel when he chose to denounce one or other of us as a callous rogue or vagabond; he was only earning his living and doing his best. We explained that the counsel who represented our side really knew the facts of the matter and could be relied upon to give a fair picture. As for any reproof from the judge at the end of the case, ah well, that should be taken in the spirit in which it was intended–he was only joking, especially in any reference to her sons.

Bessie had her own attitude to our professional activities, and that was why we weren't too keen on her talking to the profile writers. When asked the usual inane question 'how she felt' when her sons were simultaneously editing three national newspapers of vastly disparate types Mrs Cudlipp would reply, 'Well, I was very relieved

when they didn't all become bank clerks. The danger of embezzle-
ment, you know.' Perhaps she had suspected what had happened to
some of the small change on the mantelpiece.

The day I left Howard Gardens Secondary School at the age of
fourteen Mr Mathias, the cleverest teacher in the prison, stopped me
in the playground and said, 'Well, and what on earth are you going to
do?' The confines of his profession at middle level had turned an
intellectual into an embittered cynic, condescending and sarcastic to
the young. The only relief for his frustration was the request now and
then to review for a pittance for the *Western Mail* a book of significance
beyond the nous of the dull dogs of the resident staff. When I replied
that I would be a journalist, sir, Mr Mathias said, 'I have read now
and then a humorous essay by you, usually in indecipherable handwriting, but good heavens, boy, you need far more than an errant
sense of humour to review books for a newspaper. You need knowledge–where is your knowledge?'
I was going. He was staying. Even at that age I sensed his envy as I
walked to the gates and he returned to the classroom to mark more
indecipherable papers and prepare more lectures about subjects
which bored him for pupils whose minds were wandering and were
for the most part waiting to escape as soon as the law would allow
them. When I called at the school as a freed slave a year later to report
some event for the Cardiff *Evening Express*, Mr Mathias was good
enough to smile in acknowledgement.

Where, in May of 1926, when I was viewing the General Strike
from the back seat of the commercial traveller's car in Ebbw Vale,
were some of the other characters who appear later in this narrative?
How were they affected by the catastrophe, what part did they play
and on which side of the barricades?
Aneurin Bevan then lived in Tredegar, a few miles from Ebbw
Vale; he was twenty-nine, a rebellious member for the second time of
the Urban District Council. He was frantically organising concerts
and displays as a union official to raise money for feeding centres for
the distressed pit workers and their families. During the Nine Days,
when the *Western Mail* launched what he considered to be an obscene
attack on A. J. Cook, he led a procession of protest to Waunpound,
the mountain between Ebbw Vale and Tredegar, where copies of the
paper were ceremoniously burnt and buried, Nye delivering the mock
funeral oration.

Winston Churchill was fifty-two, Home Secretary in Stanley Baldwin's Cabinet. The whole of the national Press was closed down and he emerged in triumphant exhilaration editing the official pugnacious *British Gazette*. Herbert Morrison, thirty-eight, had been secretary of the London Labour Party for eleven years, and because of his experience in the circulation departments of newspapers was selected as the despatch organiser for bulletins and orders to the strikers in London and the Home Counties. Ironically, his first job was to send out the order calling off the strike. Hugh Gaitskell was in his second year at New College, Oxford, recognising the General Strike as the turning point of his life. He was not among the hordes of dons and undergraduates who dashed to the cities to drive the buses as strike-breakers. He worked for the strikers, collecting and distributing the *British Worker*, living on tenpence a day and eating at fried-fish shops. Harold Wilson was ten, moving from Royds Hall School in Huddersfield to Wirral Grammar in Cheshire. Already in the Wilson family album was a prophetic photograph of Harold in short trousers on the steps of No. 10, taken two years earlier by his father during a London visit on the motor-bike and side-car.

Cecil Harmsworth King was twenty-five, shyly pecking around in minor jobs in the Harmsworth family newspaper empire of which the *Daily Mail* was the flagship, learning about reporting and advertising, poking his nose in where he wasn't wanted and wasn't encouraged.

2

My Redeemer Liveth

There is a formidable assault course in journalism to enjoy or endure before you can invite yourself to a confidential pow-wow with the Prime Minister over his proposals for dealing with the current crisis. Or fly to Tokyo to meet Mr Sato. Or to Delhi for a talk with Mrs Indira Gandhi. Or ask for Mr Soldatov at the front door of the Soviet Ministry for Foreign Affairs in Moscow. Or walk nervously past the lions in the courtyard at the Palace at Addis Ababa on your way to chat up the late Lion of Judah. Or sign up Winston Churchill and David Lloyd George as contributors. Or meet the President of the United States in the White House in Washington to discuss the war in Vietnam, off the record.

A jovial confrontation with Mr Khrushchev at a caviare and vodka nosh-up in St George's Hall, the Kremlin, is not a daunting experience when one has run the gauntlet of dealing with the mayors, aldermen, councillors and chief constables of provincial England. Bureaucracy is exportable. There is no basic difference between the Chairman of the Finance Committee of Salford City Council and the Chancellor of the Exchequer at No. 11 Downing Street, apart from the fact that in my experience the Chancellor is less pompous.

Before the Union erected the hurdles and insisted upon a formal training period there were several ways of breaking and entering into the newspaper business. Graduates fell off university spires into the chairs reserved for leader writers on the *Guardian*, or became Instant City Experts on the *Financial Times*, or science or sociological pundits on *The Times* or the *Observer*. A number of politicians, dons, lawyers and teachers–like Mr Mathias, the book reviewer–became part-time journalists because they needed the money or an outlet for their talents. A few privileged young men, not all bright but some of them capable and diligent, became newspaper executives and later proprietors because their fathers were newspaper proprietors or, like the Harmsworths, because publishing was the family business and way of life and death. They practised walking on the water in their nursery baths.

With my modest ammunition I chose the provincial path to glory,

33

moving or propelled from one newspaper to another. The initial alternative was junior reporter on an obscure local weekly in Wales or cleaning the windows of James Howells' store in St Mary Street, Cardiff. Another possibility was boy usher in a brown uniform with buttons and pillbox hat at the *Capitol Cinema*.

My own apprenticeship was brief. My first newspaper was the *Penarth News*, a weak weekly produced by regular miracles in a prosperous seaside town. Penarth was a dormitory of Cardiff, five and a half miles s s w, comfortably middle-class, the pleasant retreat of business executives, bank managers, insurance brokers and such-like who returned more or less punctually every evening to their three-storey houses, well-dressed wives, well-spoken sons and well-scrubbed daughters who knew how to talk with unaffected charm and walk with grace and assurance at an early age. Young girls did what Mummy said, at least within her purview, were home by ten, and did not needlessly provoke a wigging from Daddy. It seems an aeon away from the current age of porn and pot, wife-swapping and male strip-tease japes for bored and jaded housewives.

At the week-end the bucks played golf or talked about cricket and the does busied themselves with preparing Sunday tea parties or cocktails for their friends and dabbled with embroidery and genteel handicrafts. There was a sprinkling of 'uppers', shipowners or mine-owners like the Corys, to remind them that higher planes of affluence still existed and were attainable, with just a little bit of luck.

The local distractions were relatively harmless; religion for the old, bridge for the middle-aged, tennis for the young matrons and unwed semi-virgins, and swimming for the teenagers. The assumption was that the working classes would continue to labour in the less congenial jobs like digging coal, collecting garbage, running trains, driving the Cardiff trams, delivering the post. The other assumption was that a strong Tory Governemnt would soon deal with any non-sense. It seemed a shame that people like A. J. Cook and Aneurin Bevan were born at all. Life was as pure and bracing as the sea air in Penarth. Sodom and Gomorrah were a Bible away.

The circulation of the *Penarth News*, hopefully, was three thousand, and it announced with pride under its masthead that it was incorporated with the *Glamorgan News*, the *Dinas Powys News* and the *Sully Sentinel*. The Proprietor and Editor was Mr Joseph Kemp Foster, a reporter on the *Western Mail* in Cardiff, who had resolved to launch his own newspaper business. If Northcliffe could do it and achieve some success with the national *Daily Mail* why shouldn't J. Kemp Foster? He was a hard-working, humourless and disappointed man whom fortune had not favoured. The *Penarth News* boasted that it was 'Circulating in Cardiff's Wealthiest Suburbs', but none of the wealth brushed off on to the newspaper itself. It was plagued by financial crises which Mr Foster could not over any appreciable period such as a week subsidise from the milk-round he also owned in Llandaff. He developed through anxiety the nervous twitch, the evasive eye, and the quick darting pace of the unblessed entrepreneur whose revenue rarely catches up with his debts. It was to Mr Foster that the signature of my father Willie solemnly indentured me on the paper where my brother Reg was already the chief and only reporter. The correspondence is not preserved for posterity in the Records Office but it is of mild sociological interest:

May 9 1929

Dear Mr Cudlipp,

Your son's probationary period of six months is finishing, and he informed me he would like to have this included in any arrangement that may now be made as to his immediate future here.

I therefore propose taking him as my pupil reporter for two-and-a-half years at the pocket money salary (in lieu of premium) of 5/- per week for six months, 7/6 per week the second year, and 10/- per week the third year.

I am not providing any more season tickets, but have offered him a share of Press Association remuneration with the opportunity of special experience in that direction.

Yours faithfully,

J. K. Foster

J. K. Foster had mastered the science of cost-effectiveness long before the time-and-motion mandarins of the 1960s because whatever the cost he had no effective alternative. He couldn't spread the overheads to the *Sully Sentinel* because it didn't exist. The probationary salary or pocket money of 2/6 per week plus the season ticket of 2/6 per week, totalling 5/- per week, now became the salary or pocket money of 5/- per week, the same total. Mr Clive Jenkins and Mr Jack Jones were unknown as negotiators in South Wales in the late 1920s. The new deal was not up to Lockheed standards, but it was the last straw that broke the camel's back. The *Penarth News* went bankrupt in October five months later.

Mr Foster fulfilled his side of the binding contract. When he was not engaged in fobbing off the creditors, cadging newsprint on a promissory note, asking the printer for more time to pay, canvassing advertisements at cut-price rates, or freelancing for other newspapers to try to make ends meet, he kept a strict eye upon me, always referring to me flatteringly or disapprovingly, according to the intonation, as 'Mr Cudlipp'. It was a gentlemanly profession before the Murdochs arrived.

A junior's duties on a small-town weekly do not offer much scope for the daring or original. I graduated from the Boy Scout Notes and Church Notes to covering the wheeler-dealing of the less exciting sub-committees of the Town Council. There was the evening call at the police station to ask 'Anything doing?' When invited to buzz off, I buzzed. But I usually knew what was 'coming up' in the court the next morning: wayward revellers, retired and frustrated colonels suspected of the ancient art of indecent exposure, motorists who had jumped the crossings or parked on the wrong side of the promenade. Their tarnished names were in my dog-eared notebook before they had been Found Guilty and publicly paraded in our next issue. Their minor follies were recounted in excruciating detail for the titillation or deterrence of their neighbours.

I perpetrated my first libel when I was 'on probation' at the age of fifteen. The Saturday football match which ensnared me as a sports reporter seemed innocent enough: Penarth versus Barry, two local teams in a punch-up in a lowly league.

Knowing nothing and caring less about soccer, or for that matter rugby or any other game, I mingled in the rain among the sparse crowd to eavesdrop on remarks I could produce as my own in my report of the match. The result was Barry 5, Penarth 0, and then I got my Big Idea, inspired by a raucous shout from a Penarth supporter. The facts were straightforward. The referee was from Barry, the home town of the visiting team, and Barry had won. Only a dolt could have hesitated over the introductory paragraph, and to get on in journalism you have to establish fairly soon that you are not a dolt:

> 'Few of the Penarth supporters,' I wrote, 'were surprised at the 5–0 result of Saturday's clash' (it sounded better than match) 'with the team from Barry. Nor were any of the Barry supporters surprised. After all, the referee himself came from Barry.'

I accept in retrospect that the 'ref' reasonably considered this damaging to his reputation. There was some alarming talk about a writ, but fortunately he knew as much about libel as I knew about soccer. He settled for a letter in the readers' correspondence column severely castigating the bias of my report. It was signed 'Fair Play', and was written by me.

There were regrettably two occasions when I incurred Mr Foster's disapproval.

Publication night of the *Penarth News* was an uncertain event because the electricity company cut off their supply to our linotype and flatbed machine when bills were unpaid. News reports appeared in the paper weeks after the events merely because they had been set in type and the type could not be wasted. Advertisements were repeated free of charge because there were no new ones to take their place and the paper looked mean and unsuccessful without them.. These eccentricities were, however, no alibi for the junior reporter when I failed to deliver the results of a swimming gala in time for publication in the current week's issue. I had fallen in love with Bunny Parnell, who was known in our headlines as Penarth's Channel Swimmer, and had foolishly invited her for a trip in a rowing boat when the gala ended. Later, equally foolishly, we married, but Mr J. Kemp Foster was in no mood for romance.

'I do not want to act hastily, Mr Cudlipp. I shall see you at ten o'clock tomorrow morning.'

Then came the awful verdict. 'You have let the paper down. I suspend you for two weeks, Mr Cudlipp. Without pay.'

The second occasion when I aroused the Editor's displeasure was when Mr Foster asked me to deliver parcels of newspapers in the porches of half a dozen shops, plus a couple of quire for Wyman's bookstall at Cardiff Central Station the next morning. I said nothing, but visibly demurred. After all, I was training to be a journalist not a paper boy. 'Mr Cudlipp,' said Mr Foster, 'do you know that the early issues of *Answers* were delivered to the shops by Northcliffe himself? Are you too proud?'

By the time the *Penarth News* went bust, perilously soon, I had learned more about death than life.

The local undertakers at that time were a source of malicious gossip about each other, intense in their rivalry to supervise the obsequies of the best-connected corpses. I had to crawl into their confidence to hear the first tip-off of a death, a piece of intelligence of commercial rather than editorial significance because Mr Foster paid his reporter a commission on any obituary notice booked for the classified columns. I had to arrive quicker than Ralph Champion of the superior *Penarth Times* to secure this essential bounty. The secret was being on the spot when the undertaker's men were laying out the corpse so that I could gather the details of the uneventful life of the departed from the widow and relatives for the editorial write-up and, of greater importance in the survival stakes, collect the money for the classified ad. I became an expert at drafting the words at so much a line. To encourage sympathy and trust I never declined to view the body when invited. My stock remarks were 'How peaceful he looks' or, if a woman of reasonable age, 'How beautiful'. The editorial obit, a different exercise, usually ended with a puff for the undertaker on the theme of 'The funeral arrangements are in the hands of . . .' This would ensure early information when his next client bit the dust.

A bandolier of clichés was worn for the reporting of non-events, but I did not think it funny at the time; I was anxious to demonstrate to Mr Foster that I had got it right. 'The bride and groom left for their honeymoon in the South' with a capital S meant they were going to Weston-super-Mare or Minehead on the other side of the Bristol Channel by paddle-ship but was intended to imply a sun-baked villa among the mimosa at Cannes or Monte Carlo. 'The bride and groom left for their honeymoon at an undisclosed destination' meant Barry Island six miles away.

Mr Foster had no need to send for his reporters when announcing the week's assignments because we all worked together in a one-room editorial office. The Editor was perched on a stool, crouching over the sloping top of his pulpit desk. Brother Reginald and I sat at the reporters' table (also, later in the week, the sub-editors' table with the same personnel, and later still the newspaper despatch table with the same personnel). Suzie Foster, the Editor's daughter, had a smaller desk at which she made the tea on an electric ring, counted the unsold copies, opened the post with girlish optimism and sent out the bills, cosseted Daddy and kept him in touch with the milk-round's progress in Llandaff and audited our expenses. They were never allowed to exceed sixpence without a searing probe on the theme of 'If you had gone earlier, don't you see, you could have caught the cheap-fare workmen's bus.' Occasionally the cast in the minuscule office would be increased by the arrival of the linotype operator from the cell next door, querying some illegible copy of mine or cadging a cup of Suzie's tea.

It was like the magnificently funny scene in the Marx Brothers' film when Groucho and Harpo are joined in a cabin on the cruising ship by a hundred other zanies. But the *Penarth News* was no laughing matter.

The telephone was sited on the Editor's desk, and owing to the cost-effective rules there were even fewer outgoing than incoming calls. 'Councillor Adams lives only three miles away,' Suzie would scold, 'why not walk?' The ringing of the phone bell was therefore the signal for excitement though not hilarity. The pantomime that followed gave the caller the impression that he was connected to a multi-line switchboard at the nerve centre of a towering complex where our important newspaper and its associate publications were produced. The Editor was projected as the Grand Mogul, remote, in conclave with executives and technocrats in his opulent office suite on some floor far above the mechanical chatter of our linotype machine, an eminence not easy to reach and whom it was not always wise to interrupt.

I was usually deputed to answer the telephone because the call was never for me:

'Yes, sir (or madam), this is the *Penarth News*.'

'I want to speak to the Editor (or Chief Reporter).'

'Your name, please? Very well, I will see if the Editor (or Chief Reporter) is available. Please hold the line, sir (or madam).'

The procedure was to tap the instrument several times sharply with my pencil to simulate the plugging and unplugging of switches, with appropriate dialogue that could be overheard by the caller.

'Yes, sir (or madam), the Editor (or Chief Reporter) *is* available. I will put you through now.'

After a few more sharp taps on the instrument the telephone was handed to the Editor who was a foot away from me or to my brother who was four feet away. Then I resumed my vivid account of the annual Presbyterian Church Bazaar.

My inefficiency at shorthand was concealed by a robust memory and a facility for thinking up the original angle. I absorbed from my brother the art of draining information from tight-lipped officials by pretending to know more than I knew, and rapidly acquired the science of being the Instant Expert.

I therefore affected to be unperturbed at Mr Foster's two hours' warning that he wished me to cover the *Messiah* at Dinas Powys one evening. When he told me he wanted 3,000 words my first thought was that it must be the Second Coming. He explained that it was an important event he had intended to report himself, but a certain matter had unfortunately arisen; no doubt a pressing creditor had caught his evasive eye. The ticket–it was never two in South Wales: one ticket, one telephone, one linotype machine, one Channel Swimmer–was pressed into my hand. Nowadays I could cover Judgment Day in a ten-line paragraph, but the reverse order of 3,000 words on the Second Coming was, in spite of my professional nonchalance, disconcerting. I was relieved to read on the ticket that the *Messiah* was an oratorio by G. F. Handel (1685–1757) to be performed by the Dinas Powys Choral Society.

During the rendering of 'I know that my Redeemer liveth, and that He shall stand at the latter day upon the earth,–immediately after the Hallelujah Chorus and shortly before 'Behold, I tell you a mystery'–the idea emerged and I knew that my Redeemer also liveth. The names and addresses of the whole of the choir would surely produce 1,500 words and fulfil half of my mission. That was achieved by standing at the door of the church hall with a notebook as the choir dispersed, recording the name of their houses as well as the street. *Mon Repos, Chez Nous, Dunroamin*–all words, and I needed words.

I called in at Cardiff Library before catching the train from Cardiff Central to Penarth the next morning and casually requested a glance at any books they happened to have on Handel and the *Messiah*, 'not to be taken away'. They included *Grove's Dictionary of Music and Musicians*, and I swiftly scribbled my notes:

'Masterpiece. Incomparable grandeur.

'Revelation came to Handel as he wrote it: "I did think I did see all Heaven before me, and the Great God Himself." (Must work this in.) Conductor must now make personal interpretation: no conductors in Handel's time.

'Handel wrote it in London. (Did he ever visit Dinas Powys?) Naturalised as British citizen in 1726. Scored strings only. Kettledrums and two trumpets added for a few items, with Handel himself playing the organ. Other instruments added later.

'Three parts: the Prophecies and the Narrative of the Nativity; the Passion and the Resurrection; Man's hope of his own resurrection.

'Mention that when George the Second heard the first performance of *Messiah* at Covent Garden he was so emotionally aroused by Hallelujah Chorus that he rose to his feet and remained standing until its last notes. Don't mention he didn't know much English.'

Electricity permitting, it was publication night.

The report began: 'Handel was born in Halle, Saxony, in 1685 and did not become a British citizen until 1726. It is not known whether he visited Dinas Powys but he was there in spirit last night when his masterpiece of incomparable grandeur was given the most spirited rendering I, or any others present, have ever heard . . .' I prayed that my Redeemer had arranged that Dr Grove did not liveth in Penarth.

Mr Foster nudged me the next morning, beckoned me to follow him, climbed on his stool and placed his hands upon my shoulders.

'I must congratulate you, Mr Cudlipp. I did not know you were a music critic as well as a soccer expert.'

Then, with a twinkle in his eye: 'How much are we paying you now?' It was all happening, and so soon. The great rise, a fortune, *success*.

'Five shillings a week, sir, but now without the season ticket from Cardiff.'

The twinkle broadened into a smile as he took my hands in his. He said, 'I'm glad.'

The poster of the *Penarth News* displayed in the village of Dinas Powys announced

MESSIAH TRIUMPH:
FULL NAMES OF CHOIR

I wrote the poster myself with a thick black crayon, but that week the *Penarth News* expired. Mr Foster was able henceforth to concentrate upon the milk-round in Llandaff. Ironically and unjustly his failure was my salvation.

The collapse of the *Penarth News* released me from my three-year apprenticeship and I was on my way, wondering what if anything would turn up next. I was henceforth able to carry around with me the testimonial signed by the Proprietor and Editor, Mr J. Kemp Foster. I still possess it. It might still be useful.

October 12 1929

'I have pleasure in stating that Mr Hugh Cudlipp has been employed on these newspapers for the past year and has assisted generally in the gathering of local news, the reporting of Council meetings, social functions, etc.

'He is strictly temperate, a hard worker, takes a fair shorthand note, and is well informed on musical and dramatic subjects.

'I have only parted with him on relinquishing proprietorial control of these journals, and strongly recommend him.'

Like Lloyd George and Aneurin Bevan and other humble Welshmen, I had seen London. The magnet to them was political power; London to me was the city where the national newspapers were created and published. Mr Foster's written and signed evidence of my strict temperance at sixteen was a slender passport to Fleet Street: indeed, it could have been a disadvantage. Who, in any case, could have got pissed on five bob a week? I needed more Oscars before I could knock on the door of the Press Lords.

An evening newspaper in Cardiff was good enough to employ me and there I learned more about death, more about the death of newspapers and the acute vulnerability of Editors. I omit the name of the newspaper and of the principal character in this grim experience because I would not wish to cause pain to his relatives.

The cast in the drama is compact:

The Editor

The Editor's Secretary (his daughter)

The Junior Reporter (me)

The Penarth Channel Swimmer

The Penarth Channel Swimmer's mother

The situation which led to my involvement was also simple. The Channel Swimmer suddenly arrived in Cardiff with my future mother-in-law and phoned from the office reception desk suggesting a coffee. The Junior Reporter was skint and therefore had to get his meagre expenses countersigned immediately by the Editor. The Secretary, who was a charming lady for whom I had a glowing affection, worked in the annexe to the Editor's office.

'Take the expenses in yourself, Hugh. I'm sure he will sign them right away.'

There was no 'Come in' when I tapped on the door so I stood on tiptoe to peep into his room above the frosted glass. The first thing I noticed was the blind cord, taut and at an angle which defied the force of gravity. I then observed that the roll-top desk had been pulled out from its usual position. There was no sign of the Editor until I opened the door. He was sprawled on the floor with his head held higher than the rest of his body by the blind cord tied around his neck. He was redder than usual in the face, certainly dying or dead.

I closed the door and ran to the Chief Sub-editor, a man who was notorious for his stories of his own steely courage in World War One. When I informed him that the Editor was hanging in his office he fainted and slid off his swivel chair. I grabbed the News Editor and said, 'Come with me—quickly.' I cut the blind cord with a Boy Scout knife attached to my belt. The Editor was still breathing. He was taken to Cardiff Infirmary by ambulance—and survived.

An hour later the staff were told what the Editor already knew, that the two evening newspapers in Cardiff were amalgamating and that 'Employees who have been in the service of the company for long periods, especially ex-servicemen with families, will receive special attention.' I had been on the newspaper six months and was one year old when the Great War was declared.

Mother-in-law paid for the coffees after waiting an hour for the Junior Reporter to arrive at Rabbioti's café next door to the office. She looked at me unbelievingly as I spelled out my sixty-minute alibi and asked her if she had any idea how long it took to get to Manchester by train.

A discouraging beginning in a way, but in Manchester I really learned what journalism was about and much more of what life rather than death was about. I met most of the first-class operators who were later to fill the Editors' chairs on the newspapers in London: Manchester was the recruiting ground for talent for the 'nationals', a good place to be.

As a young reporter in that city I wrote my one and only story that, in nearly fifty years of newspaper work, was ever suppressed—or, to be more accurate, prominently displayed in the early editions and juggled out of sight in the 'final'. The paper was the Conservative *Manchester Evening Chronicle*, owned by Lord Kemsley and other members of his family. Lancashire was embroiled in a protracted lock-out or strike in the cotton industry and I was sent in a car on a lightning tour of the mill towns—Oldham, Rochdale, Bury—to report on the mood and spirit of the workers that day. How defiant? Were they about to cave in? What were they really thinking? I discovered that they were defiant indeed and positively not about to cave in. I interviewed dozens of them in the various towns and was moved by their resilience. The pawnbrokers' shops were filled with pledged possessions, the bookies' runners were idle, and the wives (most of them spinners or weavers themselves) told me the secret of how to make a hot-pot go further by adding water.

43

It was a scene of unrelieved drabness, but colourful in human terms, and the story dictated itself as I phoned in to the office in Manchester section by section from the telephone boxes along the route. On the return journey I stopped the car at Bury to buy the *Chronicle*, and there was my story, a page-one lead, sympathetically and spectacularly headlined by the 'splash' sub-editor who was also, no doubt, more sympathetic to the cotton workers than to the employers.

I arrived back in the office, groping around for the final edition with the complete and polished version. I was surprised and somewhat alarmed to see that my work of art had entirely disappeared from the newspaper, replaced by a story transparently of no importance. Worse, there was an envelope addressed to me on the notice board containing a brief note from Nathaniel H. Booth, the Managing Editor. Would I call downstairs to see him when I returned.

'It was a great story,' said Norman Calvert, the News Editor. 'Very moving. I know Natty Booth wants to see you. He's in his room.'

In moments of anxiety or crisis Nathaniel Booth sank his hands deep into the seat of his pants and scratched his backside. On this occasion he was scratching vigorously, and perspiring.

'Sorry, Cudlipp. I want you to know that I agree it was a great story, but I had to take it out of the final. The proprietors have interests in the cotton industry. And . . . well . . .'

My factual account had not been killed by the proprietors, but it was considered circumspect to erase it from the final edition which was customarily despatched to London. The vigilant Natty had seen it in time and therefore Lord Kemsley wouldn't see it at all.

In Salford in 1930 I visited slum houses that had been denounced by Engels in 1844 in his book on the English working class, condemned as unfit for human habitation. Men, women and children were still living in the same houses in the same revolting conditions. They were still living in the same houses in 1974, but they had been finally rescued a few months before I revisited Salford to make a television documentary on how some of the other half live. Houses of a similarly ghastly standard were still there around the corner, still occupied. In Choir Street, Gerry and Madeleine Evringham were bringing up their young family of four in 1974. You could sink your fingernails into the plaster. There was water under the rotting floorboards. The children excitedly called their mother one morning to see 'the pretty coloured flowers' suddenly growing on the wall of the sitting-room.

They weren't fibbing; the flowers were there all right, in mauve and scarlet. *Fungi.*

Blackpool, where I worked for a while as a district reporter, was more instructive than a year at a university. I met the British working class on holiday before they discovered the Costa Brava, wearing 'Kiss me, Sailor' paper hats and blowing bubble gum and cramming into the ear-splitting song-plug booths when it rained, or into the Zoo at the Tower or the bars at the Winter Gardens. The Golden Mile with its raucous exhibitions and barkers with hailers and massive coloured posters luring the crowds to step inside and splash a tanner. 'See the Unfrocked Rector of Stiffkey Burning in Hell.' When he was Fasting Unto Death the miserable little runt, disguised without his clerical collar, used to meet me after the evening's show for a beer and sandwich in the pub. Regrettably, the Reverend Harold Davidson (the Prostitutes' Padre) was no Daniel: when he appeared in a lion's den at Skegness in 1937 the clumsy ass trod on its tail and was mauled to death. 'Freaks. Midgets. Albinos.' Champagne on draught in Yates' Wine Lodge opposite the north pier. 'The Fattest Woman in the World, Straight from Coney Island, America.' Jumbo ice-cream cornets and candy floss and pink peppermint rock stamped right through with the name of Blackpool. 'Mitz, Morris and Akka, the famous Hollywood Apes.' Dirty postcards—'I've lost my little Willie' and 'Cock Inn, that's what I want.' The plump nudes, who couldn't wobble (unless you made them giggle and wiggle) without breaking the law, portraying 'The Judgement of Paris and Other Renowned Masterpieces'. Phoney auction sales flogging junk, the Original Gipsy Rose Lee, and 'The Genuine Buffalo Bill' (from Leeds). Beach shows, treasure hunts and the *Daily Mirror* Eight, a sprightly team of high-stepping go-go glamour girls touring the seaside resorts to save a dying newspaper.

In Blackpool at that time I was also able to acquire some knowledge of municipal graft.

II
THE
TURBULENT
NEWSPAPERS

3

The Glorious Gamble

I was early at the barricades of the Tabloid Revolution.

In July 1935 a classified advertisement appeared in the *Daily Telegraph* seeking 'bright assistant features editor with ideas able to take charge,' and my brother Percy, then Editor of Beaverbrook's *Evening Standard*, nudged me to apply. After all, they couldn't offer me less than 'the minimum' I was then being paid at the London office of the *Sunday Chronicle*, another Kemsley newspaper to which I had graduated from Manchester. They might offer more. The title of the newspaper was not disclosed, and when Basil D. Nicholson, the new Features Editor of the *Daily Mirror*, phoned me to say that it was he and that newspaper who had inserted the bait I was inclined to allow the matter to end there.

The *Mirror*, with the single exception of the *Daily Sketch*, produced in the same Kemsley stable where I was working, was Fleet Street's most identifiable lame duck. But when we met there was something intriguing about Basil D. Nicholson. He was a character straight from the pages of any of Evelyn Waugh's later novels, wearing a green tweed suit and octagonal spectacles. He had left J. Walter Thompson, the American advertising agency, to join the *Mirror* as a journalist, and the magic words he uttered were: 'We're going to turn the *Mirror* into a real lively thrusting tabloid newspaper. We haven't started yet.'

'Like what?' I asked, and he took me to his room to show me, surreptitiously, copies of the New York *Daily News*.

'Why does the ad say "able to take charge"?' I asked, and Nicholson replied that he didn't expect to last long there himself the way things were going.

'Can you start today? Otherwise I might be fired before you get here.'

My departure from the *Sunday Chronicle* took no time at all. In spite of James Wedgwood Drawbell's efforts Lord Kemsley (the issue went to him, quite incredibly) would not up my take-home pay by more than ten bob though I would have been prepared to stay for an extra quid.

I reported for duty on August Bank Holiday Monday, 1935, at the age of twenty-one. William Connor, later renowned as the daily columnist Cassandra, arrived the same day from J. Walter Thompson, where he had been copy-writing the Harpic account. So did Peter Wilson from *The Times*. Connor and Nicholson had visited the *Mirror* office a year or so before with an introduction to the Advertisement Director, unsuccessfully trying to sell a strip-cartoon.

The largest type on the front page of the paper that day was still in a modest 48-point, and two others of the page-one headlines were in sedate old-fashioned italics, soon to disappear. The boast to be 'The Daily Picture Newspaper with the Largest Net Sale' was a toot on a tin whistle, for its only rival was the *Daily Sketch*. I was already adept at slinging type, writing bright headlines and chopping pictures in the right place, a graduate from Jimmy Drawbell's finishing school on the *Sunday Chronicle*, so there was nothing in the technical sense that worried me one jot. The problem was to sense the atmosphere and sense it accurately. It was impossible to discover at that time who was in charge, what the policy of the *Mirror* was or indeed if there was a policy at all.

Alfred Harmsworth, the first and only Lord Northcliffe, conceived the paper in 1903 as 'The First Daily Newspaper for Women', edited and staffed by ladies of breeding from the high-class weeklies. 'So mad a frolic,' he wailed as the circulation crashed from the first issue's 265,219 to 24,000 within three months. It dealt with everything from the stitching of a flounce, how to make *consommé aux nids d'hirondelles*, to Imperial defence. Northcliffe cried 'Enough' when his losses passed £100,000, declared angrily that women couldn't write and didn't want to read, and called in Hamilton Fyfe as Editor and Kennedy Jones to start all over again.

'You can't imagine the things I had to blue-pencil,' Jones told his friends. 'Two people acting at Drury Lane got married and went on acting as usual–they didn't go away for a honeymoon. The paragraph about this ended: "The usual performance took place in the evening."' When a letter about French affairs was sent daily from Paris the original headline, written by a lady, was set up in type but did not appear: it was changed to 'Yesterday in Paris'.

Kennedy Jones decided 'The monstrous regiment of women must go,' and Fyfe set about the distasteful task. The rape of the Sabine women was a mild pleasantry in comparison. 'They begged to be allowed to stay,' he said. 'They left little presents on my desk. They waylaid me tearfully in the corridor. It was a horrid experience, like drowning kittens.'

The saviour of the newspaper was an eccentric technician named Mr Arkas Sapt who knew how to fill a paper with photographs printed on high-speed rotary presses. The *Daily Illustrated Mirror*, the first half-penny daily publication of its kind, appeared on January 25 1904 and was selling nearly 290,000 copies a day by its first birthday. Hannen Swaffer was its first Art Editor and Harry Guy Bartholomew became an Assistant Art Editor. The paper made history by publishing a double-page picture of the dead King Edward VII, eyes closed, hands folded, and at his elbow a spray of white roses placed there by his Queen. 'The picture can only go in one paper, the *Mirror*,' said Alexandra, 'because that is my favourite.'

In 1914, preoccupied with *The Times* and the *Daily Mail*, both closer to his heart, Northcliffe allowed the *Mirror* to go to his younger brother Harold Harmsworth, the first Lord Rothermere, a money maniac who regarded the newspaper and its companion the *Sunday Pictorial* as sources of funds to invest elsewhere.

Presiding over the doom of the newspaper in the 1930s was a triumvirate. The first member was John Cowley, the scared Chairman who represented the controlling shareholder, Rothermere. As caretaker he besought his colleagues to take care, and the delivery of a writ, even by a firm of crooked solicitors on behalf of a notorious scoundrel, would disturb his sleep at nights. The second was Wallace Roome, General Manager, a hail-fellow-well-met smoothie whose sincerity couldn't be trusted an inch but who was pleasant to have a drink with; the third was James Lovell, a pleasant, indeed a good man with a beguiling smile and half an inch of cigarette stuck to his lower lip. His mission in life was to obstruct any expenditure on anything at all, forever mentioning 'the bawbees'. Cowley and Roome did have a publishing background of considerable experience but little distinction. Cowley began as a cashier and his name was in the imprint of the first issue of Northcliffe's *Daily Mail* as General Manager, but a personal adventure with Edgar Wallace into the evening newspaper field flopped.

The death rattle in the throat of a national newspaper is first heard in John o' Groats and Land's End when the local general store cuts its supply below a quire, and this was now happening on a grander scale throughout the country. By 1933 the *Mirror* was losing

70,000 customers a year and there was a musty smell in its head-quarters–Geraldine House in Fetter Lane, off Fleet Street, a wedding-cake edifice, hopelessly impractical as a publishing house.

Of more significance in the future than the Triumvirate were two other directors, Guy Bartholomew, looking mischievous and busy but doing nothing of any significance, a talented man watching time go by, and Cecil Harmsworth King, ambitious but frozen out and achieving anything he did achieve by machination. When he became a director of the *Mirror* company in 1929, and for many years after-wards, the financial figures of the company were not disclosed to him by the Triumvirate; as Advertisement Director he had the unpleasant task of convincing advertisers the circulation was around a million, which they knew it wasn't, instead of nearer 700,000, which they suspected, and he was allowed no expenses to wash down the lie with a bottle of Château Latour over a lunch table at the *Savoy*.

The unhappy Editor, L. D. Brownlee, was a former schoolmaster and Oxford Blue, interested in cricket, full stop. Any future for the newspaper could only arise from an uneasy connivance between Bartholomew and King, mutually unfriendly and untrusting.

The impending disaster was grave enough for them all to be fired, and certainly nothing could be achieved without the disappearance of Brownlee; 'If in Doubt Fire the Editor' is usually a rallying call that will eventually muster sufficient support for some semblance of action, and this was an objective which the subtle Cecil could handle more adeptly than the clumsy Guy Bartholomew. Bart's motives would be obvious, to hold the editorial reins himself; King could adopt the more disinterested stance of an advertising director plead-ing for circulation figures that would attract sufficient advertising to keep the business alive. The frustration of a man who had been refused executive power of any sort until he was thirty-three had schooled him in the art of patience.

Brownlee is an excellent fellow, King would concede, but is he in the right job? Are we being fair to Brownlee himself? He might have a mental breakdown the way things are going and we don't want that on our conscience. It would surely be kinder to give him a hint after Christmas than before, don't you agree? Who is the best among us to tell Brownlee–surely not Bartholomew? Shall I, or you, or you?

Cecil King, disliked by the others because of his unruffled public school and university background, unpopular in the Harmsworth family but still of it, was ideally equipped for the undermining role; after a passage of time people began to wonder why Brownlee was still coming to the office, and Bart was content to enjoy the intrigue without any personal risk.

The Cecilian chant continued. The real problem is really no longer Brownlee–he will obviously be happier with a generous cheque and more time to dally at Lords. The problem is who will follow him as Editor. Bartholomew? Over Cowley's dead body? Then why not Cecil Thomas as Editor with Bart in another role but not directly responsible for what is being printed *that* night?

Thus Bart became Editorial Director in 1933 more by assumption than by design or grateful elevation by the Triumvirate. Cecil Thomas, cherubic, courteous, unobtrusive and tranquil, the son of a Cambridgeshire rector, assuaged Cowley's fears of what might happen in the newspaper and assured him that all was in good taste. He formally succeeded Brownlee as Editor in 1934, but it was Bart to begin with, and later others, who edited the Editor. Cecil Thomas was financially treated with degrading meanness and was allowed no expenses by Bart; nor was he treated with respect in other ways. He was good-natured and needed to be, for one of Bartholomew's favourite tricks involved a plank of wood as a prop. In the presence of a member of the staff or of a petrified visitor Bart would creep up behind the Editor and crash the plank on his bald head. The weapon was five feet long and a foot wide, and those beholding the homicidal attack for the first time felt faint. The plank was made of balsa wood and weighed less than cardboard. The act was symbolic, but I always suspected that it hurt the Editor more than he cared to admit. 'It's bloody silly, really,' Cecil Thomas complained to me, 'but Bart enjoys it.'

There is no point in conducting an autopsy on a newspaper that nearly died, indeed in its existing form did die, but it became significant not merely in publishing circles when it was revived by the kiss of life. 'Guy Bartholomew had ideas, I had good judgement, so we put our heads together;' that is Cecil King's description, true so far as it goes, of how the new thinking began.

The putting together of these particular heads was no simple matter. Facially they were both strikingly handsome but the contents were mentally dissimilar by every known test. King's middle name 'Harmsworth' meant what it said; he was the nephew of Northcliffe and Rothermere and his mother was Northcliffe's sister. The physical resemblance between Bartholomew and Northcliffe was apparent and Bart's mannerisms and behaviour were reminiscent to those who had known the great Alfred. He was not one of Northcliffe's handful of illegitimate offspring, though he did not go out of his way to deny the rumour. He was rated as a bastard in every other sense, why not Northcliffe's? Less romantically, at the time of its Caesarian birth, he joined the paper from the engraving department of Northcliffe's *Illustrated Mail*. Bart was inventive, energetic, conspicuous, a show-man, a born newspaperman but not a journalist in the sense of being able to write a sentence and knowing what it meant. At one of the two *Mirror* board meetings over which Northcliffe presided he appointed him a director at twenty-eight, and from then on his colleagues had to pay the price for his inferiority complex, on some occasions a heavy price indeed.

Cecil King was a Wykehamist, burnished at Christ Church, Oxford, aloof and lonely but seeking no one's company, intrigued in an intellectual fashion with the human race and its problems but incapable of meeting it on terms of parity. During vacations from Oxford and in his post-Oxford days he had dabbled at this and that in the Harmsworth publishing empire, unhappily knocking on doors as a reporter in Glasgow, importuning advertising agents for the *Daily Mail* in London, tasting the sour fruits of nepotism, biding his time, and trying on dying men's shoes.

The New York *Daily News* was launched on Northcliffe's advice as a carbon copy of the London *Daily Mirror*, but by now was far more successful than the original. It was studied and visited, and the message was clear. The *Mirror* was a *picture* paper with news, de-signed to be bought as the second choice with a more serious news-paper, but the NY *News* was a *newspaper* with pictures, custom-built to be bought by a vast new audience of people lower down the scale of literacy, most of whom bought no newspaper at all until it arrived on the stands. It was also apparent that the leading American ad-vertising agencies, with their sales appeal to the masses in strip-cartoon form, had evolved a technique which the editorial pages of a pop newspaper would be wise to emulate. J. Walter Thompson were the masters of the new 'art' form, so it seemed prudent to acquire some of their know-how and talent: they were skilful exponents of marketing, consumer research, 'point of sale', and newspapers had a lot to learn from them. They were even willing to promise their support with advertising.

This was the birth of the tabloid revolution in Britain, but it took two more years for the thinking to simmer, the courage to rise, and to attract the nucleus of the staff who were to transform the *Mirror* into the most turbulent and commercially successful newspaper anywhere in the world. The first day Bart performed as Editorial Director was Tuesday, November 29 1933, and the next morning's headline was:

TRIAL BY FURY–U.S. LYNCH LAW
Frenzied mob storm another gaol.
Soldiers' Bombs Defied.

It was a study in mass lunacy, startling at that time but in content far less gruesome than the coverage of wars and terrorism and violence that are today the commonplace fare on television news screens every evening. It was the first indication that the genteel *Daily Mirror* intended to expose unpleasant truths as well as to report the titillating niceties. There were two pictures, small by modern standards. One showed a well-dressed mob in San José, California, battering in the doors of the county prison prior to the lynching of two alleged kidnappers; the Governor publicly pardoned the people involved and said 'it was a fine lesson to others'. The second picture showed the body of one of the lynched men hanging at the end of a rope, a spectacle cheered by the onlookers. Curiously, it was my account in *Publish and Be Damned* of this publication by Bartholomew that led Victor Gollancz to refuse to publish the book. In a moment of aberration he must have thought the *Mirror* or I believed that lynching was good for the soul.

Advertisers complained that the tone of the newspaper was occasionally conflicting with the softer sell of their products, but the circulation went up. Bartholomew knew that a brasher age and a wider appeal to the public, especially the young, called for a brasher newspaper technique. In November 1934 he began to

SHOUT

louder in condensed sans headline type, projecting the evolving personality of the newspaper. John Cowley trembled and Fleet Street wondered what was going on.

When I arrived at Geraldine House in 1935 the *Mirror* was a hotchpotch of conflicting schools of thought, and schools of no thought at all. Bart's emergence in 1933 with his lynching pictures had not yet set a style in a consistently robust selection of news and pictures, and I was told by Basil Nicholson that certain of the existing features (I called them the pages in invisible ink) were sacrosanct. Among the untouchables was the editorial, expressing the paper's opinions, at that time decreasingly Right-wing but still tastefully written by the eccentric bibliophile Richard Jennings, later to become the passionate advocate of Churchill and then his scourge in office. The readers' letters were hand-picked for their inoffensiveness and middle-class smugness. The gossip page was a diet of refined, soporific chit-chat on social and booksy affairs. Was it generally known that George V was an enthusiastic philatelist? Who was the tiniest débutante, the best-dressed Member of Parliament, the tallest Cabinet Minister, the most handsome bishop? The swans on the lower reaches of the Thames were mating.

Those were the ingredients retained in the evolving paper to pacify John Cowley, in the hope that his eyes would not wander too far over the rest of the paper which in the next two years was to undergo an astonishing transformation, eventually swallowing the whole.

'All these readers' letters are dead,' I said to Basil Nicholson. 'Do you think we could run a rival letters feature in the same paper called "Live Letters", attracting younger readers, giving snappy replies to their queries?' The devious approach appealed to Basil and Bart.

The next citadel to fall was the gossip page and I was put in charge, tackling the problem rather rashly and inevitably upsetting the Chairman. Three weeks after I arrived the readers of the page lost touch with the swans and were informed that Queen Ena of Spain had shocked the guests at a dinner at the *Savoy* by using a toothpick after the succulent savoury and before the dreary orations. Also that Elsa Lanchester, the actress, had found it absolute hell to dance at the *Dorchester* Charity Ball because of her screaming corns. When the item appeared her husband Charles Laughton came through on the phone, asking if I were the editor of the gossip page. I replied Yes, with suitable pride. 'Sir,' he thundered in his *Mutiny on the Bounty* voice, 'sir, I am coming immediately to your office in a fast car to horsewhip you.' I continued, a little nervously, writing a paragraph about a millionaire who had given his dance partner a double-decker bus because he liked her tango.

The front page blossomed out into one-inch deep black headlines ('MARRIAGE AT 9 SHOCKS U.S. WOMEN') and the news pages were now filled with condensed items of maximum interest to the maximum number of readers. This was the work of Roy Thistle Suffern, who never had his share of the credit or the blame. During the two years in the front line at the *Mirror* when the tabloid revolution got into its stride my principal contribution was to humanise the feature pages and enjoy myself thinking up the wacky and controversial ideas. I amassed a team of psychologists, soothsayers, doctors, pet experts and scribbling priests whose services were at my command by merely picking up a phone and later despatching a cheque. I engaged Godfrey Winn to pour out his heart to our women readers on 'my very own page' every day. Cassandra called the whole thing 'Cudlipp's Circus'.

Winn described his embroilment with the *Mirror* in his autobiography:[1]

'I had no idea that, behind the scenes, the *Daily Mirror* was in the process of a far-reaching upheaval, having a giant face-lift which was to change its image completely, so that it was to become one of the most powerful and at the same time one of the most responsible media for influencing public opinion in the world... How should I have known? Out of the blue, I was rung up and taken out to lunch in a small Fleet Street restaurant called *The Wellington*, by a young man, several years my junior, with a head of dark curling hair set above a wide forehead, and the deep-set Celtic eyes of a visionary turned fanatic who gave me the impression at sight that if anyone touched him, electric sparks would shoot out in every direction.'

Sorry about that; it was me.

The environment was more robust than he had been accustomed to in the sedate magazines for women. The writing of a page a day of abounding variety and changes of mood, a one-man performance, is a gruelling task. The tantrums were daily and the weeping weekly, but Winn was a superlative journalist. When I left the *Mirror* for the *Pictorial* he was suborned by John Gordon to write a page in the *Sunday Express*, and on the day he arrived there the principal shareholder phoned him: 'Well, this is Lord Beaverbrook speaking. I have been informed of your arrival and I would like to invite you to come and dine tonight. Eight o'clock at the *Colonial Hotel*.' Beaverbrook was a master of the All-embracing Gesture, at his best a journalist among journalists. This was the reason why the dynasties of Fleet Street, hiring talent but keeping it at a respectful distance, could never fathom the loyalty he commanded from his Editors and principal writers. The professional Godfrey Winn, instantly absorbed like any other actor into his new role and facing his new audience, dis-

[1] *The Infirm Glory* by Godfrey Winn, Michael Joseph, 1967.

missed his long run in the Geraldine House Extravaganza with unusual modesty: 'In actual fact,' he admitted, 'it didn't make a single copy's difference.' In actual fact the readers of the *Mirror* had at this stage become addicted to a daily drug, the newspaper as a whole, as sedative in places as pethidine and as stimulating in others as cocaine or alcohol. They were not disposed to endure the withdrawal pangs of changing their allegiance to another newspaper to follow a star.

There were other ingredients. The newspaper involved itself intimately in the lives of its readers:

> Are you glad you married, or sorry? What was the most embarrassing moment of your life? Tell us about the worst nightmare you ever experienced. Tell us about the skeleton in your family cupboard, the misdeed you are ashamed of. Tell us about your Greatest Adventure. What are your Eight Sane Rules for Happy Marriage?

We announced an anthropological investigation into 'this love business', and 50,432 women readers filled in the questionnaire. Their unabashed frankness to their favourite newspaper revealed, among more personal matters, that the first kiss, on average, came five months after the first 'hello' and was received at the age of fifteen and a quarter, usually between six p.m. and midnight. A similar investigation today would yield different results; for kiss read coitus. But the point of it all was that the *Daily Mirror* was now dealing with life as it was and is lived by ordinary people, spotlighting the things they really talked about and which deeply concerned their families. We were developing a service that would cater for their needs from the cradle to the grave.

If it had merely become a more popular newspaper it would have been no more interesting than Coca Cola or fish and chips or Tampax. It assumed a self-importance and then a national importance which nearly, by a hair's breadth, led to its total suppression during the war and endless skirmishes with the Establishment and the unions after the war. But the immediate problem was to make it sell and succeed. It is nonsense to pretend that anybody at that time was casting himself in the role of a sage or a prophet or a political force to be reckoned with, or even regarded the paper as an essential social or political service.

A closer look at the people there on St Crispin's Eve is interesting in view of subsequent events.

In his brief time on the *Mirror* Basil Nicholson made a major contribution, encouraging strip-cartoons and advertising techniques, reminding me and others that we shouldn't think our potential readers were as clever as he was. He was forever deriding orthodox newspaper thinking. He had been schooled in the advertising world to appeal to the greed and envy and fears of the lowest common denominator, and cared little about the wider responsibilities of journalism.

During our brief time together I produced the most extraordinary headlines for the *Daily Mirror*, inspired by the ravings of the more excitable American newspapers and magazines; hell, I thought that was what they wanted.

BOSSY WIFE GETS HUSBAND'S GOAT– HE WANTS A VAMP AT 40!

MATCH-MAKING MAMMIES SHOO SPINSTER LOVELIES TO GIBRALTAR TO GRAB A JACK TAR HUBBY

REVELLER VANISHES FOR DAYS– COMES BACK AS POP-EYED DRAGON SHOUTING 'WHOOPEE! WHAT A NIGHT!'

I wouldn't have passed one of the headlines myself then or since, but Nicholson received them with maniacal glee, Bartholomew occasionally recognised me but said nothing in the corridor, and Cecil Thomas smiled at me as well as at everyone else.

Six months after my arrival Basil beckoned me to go with him to the roof. The wind was at gale force, it was raining, and it was impossible to light the giant Corona he had thrust into my mouth.

'Bartholomew has fired me,' he shouted. 'He wants to see you now. I think they want to give you my job. Take it, or everything we've done will be wasted. All the other people here are fools.'

Basil was fired because time and again he had been ordered to tone down our handiwork, my handiwork, and simply didn't care what the directors thought. Probably Bartholomew didn't like green tweed suits and people who tried to pry under his cloak of mystery and secrecy by asking questions he did not wish to answer.

The fact is that nobody edited the *Daily Mirror* in its formative years. The Editor, Cecil Thomas, who was reputed in his earlier days to have been a ferocious chief sub, screwing up badly handled copy and hurling it at the perpetrator, now strolled around having an amiable word here and there, never initiating or killing an idea good or bad or expressing a view without looking over his shoulder. Bart, the symbol and spirit of the revolution, controlled the strip-cartoons and pictures, walking prominently once a day through the editorial floor but talking to no one, displaying his authority by mindless sackings and acts of individual cruelty, issuing threats sometimes through third or fourth parties to individuals to 'watch their step'. Roy Suffern evolved and ran the news pages, and one of his sub-editors at that time was Edward Pickering, who followed me in the 1970s as the head of Mirror Newspapers. I ran the features. The leader writer, Richard Jennings, wrote his own editorials. Cassandra edited his own column and Philip Zec later on evolved his own cartoons, collaborating with Cassandra on the captions. If there was a master-mind, or even two master-minds, behind the operation it was not readily apparent to the guerrillas who were aiming the hand grenades and holding up the public to ransom.

It was a gamble but a glorious gamble, conducted in the edgy atmosphere of an unlicensed gaming club expecting a police raid. There were furtive side-glances among the players and a code of nose-tapping, keep-it-to-yourself secrecy. 'Don't put it in the first edition, wait till Cowley's gone home.' 'It's better if Bart sees it the first time in the paper in the morning.' 'I told Cecil Thomas, so it won't come as too much of a shock.' The hurly-burly was presided over by The World's Greatest Illusionist, Harry (The Only) Guy (The Unbelievable and Unrepeatable) Bartholomew. Occasionally he would snooze or enjoy a tipple or stay the night in a small flat on the fourth floor of Clifford's Inn, two hundred yards from his office, a hideaway nobody was supposed to know about from which he could suddenly materialise at any hour of the night in the event of a war, a national disaster or a Royal crisis. The retreat was overlooked by my flat on the top floor of the same apartment block. I therefore knew he wore corsets, a damaging titbit I thought it prudent to keep to myself. On several occasions I saw him roll them on, and on one occasion with the reluctant aid of the rector's son, the Editor.

The greatest simplification of the *Mirror*'s turmoil in those early days comes from Cecil King, writing later in life. 'Of course,' he wrote, 'when starting out to create a new kind of newspaper, I had no real idea where I should end up—certainly not with a total sale of *Mirror* and *Glasgow Record* verging on six million a day.' The use of the word 'I' in this context was a slip of the quill. On other occasions and in the same book, *Strictly Personal*,[1] he recognised Bartholomew's essential role and was more than generous to the inner circle. Five pages earlier he recorded that he and Bart 'put their heads together', and one page earlier, writing of the succession to the Chairmanship, after John Cowley's death in 1944, he acknowledged that 'Bart had done more than anyone else at that stage to resuscitate the paper.' King's contribution during the revolutionary years was of major importance not so much as the visionary but as the elegant wheeler-dealer, becalming the Triumvirate, expediting the emasculation or isolation of the duds, first-aiding Bart's erratic confidence and diverting him from the sillier and merely mischievous excesses, shocking for shocking's sake. As the only intellectual around he had the temperament and time for contemplation, but the conclusions he reached by thought and knowledge were identical with the conclusions reached by others through instinct and conviction, doing what comes naturally. One of his conclusions was: 'If we were to move the *Mirror* into a new market it would have to be the working-class market.' Exactly. 'Our best hope was therefore to appeal to young working-class men and women, and in general the least educated part of the population.' Precisely. 'If this was the aim, the politics had to be made to match.' Socialism was good for business? The *Mirror* never went as far as embracing the materialist concept of history, but never has a more materialist motive been vouchsafed for what it eventually did advocate. King in his ivory tower was playing chess, but the boys in the backroom were playing ludo and shove-halfpenny; they were building a platform from which they could express their thoughts, not calculating thoughts that would build a platform.

In March of 1931 Rothermere wrote to John Cowley:

'I wish you to understand most clearly that, in future, the *Mirror* and *Sunday Pictorial* businesses are entirely under your and your colleagues' control . . . PS Of course, all vacancies on the Boards of the two companies will be filled by you.'

Cowley continued to represent the controlling shareholder until 1935 when Rothermere, believing that the *Mirror* was going broke and would cease publication, ordered the sale of 80,000 out of 80,450 shares held in the *Mirror* by the Daily Mail Trust, of which Cowley

[1] *Strictly Personal* by Cecil H. King, Weidenfeld and Nicolson, 1969.

was a director; he also disposed of his personal share holding sporadically on the Stock Exchange. King tells us that Rothermere 'was not a man of integrity and used his newspapers to boost the shares of the *Mirror* so that he could sell out.' A nephew cannot be expected to control his uncle's financial chicanery however much he may deplore it, but is he also obliged to swallow Uncle's politics without demur, even when those politics become alien to the British way of life?

On January 22 1934, in the interim period between handing over power and finally bowing out, Rothermere wrote–or caused to be written, and then signed–a special article in the *Daily Mirror* entitled 'Give the Blackshirts a Helping Hand', supporting Oswald Mosley:

> Timid alarmists all this week have been whimpering that the rapid growth in numbers of the British Blackshirts is preparing the way for a system of rulership by means of steel whips and concentration camps.
>
> Very few of these panic-mongers have any personal knowledge of the countries that are already under Black-shirt government. The notion that a permanent reign of terror exists there has been evolved entirely from their own morbid imaginations, fed by sensational propaganda from opponents of the party now in power.
>
> As a purely British organisation, the Blackshirts will respect those principles of tolerance which are traditional in British politics. They have no prejudice either of class or race. Their recruits are drawn from all social grades and every political party.

Far from being an article of personal opinion it ended with a list of the addresses of Blackshirt premises where embryo Fascists could enrol for membership, and it was succeeded by another piece, 'Hurrah for the Blackshirts': 'Young men may join the British Union of Fascists by writing to the Headquarters, King's Road, Chelsea, London, sw.'

Cecil King had been a director of the *Daily Mirror* since 1929 and Bartholomew, now Editorial Director, had been on the board since 1913. His name appeared in the first wages book of the paper in 1904: 'H. G. Bartholomew, 30s.' They had already put their heads together in 1933 and decided that the best hope for their dying newspaper was to appeal to young working-class readers and that 'the politics had to be made to match', that is, to support the Labour Party. Did either oppose in 1934 the publication of Rothermere's Fascist tirade, degrading the *Mirror* to the status of a recruiting sergeant for Mosley? Did either mildly propose that another view of the Blackshirts might be published in the same newspaper? Did either indicate an intention to resign with a public statement saying why? Cecil King did not keep a diary until the war, so we are unaware of his private thoughts at that time. The only explanation of the silence is that they knew or hoped that the end of the Rothermere influence was near at hand, and that in their resurrected *Daily Mirror*, matching the politics to the commercial aim, there would arise an occasion for retribution. By 1934 the ultra Right-wing ravings of Rothermere had become an affront to democracy. 'His enthusiasm for Hitler was deplorable,' wrote Cecil King many years later, but it was deplorable *then*, in 1934. Uncle Harold proclaimed, principally in the *Daily Mail* but reflected in the *Mirror* and *Pictorial*, that 'nearly all the news regarding the Nazi regime published in our most responsible journals is pure moonshine,' 'We and the Germans are blood kindred,' 'Herr Hitler neither drinks, smokes nor eats meat.' He supported and eulogised the Nazis and Mussolini's regime in Italy and told the public through his newspapers that 'The (British) Blackshirts will stop war.' Not a single member of the Harmsworth dynasty raised his voice on a single occasion in protest or stood up to be counted; nor did a single one of them join Mosley's Blackshirts. The fireball Bart merely swallowed his medicine like a yes-man.

Was Socialism good for business, better for business than Fascism? If the political and sociological philosophy of the new *Daily Mirror* had been generated solely by calculating directors and written to order by hack journalists the insincerity of the exercise would have been blindingly apparent.

The roaring radicalism of Bartholomew, if it ever existed, and the 'anti-Toryism' of Cecil King, if it had yet emerged, were effectively subdued in the 1935 election. That Parliament endured for nine years, six months and twenty-five days. It was dissolved on June 15 1945 for the first election after the war. It began as the National Government of Stanley Baldwin, majority 247, ended as the Coalition Government of Mr Churchill, and was followed by the Labour Government of Mr Attlee, majority 146.

The following political dialogue between the *Mirror*'s strip-cartoon characters was recorded on the leader page of the newspaper on November 9 1935, five days before the polling and a few months after I reported for duty:

John Ruggles: Who reduced unemployment? And the income tax? Who reduced the price of beer? STANLEY!
Gladys Ruggles: I put my trust in Mr Baldwin.
Jane: Hip! Hip! Hooray!

Cecil King's sympathies, as he tirelessly said, were with the underdogs of society. But it was important for the success of the new *Daily Mirror* that the underdogs barked for themselves unpampered and unmuzzled, and the arrival of Cassandra and myself in this scene of the First Act was therefore propitious.

I developed a permanent affection and respect for Cecil King that lasted, with few explosions, for the rest of our lives. Nobody was more active in expanding my knowledge and experience and giving me opportunities to utilise such talents as I had. The professional association worked with harmony also because I, an amateur but enthusiastic psychologist, was aware of the filial problems which imprisoned him and of his total inability to enjoy either the balm or stimulus of mental nudity in the presence of another.

Bartholomew, with maudlin contrition after the deeds were done, punished me for the unpremeditated crime of being his only visible editorial successor. The forfeits he exacted for this misdemeanour were typical in their pettiness. He sacked Eileen Ascroft, a major feature writer on my staff who was doing a brilliant job for a pittance. He observed I was in love with the girl, and we began our happy marriage at the end of the war, five years after the death of my first wife. The grounds for Eileen's abrupt dismissal from the *Mirror* were that she, with half a dozen others including me, had played darts at a modest office beano, using the oak door of his office as a dartboard. And then, for an encore, he fired me from the Editorship of the *Sunday Pictorial* in 1949.

These are not valid reasons for sustaining any fiction that does less than justice to Bart's true role in the re-creation of the *Daily Mirror* in the mid-Thirties: it was the paramount newspaper achievement in the twentieth century so far, and success has many fathers.

There is The Curious Case of the Three Dots in the book written by Maurice Edelman in 1966, fifteen years after Cecil King had succeeded Bartholomew as Chairman and four years after Bartholomew's death. The book, *The Mirror: A Political History*,[1] was conceived by King as a record of what the newspaper had been saying on the important issues over the years, and I proposed the author. When

[1] *The Mirror: A Political History*, Hamish Hamilton, 1966.

Hugh, right, at the age of six
with his sister, Phyllis.

The Hollywood-style pressman on the left is myself at 17,
district reporter in Blackpool in 1931 for Kemsley's newspapers. Third from left, my assistant Bill Boyle. Fourth,
Moishe Saidman, staff photographer. The picturesque Crossley
truck delivered the Manchester *Evening Chronicle* to Blackpool
at high speed. Holding it up is Jimmy Byrne, Circulation.

At 18, the suspicious Sub-editor of the
Evening Chronicle in Manchester.

Maurice Edelman was dealing with the influence of the newspaper in the war years he quotes a passage from A. J. P. Taylor's *English History, 1914–1945*:

'There was (during the War) no cheap organ of hate on the (Horatio Bottomley) *John Bull* model. The war had one important outcome in the newspaper world. For the first time the masses— other ranks in the forces and factory workers—read a daily news— paper, and this carried the *Daily Mirror* to the top of the circulation list. The *Mirror* was popular in a special sense. Previous popular newspapers, the *Daily Mail* and the *Daily Express*, were created by their proprietors, Northcliffe and Beaverbrook—men not at all ordinary. The *Mirror* had no proprietor. It was created by the ordinary people on its staff . . . The *Mirror* was, in its favourite word, brash, but it was also a serious organ of democratic opinion and owed its success as much to its sophisticated columnist Cas- sandra as to Jane, its strip-tease strip-cartoon. The *Daily Mirror* gave an indication as never before of what ordinary people in the most ordinary sense were thinking. The English people at last found their voice, and the historian is the more grateful for this voice since the Second World War, unlike the First, produced no distinctive literature.'[1]

The Three Dots indicate the omission of the praise I now italicise in the passage published by A. J. P. Taylor:

'It was created by the ordinary people on its staff, *and especially by Harry Guy Bartholomew, the man who worked his way up from office boy to Editorial Director.*'

I did not notice the omission when I read the proofs of the book, but it was observed by that awkward but diligent sleuth now known as Lord (George) Wigg who wrote to me about it. The opportunity did not arise for me to ask Maurice Edelman before his death in 1975 why he considered this forthright recognition of Bartholomew by an historian of repute inappropriate for his book. It did not accord with Edelman's own view that 'Northcliffe invented a style of journalism for mass circulation which King continued.' It did not, admittedly, fit naturally into his general theme: 'Without King's intervention and his political influence on Bartholomew, the *Mirror* might well have remained a ragbag of Right-wing attitudes, lingering on from the

[1] *English History, 1914–1945* by A. J. P. Taylor, Oxford University Press, 1965.

Rothermere dispensation.' (Not in Cassandra's column, or in my pages, or in Philip Zec's cartoons.)

'King,' wrote Edelman, 'took the amorphous potentialities of the paper and translated them into political power. Far more effectively than any of the press lords of the old establishment, he was to make a newspaper a decisive electoral factor. King was interested in clear exposition. That is why, despite the difference between his background and that of Cudlipp and Bartholomew, he found a common denominator with them in making the *Mirror* the paper of the ordinary man, interested in his day-to-day living and the affairs which determine it. His natural ally in this was Cudlipp, the young and exuberant ideas man who was also absorbed by the political revolution that was going on in Britain. He [King] was less sympathetic towards Bart.'

How far King's influence subtly conditioned Bartholomew during the tabloid revolution no one knew except the two men, but in my estimation at the time and in retrospect the influence was greater than Bart admitted, which was zero, but was not so great as Cecil assumed in later years and Maurice Edelman immortalised. Even if Bartholomew had been receptive rather than resentful, his brainpower was a formidable barrier to incoming or outgoing messages, especially of a political nature. Any wisdom injected into him by King stayed where it was deposited and was never passed on to the men and women who were making their marks on the paper. Early in the war, before the Japanese were committed at Pearl Harbor, Bart asked me when I was going to publish an article attacking the Japs, 'the Communist bastards'.

Bart was a romantic liar, claiming according to the occasion half a dozen origins probably all of which were fanciful. He told Ellis Birk and Philip Zec, the superb cartoonist, that he was Jewish, but apparently with no deeper motive than making everybody feel at home: if the Chief Corrector of the Press at the *Mirror* had been an Arab, Bart would have mentioned casually to him that he was Lawrence of Arabia or Abdul the Damned's younger brother. The Births of Bartholomew were in the same class as the War Careers of John Gordon. I heard them all, from both. That Bart could hardly spell, and that his knowledge was limited, was true; anybody who received a letter from him in his own handwriting, or heard him expound on any subject other than photography or photo-engraving, was aware of this. I do not differ from King's assessment:

'Amusing and at times brilliant, but a dreadful man to work with or for. He enjoyed spying on people, and so our telephones were tapped and our letters read. Any critical remark about any member of the staff would be passed on by Bart to create mischief. If no critical remark was made he would often concoct one. Setting different members of the staff–or the board–at each other's throats was a real pleasure for him.'

King's description of their relationship as based on love-hate was fanciful; King was tolerant of Bart and recognised the qualities of the man the *New Statesman* described as 'a rough erratic genius fashioned out of an extraordinary mixture of shrewdness and naïvety, toughness and sentimentality', but he was aware from long experience that Bartholomew would try to injure him 'whenever opportunity offered'. Bart's attitude to Cecil King was of unrelieved hostility, a sustained jealousy of his superior mental equipment and judgement. Why was he in the bloody building at all? I saw or heard of no occasion when love, or even mild affection, played a part.

An atmosphere of internecine warfare is not, of course, exclusive to the publication of newspapers. Nobody could garrotte an over-garrulous or over-querulous Minister more expeditiously than the unassuming Clem Attlee, or assassinate half a Cabinet with more aplomb than the urbane Harold Macmillan. Cloak-and-dagger operations are also familiar in the cloisters of Church of England cathedrals and Oxbridge universities; few can sharpen a dart more painstakingly, or tinge its tip with subtler poison, or aim it more accurately than a thwarted academic. Yet it was ironical that a newspaper that was successful because of its sense of human values, its compassion and its sincerity and warmth, should be produced in a climate upstairs of rumbling personal malevolence and rivalry, though there were others who worked on the landing or downstairs who formed lifelong friendships.

The revolution at the *Mirror* would have occurred if King had not been there, in fact as soon as Harold Rothermere faked up the share price and sold out in 1935, but it would not have been conducted so skilfully. The revolution would not have occurred at all if Bartholomew had not been there. At that time it could not and would not have been attempted by any of the existing editorial staff, a downtrodden underpaid mass of second-raters with half a handful of exceptions. For two reasons it could not have been achieved by the newcomers. They did not know the vanities and weaknesses of the ageing board of directors and how far and how often they could be circumvented or cajoled or defied; secondly, they would not have been there at all unless there had already been signs in the sky or rumours in the Fleet Street wine bar, *El Vino*, of a change in mood and a willingness by a few to take many risks. To put Cecil King into correct perspective in 1933, 1934, 1935 and 1936 is not to underestimate his influence at that time or minimise his leadership in the post-Bart period, but Bart should be buried in the right tomb and with the correct inscription, even if he was incapable of writing it himself.

His outstanding qualities were his courage in publishing, truly without fear or favour; his sparkling originality; his technically inventive mind in photographic reproduction; his skill at picture presentation; his energy, a vital asset to a newspaper.

Within a few years King's political knowledge and prescience became decisive in the group when he and I were working together on the *Sunday Pictorial*–vastly more noisy, politically, than the *Mirror* in the years that remained before Munich and Dunkirk, leading not echoing the *Mirror*. His influence on both newspapers after Bart's enforced departure in December 1951 was paramount. Over the years his guidance and foresight were as significant as Bart's visual skill at popular journalism, but the barker on the stand outside is more important than the lion inside the tent. No audience, no circus.

The fact that matters is that the newspaper changed course in the mid-Thirties, selected the correct course either by instinct or intellect or both, came out of its coma and began to breathe without artificial aid. The public response, much to the relief of King who was trying to placate the advertisers, was immediate. It attracted new and younger readers, and at a swifter rate than it lost old readers through natural causes or shock at the bizarre tone of its contents. The fall-out of retired colonels, headmistresses and bank managers' wives in Cheltenham, Bournemouth and Leamington was noticeable and their letters of protest were a joy to read.

4

A Noisy Conspiracy of Silence

The principal difficulty in working for Bartholomew was the conspiratorial silence. The operation had to be conducted without any other newspaper knowing anything about our activities and plans, such as they were. He liked the opposition to think we were mad, which they frequently did and we occasionally were.

He was never seen at functions in any strata of society and his sole companion was his own inferiority complex. He avoided his equals in other industries and in his own industry, and therefore acquired no knowledge at all. He did not know what to say to them and regarded their questions as an intrusion. He did not make speeches because he could not make speeches. The role of the unsmiling and inscrutable sphinx was to his liking.

When he visited New York after the war he whispered into the ear of John Walters, our correspondent in America who met him at the liner, 'I am Colonel Bartholomew on the passenger list. I have nothing to do with the *Mirror*.' When we travelled together in a Sunderland flying boat to Australia with the financial director, James Cooke, Jimmy Lovell's successor, he imposed rules of caution; no surnames, no mention of newspapers, preferably no dialogue at all. 'Call me Guy, nothing else.' As he dozed off the Australian sitting with us asked, 'Who's your friend?' I told him that Bart was a well-known English bishop, incognito, and the Aussie replied, 'Well, he is certainly a fine old gentleman, a very fine old gentleman indeed.' It was a twelve-day journey and our fellow passenger was later surprised at the bishop's language in the hotel bars when we touched down off Syracuse, and then on the Nile and the Ganges.

To be observed by Bart in the presence of a journalist on any other newspaper was to invite a warning, through another party, to watch one's step; to be mentioned by name in a trade periodical was usually fatal. By the time Hannen Swaffer mentioned me in his *World's Press News* column as his 'favourite journalist' I was editing the *Sunday Pictorial* and temporarily beyond Bartholomew's immediate grasp: there would have been no doubt about my fate if he had been boss at that time of the whole shooting match. To survive with Bartholomew it was necessary to be more anonymous than he, though it was difficult not to be known by the contributors. Walking alone was an elaborate and immature charade.

The folly of conducting a newspaper in secrecy was apparent as soon as the new *Mirror* came face to face with its first national crisis in 1936, the Abdication of Edward VIII because of his love for the divorced and remarried Mrs Wallis Warfield Simpson. The *Daily Express* and the *Daily Mail* knew step by step what was happening behind the scenes at Buckingham Palace and Downing Street. The King was consulting Lord Beaverbrook, who had first heard from my brother, Editor of his *Evening Standard*, that Mrs Simpson was suing for her second divorce at Ipswich Assizes on the grounds of her husband's adultery. Esmond Rothermere, who had succeeded his father as Chairman of Associated Newspapers (*Daily Mail*), was also consulted in the dual role of friend and Chairman of the Newspaper Proprietors' Association. Edward sought their co-operation in protecting Wallis from 'sensational' publicity and later on in the saga on how to parry the Prime Minister, Baldwin. Churchill was advising the monarch and he was in close touch also with Beaverbrook. *The Times* was in daily and later hourly contact with Baldwin. The *Daily Mirror* had no contact with anybody who knew anything, not even with a footman at Buck House.

When Mrs Simpson's second divorce was imminent in England in October the King achieved 'the miracle I desired–a "gentleman's agreement" among editors to report the case without sensation'. The gentleman's agreement among editors was a pact among proprietors and personal friends of Edward not to give the divorce case any prominence in their publications and not to mention in that report Mrs Simpson's friendship with the King.

The American newspapers were already making references, no longer veiled, to the new King and Mrs Simpson 'making woo' and to the 'suppressed rage in the Royal household' at the course of events. The British Press were straining at the leash, guilty that they were still withholding from the public news which was now a matter of common gossip and common concern among the Establishment and in Fleet Street taverns.

Bartholomew decided to act alone. On the morning of December 3 the nation heard for the first time of the secret historic struggle then at its height between the King, the Church and the Cabinet and was told at last that Edward VIII wanted to marry Wallis Simpson. The

same morning the other newspapers, notably *The Times*, were still
pontificating about 'King and Monarchy' and constitutional principle, deploying innuendoes but nowhere telling their readers that
somewhere in the grounds of the King's country house, Fort Bel-
vedere, where the lovers avoided the rude gaze of Parliament and
public, there was no doubt an oak tree etched with the simple truth
'Wally loves Teddy'.

Bartholomew was right to break the veto and publish the facts, and
it was fascinating to observe in the office the clandestine relish with
which he set about his task, prolonging the love-play and timing the
climax. This was the supreme orgasm in the life of a man governed
by a psychopathic passion for mystery, concealment, intrigue and
surprise. There was a noble cast for the greatest act of The World's
Greatest Illusionist, a perfect script and a vast audience; the human
race (less, possibly, the Chinese and the lost tribes of the Amazon)
was standing on tiptoe. The first two editions of the *Mirror* contained no reference to the crisis, for it was necessary–I'm sure you'll
understand–to ensure that Chairman John Cowley had left and was
safely tucked up in bed with his toddy. An elaborate network of
espionage monitored his progress by car during the evening and his
final whereabouts.

I worked in the room next to Bart's, but he telephoned. 'Cudlipp?
Bartholomew. Do not leave the building. You'll get a call in the next
hour but don't ask who's phoning you. He'll tell you Cowley's son
has left the office. When you get the message put your head round my
door–but don't say a word if anybody is with me. Better still, say
nothing at all, even if I'm alone. Understood?' Cowley's son worked
in the Circulation Department or thereabouts and Bart had arranged
that a copy of the first edition, the 'nothing doing' issue, would be
wedged into his hand and that he would be told he was not required for
late duty; there was the possibility that he might take the later
editions home to show his father. When the message about young
Cowley's departure arrived I put my head around Bart's door, said
nothing as instructed, but made the sort of Chester Conklin grimace
which indicated that everything, whatever everything might be, was
going well. He was alone, but I did not break my Trappist vow.

'Sit down, Cudlipp. Can I trust you?' I instantly put on my Of-
course-you-can-trust-me mask, an essential part of the journalist's
working kit or fool-bag. 'We're printing it tonight. Don't tell a soul.
Don't ask or answer questions. Don't answer your phone from now
on even if I ring.' I understood, or maybe.

Roy Suffern, the Night Editor, was darting along the corridor rather frequently from the editorial room to Bartholomew's HQ, but when we passed in the corridor we exchanged no message more incriminating than 'Hello', with me risking 'See you later'; neither knew how much the other knew, or how little both of us knew.

The third edition spoke of Baldwin's 'audience of the King on urgent and political matters not connected with foreign affairs'. Next there were hints of 'grave issues'. I noticed at this stage that Bartholomew, who had vanished from the office for two hours, materialised in the corridor in passage to his room; he was wearing an Anthony Eden hat and a lounge suit pulled on over his blue-striped pyjamas. It was not until the final edition came off the presses at 3.53 a.m., too late to give the rival newspapers the courage of Bart's convictions, that the facts were revealed with a portrait of Mrs Simpson. The headline was:

THE KING WANTS TO MARRY MRS SIMPSON. CABINET ADVISES 'NO'

It was a pleasant evening. The type on the front page was the biggest and blackest the *Mirror* had used to that day and its policy on the crisis was unequivocally on the side of the King and his right to choose his own wife.

During the campaign I was able to take over the front page with some strident opinionated headlines:

God Save the King! TELL US THE FACTS, MR BALDWIN!

And at the bottom of the page:

THE NATION INSISTS ON KNOWING THE KING'S FULL DEMANDS AND CONDITIONS
The Country Will Give You the Verdict

It was the first occasion on which the paper's *views* pushed the *news.* off the front page, a device I was to use many times when I edited my own newspaper. Two pages inside were devoted to the stories I had assiduously collected from the American Press. 'These were the lies,' the headline proclaimed, 'which poisoned world opinion.' There was another 'first' during the crisis. Cassandra, who had swiftly acquired his style and stance on public affairs, emerged for the first time in a national crisis with a full-page article called 'I Accuse' and we worked together on the project:

> I am writing about what I regard as the biggest put-up job of all time. I accuse the leaders of the Church of England of placing our King in a position from which it is almost impossible to retreat. I accuse the Prime Minister and his Government of manoeuvring with smooth and matchless guile to a desperate situation where humiliation is the only answer.

Cassandra ferociously attacked the hypocrisy of the aristocracy in condemning the King's projected marriage to a twice-divorced woman, referring in passing to their own 'sorry pageant of adultery and divorce'.

Two days later I was able once more to escape from my cage in the Features Department and book another front page:

45,000,000 DEMAND TO KNOW –AND THEN THEY WILL JUDGE

We were demanding the answers to five pertinent questions. There could be no doubt any longer about the new class-consciousness of the *Daily Mirror*, or any doubt that it had swopped classes and causes for good. There would be no more recruiting campaigns for Oswald Mosley's Fascists and the bottoms of the Continental dictators would never be licked again. Mr Baldwin crossed the Editor off his visiting list and the Tory Party lost a faithful but feeble friend in the Press, the old *Daily Mirror*.

As any alchemist in the Middle Ages would have known, all that glitters is not gold.

Did the Mirror *know on this occasion what was going on behind the scenes?* No. Cecil King's assessment of the situation in which we found ourselves was more perceptive than Bart's. Bartholomew had enjoyed the Pyjama Game, but King was thinking of the future, when the *Mirror*, if it were to be taken more seriously, must take itself more seriously. 'We had, of course, no useful contacts of any description,' he wrote in *Strictly Personal*. 'In so far as the paper (in the past) had anything of the kind, it depended on Rothermere. When he withdrew, he left nothing behind. This was brought home to us in a very marked form at the time of the Abdication. Cudlipp and I vowed never to be caught in the dark by some crisis like this ever again.' Nor were we. I observed that Cecil King, a student in his Oxford days of constitutional history, was the only man in the office who could talk knowledgeably about the possibility of morganatic marriage, by which device Mrs Simpson could have married the King without herself becoming Queen.

Advocacy was not enough: I learned that the brief was as important as the rhetoric. King's claim that over the years we acquired better sources of information over the whole field, political, diplomatic, financial, scientific, etc. than any other paper might well be disputed by any other paper, but it was not an idle boast.

Was the Mirror *right to break the self-imposed veto and tell the public, who footed Royalty's wages bill, what was going on?* Yes.

Some years later in a newspaper trade journal Editor Cecil Thomas emerged from his cocoon, and it was a pity he did not emerge more often, to make some forthright points about the paper's performance on the Abdication crisis:

> What is a newspaper? Does it or does it not exist to provide news for its readers? Well, then . . . are news editors to be asked to say that this or that is not 'nice news'? Are they to be constantly acting as nursery censors? A news editor with that type of mind would be like a general with a conscientious objection to killing. The truth is that the London Press is already too niminy-piminy, too nice altogether, too refined, too ready to leave out, too reluctant to print without fear or favour. Just recall, they said nothing at all about Mrs Simpson until December 3 when the *Daily Mirror* gave her name and picture. Then all, with terrific unanimity, came out next day with pages about her. A newspaper that wishes to retain the confidence of its readers should be ruthless and remorseless in revealing all the news it can get.

It was a splendid statement of the attitude of the new *Mirror*. The paper would no doubt have taken the same line, espousing the King's right to a personal choice on a very personal matter, even if it had been able to tap every phone line between Buckingham Palace and Stornaway where lived Lord B., and Warwick House where lived Lord R., and also if it had been privy to the pow-wows between 10 Downing Street and Geoffrey Dawson of *The Times* and to the 'distressing talks' between Archbishop Lang and the ailing King George V about his heir apparent's infatuation. But the *Mirror* knew no more about these negotiations than any of its readers. This was the price that had to be paid for walking alone in step with Bartholomew, or respectfully three paces behind him.

Was the Mirror *right to support a wayward King against an anxious Establishment which on this occasion correctly assessed the character of the monarch and the mood of the people*? Maurice Edelman summed up the situation:

> 'Contrary to Edward's belief, his conduct was disapproved in wide circles. There were rumours on the Left that through the influence of his American friends he had undue sympathies with Nazi Germany. He had spoken disparagingly of the League of Nations. In June 1935, he had addressed the British Legion and proposed that a deputation of ex-Servicemen should go to Nazi Germany on a friendship mission. On top of it all, Prince Charming seemed to have turned into a middle-aged playboy.
>
> '"Every time I dipped into the bran-tub of provincial opinion," said Dalton, "I pulled out a puritan."'

It is possible to be instinctively wrong. If our politics had to be made to match our new readers, 'the young working-class men and women and in general the least educated part of the population', we would have to do better than that. Yet the circulation of the *Mirror* increased more dramatically than that of any other newspaper during the Abdication crisis, and when the curtain fell it retained more of that increase than any other paper. The newspaper had put the wrong case, but its style and presentation were exciting, and the greatest story for many years had provided the opportunity to develop its new technique in all its compelling, even garish, appeal to the masses.

'This is the moment we keep our heads down,' Cassandra said to me, 'but I have other causes in mind.' The Bartholomews, the Cassandras and the Cudlipps left it to Richard Jennings to heal the wounds in three sober editorials. Words like 'insists' and 'demand' and accusations of political manoeuvring gave way to earnest pleas for time and patience, sympathetic to Edward's dilemma but asking questions about the true national interest and recognising Baldwin's concern for the institution of monarchy. The paper was now a less enthusiastic member of what Beaverbrook called the King's Party, and when Baldwin announced to Parliament that a morganatic marriage would be unacceptable an editorial acknowledged that 'Mr Baldwin's position in this matter has been one of extreme delicacy and difficulty.'

Good old Jennings. The Duke of Windsor waited until 1951 to sell his memoirs, *A King's Story*, to the *Sunday Express*, like any other transient notoriety. The *Mirror* turned its attention to international issues of greater importance than a domestic abdication: the rising menace of Hitler and the coming war.

This was a matter on which I was better informed than morganatic marriage.

In the gathering storm the new *Daily Mirror* came of age mentally, establishing itself as a voice of national significance. Our interpretation of events was perceptive and mature. Vastly more so than the *Daily Mail*, pro-Nazi and pro-Fascist under the odious influence of the first Lord Rothermere. Vastly more so than the *Daily Express*, saddled up to the moment the sirens wailed in London one Sunday morning in September 1939 with Lord Beaverbrook proclaiming 'There Will Be No War,' dispensing bromides to a nation that needed pep pills. Yet the most curious contrast was between the *Mirror* and *The Times*, which took leave of its senses for six years under the guidance of Geoffrey Dawson. He had been Editor from 1912 to 1919 during Northcliffe's ownership and was brought back to the chair in 1922 by the Astors with unhappy consequences in the 1930s.

The basis of the argument was simple enough–when and by what means the injustices to Germany under the Treaty of Versailles . could be redressed, and how far Europe and the world were prepared to yield to her other aspirations without a fight. The arrival of Adolf Hitler as Chancellor of Germany on January 30 1933 was followed by his Nazi Party's total absorption of the national administration in less than two months. The argument ceased to be academic when Hitler embarked upon his programme of tearing up the Versailles clauses one by one according to the gospel of *Mein Kampf*.

The Times delicately stated its position in an editorial on June 28 1933: 'Europe in fact is placed in the dilemma of having to refuse to force what reason suggests should at least in part be conceded, or else of yielding to extremism what earlier was refused to moderation.' The policy of *The Times* and the inner Tory clique signposted the *autobahn* to Munich. Appeasement, conceding not generously from strength but from weakness and fear, was ennobled in fine words in editorials in *The Times*, camouflaged as lofty and disinterested statesmanship. The cringing obsequiousness of that newspaper at that time was unveiled in a confidential letter in May 1937 from Geoffrey Dawson to the acting Berlin correspondent of *The Times*. Mr Chamberlain had just succeeded Mr Baldwin as Coalition Prime Minister and Mr Dawson was discomfited by criticism voiced by the Nazis at some inadvertent item in the Thunderer which had fallen short of idolatry.

'It would interest me greatly to know precisely what it is in *The Times* that has produced this antagonism in Germany. I did my utmost, night after night, to keep out of the paper anything that might hurt their susceptibilities. I have always been convinced that the peace of the world depends more than anything else on our getting into reasonable relations with Germany.'

The contents of the letter were not disclosed[1] until years after the war was over.

There were certainly no skeletons to rattle in the *Mirror*'s cupboard after 1934, no shameful letters to be disgorged years later. Even before Rothermere's departure as chief shareholder in the paper, the fastidious Richard Jennings, the leader writer, emerged with a staunchly independent attitude to the thugs who had seized power in Germany and were threatening to overrun and overrule Europe and, eventually, subjugate Britain. He had acquired a veneer of intellectual radicalism in his years at Oxford and had absorbed all that is good in English culture. His style when I arrived on the newspaper was testy, pinpricking and teasing rather than provoking. Hitler didn't know it, but he transformed a gentle bibliophile into a ferocious anti-Nazi. The metamorphosis of Richard Jennings was startling to behold: nobody could have anticipated that the answer to the jack-booted stormtroopers goose-stepping along the Unter den Linden would have come from the literary editor of the formerly genteel *Daily Mirror* in London, shuffling fussily around the office in his soft carpet slippers.

Jennings had no taste for the new people on the *Mirror*, or indeed for anybody other than the Sitwells, but he did invite me to his little office, a bric-à-brac shop full of books and minor *objets d'art*, where he told me surprisingly that I was welcome when I wished to 'escape from Bart's madhouse'. The only political influence I could exert just then was to encourage the lonely Cecil King principally by listening, sustain Cassandra by implanting ideas, and exchange views with Jennings. As Features Editor I was in charge of the joy department, but unlike the Nazis I preached 'Joy through Strength' instead of 'Strength through Joy'.

---

[1] *History of* The Times, *1921–1948*.

77

Churchill, in search of acolytes, was also observing Jennings. When Winston warned Britain in 1932 of the danger of a rearmed Europe, Jennings responded, writing under the initials 'W. M.' (William Morris?) From then on Churchill and he preached from their different platforms that the dictators meant war. Be strong, rearm, seek allies, appeasement could lead only to disaster.

Adolf Hitler became President of Germany as well as Chancellor an hour after Hindenburg died on August 3 1934. In the *Daily Mail* Lord Rothermere, the first Englishman to lick his boots, published an interview with Hitler proclaiming devotion to the cause of peace. The *Mirror* reminded its readers of another famous interview with the former Kaiser published in the *Daily Telegraph* in 1908, but it took the rational view that no great and populous nation could be permanently kept in subjection to the terms of a vindictive peace treaty. 'When they strove to fulfil the terms of the Treaty, they existed miserably. It is mere humbug, therefore, to reproach them for defying the Treaty–if they can. We shall get nearer a hope for peace if we recognise these realities.' German rearmament was a different matter, 'particularly in view of the collective or herd hysteria of her people'.

Hitler gave a pacific interview to the *Daily Mirror* in February 1936, and marched into the Rhineland a week later, offering twenty-five-year peace treaties with his neighbouring countries. The newspaper itself now embarked upon a wobbly period. It had never advocated war–it had, like Churchill, preached preparedness. In retrospect the Hitler interview, again expressing his devotion to peace, is seen as a lie, but it beguiled the *Mirror*: 'It Must Not Be War. Hitler's Peace Plan Should Succeed.' On March 9 1936, it unaccountably published this drivel:

> Who will be caught again by lying twaddle about war to end war, and about our sacred honour and our solemn oath? The futile pacts and obsolete treaties may lie in pieces wherever Hitler or anybody else has thrown them. Better flimsy fragments of imbecile documents on the ground than millions of rotting bodies of young men.
>
> The latest week-end crisis does *not* mean war–for us.
>
> The time has ended for the making of further pacts, guarantees, agreements, understandings and whatnots in defence of an impossible system, which seeks to perpetuate the ludicrous settlement of the revengeful post-war years. Those arrangements still divide Europe into water-

tight compartments of victors and vanquished, the satiated
and the rebellious. Statesmen talk about 'our' signature
here, there and all over the world. Whose signature is it?
Not that collectively of the millions who would perish in
another war. The signature merely of a few muddled and
terrified politicians.

It was a pacifist's charter, a ludicrous undermining of the right and
duty of elected governments to represent their people and speak in
their name in grave matters of war or peace. I don't suppose there is a
newspaper in the world that has not somewhere in its files a campaign
or an article or an editorial it would prefer not to exhume. Perhaps a
day might usefully be set aside each year for a bonfire of bad ideas, or
bellicose attitudes, or mistaken information, or unfair attacks, or
indefensible intrusions. Maurice Edelman was right to describe that
editorial as contemptible and the month of March 1936 as an unhappy
descent in the *Mirror*'s political judgement, 'the nadir of its political
sagacity'. It suddenly advocated that Britain should try reason with
the President-Chancellor of Germany and steer clear of alliances on
the Continent: Geoffrey Dawson must have thought he had converted
another newspaper to march under his banner of appeasement. After
Mussolini's seizure of Abyssina the *Mirror* even expressed the belief
that a new phase was about to begin in Europe and that peace might
yet be reconstructed on a more confident basis.

Bart–or King? Or Jennings on his own? The mad month closed
with 'W. M.', reminiscent of the style that identified him before he
became the Man Hitler Changed, writing of the joys of spring:
'Nature is already in a merry mood. The daffodils and the primroses
are out and the lambs are skipping in the sun ... What does the world
and his wife want? Merely to get on with their work and play.'
Goebbels must have chuckled.

I had no power or responsibility beyond my domain and Cassandra
had no influence beyond his column. I record this sorry occasion to
dispel any claim that we, collectively, were always or nearly always
right on that newspaper. When I invited myself to Richard Jennings'
bric-à-brac shop upstairs to discuss the curious change in policy he
said, 'One has to try for peace, hasn't one?' He handed me a slim
volume of poetry. 'Did you ever read Humbert Wolfe's *Requiem*?
Came out a long time ago, 1927 or something like that. You'll like it.
Let me have it back later.'

Jennings and the *Mirror* recovered their sanity, rudely jerked back to reality by the opening of the three-year Spanish Civil War in the summer of 1936, establishing yet another Fascist dictator-state in Europe, and by the first of Winston Churchill's series of thunderous warnings of what was happening in the world around us and of the shape of things to come. Jennings wrote:

> Churchill can claim credit for having drawn Mr Baldwin's somnambulist attention to the huge, the inexplicable armaments of Germany. He speaks with authority, as one closely concerned with the technicalities of war. Thus yesterday we seemed, indeed, to be back in the dark war age—with Mr Churchill again demanding his state of emergency and clamouring for a deputation to confer with the Prime Minister. It is depressing to have to admit it. But Mr Churchill is right.

On April 1 1938 Cassandra wrote:

> Before this visit to Germany I always had a sneaking feeling that there was a strong undercurrent of opposition to Hitler.
> I am now certain that I was wrong.
> I know now that this man has the absolute unswerving confidence of the people.
> They will do anything for him.
> They worship him.
> They regard him as a god.
> Do not let us deceive ourselves in this country that Hitler may soon be dislodged by enemies within his own frontiers.
> Germans regard him as the greatest figure in their history.
> Better and greater than Bismarck.
> Infinitely superior to Frederick the Great.

Cassandra had been visiting Germany frequently since he joined the newspaper in 1935, steadfastly warning Britain and his readers, the future soldiers and airmen, that the Nazis were ready, not preparing, for war.

5

---◆◆◆---

'Editor: Private'

Cecil King had always been civil to me during those first two years at the *Mirror*. He restricted the dialogue to the business in hand, occasionally with a twinkle in his eye, discussing newspapers in terms of strategy rather than of instant ideas. It was apparent that he didn't like anybody very much and also apparent that he didn't particularly dislike me, though we would not be going out on the tiles together or painting the town pink. He knew a Good Idea, especially a mischievous idea, when he heard one and indeed would think up a mischievous idea or two himself; he said he enjoyed 'putting the cat among the pigeons'. Example: 'Why not explain to our readers what, if anything, the political parties stand for, an impartial exposition'–adding archly, 'including the Communists?' It was easy for either of the Cecils, King or Thomas, to explain to Chairman Cowley that it would have been construed as bad taste if the Reds had been left out, or unwise for the new *Mirror* at that stage to have invited charges of partiality or, heaven forbid, suppression: it was a tedious chore but it did not call for any device more sophisticated than a white lie. For my part I enjoyed discussing the Communist Cause with a comely and wholesome Eton-cropped graduate, who believed in free love, from their King Street headquarters.

Cecil's Law on tabloid journalism was uncomplicated, though to him it was far from being a Wykehamist's whim; he had really thought it out and studied the problem, for Cecil never jumped to conclusions. Here it is, in his own words:

> 'The criterion I used to apply was to ask of a paragraph if it was of interest to, or intelligible by, a bus-driver's wife in Sheffield. If not, then it should not have been printed. This criterion excludes a certain amount but, more important, imposes on a great deal more a high standard of simple clear English.'

I got a little tired of hearing about the bus-driver's wife in Sheffield. It wasn't dauntingly difficult for a commercial traveller's son from Cardiff to chat up a bus-driver's wife in Sheffield or anywhere else the Wykehamist might choose to mention without notice of the question: the proletariat spoke the same language. But before we depart from this highbrow seminar on Communicating with the People I should warn the present Editor of the *Daily Mirror* that if he is still mindful of Cecil's Law he should be printing the Sheffield edition in Hindi and Urdu. Cecil has retired to Dublin, but I would not like Mike Molloy to be the unhappy recipient of a cable in Gaelic telling him that certain paragraphs 'should not have been printed' in English because they were unintelligible to a bus-driver's wife.

King was keenly aware of the necessary ingredients of spice and audacity and enjoyed the fun of publishing as well as its more serious aspects. Nobody confused him with the Laughing Cavalier, but he did have a sense of humour, 'Irish,' he explained. He enjoyed talking about my human ideas for the feature pages, eccentric by previous standards on the paper, uninhibited by anybody's standards at that time; and we were appealing to the young, of which he specially approved:

> Knock! Knock!
> Who's there?
> It is the younger generation.
> What is your ambition?
> Youth is painfully fighting for an outlet which will offer escape from obscurity into the public eye. The *Mirror* is offering that outlet.
> If you are under twenty-five and have something to tell the world about yourself and what you want, send in your entry, now: Write 100 words on 'What I Am', 100 words on 'What I Can Do' and not more than 200 words on 'What I Want to Do'.
> Address your entry to 'Ambition'.

I specialised in this sort of persuasive word-economy; delete 'specialised', it came naturally. The value of the conversations with King did not rest so far as I was concerned upon our exchanges on tabloid journalism, of which I instinctively knew more than he could ever intellectually learn, but on his wide-ranging views about the world in general, his knowledge of politics, his Time Machine forays into the future: where would Britain, Europe, the civilised and uncivilised world be in five years, and where would our newspapers be, saying what and to whom? And there were the mistakes the great publishing houses of Fleet Street had made in the past and were still making. We talked of Northcliffe, Beaverbrook, Camrose and the other pioneers in their particular spheres, and of war and peace and human rights and social injustice and vested interest. These were the fascinating areas of which King knew almost everything and I knew little.

'Cudlipp at that time had little education, no foresight, but a galaxy of journalistic gifts . . . he has a gift for timing which is quite beyond price in a daily paper. Over the years he has acquired an excellent education, and has picked up from me a habit of looking ahead which, once acquired, cannot be forgotten.'[1]

King was my tutor, Bartholomew my tormentor. A sustained conversation with Bart about anything of any consequence was out of the question; dialogue was conducted in expletives, abruptly begun, abruptly ended; he did not have a surfeit of charm to squander on superiors or underlings. Power had come to him late in life and it was his, and his alone, to monopolise. Often we would be in the same wine bar early in the evening, *El Vino* in Fleet Street, Bart with Cecil Thomas and one or two of the commercial people who were his toadies or spies, I usually with Cassandra when he had finished his column, dropped a carbon into my room, and sent the copy to be set. There was usually a cold and suspicious look of recognition but he rarely joined us or invited us to join him; he was more friendly to Cassandra when I was not around. Was I seeing too much of King? Was I a King's Man?

A closer relationship with Cecil was inevitable whatever the consequences. He found it difficult or imprudent to dispense friendship; the cautionary rule of the Harmsworths was that last year's favourite might easily become this year's encumbrance, making it difficult to make changes. In spite of this professional reticence and the social moat he built around his castle, where he chose to reside and contemplate alone, I found it possible when necessary to raise my voice and shout across the drawbridge.

One morning in September 1937 Bartholomew put his head around the door between our rooms and beckoned me in, an unusual ploy. 'Here's a laugh,' he said, 'Cecil King is going to send for you shortly and ask you to become Editor of the *Pictorial*. As if you'd leave the *Mirror*! Come and see me afterwards.' I was not accustomed to such comradeship and warmth.

[1] Cecil King in *Strictly Personal*.

The situation between the two men is now familiar, based exclusively on mutual suspicion. But Bartholomew's attitude to the *Sunday Pictorial* was in a different category of human high tension; it was risky to be near him when the name of the paper was mentioned and there was reason for his anger. The two newspapers were then owned by separate companies holding a controlling interest in each other; they shared the same offices and plant, the same Chairman, and several directors served on both boards. The *Mirror* under Bart was now roaring away, all set to become the world's biggest daily seller, but in 1934 he had not been asked to take over both newspapers and by September 1937 the *Pictorial* was still languishing, its circulation having dropped from 2,416,981 in November 1925 to 1,336,000. The revival of the *Pictorial* had not been offered to Bartholomew. The Triumvirate of Cowley, Roome and Lovell wanted to cling on to at least one newspaper, prim, conservative, inoffensive, which would not embarrass them in their clubs or among their week-end social friends; the fact that the *Pictorial* was near the abyss of financial disaster was to them a secondary consideration. Bart had sufficient power, too much already for their comfort. Yet the problem would not go away. Cowley was finally talked into agreeing in 1937 that Bart should be made Editor of the *Pictorial*, but when the directors met to resolve the matter Bart was so insulting to Cowley that he refused to make the appointment. I knew nothing of this meeting, nor was I informed at that time by anybody of the lethal condition of the minefield. On the roof in Fleet Street one needs more lives than a cat and a charmed life is an asset. King was appointed Editorial Director of the ailing Sunday and Bart looked forward to what he hoped and thought would be the Wykehamist's crash-dive.

King phoned me with his polite request, 'Would you like to pop down?' presumably unaware that I had already been alerted by Bartholomew. He explained the problem with his usual patience. His discourses with the existing Editor, David Grant, did not seem to be getting anywhere at all. If an idea was mentioned it would not be resisted but the execution of it would be so appalling or half-hearted that the idea itself was made to look ineffective or even silly. The paper was in a locked-in position with all the wrong writers on long contracts. Something had to be done, and quickly, about the *Pictorial*, or the group itself would be in deep trouble. David Grant was 'a nice enough chap', principally interested in golf, but King had reached the end of his tether and Grant was departing.

'Bart,' said Cecil King, 'has agreed that I can have any of the

Mirror men as my Editor. Will you agree to be Editor of the *Sunday Pictorial*? It is only fair to warn you that we won't be getting any help from Bart.'

I said: 'Yes—when?'

Among my more dramatic one-scene dramas on newspapers I retain a nostalgic memory of the meeting shortly afterwards with Harry Guy Bartholomew; the pity is that it wasn't filmed or taped or photographed or even witnessed.

'Yes, yes, come in,' he said when I phoned. He couldn't wait, but the benign smile which I had rarely seen before and never saw again did not remain for long.

'Seen King?'

'Yes.'

'Did he offer you the job?'

'Yes.'

He was in a boisterous mood, banging his fist on the table and laughing in a humourless fashion.

'What did you say, Cudlipp?'

'Yes.'

In the closing stanzas of a menacing harangue, Bartholomew, now almost breathless with rage, eyed me distastefully and said, 'I'll tell you this, you'll not get any help from me—no help at all. That's all.'

It was a promise he kept until he fired me in 1949. I always knew that retribution was in store.

The historian of what happened Upstairs after this significant day is Cecil King:

'Bart said I could have any of the *Mirror* men as my editor (this was typical of Bart), he had interviewed any possible editors and told them if they accepted any offer from me he would do his best to ruin them. However, I invited Hugh Cudlipp to be editor and he accepted. He was twenty-four. This infuriated Bart, who kept us out of the *Mirror* as far as possible and was obstructive in every way. What annoyed him more than anything was that the *Pictorial* sale soon started going up, and for many years kept 200,000 in front of the *Mirror*. This was infuriating (*a*) because the *Mirror* was his paper, (*b*) because he hated the *Pictorial* anyway, but (*c*) because the continued success of the *Pictorial* underlined the fact that he was neither entirely indispensable on the *Mirror*, nor was he wholly responsible for its success.'[1]

[1] Cecil King in *Strictly Personal*.

It was High Noon in Fleet Street and I was a walking target; so, on a loftier and safer plane, was Northcliffe's nephew. Adversity creates strange bedfellows, but it wasn't discouraging to be able to stick a sign on the door of my new office saying 'Editor: Private' at twenty-four; nobody else, anyway, had ever had the nerve or opportunity at that age on a national newspaper, even a dying one. I admired King's courage, or suspected the depth of his desperation, in appointing me. If his judgement had been wrong or his prayer not answered it would have been publicly known with supersonic speed; half a dozen issues of the new *Sunday Pictorial* would be enough to establish the folly of it all. The divine right of the Harmsworths to put the head of the offending Editor on the block of the guillotine would not have sufficed in this case, not with Bartholomew knitting near by. If the mission had failed, little more would have been heard of Cecil Harmsworth King for the rest of his living days and nothing at all more of me.

To Bart I was the traitor to an inner magic circle he had never invited me to join, which did not visibly exist, and to which if it did exist nobody except Harry Guy Bartholomew belonged. Yet a few days after our 'That's all' confrontation he asked me to see him again. He was in a mood of brooding tranquillity, known to sailors as the eye of the storm, merely transitory, making an unexpected offer.

'You can take only two *Mirror* men with you to the *Pictorial*.'

I chose the two not only for their potential talent but for their high-voltage dispensability from Bart's point of view.

'Peter Wilson.'

'Yes.' I knew Bartholomew had been at odds with Peter's father, Freddie Wilson, who had worked for the *Mirror* years before. I also knew that Freddie Wilson had been a close friend of Wallace Roome, the suave General Manager, one of the Triumvirate who had thwarted Bart from any discernible power on the paper until he had been soured.

'Stuart Campbell.'

'*Yes.*' I knew that Campbell, working somewhere on the News Desk, had been goaded by *his* frustrations into becoming a zealous and belligerent officer of the Union. '*Yes,*' Bart repeated, 'but he will cause you a lot of trouble. And I will release them both immediately. I don't want to see them. You tell them.'

Peter Wilson, given his chance at last, and swiftly announced by me as the Man They Can't Gag, became in a short time the finest and most versatile sports writer in the British arena, a colourful boxing commentator without equal even in the United States, where Paul Gallico and Damon Runyon, sire of the Lemon Drop Kid and Harry the Horse, had sponged the blood from their lapels as reporters at the ringside. Among my favourite headlines was the one we wrote together in rather large type for Peter's report on the love-in between Bruce Woodcock and Lee Oma, the horizontal cardboard man from Detroit:

OMA? COMA? AROMA!

Stuart Campbell master-minded the methods of detection and the techniques of proving malpractice which were required first to trap and then to expose an impressive number of the price profiteers, ration-dodgers, petrol thieves, racketeering landlords and other scum who float to the surface of a nation in travail: many of our liberties were cheerfully put in pawn during the war, but unfortunately the law of libel was not suspended for the duration. Campbell was the obvious man to select as Editor of the *Pictorial* when I vanished into the Army at the end of 1940, but for the five years of my absence elsewhere King and he conducted a private war of their own. He later became the outstanding investigative Editor of *The People*.

The anaemic *Pictorial* was passing peacefully away on Sunday mornings, wet or fine, and its transformation into a volatile Sunday tabloid with a future had to be conducted more dangerously and quickly than the rescue of the *Mirror*. A daily newspaper can change its mood in more leisurely fashion, following the sensational with the sentimental next day, correcting an overdose of politics with the antidote of human interest in the next issue, quietening excesses or stimulating a few dull efforts with immediate effect. A Sunday newspaper appeared only fifty-two times a year.

The metamorphosis had to be effected with the rudeness which attended the birth of Gargantua, delivered through his mother's left ear. Gargamelle, daughter of the King of the Parpaillos, did not go into labour until the eleventh month of her pregnancy and only then as a result of eating too much tripe. The *Pictorial* was in the same plight. It had to be surgery without anaesthetics.

The paper was respectable and virginal and I read with mounting dismay the issue that appeared the week before I took over. 'Dismal, isn't it?' said King. 'Why didn't they know, why didn't they do something about it?' An editorial asked the searching question, 'Should prospective brides produce before marriage a certificate testifying to their prowess in home management?' but the reply to the question was not disturbing: 'Give and Take in married life is an adequate substitute for diplomas.' Old Timer took a whole page to deal with 'Early Crops of Tomatoes', and the Radio Parson of the time, the Reverend W. H. Elliott, asked: 'Is Most of the World Mad?'

The *Pictorial* was a conspiracy to make the English Sabbath duller. The jokes page, my God, the jokes page! 'Nuts and Wine' it was called, and one and all warned me I would kill it at my peril, but I threw thirty chestnuts on the fire the first week I took over.

Another Howler

Deerstalking is the animal conversation between stags.

Canned music

Employees in a tinned fruit factory are encouraged to sing whilst at work. They just make merry while they can.

Reading them again does not convince me that the decision was unduly bold. It did not take long to discover that the principal protagonists on the newspaper for the sanctity of 'Nuts and Wine' were those paid extra for manufacturing the atrocious puns at the rate of two guineas a groan. For the same reason there were three ineffective short editorials for extra pay every week which said nothing instead of one that said something worthwhile or important. When the perks were consolidated into the take-home pay the resistance collapsed, and the other walls of Jericho fell at a loud blast.

The staff began to warm to the newcomer, and when the sale almost immediately began to increase they admitted to me one by one, not in the hearing of the others, that it had all been a bit of a racket and it really was time things changed. My more astonishing discovery was that two or three of the top executives on that sanctimonious, blue-pencilled Sunday newspaper had been making money on the side with the connivance of the Editor as the creators, publishers and contributors of a bluish sex-mad magazine called *Razzle*. That sort of insincerity can never produce a newspaper which matters a damn to anybody: the entertainment side of the old *Pictorial* was unfunny and the serious side farcical.

The weekly political article, written by Mr Collinson Owen, was so lamentably Right-wing that it had no relevance to current affairs; it was worrying away that week about 'Left-Wing Cans on Tail of Our Foreign Policy', and believe it or not the man who was alleged to be tying on the cans was that capricious revolutionary Anthony

Eden, the young Foreign Secretary. Out it all went, including Pip, Squeak and Wilfred, though I should have modernised that famous strip-cartoon instead of being cruel to animals.

Cecil King was able to report to the Triumvirate that all was well on the circulation front; they were older and more dithery and more scared than ever, but still there (Cowley, with outrageous insensitivity, clung on until he died at seventy-four in 1944). Bartholomew thought up several novel ways of displaying his anger apart from ignoring me in or out of *El Vino*. The *Pictorial* staff was tucked away in No Man's Land, overcrowded in depressing brown-paint surroundings. When I requested the small room of a *Daily Mirror* executive to work from on Saturdays, nearer the editorial production floor we took over on that one day, the answer predictably was No; former friends and professional acquaintances on the *Mirror* were warned to watch their step and advised not to be seen with me. Cecil King, as a director, was treated more savagely and with indignity: he was barred from the *Daily Mirror*, though a director of that newspaper, and could keep contact only by subterfuge or accident. He could not and did not exercise any meaningful influence on the daily newspaper, political or otherwise, until 1939, and then only on sufferance. There were benefits in being a Harmsworth, but one had to put up with the weather conditions: there was no escape to the Aitkens or the Berrys or the Astors, no trap door.

But there were compensations. Cecil and I were running the *Sunday Pictorial*, it had been saved and was already flourishing. There was no Bartian inferiority complex on my part in turning King's knowledge and notions, or anyone else's, into roaring original journalism in that period which climaxed in the war. The *Mirror* still had Cassandra and it still had Richard Jennings. The *Pictorial* developed its own Sunday-paper techniques—and we all had Hitler and Mussolini on the other side. A sour frown from Bartholomew in Fetter Lane was a minor price to pay for such freedom.

At this stage of the proceedings King introduced into our relationship a hint of togetherness which was rather out of character. He was always in the office on Saturday nights when the *Pictorial* was being produced, edition by edition, hopefully with improvements each time. It was the proudest and most anxious moment of the week for him, and my busiest. Nevertheless we customarily dined together at the Martinez Spanish Restaurant in Swallow Street, and I always had my share or more of the two bottles of claret.

Deservedly so, because the response from the readers was swift.

Here are the yearly circulation figures:

1937	1,340,900
1938	1,443,700
1939	1,580,000
1940	1,702,500

The *Sunday Pictorial* was no longer a newspaper in distress.

6

The Change of Winds

On the front page of the year's first issue in 1937 the *Pictorial* addressed its inattentive and dwindling readership with an exclusive item:

BRASS BANDS PLAY TO CATERPILLARS

The news was of some interest to music-lovers or music-haters, according to their attitude to brass bands, and possibly to amateur entomologists and any other larvae that happened to be passing by that Sunday morning.

The front page headline in the first issue of 1938 dealt with a murder which was of maximum public interest at the time:

MONA TINSLEY'S SPIRIT
LED HER SLAYER TO THE GALLOWS

The shop was under new management. The newspaper had suddenly discovered the human race: somewhere inside the same issue I whispered–'Shush-h-h, This is Baby's Page'. What made it different from the other popular Sunday papers was its political awareness in an intensely political period, its social savvy and its brash confidence.

A major happening in February 1938 yielded a scoop of some world-wide significance which ensured that henceforth the paper would at least be read by its rivals on publication night. There is nothing like a scoop for reviving the spirits and stimulating the hopes of the staff of a newspaper which has not excited any interest or comment for a decade within or without the industry; and it was a political scoop at that.

In 1935 Anthony Eden, then Lord Privy Seal, had been appointed Minister Without Portfolio for League of Nations Affairs and in the same year Secretary of State for Foreign Affairs, serving under Baldwin and later Neville Chamberlain. The estimation by Harold Macmillan of his contemporary's commanding position at the age of thirty-eight puts Anthony Eden in true perspective: 'His fine war record, his charm, his versatility, his pre-eminence in debate, his appeal to men and women of all parties; all these made him an out-standing figure.' His policy was firm resistance through the League of Nations, and when that failed through alliances with the world's two greatest powers, to the expansionist plans of the Germans, the Italians and the Japanese. Baldwin was indifferent to foreign affairs and Chamberlain merely ignorant, but such was his vanity that he re-solved to conduct these matters himself, meeting his adversaries face to face (and encouraged by *The Times* to do so), acting, not in partner-ship with his experienced Foreign Secretary but on occasions behind his back. In July 1937 he had written personally to Mussolini, his first move in a hopeless gambit to prise the Axis apart, recording in his diary that 'I did not show my letter to the Foreign Secretary for I had the feeling that he would object to it.'

Cecil King and I were aware from different sources of the growing disaffection between Chamberlain and Eden over Italian affairs, and there were hints in some of the newspapers of Eden's growing irrita-tion. The preponderance of Cabinet opinion, massively misguided, was against him. At midnight on Saturday, February 19 1938 I telephoned him at his home with suitable apologies for arousing him so late.

'Quite all right, Cudlipp, I'm not in bed.' *Clue Number One.*

'I understand, Mr Eden, you have resigned as Foreign Secretary.' There was a pause. *Clue Number Two.* And then–

'Oh.' *Clue Number Three.* Any fool knows the difference between Yes and No, but a newspaper man of any merit must be able to divine the degree of admission indicated by that inadequate shield 'No comment'. No fool could have misinterpreted the exclamation 'Oh'; the pause and then the intonation indicated his surprise that the secret could have reached the Press so quickly. There were no parrying questions from Anthony Eden along the lines of: 'And who has told you this curious information?' There was no denial, *Clue Number Four.* That was the most significant clue of all, and *Clue Number Five* was that experience had taught me that at midnight, especially with honest men like Eden, the instinct for stratagem or evasion and in particular downright lying is at its lowest ebb.

I did not want to prolong the delicate moment and thereby risk a personal request to withhold the news 'in the national interest' until this or that had occurred or until something had been said or confirmed in another place. Yet, on the eve of what we knew was expected the next day, another raging speech by Hitler, I could scarcely announce exclusively the resignation of the British Foreign Secretary on a matter of transcending principle merely on the evidence of the one word, 'Oh'.

I chanced a parting sentence: 'I realise there may be further talks and the announcement will not be made until tomorrow, and apologise again for disturbing you tonight and so late.'

Still no denial and another pause.

Clue Number Six: clearly an announcement *was* going to be made the next day.

'Good-night, Mr Eden.'

'Good-night, Cudlipp.'

I wrote the front-page headline for the last edition—

EDEN
RESIGNS

But had I sufficiently considered and probed the word 'Oh'? If Eden had in fact resigned on the moral issue of accommodating the Nazis or resisting, capitulation or defiance, surrender or war, why would he wish not to say so? He would no longer have reason to pander to the susceptibilities or timing of a Prime Minister who had rejected his counsel and, worse, double-crossed him in high office. Did 'Oh' not only indicate surprise but also that he had not yet made the irrevocable decision, that he had in fact resigned but had been requested by Mr Chamberlain to reconsider, to sleep on it, and that when I telephoned him at midnight he was engrossed in that agonising process? I thought it prudent to add a sub-heading:

CABINET WANT HIM TO STAY
TODAY'S TALKS WILL DECIDE

After I had written the story I telephoned Cecil King at home, an unusual event because he drew the curtains at an early hour, and told him the exclusive news. 'This is a major scoop,' said Cecil, 'how do we know at this ungodly time?' 'Oh,' I replied, 'I phoned Eden myself at midnight and he said "Oh". I will explain it all when we meet.' It was officially announced on Sunday, February 20 1938 that Mr Anthony Eden had resigned as Foreign Secretary. I have no claims like the talented lady whom King married in 1962 to be a 'sensitive' in the art, science or phantasy of extra-sensory perception: it was a journalist's hunch.

The same day Hitler made a major speech, ranting on for three hours, a marathon of Nazi self-glorification, lampooning democracy, vilifying the Jews, sneering at Christians with Bibles, and talking of

Germany's love of peace. It was the old story–'We want peace, *that* piece.' And it was no consolation to know that the wild men of Europe, bereft of any sense of honour or regard for truth in the traditional manner, would be cosily dealt with by Chamberlain, a former Lord Mayor of Birmingham, born 1869, armed with a bowler hat, an umbrella, and his own inestimable vanity, and the new Foreign Secretary Lord Halifax, born 1881, unversed in foreign affairs, the modest aristocrat, deeply religious, a Christian with a Bible.

The total ascendancy of the appeasers in the British Cabinet had now been accomplished. In the next month, March of 1938, Mr Chamberlain rattled a sabre. 'The sight of this enormous, this almost terrifying power which Britain is building up,' said the Prime Minister, 'has a sobering effect on the opinion of the world.' Before the end of the month Austria was raped by the Nazis.

Charles Wilberforce was our principal Sunday contributor. On rereading his material I find him rather bellicose, a bit of a flag-waver, but waving the Union Jack at a time when certainly someone should have been waving it. He was a passionate exposer of inertia in high places, Old-Men regimes were anathema to him, and he pleaded for the resurrection of British spirit and pride; his text was that since war was inevitable it was time the politicians did something about making victory for Britain and its Allies a conceivable outcome. The country was infested by German spies, and the Nazi High Command were well aware that Chamberlain's boast of this enormous, this almost terrifying power that Britain was building up was still a propaganda myth. Hitler was not terrified and the British people were still being shamefully misguided. 'Our Army,' wrote Wilberforce, 'is still only playing soldiers, with 1918 mentality still in command, 1918 weapons still in use, and 1918 transport still favoured.' The politicians at the helm were still deluding themselves that speeches could make the world safe for democracy. '*Freedom* of speech–to answer Hitler with confusion. *Liberty*–to make an appalling muddle of defence. That is the Britain we are expected to be proud of.' There was still much to be done. 'Churchill, the one man Hitler fears, is still not in the Cabinet. Russia, the one country we must embrace in the peace bloc, is still an issue clouded with political quibbling and nauseating diplomatic niceties. Must the people also force these obvious steps upon the Government?'

It is a record that bears examination, and the only other newspaper that was pressing the Government for immediate action with the same fervour and inside knowledge of the nation's infirmities was the *Daily Mirror*. As time went on they were to pay for their enthusiasm and their patriotism when the patience of the British politicians was exhausted, and censorship and then suppression were threatened.

In September of 1938, the month of greatest international anxiety until war began exactly one year later, Wilberforce wrote during the period of Neville Chamberlain's three flights to Germany to meet Hitler face to face at Berchtesgaden, Godesberg and Munich:

> Now that for the moment the tension seems to have eased slightly–for while there are conferences there cannot be war–we can breathe more easily again, with the hope that some way will be found to avoid a war no single person in Europe wants . . .
>
> Now we have a pause from strain, we must find some means of regaining the respect of the Dictator countries. Not by giving in to them. Not by joining with them in an international brawl. Not by surrendering our traditional principles of freedom. But by restrengthening ourselves, by restoring our own faith in our destiny. And by recovering our morale and self-confidence.

Wilberforce was never content with pious thoughts and exhortations. Whether the country liked it or not it had to be put on a potential war footing; you cannot reason with a lunatic with his finger on the trigger. The measures he advocated were National Registration for every man and woman with a view to conscription for labour and military service in case of war (Hitler had proclaimed conscription in Germany on March 16 1935); the vast extension of food-growing in the country; a recruiting campaign for the Territorial Army; the arming of the defence forces with the latest and most scientific weapons; the completion of air-raid precautions. The message was– '*Britain Must Wake Up!*'

What happened at the meetings in Germany was what always occurs when a rabbit presents its visiting card to a ferret. A week after the signing of the Munich Agreement in the early hours of September 30 1938 Wilberforce said one of the lessons that Hitler had come near to demonstrating was that the leisurely and disputative Parliamentary system had disadvantages in a war situation.

I was invariably in accord with Charles Wilberforce's philosophy and ensured that his trenchant articles were given prominence whenever he had time to write. And he was given facilities that all other writers on newspapers envied–late delivery of copy, up-dating of facts to the last minute of going to press, global freedom of expression, lunching with the Editor every day and intruding upon the privacy of his office without knocking at the door. I was Charles Wilberforce. Cecil King, condescendingly and never in the presence of Mr Wilberforce himself, referred to Charles as his mouthpiece; Mr Wilberforce, a vain fellow, regarded Cecil King as his legman, but as the impartial Editor I had the sagacity to marry one man's words with another's foresight and frequently with my own convictions. At all events, I knew that Mr Wilberforce would never desert the *Pictorial* for another newspaper unless I took him with me.

It was a healthier partnership than that which existed between the first and unlamented Lord Rothermere and the hypocritical Horatio Bottomley who wrote for him during the First World War in the same newspaper. The two gentlemen met while dining at separate tables at the *Carlton*; to impress his friends Rothermere called across, 'I have long been waiting to meet my chief contributor,' to which Bottomley replied, 'On the contrary, I have long been wishing to meet *my* chief contributor.'

The agreement between Germany, Great Britain, France and Italy at Munich on September 30 was reached and signed at a meeting to which no Czechoslovakian minister was admitted. Sudetenland, then part of Czechoslovakia, was ceded to Hitler without a fight in the vain hope that it was the last of the Nazi demands and that future disputes would be resolved by a gentlemanly international cabal.

I was determined that the *Pictorial* at least would play a noisy part in awakening Britain from the Munich euphoria. It was ammunition for Beaverbrook's tranquillising campaign that there would be no war at all, and heaven-sent fodder for the pro-Nazis in high places in Britain who presented Hitler as a statesman seeking justice for his people and no quarrel with us. The haze had to be blown sky-high.

I have always used the front pages of any newspapers I could lay my hands on for pamphleteering as well as for the presentation of news. The technique was simply to use strong words and compelling type that would hammer home the message not only to the millions who bought the paper regularly but to the millions who would catch a glimpse of the headlines on the shop counters, the railway bookstalls, the street corners, the trains and buses. The essential was that the message would be in tune with public hopes or fears, or so startlingly opposed that the audience was intrigued to know *why*. The second essential was that the message or warning would be proved to

Cassandra (William Connor), left, and me on a flight to
Scandinavia in 1936.

An informal family snap of the three brothers who became
Fleet Street Editors–Reg (*News of the World*), Percy (*Evening
Standard* and later *Daily Herald*), Hugh (the Mirror Group).

In the office, editing the *Sunday Pictorial* at the age of 24.

Cassandra, Peter Wilson and I joined the new *Daily Mirror* the same day in August 1935. This picture was taken at a celebration dinner 25 years later.

be right and justified within the fickle limits of public memory. The source of the power and influence of the *Mirror* and the *Pictorial* before, during and after the war is that they were right on so many significant issues.

A fortnight after Chamberlain returned triumphantly to London waving his piece of paper–'Peace with honour. I believe it is peace in our time'–I said to the News Editor, which surprised him, that I hoped there would be no news of paramount importance that Saturday. I had prepared a front page dominated by a picture of Dictator Hitler; the arrogant bully in Nazi uniform, not the Hitler who beguiled his visitors to Berchtesgaden with a charade of charm and patience between his performances as the screeching paranoiac at Nuremberg rallies. The picture was rivalled in prominence by the words:

BRITAIN REVOLTS
No more bootlicking is nation's verdict

There was an increasing awareness in the country that the leadership at Westminster was leading only to disaster, and the front page encouraged such awareness. The timing was right. While other newspapers were still acclaiming Chamberlain and his statesmanlike genius in averting war, I described Munich as shameful.

The timing of New Year's Day 1939 was due to a higher authority: it was a Sunday, another chance not to be missed. The headline was:

BE READY BY SPRING!

The story warned that Hitler had alerted his general staff to make all preparations for a major move in March. I wrote the introduction: 'Other papers know as much as we do. They do not tell. They do not wish to alarm the British public. Neither do we.' But . . . 'We think you should know the facts, for without armed strength there can be no such thing as a Happy New Year.' Bernard Gray, already earmarked and studying to be our war correspondent before war was declared, carried on from there and wrote the rest of the message based on what he had seen in Germany and learnt from his contacts on the Continent.

There were now two turbulent newspapers.

As Hitler continued to tear up the map of Europe and throw the pieces to the wind, we continued to probe the inadequacies of Britain's defences, bewail the stupefaction of the Chamberlain administration and press for the entry of Churchill into the Cabinet, the man who had prophesied the gathering disaster and remained in the political wilderness because of the jealousies of mediocre men.

Ten days after Hitler began his conquering march in March 1939 I wrote in the *Sunday Pictorial* under the name of Charles Wilberforce an article motivated more by desperation than hope, entitled 'Does He [Mr Chamberlain] Think We Are Cowards?' What a sinister and melancholy year this was for Britain. In all time there had been no more miserable tale to tell of delay, confusion, suspicion, incompetence and stupidity. Ten days had passed since Hitler's tanks began to rumble eastwards and there was still no military alliance between Britain, France, Russia and Poland, still no cry of 'Thus far, and no further,' still no step to make National Service compulsory in Britain, still no harnessing of the energy of the unemployed. Eastern Europe was falling like a pack of cards because there was no Grand Alliance. How could those countries, overwhelmed one by one, resist the power and speed of the Nazi *blitzkrieg*?

> I implore the leaders of this country to bring about the military alliance that will ensure our future and to introduce the Compulsory National Service that will organise us to do our part. And they must do these things without delay.
>
> OTHERWISE, IF WE ARE EVER FORCED INTO FINAL COMBAT WITH ONLY A SLENDER CHANCE TO WIN THE STRUGGLE A GRIM HOUR OF RECKONING WILL BE AT HAND.
>
> It is then that the people of Britain will have to deal with the false prophets and the manufacturers of soothing lies...
>
> They all have names, these people whose stupidity is sabotaging our strength. And not all of them are statesmen.
>
> We may pray that the hour of reckoning will never come upon us. We may pray that it will never be necessary for the people to turn upon them in their wrath and condemn them. But let us say this now, and say it frankly: if ever such a time does come it will take more, much more, than the ignorance of these prophets of blind optimism to explain away their conduct.
>
> Let us realise *now* that nothing must be allowed to hold up this bold stroke for Peace and Security ... Let us GET ON WITH THE GREAT TASK WITH NO MORE DELAY.

These were powerful, even threatening words. King and Cudlipp were no longer in the position they were in with Bartholomew during the Abdication crisis–knowing nothing, hearing nothing, seeing nobody, suspecting everything. King's subjects were history and politics and mine were instinct and politics. Basil Liddell Hart, the best military brain of our time, and General 'Boney' Fuller were contributors to our newspapers and friends of mine; the military writings of both of them on modern warfare had been studied and absorbed by the German High Command and shamefully neglected in Britain. King and I travelled to Totnes, Devon, for long talks with Liddell Hart; he was consulted by Lloyd George, Churchill and Leslie Hore-Belisha, the War Minister, and we were therefore as well informed as they. During 1939 and until January 1940 I wrote a number of Hore-Belisha's speeches. We had the advice of another friend, Robert Vansittart, at that time Chief Diplomatic Adviser to the Government, unheeded in his warnings about Germany's true intentions and ignominiously pushed into the background.

Eileen and I dined with Van and his wife often at their home in Denham, Denham Place, and he and I occasionally lunched at Madame Prunier's in St James's: oysters were his staple diet. The serenity of Sarita Vansittart, a woman of quite captivating charm, was rarely disturbed even as the crisis developed.

'Don't you agree, Hugh,' she said as she sent the tabasco sauce on its round at Denham Place, 'that it would be so much nicer for all of us in the world if only everybody believed in peace?'

'Well . . . yes, Sarita, I do.'

'The problems that arise hurt one so deeply,' she said, after National Service had at last been imposed. 'I haven't told you yet, Van, that the first of our five gardeners has been called up.' I remember my brother Percy, then Editor of the *Daily Herald*, telling me a similar story about Attlee's discomfort when rationing began and restaurants were severely restricted. 'After all,' said Clem, 'one must take one's wife somewhere to dine.'

The significance of Vansittart was that, like Churchill and our newspapers, he was vindicated by events.

In midsummer of 1939 our writers were joined by a distinguished contributor who was soon to play the dominant role in the nation's affairs. In July King and I went to visit him at his home at Chartwell, near Westerham in Kent, when he was in his eleventh year of exile from the counsels of the Tory Party, a great figure in the minds of the

British public but cosseted by a mere handful of political friends. Among them were Lord Beaverbrook, Bob Boothby, Professor Lindemann and Brendan Bracken, and prominent among his admirers and supporters were the *Daily Mirror* and the *Sunday Pictorial*. King and I had agreed in April to launch a campaign to urge the inclusion of Winston Churchill in the Cabinet, and I wrote a front-page piece condemning the personal and political feuds which still deprived the country of his services. When the article appeared Churchill sent a message, anxious to know the public reaction. I sent him an appraisal of the vast pile of letters from readers and a fervent thank-you telegram arrived in response.

We were provided with tea, and Churchill, inspired by a double whisky, paced the room for an hour haranguing us about the calamitous events about to engulf the nation. '*Nothing can save us,*' he said. '*Nothing—except the hammerblow of circumstance.*' There was nothing but applause from him on that occasion for the sustained criticisms in the *Mirror* and *Pictorial* of Chamberlain and the mediocrities in his Cabinet. Churchill spoke of them, one by one, almost without exception, in terms of contempt or pity. His first *Mirror* article began with a warning to Germany:

> Let there be no delusions in the Nazi party and among its grim chiefs that, for instance, Poland, the Baltic States, the Ukraine, Hungary and Roumania could be overrun, and that the aggressors could then turn round and make peace with the Western Powers.
>
> Napoleon, sword in hand, sought victorious peace in every capital in Europe.
>
> He sought it in Berlin, in Vienna, in Madrid, in Rome and finally in Moscow.
>
> All he found was St Helena.
>
> There were years in that struggle when England stood quite alone, all the world against her.
>
> The unaccountable delay—whoever is to blame for it—in concluding an all-in alliance between Britain, France and Russia, aggravates the danger of a wrong decision by Herr Hitler.

His final article in August, the month before war was declared and he was at last invited to join the Cabinet to rule the Navy, was entitled: 'At the Eleventh Hour'.

There was entertainment and mass interest as well as fury in the expanding *Pictorial*. Glamour. Even spiritualism, probing rather than exposing. And, of course, crime, astrology (for fun, not to be taken seriously), and sentiment, and the finest cuddly baby pictures taken then or since by any photographer in the world, a camera artist with the intriguing name of Torkel Korling. Yet the dominating theme was the momentous happenings in Europe, the sloth of the British Government, and the coming conflagration.

'A Charter for the New Britain' reflected the more permanent philosophy of the newspaper and its closeness to its readers. The war would be the end of a social era which had scarcely been a matter for pride or complacency. The war, and what then? The abject surrender of the enemy was not of itself an inspiring war aim. The fighting men and their bombed and battered families at home, and the factory workers and the miners, needed something more uplifting and socially just to look forward to as the Promised Land than a repetition of the wintry regimes of Mr Baldwin and Mr Chamberlain in the 1930s. They were beginning to question the omniscience of the Establishment and the notion that the Tory Party was the natural Government. The collapse of political leadership in the past decade and the continuing power of proven incompetents encouraged their rebellious thoughts.

Who *were* the leaders of the nation?

Charles Wilberforce examined the *dramatis personae* of Parliament on August 6 1939. The House of Lords was still exclusively hereditary, and a considerable proportion of the House of Commons could scarcely be described as commoners.

55 Members of Parliament supporting the Government of the day were related to the peerage.

Half the leaders of the Conservative Party had cousins on the back benches.

Of 236 Tory members:

18 were heirs to peerages;
13 were the younger sons of peers;
24 were blood-relations of peers;
24 were baronets; and
64 were knights.

Mr Simon Haxey, author of *Tory MP*, whom Wilberforce quoted, had also discovered that though only one per cent of British boys went to Eton or Harrow, thirty per cent of Tory MPs at that time had been educated at one of those expensive schools. The *Pictorial* reminded its readers that when the call first came to Mr Stanley Baldwin to form a government one of his first thoughts, he said, was that it should be a government of which Harrow should not be ashamed, and the newspaper added, 'What damn nonsense!'

Charles Wilberforce's next contribution (August 13 1939) made the popular *Pictorial* even more unpopular Upstairs. With more courage than most newspapers, a warning was issued to 'Hitler's friends in Britain'. He named the wealthy aristocrats and titled gentry who through conviction, naïvety or stupidity fawned around the Nazis, hobnobbed with von Ribbentrop in Berlin and invited him back to their stately homes in England. These people were explaining away the Führer's smash-and-grabs as the valid redressing of injustice. They were beseeching their fellow citizens to believe in his protestations of peaceful intention. The dictator gained a misleading impression of the effeteness and gullibility of the British from the antics of these simple folk, but their influence in high places was as great a factor as 'There Will Be No War' in slackening the pace of the country's preparedness. David Low got it right in a brilliant cartoon showing Lady Astor, J. L. Garvin of the *Observer* and Lord Lothian, wearing newspapers as *tutus*, performing ballet gyrations to a gramophone record of Nazi foreign policy. The conductor was Goebbels.

On the Sunday morning of September 3 1939 the Prime Minister addressed the nation on the radio at 11.15. An ultimatum had been delivered to the Germans at nine that morning, expiring at eleven. Britain was in a state of war with Germany. 'I cannot believe that there is anything more, or anything different, that I could have done. It is evil things that we shall be fighting against, brute force, bad faith, injustice, oppression and persecution. And against them I am certain that the right will prevail.'

The sirens sounded over London as we rushed out a special edition of the *Pictorial*. I noticed, as we were ordered to move to the basement, accompanied by the anxious Mr John Cowley, that the air-raid shelter was in a state of hopeless disarray and incompletion. Had we been too busy warning others?

It was a false alarm.

'Everything I have worked for,' said Mr Chamberlain to the House of Commons that day, 'everything that I have hoped for, everything that I believed in during my public life, has crashed in ruins.'

As a peacetime Minister since 1922 Neville Chamberlain had

served the nation in three separate departments including the Treasury. His talents as an administrator were considerable. As Prime Minister in a situation visibly and inevitably leading to war his principal characteristics of smugness and vanity were disastrous. The only words of his I read or heard from his own lips that bore any resemblance to fact or realism were uttered at a meeting he held for Editors, including me, at No. 10 Downing Street shortly after war was declared.

'The Press can greatly assist us,' he said, 'in educating the public about the situation. People may think it will all be over and done with quickly and that we shall soon be back to normal. I have to tell you the Cabinet believe it will be a long war. At least three years. I do hope what you write in your newspapers tomorrow will convey this mood.'

I left the brief conference at Downing Street that day with one solid conviction. Anything newspapers could do to accelerate a change in the leadership was a patriotic duty. The greatest obstacle to victory or even survival as a nation was Mr Chamberlain.

7

Lloyd George: Pétain in Waiting?

One of the rich rewards for an Editor of a national newspaper, granted a little more than average energy, is that he can always know what is going on, even if he misinterprets the scene. He can see anybody he wishes to see by writing a convincing letter or inviting him to lunch, preferably in a private room. With the exception of Baldwin and Chamberlain, I have therefore personally known all the Prime Ministers of our time, and since the war all the leading Cabinet Ministers and political personalities who mattered or might matter. Only an ass, or a bore, or an Editor who can't be trusted, is seen only once. The contacts ripen if there is an exchange of thought rather than mere questioning or listening.

There was no irrevocable committment to the policy of this or that Party. Regardless of Party we criticised what we thought was wrong, and threw three or two hats in the air, or one, when things were going right from the *national* point of view. Such a policy made easier our contacts with the best men in all Parties, and only on one occasion and by one man was the basis of confidence shattered. That was when Cecil King, of all people, decided to kiss (or kick) and tell in his declining years.

The formal declaration of war should have involved, in all conscience, the immediate resignation of Neville Chamberlain. All that happened was that his Cabinet was strengthened by the admission of Winston Churchill as First Lord of the Admiralty. Anthony Eden was back as the Secretary of State for Dominion Affairs. The old gang were still substantially in power playing musical chairs, with rewards for the faithful Municheers; some were unaccountably promoted.

There was one personality of significance outside the Government who, according to events, might still be called upon to play another historic role. 'The Man Who Won the First World War' was now seventy-six, but still a Member of Parliament.

In these darkling days there was ample cause for depression and defeatism, none more stark than the signing of the Nazi-Soviet Pact on August 23 1939. The half-hearted, low-level negotiations conducted by Britain and France with Russia from May to August had petered out in confusion and suspicion. Lloyd George had pressed for a Soviet alliance, was dejected by Chamberlain's failure to grasp the initiative, was pondering the possibility even at that late stage of a bargain with Hitler. Lloyd George's stance at that moment was ominous. He was counselling the Government not to reject any offers of peace that Hitler might make, and indeed was about to make. He urged the calling of a world conference to face and determine the issues confronting the European powers. After the partitioning of Poland between Russia and Germany on September 29 the peace offer did come from Hitler and was firmly rejected by Chamberlain. In France, weak, divided and suspicious of the British Government's real intention, the offer was tempting. It was apparent then, and more so in retrospect, that peace at that time could only have been achieved on terms so degrading that democracy could not have survived. And how long would peace have lasted?

When Lloyd George talked in the Commons of such a deal most of the Members were astonished. 'I deeply deplore and regret this speech,' said Duff Cooper, 'it will go out to the world with his name at the head of it–a suggestion of surrender.' The frown on the face of Winston Churchill signified that he agreed with Duff Cooper, and from the Socialists also came condemnation of the timing and wording. It was clear to me that the duty of a popular paper was to give the widest possible public airing to the issue and to come down thunderously on the side of No Surrender.

The piece I wrote on October 15 was headlined 'A SHAME-FUL SCHEME: WE ACCUSE LLOYD GEORGE.' The motives were obvious; to support Neville Chamberlain when for once he was right about the war and to expose Lloyd George when for once he was wrong. The weapon I chose was ridicule, the weapon he would have chosen himself. My theme was unflattering. Instead of resting his seventy-six years in retirement, a gentleman farmer with nought to trouble him except his crops and the price of pigs, David Lloyd George was so eager to return to the scene of his former glory that he was willing to wear even the mantle of surrender. He was prepared to bargain with the dictator who had broken nearly every promise he had made. The same views expressed by younger men without his record, I wrote, would merit the charge of funk. Lloyd George, the old war-horse, was feebly pawing the ground like Ferdinand the Bull, awaiting the postman at Churt with his daily mailbag–'simply armfuls'–from others who were unwilling to galvanise the nation to face another challenge. He was no longer able, as Churchill said of him in the last Great War, to view every day as if it were 'filled with the hope of the impulse of a fresh beginning', no longer eager to 'grapple with the giant events', to strive to compel them; no longer 'undismayed by mistakes and their consequences'. The time had come for 'The Man Who Won the Last War' to pass on the torch. This was the twilight of a god.

The picture which illustrated the article showed him with his hands held aloft, fingers apart, in a typical oratorical pose. The caption was the one word–'SURRENDER?'

There was overwhelming reason for Lloyd George's gloom, and what he had already written and said in Parliament about the course of events had been justified. The days of Chamberlain's Premiership at last were numbered, and the emergence of Winston Churchill could not much longer be delayed even on the most pessimistic prophecy. But Lloyd George had less faith than the British public in what Churchill could do, and less hope than any living soul that Britain could end up among the victors. Nor was his attitude conditioned solely by the abysmal record of the Baldwin and Chamberlain administrations. He had met Adolf Hitler and the effect of the mesmerism had lingered. For the occasion, honoured that the greatest living statesman had travelled to Germany to pay court, Hitler suppressed his fanaticism and exuded sincerity and sweet reason.

In the autumn of 1936, when he had completed the sixth and last volume of his *War Memoirs*, Lloyd George succumbed to the pressure from Joachim von Ribbentrop, then German Ambassador to Britain, to visit the Fatherland and meet the Führer.

The first of the two meetings between Hitler, forty-six, and Lloyd George, then seventy-three, took place on September 4 near Berchtesgaden in the Bavarian Alps. Hitler clasped his hand as he stepped out of the car and led him up the stone steps to his spectacular chalet. They talked for three hours on the future of Europe, the menace of Bolshevism, the recognition of German equality, an air pact between Germany, France and Britain, rearmament, Spain, national finance and plans to deal with unemployment. To members of his entourage Lloyd George said that Hitler was a great and wonderful leader, the Saviour of Germany; he was fascinated by 'his gestures, his eyes, his voice, his talk'. One of his companions on this journey was Thomas Jones, who served under four Prime Ministers as Deputy Secretary to the Cabinet. The next morning he told Jones, 'Hitler is a remarkable man. His head has not been turned by adulation. He seems essentially modest.' At the second encounter, that day, Lloyd George was not displeased by Hitler's compliment, 'that it was realised in Germany that if the war was won by the Allies it was not due to the soldiers but the one great statesman, Lloyd George . . . Lloyd George, speaking with a tear in his throat, was deeply touched by the tribute of the Führer and was proud to hear it paid to him by the greatest German of the age.'[1]

The chilling spectre was of David Lloyd George sharing in 1940 the same mantle as Pétain when France sought an armistice. The hero of Verdun, *Ils ne passeront pas*, became the Nazi collaborator and puppet. Was there the possibility that Lloyd George could be persuaded into entering the national scene in a positive role instead of counting the months to defeat and surrender? Cecil King and I agreed that if indeed he would make a contribution to national morale we would be performing a service in encouraging him to do so.

I spoke to his secretary, and Lloyd George agreed to see me for lunch at home at Churt on January 3 1940. He arrived promptly at one o'clock after a walk around the farm with Miss Frances Stevenson. She was the secretary with whom he was living, the lady who became the second Mrs Lloyd George in 1943 and later the Countess.

Over a whisky I was able to tell him, as if he cared, that at the age of seventy-six he looked singularly like the Lloyd George who was framed in passe-partout on the wall of our living room when I was a kid at 118 Lisvane Street. 'It is wise in politics to decide what you're going to look like and then never falter,' he said. 'Otherwise you are regarded as untrustworthy, even shifty.' There are of course other reasons why some politicians are regarded as untrustworthy or shifty, and during his long career Lloyd George provided some notable and notorious examples. I mentioned that I first heard him speak at the Free Trade Hall, Manchester, during the 1929 Election: 'If there were any passages in the *Manchester Evening Chronicle*'s long account of that oration which you did not in fact make, or wished you had made, it was entirely my fault. I was on a four-man team of reporters to take it all down, and when my turn came you were talking quicker than my shorthand.'

There was snow on the ground and he asked me if the car had skidded on the way down, and while I was answering he began to talk

---

[1] *Diary with Letters, 1931–50* and *Lloyd George* both by Thomas Jones, Oxford University Press, 1970 and 1951.

about Russia. Here is what was said at the private meeting. I found it all locked away with other papers in a drawer when I returned to London in 1946 when the war was over. It was marked 'Confidential, not for publication':

'"See today's news? What do the optimists say about that?" He was referring to the announcement that Germany was sending military advisers to Moscow and the rumour that 200,000 German experts were to reorganise Russian industry and transport.

'"What happens when you try to tell the truth about the war?" he asked. "Fellows like you call me Ferdinand the Bull–a pacifist– or a defeatist.

'"What can a naval blockade by Britain achieve now? Russia has already promised Germany one million tons of fodder and half of it has been delivered. I keep pigs. One million tons of fodder would feed all the pigs in Britain for one year. But I can scarcely get fodder for my own pigs now."

'We went to lunch–pea soup, boiled silverside of beef, etc. with apple dumplings to follow. Then celery, "grown on the premises", said Lloyd George. Eating soup, he makes a noise like an Indian typhoon. As much falls out as goes in. A little of the silverside was deposited on his waistcoat.

'Discussing the events of the past ten years, he sneered at Baldwin and Chamberlain, "A second-rater," he said.

'"Then why not criticise him frankly in public?" I asked.

'"Oh, I wouldn't like to make a personal attack upon him." He meant this: it was not a cynical remark.

'"How long will it be before Chamberlain vanishes from the scene? I think he is a peril to the nation's security, and the sooner he goes the better."

'Lloyd George's reply was: "It will take longer to get rid of Chamberlain than you think. It took two years for Asquith to go in the last war. He was an abler man, and there were more alternatives at hand. I told Churchill three weeks ago that he was unwise to take the job at the Admiralty. If he succeeds in sinking all the German U-boats, he'll be very popular. But what if they launch four hundred new ones? What if there are serious reverses? Winston will get it in the neck."

'Before lunch was finished his secretary, Miss Stevenson, departed; she was having tea with H. A. L. Fisher who lives nearby.

'Here are other views he gave during our subsequent talk:

'"I think the registration of another 2,000,000 men for calling up is a grand thing. It would be a fine thing if every young man in this country underwent six months' training. A nation prepared would never be frightened of war." When I asked him what message he would give to these young men, his eloquence dried up, and he said rather vaguely that he would tell them to "Stand By and Be Prepared."

'Of Churchill he said: "He is very bad at picking men." He suggested Churchill would pick men he liked and would not worry about their actual ability as much as Lloyd George did in the last war.

'"I brought in outside talent such as Smuts," said Lloyd George. "That's what ought to happen now."

'"We are not worrying enough about India. Nehru is a Communist and a very brilliant man.

'He thought that Italy would probably remain neutral throughout the war. "Italy is making lots of money as a neutral now," he said.

'We went on to discuss finance and the bankruptcy of nations in relation to warfare. "I don't believe finance is a vital factor—and never did," he said. "For years they told me Mussolini could not succeed because of his huge budget deficiency. They told me too that Hitler would crash economically, unable to finance his industries. Well, everybody knows what has happened now!"

'Lloyd George did not seem to be worried so much about Russian aggression in Scandinavia. "After all, the bulk of the products of these nations went to the Central Powers in the last war," he said.

'He was much more concerned about a Russian thrust to India through Persia. He regarded the pact with Turkey of paramount importance, but he said that the Turks were not good fighters outside their own country. "The last war established that."

'Of the French and German armies, he said:

'"I think the French Army is better. You must remember that it takes ten years to make a good NCO. When I was in Germany in 1936 a thing I particularly noticed was the youth of the NCOs. I do not think they will be as good as the French."

'Talking of Churchill and Poland, he said:

'"Of course, this is not for publication, but I will tell you privately that Churchill telephoned me three weeks before the war and told me Hitler's latest terms for a Danzig settlement.

Winston said, 'I think they are not unreasonable,' and I agreed with him."

'Discussing the state of exhaustion into which the country would be forced by a prolonged war, he said: "It is when a man is exhausted that the bugs get at him. It might be typhus, or influenza. Or a Communistic bug, or a Fascist bug. Or some new bug we have never heard of.

' "The Polish Army was rotten. They had not even dug trenches. And who was it who received the retreating Polish armies in Roumania? None other than their Commander!

' "We should have called a halt when Hitler interfered in Spain. The people who say Hitler is a fool are mad themselves. He's not epileptic. He has a fine head."

'After these preliminary skirmishes Lloyd George got down to his view of the situation as a whole. As he delivered this lecture he paced up and down the room waving his arms about and became very excited and angry.

' "This is a damn crazy war," he said. "For years the menace of Germany has been rising, but what did Baldwin do? He was too lazy to make a great decision. He thought it would shock the people of this country too much. He didn't have the courage that was necessary in a Prime Minister at that moment. We let Manchuria go to Japan. We allowed an interference in Spain, in spite of the peril to our Mediterranean sea routes which a Franco Spain would cause. We did nothing about Austria–nothing about the Rhine– nothing about Czechoslovakia. And then, when it was strategically and emotionally impossible for us to do a damn thing, we cried a halt at Poland. Traditionally, Britain had never guaranteed a Central European Power–what made Chamberlain think it was suddenly possible to fulfil such a pledge now? I told him that in the House of Commons, but he wouldn't listen.

' "I have constantly warned the country about the growing alliance between Germany and Russia, but they wouldn't listen to that either."

'I asked him some frank questions about his suggestions shortly after the outbreak of war, that we should "negotiate with Hitler". I told him I did not consider Hitler's Peace Offer a genuine one, that he would have struck again. Would it have been possible, I asked, to rouse the people of this country to a war effort a second time? It seemed to me difficult enough to do so the first time. This was his reply:

'"I believe Hitler really wanted peace when he made that offer, and I would have negotiated. But what happened? We slammed the door in his face."

'He then began to discuss the war objectively and to prophesy what would happen.

'"People called me a defeatist," he said, "but what I say to them is this: *Tell me how we can win*! Can we win in the air? Can we win at sea–when the effect of our naval blockade is wiped out by Germany's connection with Russia? How can we win on the land? The Germans cannot get through the Maginot Line. When do you think we can get through the Siegfried Line? Not until the trumpet blows, my friend.

'"Even if Hitler marches his troops into Holland and Belgium it will be to get nearer England–to build submarine bases and aerodromes; not, in my view, to invade France.

'"In what field can action be decisive for either side? In none. Hitler cannot win any more than we can, and he has the brains to see it. So what will happen? The war will drag wearily on. There will be no spectacular appeals to the emotions. The people will become bored and dreary. And in the end they won't stand for it. There is no excitement in a war like this. In the end they will demand peace."

'He did not think this would be in 1940, but thought the stage might be reached in 1942 or 1943.

'"I cannot write what I believe to be untrue. I cannot tell the public that we will win, when I think that a victory is impossible for either side. This view has been forming in my mind for many months, and I wanted to do all I could to hold Europe back from this horrible mess. Then–what did I find? I found that Liddell Hart had come to the same conclusion. Liddell Hart is a great man– he is the greatest military writer of our time. And he is a philosopher, and a man of courage too. I admire him more than I can tell you. He was Military Correspondent of *The Times*, and he refused to carry on because they wanted him to write a lot of optimistic slush.

'"Oh yes," said Lloyd George, "I know a lot about newspapers and what their advertisers want. I think it is a terrible thing that newspapers should be controlled in this way and should not have the courage of their convictions. Liddell Hart has made a great sacrifice–which is more than I have done yet. He is ill now–sick with anxiety."

'I tried to encourage Lloyd George on more constructive lines.

'"I agree with your analysis of the situation, and with Liddell Hart's," I said, "but is it enough to diagnose the complaint and not attempt to cure the patient? What would you do if you were forced to be Prime Minister now?"

'He walked up and down and dodged the question. When I brought it up again later he made this reply:

'"That's all very well. It's all very well for the country to get in a devil of a mess and then to ask somebody to pull it out when it is too late. And it is too late. Nothing can be done—nothing at all."

'We discussed his own plans for the future.

'"What's the good of making public speeches or writing articles?" he asked. But after I had urged him on for some minutes he became more specific.

'"The only thing to do now is to go on convincing the public of the horrible muddle we are in—they don't know the half of it."

'What then?"

'He began to talk of peace again. The time would come when we would be in a more favourable position than now to talk about peace.

'I tried again: "But isn't this true? When that moment comes the less our *need* for peace the greater chance we will have of acquiring it? Mustn't we, in the meantime, get the strongest possible Cabinet, find new talent, and build up as mighty and as resolute a nation as we can?"

'It was difficult to get him to show any interest in constructive planning.

'"I am not a pacifist," he said, *"but how can we win?"*

'As I was leaving he said that he had been frank and had told me as honestly as he could what his position now was. It is my view that Lloyd George thinks we will lose the war.'

Lloyd George wrote a series of articles for the *Sunday Pictorial*, but in a mood less defeatist than his private thoughts. He was offered Cabinet office but refused. He also declined an invitation to be Britain's Ambassador in the United States. He formally retired from public life at the end of 1944 and died at eighty-two at Llanystumdwy on March 26 1945. Thirty-three days before Mussolini was executed by his own compatriots on April 28. Thirty-five days before Adolf Hitler committed suicide on April 30. Thirty-seven days before Berlin fell to the Allies on May 2, and forty-two days before all the

German forces surrendered unconditionally on May 7, to take effect the next day, Victory in Europe Day.

Britain emerged on the victorious side in the second of the two world wars in less than half a century.

There was no vacancy for a British Pétain.

8

Carpeted—by the War Cabinet

1940 was, surely, the momentous year of the Hitler war, make or break for Britain. It is puzzling to comprehend what anybody is worried about in Britain in the 1970s when we are merely the victims of our own indolence, indecision and unrealism.

Every man, woman and evacuated child had his or her own 'Nineteen-Forty', and mine was less spectacular than some. It began with a Chamberlain-must-go campaign and a Churchill-for-Premier campaign, both of which, unless history is lying, succeeded. I was severely mauled with my colleagues at a series of War Cabinet meetings presided over by Churchill in the month of October, and was delivering coal in the December snow in a 15-cwt truck as a private to the officers' wives at Catterick Camp in Yorkshire.

What precisely were the turbulent newspapers, especially the *Sunday Pictorial*, telling their readers during 1940 that aroused the wrath of the Cabinet to a pitch that led to their first threat of censorship of comment in national newspapers?

The general theme of my weekly article was based on the current thoughts of Cecil King, or on my own current thoughts, or a mixture of both. When the final product emerged on Saturday mornings in time for printing at night, Cecil never flinched. On rereading these contentious pieces I conclude that we certainly had the courage of our convictions and that a better, or worse, combination could not have been assembled at that time.

My texts were the urgent advancement of Winston Churchill to the Premiership, the absorption of the unemployed into the war effort, the imbecilities of Britain's propaganda at home and abroad, the creation of a Citizen's Army, and any other matters that seemed of national importance at the time. Above all, we conducted a strident campaign against the retention of the Municheers in the Coalition Government formed in May when Germany invaded Holland and Belgium. All patriotic stuff, one would have thought, most certainly not displeasing to Winston Churchill.

But there were no more thank-you telegrams from Mr Churchill once he was installed at No. 10. The two newspapers had conspicuously been his allies in warning Britain of the Nazi menace. Far from incurring Winston's ire they had enjoyed his connivance, and one of them, the *Daily Mirror*, had become his own public platform in 1939. Yet a few months after he was appointed Prime Minister his disciples were viewed with glowering suspicion for continuing to preach the same gospels with the same fervour. What Churchill regarded as patriotism of a high order in 1939, and indeed until the moment of his personal power, became subversion and sedition of a low order in the winter of 1940. The First Column became the Fifth Column. And the men in the Tory Party who had cynically excluded him from office had now become, for political reasons and *Party* political reasons, his trusted friends. An attack upon them was now an attack upon him, and his patience—like Hitler's—was soon exhausted.

How guilty *were* the two newspapers of the sinister motives attributed to them before the end of the year by the new Prime Minister?

One of my first campaigns was to launch a weekly column entitled 'Truth', to expose the inept fairy tales about the war appearing in the other newspapers, 'news' items or views purporting to prove that Hitler was 'cornered', that he was already quarrelling with Stalin, that the German Army was on the verge of revolt and the Red Army a humiliating myth. The *Sunday Express* was telling its readers:

RED ARMY BOGEY BURST
Bombs fail to explode: Tanks old and thinly armoured:
Soldiers machine-gunned into obeying orders

Old men in power, with due respect to our own ageing Chairman, John Cowley, was another target that appealed to me. *'They can't win the war by themselves. They refuse to make way for the young. So what can be done? How can they have the vigour to outwit the German war lords?'*

> Hitler is fifty.
> Ribbentrop is forty-six.
> Goering is forty-seven.
> Goebbels is forty-two.

THE AVERAGE AGE OF GERMANY'S WAR CABINET IS FORTY-SIX

One of the troubles in pre-war Britain was the Old Men clinging to power in the Services as well as in politics and industry. The railway networks were domestically the lifeblood of a nation at war, but a medical examination of their boards of directors in the Roaring 1940s could only have been undertaken by a gentle and experienced geriatrician.

'A few days ago,' I wrote, 'the Great Western Railway held its annual company meeting and there were three long rows of directors lined up on the platform.' I should have called it the Great-great-great-Western Railway.

> How many knew the business? The Lord only knows. One of them, Sir H. M. Jackson, is eighty-four. The deputy chairman, Lord Palmer, is eighty-two this March . . . On the Southern Railway the position is even more dismal. Sir Charles Morgan wins the marathon race at eighty-five . . . And the LNER? THEY HAVE A DIRECTOR WHO IS EIGHTY-SIX.

The railway problem at that time was not the wisdom or otherwise of nationalisation but a bottle-neck in embalming.

The conduct of the war itself remained the centre point of the nation's anxiety, expressed in the *Pictorial* week after week. Mercifully in May one of the regular items on my agenda could be erased, the continued Premiership of Arthur Neville Chamberlain. There was no a'sighing and a'sobbing, but who killed Cock Robin? There is an exultant entry in Cecil King's war diary on May 10:

> 'So at last my campaign to get rid of the old menace has come off. I consider this is the best bit of news since war was declared. I do not think Churchill is young enough to win the war, but he is immeasurably better than Chamberlain. The *Sunday Pic* was the paper that hammered away at getting Churchill into the Cabinet, a campaign that the other papers took up and that got him in. Then on October 1 last the *Sunday Pictorial* had a very good page article by Cudlipp announcing that Churchill would be the next Premier. We shall reproduce part of it to show how right we are.

But newspaper boasting apart, it was a long shot when it was made and it has come off!'[1]

I would not stake our claim so extravagantly. There were other forces at work, primarily the march of events. Finland agreed to Russia's demands and made peace on March 12. Once more the Allies, France and Britain, had failed to go to the aid of a small country. The event was followed by Chamberlain's ludicrous statement that time was on our side and that 'Hitler has missed the bus'. Germany invaded Norway on April 9 and British troops landed near Narvik on April 15. The amphibious expedition was conceived and executed in confusion, inadequately manned, crippled by divided command, deprived of superior air power. Public dismay and disgust at the disaster reached dangerous proportions. There were also powerful forces in Parliament, dissident groups chaired by Leo Amery and Clement Davies and others, who were now more openly demanding new leadership and a new government. The secret talks that had been taking place in clubs, some of which I had attended with Clem Davies and Hore-Belisha after he had been fired as War Minister, had become an open conspiracy.

The decisive debate in the Commons took place on May 7 and May 8, portrayed in detail in dozens of memoirs by those who were in the ring or at the ringside. Admiral of the Fleet Sir Roger Keyes, the hero of Zeebrugge, addressed the House in his full naval regalia, attacking the Government and the Admiralty for not firing its way into the Trondheim Fjord. Leo Amery, a great Parliamentarian and patriot, made the speech of his life, stark in its logic and ferocious in its marshalling of the case against the bedraggled Chamberlain regime. Cromwell's burial oration for the Long Parliament supplied the burial words for Neville the Unready:

'You have sat too long here for any good you have been doing. Depart, I say, and let us have done with you. In the name of God, go!'

The sensitive issue was the position of Winston Churchill as First Lord of the Admiralty, more than any single Minister the architect of the ill-starred adventure. The cry of 'Another Dardanelles' would have tarnished his reputation even with the public who were now impatient for him to take over the leadership.

---

[1] *With Malice Toward None: A War Diary* by Cecil H. King, Sidgwick and Jackson, 1970.

Characteristically he had told Harold Macmillan half-way through the debate that he had signed on for the voyage and would stick to the ship, and he interrupted Lloyd George to say emphatically that he took his full share of the burden. 'The Rt. Hon. Gentleman,' said Lloyd George, 'must not allow himself to be converted into an air-raid shelter to keep the splinters from hitting his colleagues.' To Chamberlain, Lloyd George was lethal, too lethal for the taste of some in the crowded House:

'He has appealed for sacrifice. The nation is prepared for every sacrifice, so long as it has leadership. I say solemnly that the Prime Minister should give an example of sacrifice, because there is nothing that can contribute more to victory in this war than that he should sacrifice the seals of office.'

It was the end of Chamberlain as Prime Minister, yet the enormity of his vanity was not apparent until the next day, May 10. He regarded the sudden Nazi invasion of Holland and Belgium as a reason for delaying any political changes in Britain, but stronger minds prevailed.

Cecil King's campaign to get rid of the old menace had certainly 'come off', but others were there on the battlefield who had the stomach for the fight and lived to strip their sleeve and show their scars. The turbulent newspapers had erected the guillotine. It was Chamberlain who put his own head on the block and Parliament which released the cord that freed the heavy blade.

On May 12, two days after Churchill had been acclaimed Prime Minister and formed his Coalition Government, the *Pictorial* editorial was headed 'A Call to Arms':

Churchill is at the helm and will get on with the job of winning the war. And this journal joins with the public in hailing his enthronement.

He takes office—let us face it—at the hour of grave peril.

You may depend upon it that Winston Churchill knows the evil measure of the maniac he must outwit . . .

But we will watch this new Administration with the same vigilance with which we watched the old one.

If it has faults, we will expose them.

If there is ever any evidence that old Party loyalties or

niceties are still weakening our national effort, we will
bring that evidence before the nation.

THE VITAL NECESSITY IS THAT MR CHURCHILL
SHALL BE SUPPORTED BY THE STRONGEST, BRAVEST
CABINET THE COUNTRY CAN PRODUCE.

One impediment to national unity remained. The most notorious
of the Tory Municheers, including Chamberlain, were retained
in the new Coalition Government. It was a gesture of imprudent
magnanimity, an arrogant disregard of public and Parliamentary
opinion. Throughout his career Churchill had been a House of
Commons man rather than a Party man in the strictest sense,
but now that he was at the summit and not in the political wilderness
he was over-sensitive to the influence of the Tory machine in
Westminster in wartime. He had more enemies than friends. The
Socialists distrusted him and even at the moment of Chamberlain's
downfall wanted Halifax as his successor, not Churchill.[1] Worse,
he had undermined his own Party's confidence in his judgement on
world affairs to such a degree that his warnings on the Nazi menace
and the need for rearmament went largely unheeded. And now, as
War Supremo, Party unity became inexplicably more important
to him than national unity.

On June 23 the *Sunday Pictorial* expressed its view with a frankness
that before many months was to place its relationship with Winston
Churchill on a different plane. The editorial was entitled 'Out with
the Muddlers':

Our new Prime Minister has established himself as a
mighty leader of a nation in torment. His own effort is
prodigious, an example to soldier and citizen; and his
orations enhearten us all.

There can be only acclamation, moreover, for the
wisdom of his new appointments.

It is Mr Churchill's peculiar zeal in defending and
retaining the Old Gang which astounds his supporters
and dismays the country as a whole. He is weakening his
own Government and dissipating his own energies in
striving to make successes out of the most conspicuous
failures and muddlers of our time.

---

[1] So, for the record, did King George VI.

Neville Chamberlain, aged seventy-one, is still in the Inner Cabinet. He is the man the Germans duped; the man who thought 'Hitler missed the bus'; the man whom progressive defeat made more 'confident of victory'.

Lord Halifax is there, too. The dignified Foreign Secretary who dismally failed (if indeed he ever tried) to dissuade his chief from perpetrating the errors of the past few years.

Sir Kingsley Wood remains to govern our Exchequer; the little man who always looked more busy than he really was. The former Minister for Air whose speech charmed the nation into the belief that aeroplane production was satisfactory.

Are there any others who remain who should have gone?

Yes. Viscount Caldecote! He has changed his name, but not his brain. Caldecote–none other than that monumental failure Sir Thomas Inskip–is our Dominions Secretary, and is also leader of the House of Lords.

Sir Samuel Hoare–still there, still there!–is now the dreary advocate of our cause at this vital juncture in Spain.

THIS IS NO TIME FOR MINCED WORDS, FOR FANCY PHRASES: OR FOR RESTRAINT. THE PUBLIC WANT THESE BLUNDERERS THROWN OUT. LOCK, STOCK, BARREL–AND WITHOUT CEREMONY.

There is so much that is progressive about Mr Churchill's Government that it is a tragedy for its record to be besmirched.

Herbert Morrison inherited from Leslie Burgin a mammoth departmental mess-up. But Morrison rolled up his sleeves and cleared the confusion away. His Ministry of Supply is at last supplying the Ministries.

Ernest Bevin is another success. For Bevin, the workers are working day and night to help to win the war.

The Premier has encouraged, too, the best from the Tory ranks.

Anthony Eden is the Secretary of State for War, and his enthusiasm and idealism are assets in any Cabinet.

What about Lord Beaverbrook? There will be no war? Beaverbrook is helping to win it now. His personal courage, tenacity and mental capacities are now devoted to the nation's welfare. He is producing our planes—and producing them quickly.

Mr Churchill, too, has brought men like Lord Lloyd and Richard Law to the political forefront. But why should the courageous innovations and the successes cease here?

Similar thoughts were now appearing in the other newspapers, but more politely and by insinuation. The cause of the offence committed by the *Pictorial* and the *Mirror* was the irreverence, the brash unacceptance of the Establishment, the probing questions, and—the deadliest weapon of all—telling the truth.

Why was Mr Alfred Duff Cooper, the Minister for Information, sending his son to America when it was his job to convince the English that England was safe? The *Pictorial* figured that 'Muff' Cooper would soon have to deny or confirm that his Ministry of Mis-Information was responsible for a note which publicans had received asking them to control their customers' 'thinking', as well as their drinking. Sir Kingsley Wood was re-christened Sir Kingsley Wouldn't.

We continued to press for younger blood in high office and command, and I had the impertinence to remind Mr Churchill, the master of military history, of some interesting military facts exhumed over the midnight oil. Napoleon won his most brilliant victories over the Italians at twenty-five, complained of old age at forty-one, and was no more than forty-six at Waterloo. Alexander the Great was a renowned soldier at sixteen and died at thirty-two. William I was thirty-nine at the Battle of Hastings in 1066. Robert the Bruce, King of Scotland, was forty on the battlefield of Bannockburn when he defeated the English in 1314. Edward III was thirty-four at Crécy. Henry V was twenty-eight at Agincourt. Cromwell was forty-six at the battle of Naseby. Marlborough was fifty-four at Blenheim. At Plassey, Clive was thirty-two, and Wolfe was thirty-two at the capture of Quebec, a victory that gave Britain Canada. Wellington was thirty when he won the victory of Assaye, and forty-six at Waterloo. Three-quarters of the really great generals in history were under forty-five. I don't know what use Churchill was able to make of this information, but at the time it seemed to me worth passing on.

One particular issue, not surprisingly, was a source of irritation throughout the war to the new man at No. 10. What were Britain's aims? What was at the end of the tunnel, or, more inspiringly, the vision on the horizon? He regarded such matters as the idle talk of idealists, probably pink, of philosophers, probably pacifists, and of other barnacles on the bottom of the hull of the Ship of State. To a man of war, totally absorbed in his own finest hour, straining at the leash for the moment when he could deliver death and destruction upon the enemy, the question of 'After survival–what?' was academic, an irrelevant intrusion in the greatest game of martial chess the human race had ever witnessed.

He considered he had dealt with and dismissed the subject in his first address to Parliament and the nation as Prime Minister:

> 'I have nothing to offer but blood, toil, tears and sweat. You ask, What is our policy? I will say: it is to wage war, by sea, land and air, with all our might and with all the strength that God can give us . . . You ask, What is our aim? I can answer in one word: victory–victory at all costs.'

Whether the homes fit for heroes to live in would again be slums was somebody else's problem sometime later on, if indeed there was a later on.

He was wrong, and other minds prevailed. The public demand during the war was for reconstruction after the war. Beveridge began work on his report on social services and insurance in 1941 and produced it in 1942, with unemployment insurance for all, a free health service and family allowances as its pillars. Lord Woolton was appointed Minister of Reconstruction in 1943 with a seat in the *War* Cabinet. R. A. Butler produced the Education Act of 1944, raising the school-leaving age to fifteen and later sixteen, eventually achieved in the 1970s. Aspiration and vision were added to blood, toil, tears and sweat at any rate in domestic terms.

We reach the moment of political nuclear fission between Downing Street and Fleet Street which occurred five months after Churchill's accession to power. It is now possible with the verbatim reports of the minutes of the secret War Cabinet meetings before me to relate what precisely occurred in this parting of the ways. It was the first but not the last occasion in the war in which the Government seriously considered the censorship or suppression of one or other of our newspapers. Under the thirty-year veto, now reduced to fifteen, the War Cabinet proceedings of the 1940s were not available for Press and public scrutiny until the 1970s. We can re-examine the evidence in calmer times, and reconsider the verdict reached by some but not all members of the War Cabinet in years of greater stress and strain. The issue was not whether criticism of any sort should be allowed in wartime, or whether that criticism was justified or constructive or excessive, but whether what was written was insulting, scurrilous, seditious, malicious, dangerous, unscrupulous, sinister, encouraging a spirit of surrender and inspired by some ulterior motive.

On October 3 Mr Churchill as Prime Minister announced a reshuffle in his Cabinet after ill-health had rescued the nation from any further political exertions on the part of Mr Chamberlain: it was, in personal terms, a sad event because Chamberlain was seriously ill and died a little more than a month later. The next day the *Daily Mirror* published a comment that Churchill did not relish from an ally:

> The sifting or shunting of mediocrities or reputed successes appears to have been directed by no principle plain to the outsider, unless it be the principle that new blood must rarely be transfused into an old body.

On October 6 I wrote and signed an article in the *Pictorial*, the newspaper in which Churchill had written himself in the First World War, entitled 'The Mills of God Grind Slowly'. It applauded Ernest Bevin's elevation to the War Cabinet, Herbert Morrison's move to Home Security, and the appointment of Air Marshal Sir Charles Portal as Chief of the Air Staff at forty-seven. The newspaper complained that the rest of the Cabinet changes were a change of 'remainders'. The decisions displayed neither boldness nor originality. 'Party politics of the worst type has been the basis of this Cabinet reconstruction. Failures and mediocrities have been retained because they are Conservatives: competent men have been ignored because they are not eminent in the political Party game.' It was a lamentable charade of musical chairs in which the Chamberlainites were still being promoted. A mathematical balance of power was still being preserved. All of this, alas, was indisputably true.

There were specific references to several Ministers. 'The case of Sir John Anderson,' said the article, 'is even more confusing. For failing to solve the shelter problem, for diminishing public liberty, and for foolishly imprisoning the best anti-Nazis who have ever set foot on these shores, he has been promoted to the Cabinet of eight.'

The words that followed produced an effect I did not anticipate as I wrote them:

'Much is gained,' Mr Churchill once wrote, 'in peace by ignoring or putting off disagreeable or awkward questions and avoiding clear-cut decisions which, if they please some, offend others.

'It is often better in peace to persist for a time patiently in an obscure and indeterminate course of action rather than to break up or dangerously strain a political combination . . .'

Please read on, Mr Churchill, for these words are your own:

'In war everything is different. There is no place for compromise in war.

'In war the clouds never blow over. They gather unceasingly and fall in thunderbolts.

'Clear leadership, violent action, rigid decisions one way or the other form the only path, not only of victory, but of safety and even of mercy.

'The State cannot afford division or hesitation at the executive centre. To humour a distinguished man, to avoid a fierce dispute, nay, even to preserve the governing instrument itself, cannot, except as an alternative to sheer anarchy, be held to justify half measures.

'The peace of the Council may for the moment be won, but the price is paid on the battlefield by brave men marching forward against unspeakable terrors in the belief that conviction and coherence have animated their orders.'

MR CHURCHILL, YOU HAVE WARNED YOURSELF.

The next day, Monday, October 7, the War Cabinet met at No. 10 Downing Street, presided over by Winston in his most irascible of moods. The minutes of that meeting may now be disclosed without transgressing the Official Secrets Act, but we are solely concerned with Item 6, placed on the agenda on the Prime Minister's instructions. The item was headed, 'The Press. Subversive articles':

'The Prime Minister drew attention to an article in the *Sunday Pictorial* of the 29th September. This article, which had contained a lot of false information, had characterised the Dakar affair as "another Blunder", and had used language of an insulting character to the government. In the issue of the same journal of the previous day (Sunday, 6th October) great prominence had been given to an article published by Mr H. G. Wells in an obscure pamphlet (the Bulletin of the Labour Book Service). This article had contained a slashing attack on Field-Marshal Sir Edmund Ironside and General Viscount Gort. The general tenor of Mr H. G. Wells's article, reproduced in the *Sunday Pictorial*, had been that, until the Army was better led, we stood no chance of beating the Germans. The same issue of the *Sunday Pictorial* had contained a leading article by the Editor, containing a scurrilous attack on several members of the government, and obviously seeking to undermine confidence in the government. Much the same line had been taken in the leading article in that morning's *Daily Mirror*.

'The immediate purpose of these articles seemed to be to affect the discipline of the Army, to attempt to shake the stability of the government, and to make trouble between the government and organised labour. In his considered judgment there was far more behind these articles than disgruntlement or frayed nerves. They stood for something most dangerous and sinister, namely, an attempt to bring about a situation in which the country would be ready for a surrender peace . . .

'The War Cabinet were informed that the *Daily Mirror* and the *Sunday Pictorial* were owned by a combine. A large number of shares were held by bank nominees, and it had not been possible to establish which individual, if any, exercised the controlling financial interest of the newspaper. It was believed, however, that Mr I. Sieff had a large interest in the paper, and that Mr Cecil Harmsworth King was influential in the conduct of the paper . . .

'The Lord President of the Council [Sir John Anderson] said that he was satisfied that it would be wrong to attempt to stop publication of these articles by a criminal prosecution in the Courts. If action was taken it must be executive action, taken under the Defence Regulations, and any appeal against the action taken would be to Parliament itself and not to any court of law. He thought that whoever was responsible for these newspapers should be given a clear warning and told that the warning would not be repeated.

'In the course of discussion the view was advanced that although the articles in question were most objectionable and scurrilous, to proceed against these newspapers which made a wide popular appeal on account of their pictures might do more harm than good.

'The view generally expressed by the War Cabinet was, however, that the conduct of these newspapers represented some unscrupulous and dangerous purpose, the ulterior motive of which was certainly not the commercial motive of profit, and that a continuance of these malicious articles should not be tolerated.

'The Minister of Aircraft Production [Lord Beaverbrook] thought that an approach could properly be made through the Newspaper Proprietors' Association. This Association had considerable disciplinary powers, which he thought that they would be prepared to exercise. The Association would realise, at least as strongly as the War Cabinet, the disadvantage of action being taken by the government to suppress a newspaper, and would wish to avoid recourse to this procedure.

'The Home Secretary [Mr Herbert Morrison] said that the War Cabinet would appreciate that he was new to this matter, and had not followed the line adopted by these two newspapers. An important Parliamentary issue was involved. If these newspapers were suppressed, it would no doubt be argued in some quarters that suppression had been carried out because criticisms had been made of individual members of the government or of Generals. The government would be told that the troubles in France had had their origins in the drastic suppression of all criticism by the French government. Furthermore, he had a quasi-judicial function to exercise, and he would therefore wish for some further time to consider the matter . . .

'The Prime Minister, summing up the discussion, said that the solution which he hoped to see adopted and which he thought was generally favoured, was that two members of the War Cabinet should see the Newspaper Proprietors' Association and explain the situation to them. The articles complained of should be shown to the Association, and it should be made clear that the government was not prepared to allow continued publication of such articles. It should also be made clear that, if the Newspaper Proprietors' Association were not ready or able to take action to stop further publication of such articles, the government would have to deal with the matter in some other way.

'It was clear, however, that, before action could be taken on these lines, the War Cabinet must decide definitely that they were prepared to take action against these newspapers if necessary. In view, however, of the fact that the Home Secretary had a quasi-judicial function to perform, it would clearly be right to defer a decision in order to give him time for further consideration.

'The War Cabinet:

'Adjourned the discussion of this question to a later meeting.'

On Tuesday, October 8, Mr Churchill made the first public reference in a Commons speech to the concern he had expressed privately to the War Cabinet the day before. He described the attacks on Sir John Anderson as ignorant and spiteful and declared there was no better war-horse in the Cabinet. He referred to attacks by a certain section of the Press as vicious and malignant, almost indecent to apply to the enemy. That evening Cecil King observed in his diary that it rather sounded as if this was aimed at our two papers for taking such a poor view of some of the recent Government changes. Yes, a reasonable deduction. One that was soon to be confirmed.

On Wednesday, October 9, the War Cabinet met again, this time in the Prime Minister's room at the Commons, with 'The Press. Subversive articles' as Item 10. Here are extracts from the minutes of the second meeting:

'The War Cabinet resumed discussion of this question and had before them a Memorandum by the Home Secretary (WP (40)402) suggesting that while representations should be made to the Newspaper Proprietors' Association, this should be in the nature of a friendly appeal and not a threat of action under the Defence Regulations.

'The Prime Minister said that the articles in the *Sunday Pictorial* and the *Daily Mirror* constituted, in his view, a serious danger to this country . . . He was determined to put a stop to these attacks and to obtain protection for the War Cabinet. It would be quite wrong that two members of the War Cabinet should be put in the position of asking favours of the Newspaper Proprietors' Association.

'The Lord Privy Seal [Mr Attlee] attached importance to finding out who had the controlling interest, in order to satisfy

127

himself whether the underlying motive was definitely an attempt to exercise a disrupting influence and not merely irresponsible journalism. He regarded the matter very seriously and favoured strong action, but wanted to be sure that there was a cast-iron case. The Home Secretary was invited to take such steps as were in his power to find out the facts required . . .

'General agreement was expressed by the War Cabinet with the view that the articles in question were highly objectionable, and that, while no one objected to fair criticism, the continuance of such articles could not be tolerated . . .

'The Home Secretary pointed out that a number of other newspapers had published articles which, in their way, were just as bad . . . It was also important to avoid any debate in the House of Commons which might lead to a division on party lines.

'In further discussion it was suggested that the Minister of Aircraft Production and the Lord Privy Seal should summon representatives of the Newspaper Proprietors' Association to see them, and should explain to them that the War Cabinet were considering this whole matter and were gravely perturbed at the position.

'The Minister of Aircraft Production said that he felt quite sure that the Newspaper Proprietors as a whole would wish to see action taken to restrain the *Daily Mirror* and the *Sunday Pictorial*. These two newspapers were conducted in a manner which was damaging to the repute of newspapers generally. The Newspaper Proprietors' Association had it in their power to exercise disciplinary action, by taking steps which would add substantially to the cost of running the papers; e.g. by refusing to allow these papers to be put on the newspaper trains.'

On Thursday, October 10, I had my first inkling of the serious stance being taken by the War Cabinet. I was dining with Clement Davies, Edgar Granville and Frank Owen, then Editor of Beaverbrook's *Evening Standard*, and several others. We all met occasionally to discuss the progress, if any, of the war and to exchange ideas on how the national effort could be vastly accelerated. They had dined the night before with the Beaver who had told them (a) that Churchill had taken my article of October 6 to the War Cabinet, and (b) that the phrase in his Commons speech about vicious and malignant criticism by a certain section of the Press had been inserted by general agreement. The next morning I reported the dialogue to

Cecil King, but the same day, Friday the 11th, he had confirmation of the Prime Minister's anger on a level more official than dinner-party gossip.

In the morning Esmond Harmsworth, in his role as Chairman of the Newspaper Proprietors' Association, had been invited to meet Clement Attlee, Lord Privy Seal, with a deputation representing the Press. Harmsworth was accompanied by Lord Camrose (Chairman of the *Daily Telegraph*) and Lord Southwood (Chairman of Odhams Press, printers of the *Daily Herald* and *The People*).

Attlee, with Lord Beaverbrook, then Minister of Aircraft Production, at his side in the role of the honest broker, referred to the recent War Cabinet meetings about the contents of the *Mirror* and *Pictorial*. He said that if criticism of the 'irresponsible kind' which had appeared in those newspapers were to continue the Government would introduce legislation making censorship of news *and* views compulsory. Attlee produced cuttings from Cassandra's column. He described the policy of the two newspapers as 'subversive', calculated to cause alarm and despondency at a very critical period. He was evasive on what exactly the Cabinet objected to. There was no objection to criticism, he said, only to irresponsible criticism.

The threat was clear: compulsory censorship of *views*. The NPA deputation did not take at all kindly to the suggestion and expressed the opinion that it would wreck the Government and be most damaging to the nation's morale.

Late in the afternoon Esmond Harmsworth visited John Cowley at the *Mirror* office, to report what had happened. They were joined by Bartholomew, King, and Wallace Roome, and it was agreed that Bart and King should call on Attlee to hear the story from his own lips.

The meeting took place the next morning, October 12, at Richmond Terrace, Whitehall. There were some German planes overhead and the visitors were conducted to the air-raid shelter where they found Clem Attlee sitting on a bed reading the *New Statesman*. He said that he had been deputed to deal with the matter and that the opinions he would express were not only his own but those of the Government and 'of others'. They felt that the papers showed a subversive influence which at a critical time like that which existed might endanger the nation's war effort.

The only record of what transpired was kept by Cecil King, in his war diary:[1]

[1] Cecil King in *With Malice Toward None*.

'I asked him to give an example. He said he couldn't think of one. I said the NPA deputation had seen some of the cuttings: could we see them? He said he had not brought any cuttings along, that anyway it was not his job to watch the Press and he did not read our papers . . .

'I said we had certainly criticised the Civil Service and some individual civil servants. Was there any objection to that? He said no. My general line was to pin him down to some specific accusation. Bart's line was vague and conciliatory. Attlee was critical but so vague and evasive as to be quite meaningless. We got the impression that the fuss was really Churchill's, that Attlee had been turned on to do something he was not really interested in, and had not bothered to read his brief . . .

'I said our policy in general was to win the war at all costs—no personal or party considerations must stand in the way—and that our newspapers had contributed largely, in my view, to the war effort by the removal of Chamberlain. This had not been done by the House of Commons, let alone Churchill, but by public opinion led by the Press; and of all the newspapers we had taken the strongest line and taken it earliest. Attlee rather naturally said he entirely disagreed with my estimate of the part played by the newspapers in this affair. He said it was no part of the Government's wish to stop criticism, only irresponsible criticism . . .

'I said I thought Churchill had no objection to our kicking poor old Chamberlain, but didn't like being hurt himself. Attlee said he strongly disagreed. I said we were supporting Churchill, Bevin, and Beaverbrook, but I had to confess that our ideas of winning the war and Sir Kingsley Wood's were hardly likely to coincide. He said the Government raised no objection to such differences of opinion. At one point Attlee was doing so badly he was very near breaking off the interview. After about twenty-five minutes we rose and said good-bye: obviously there was nothing to be gained by staying any longer.'

As they strolled along Whitehall, assessing the strange and unsatisfactory meeting. Bart and King agreed that what had really annoyed Churchill and caused all the trouble was the quotation from his own book in my *Pictorial* article. He was infuriated to have been condemned out of his own mouth. King's final comment on the episode was: 'Obviously the Government will do nothing more about it, and obviously we shall pipe down for a few weeks until the course of the war alters the whole situation.'

The War Cabinet met again on October 16 at Downing Street to hear Mr Attlee's report of his mission with Mr Bartholomew and Mr C. H. King. Bartholomew, he said, had been the more reasonable of the two; King had at first tried to adopt the attitude that he did not see what harm these articles were doing. At the end, however, they had both appeared somewhat chastened and had undertaken to exercise more care in future.

'The Press. Subversive articles' was again on the agenda as Item 7 for the War Cabinet meeting on November 4:

> 'The War Cabinet had before them a Memorandum by the Home Secretary summarising the information obtained as to the principal holders of shares in the *Daily Mirror* and *Sunday Pictorial* (WP (40)430). This information indicated that no individual, or group of individuals, controlled the policy of these newspapers by means of a preponderating financial interest.
>
> 'The Home Secretary, who explained that his Paper was circulated for information only, said that the tone of these two newspapers had shown a marked improvement . . .'

Now all is known, or nearly all. What is still concealed by the Official Secrets Act from the prying eyes of the Press and the public are the contents of Mr Herbert Morrison's memorandum (WP (40)430). There is the tantalising gap in the official minutes of what, if anything, was disclosed at No. 10 Downing Street on November 4 1940. The memorandum indicated that no individual or group of individuals controlled the policy of the newspapers, but what else did it indicate? Evidently nothing sinister, for in that case it would have been instantly disclosed by Mr Churchill to justify his alarm and substantiate his charges of malice and sedition and ulterior motives. Under the regulations any government department may apply to the Lord Chancellor for a document to be kept secret for an extended period if they feel it is too sensitive for release at the end of the customary veto. You will simply have to wait for *Son of Walking on the Water*, which cannot be published because of this restriction until 1991.

The perpetual love-hate affair between politicians and the Press is often passionate, sometimes spiteful, and—as it should be—invariably uneasy. Never was this relationship more strained than between Winston Churchill and the *Mirror* and *Pictorial*. His warmth towards the newspapers in the pre-war years changed to hostility when he

became Prime Minister and became bilious during his second
Premiership in 1951.

Churchill wrote to Cecil King on January 25 1941:

'It has given me much pain to see that newspapers with whom
I have had such friendly relations, and from which I have received
in the past valuable support, should pursue such a line. It is
because of our past relations that I write thus plainly.'

The support of the two newspapers in the past had been valuable;
their criticism of his stewardship was unacceptable.

The cause of the trouble this time, in January 1941, was the
brilliant writing of my friend Cassandra, unfortunately at his best
on a theme which he relished, rumoured changes in the Cabinet.
The quality of the writing still makes entertaining reading:

By the time these words appear in print, Mr R. A.
Butler, who is Under-Secretary of State for Foreign
Affairs, may be President of the Board of Education,
which should not worry you a great deal and doesn't hurt
me either . . .

It is a remarkable system because it presumes that the
whole of the talent of the British Empire is contained
within the number of people who comprise a cricket team.

This cricket team is so good that all the batsmen can
bowl and all the bowlers can bat. The wicket keeper is
excellent at mid-on and the lads in the slips are grand in
the outfield.

Why anybody like Mr Butler, who has been working
on Foreign Affairs, should be given a job in education as
a promotion beats me.

Is a painter a better man when he becomes a plumber?

And more important, is the plumbing improved?

But to return to this remarkable flexibility and versatility
of the men who are running the war . . .

Cassandra listed in detail the nine offices successively occupied
by Sir John Anderson, the seven by Sir Kingsley Wood, and the
six by Anthony Eden.

And meet all the rest of the gang. Ex-this and ex-that—
but never ex a job!

Everybody has done everybody else's business. Every-

body knows everybody. Keep it in the family! Scratch
my back and I'll scratch yours!

The trouble is that this particular game is being
played to a funeral march.

Ours.

Miss Kathleen Hill, Churchill's personal private secretary, conveyed the news that the Prime Minister wished her to say that it was
a pity so able a writer should show himself so dominated by
malevolence. 'There is not the slightest truth underlying the
comments. No such changes have yet been considered by the Prime
Minister.'

Most of the newspapers had printed stories about the probable
move of Mr Butler to Education, and indeed he was appointed
within six months to that post. King expressed in a letter the sorrow
of one and all for giving publicity to unfounded reports and added
in a PS that Cassandra had asked for the Prime Minister to be
reminded that he (Cassandra) had been for nearly four years in the
vanguard of 'the pro-Churchill mob' and still deemed it a privilege
to be so. King included in his letter this phrase: 'Cassandra is a
hard-hitting journalist with a vitriolic style . . .' His expensive
education should have suggested a less inflammatory adjective; it
presented an opportunity Churchill would be unlikely to miss.

The reply, dated January 25 1941, acknowledged the expression
of regret. It also demonstrated, in an all-embracing and thunderous
indictment, just how far the *Mirror* and Winston had drifted apart.
He took 'the opportunity of saying one or two things which have
struck me very forcibly in reading the *Daily Mirror* and the *Sunday
Pictorial*:

'First, there is a spirit of hatred and malice against the Government, which after all is not a Party Government but a National
Government almost unanimously chosen, which spirit surpasses
anything I have ever seen in English journalism. One would
have thought in these hard times that some hatred might be kept
for the enemy.

'The second point is more general. Much the most effective
way in which to conduct a Fifth Column movement at the present
time would be the method followed by the *Daily Mirror* and the
Sunday Pictorial. Lip service would no doubt be paid to the
Prime Minister, whose position at the moment may be difficult
to undermine. A perfervid zeal for intensification of the war

effort would be used as a cloak behind which to insult and discredit one Minister after another. Every grievance would be exploited to the full, especially those grievances which lead to class dissension. The Army system and discipline would be attacked. The unity between the Conservative and Labour Parties would be gnawed at. The attempt would be made persistently to represent the Government as feeble, unworthy and incompetent, and to spread a general sense of distrust in the whole system. Thus, large numbers of readers would be brought into a state of despondency and resentment, of bitterness and scorn, which at the proper moment, when perhaps some disaster had occurred or prolonged tribulations had wearied the national spirit, could be suddenly switched over into naked defeatism, and a demand for a negotiated peace.

'I daresay you will be surprised when I tell you that as a regular reader I feel that this description very accurately fits the attitude of your two newspapers. I am sure this is not your intention, nor the intention of the able writers you employ. It is, none the less, in my judgment, the result. It amounts to the same thing, even though the intention may be the opposite.'

In a second letter he dealt with King's talk of war aims, of scanning the horizon for new ideas and ideals which might shape the world and inspire the young.

'I think it is no defence for such activities,' he wrote, 'to say that your papers specialise in "vitriolic" writing. Indeed throwing vitriol is thought to be one of the worst of crimes. No man who is affected with "vitriolism" is worthy to shape the future, or likely to have much chance of doing so in our decent country.'

In January 1941, just after I had joined the Army, the Government suppressed the Communist *Daily Worker* after a warning given six months earlier: *The Week*, a political magazine with a tiny circulation around Westminister, Whitehall and Fleet Street, was also ordered to call it a day. Mr Herbert Morrison, Home Secretary, assured the House he would discharge the great powers with which he was entrusted with restraint and circumspection.

A cartoon by Philip Zec in March 1942 caused the ultimate break between Prime Minister Churchill and the *Daily Mirror*, a controversy that excited much more interest and alarm than the demise of a Communist organ. Zec had drawn a torpedoed sailor adrift on a raft in a black, empty sea; a stark scene emphasising the horror of U-boat warfare. Underneath it, written in pencil, was 'Petrol is Dearer Now'.

Cassandra, who worked with Zec in the same room, strengthened the caption to emphasise the extra penny charge. The wording became: 'The price of petrol has been increased by one penny– *Official.*'

Philip Zec's aim was to produce a patriotic cartoon to awaken public consciousness to the grim fact that the petrol they were using, sometimes wantonly, cost men's lives as well as pennies. It was passed around in the War Cabinet Room at No. 10 Downing Street, and suspicions mounted, each member's spoken reactions creating a preconception in the minds of others. They were understandably anxious and edgy men shouldering the strain of the daily conduct of a war that was still not going well for us. To them, collectively, it appeared to be a wicked cartoon, a cruel cartoon, a deplorable and horrible cartoon. Had Zec been at that meeting in person and heard these opinions he could not conceivably have guessed that the cause of their consternation was the cartoon of which hundreds of garages had already requested copies to display on their pumps as a warning against waste.

On the morning of March 20 Bartholomew and Cecil Thomas, the Editor, were summoned to see Herbert Morrison at the Home Office. The former contributor to the *Mirror* said that he would announce the unanimous decision of the Cabinet, but kept them on tenterhooks for half an hour.

He then produced the Zec cartoon: 'In my opinion very artistically drawn. Worthy of Goebbels at his best. It is plainly meant to tell seamen not to go to sea to put money in the pockets of petrol owners.' Morrison looked at Thomas with his one eye over his glasses and said, 'Only a very unpatriotic Editor could pass that for publication.' (Thomas wanted to say in reply to that jibe, 'Well, I wasn't a Conchy in the last war like you, so I don't know how you look at things.' But Bart and he had agreed in advance, a typical Bart ploy, to say nothing.)

Then came the decision: not a shutdown but a threat. He reminded them that he had closed one paper, the *Daily Worker*, and said that it could be a long time before it reopened. 'And that goes for you, too,' said Morrison. 'You might bear that in mind. If you are closed, it will be for a long time. No further warning will be given. We shall act with a speed that will surprise you.'

The Home Secretary was stern but when the business was over he asked them to give his kind regards to Mr Cowley. As they left he was whistling a little tune to himself. The threat was formally made in the Commons later that day, and what it meant was silence or suppression. Herbert Morrison's speech in Parliament produced a shock, and the acrimonious debate stimulated uneasiness in the Services, where the *Mirror* was *the* most popular newspaper, and in the country, where it enjoyed the same affection.

Unpatriotic?

Frayed nerves had led to distorted judgement.

Philip Zec was a Socialist, and therefore passionately anti-Nazi. He was also a Jew, and passionately anti-Hitler.

Helping the enemy? When the German High Command papers, or such as were available, were examined by the Allies after the war, a document was disclosed which reduced to fatuity the view of the British War Cabinet about the *Mirror* and *Pictorial* at the end of 1940, the beginning of 1941, and the spring of 1942. The document was an order that all *Mirror* directors were to be immediately arrested when London was occupied.

In 1943, one year after he had threatened to suppress the *Mirror*, Winston Churchill travelled with his entourage to Canada for the Quebec Conference with President Franklin Delano Roosevelt. The talks were concluded more speedily than expected and Roosevelt suggested a fishing trip to fill in the time. The President, unwell at the last moment, had to call off on his doctor's orders, but Winston proceeded with the plan.

He journeyed thirty-six miles from Quebec accompanied by his wife, his daughter Mary, and the high-ranking British advisers who had attended the conference with him.

They moved in a convoy of seventeen Army cars and nine Army trucks to two luxurious fishing lodges, *La Cabane* on the Montmorency River, and *Lac de Neige* in the heart of the Montmorency timber limits. The area for miles around was patrolled by British and Canadian secret service men, camped sentries and motor-cycle police.

How do I know?

The fishing lodges were owned by the Anglo-Canadian Pulp and Paper Company.

The Anglo-Canadian Company was owned by the London *Daily Mirror*.

The *Mirror* was his host, and the Prime Minister, no fisherman, was boyishly delighted to catch a twenty-inch trout. He did not know, at the time, that it was *Daily Mirror* fish.

III

THE QUILL
BAYONET

9

'Get into that ———— truck!'

Political assault and battery is a vocational hazard for the Editors of newspapers. *Give and it shall be given.* Yet there was only one occasion when I was the subject of a question in the House.

The question came from the Conservative MP for Oxford, Mr Quintin Hogg. He asked Mr Ernest Bevin, the Minister of Labour and National Service, why Mr Hugh Cudlipp aged about twenty-seven years had not been called up for military service, and whether the Minister of Labour 'will take steps to see that any advantage granted to him is removed in order to secure the equal operation of the Military Service Acts'.

With the single exception of this occasion I have always been among the admirers of the man who became Lord Chancellor. The correspondence between us at the time, not unamusing, has already been published. In brief, the smear fell flat: the services of a valet with a white feather were not required. There were interruptions in the Commons, and then Mr Ernest Bevin replied: 'The calling up of Mr Cudlipp was deferred on the application of his employers, supported by the Ministry of Information. I understand that this deferment was against the strong desire of Mr Cudlipp himself and, as a result, his employers later withdrew the request for deferment. Arrangements are accordingly being made to post Mr Cudlipp to the Armed Forces.'

The suspicion with which I was later regarded by one or two myopic regular officers led me to believe they had read the Question and not the Answer. Or maybe just didn't believe in soldiers reading newspapers. Or didn't understand Editors. I certainly could not report for duty on the parade ground with Cecil King's letter to the Ministry of Information pinned on my battledress: 'Mr Cudlipp is extremely anxious to join one of the combatant services. So strongly does he feel that it is in this direction that his duty lies that he is prepared to resign from this firm to regain his liberty of action. Under these circumstances I feel it would be wrong for us to stand in his way any longer.'

A pressman is regarded with sufficient hostility in the Army for him not to seek also to be known as a pressed-man or as the Reluctant Recruit.

I joined in December 1940, and it was not difficult to identify on the platform in London at King's Cross (*whose* Cross?) a number of other blokes of similar age but with more family responsibilities than me, there in the flesh, clustered unhappily around them. Other types joined us at the stations on the way to Richmond in Yorkshire, a couple of miles from Catterick Camp.

We were not, in our age group, the flower of virginal British manhood. We were insurance clerks, salesmen, or something minor in the City, or unchartered accountants, or white-collar municipal workers, or wide boys, or racecourse tic-tac men or Editors. All selected fodder, for some reason or another, for the Royal Corps of Signals. I guessed the other heroes had gone through the same assessment as I had, in my case a pleasant though brief interview with a retired colonel with red tabs called back to the colours because of the crisis and now functioning as an amateur vocational psychologist.

'Cudlipp. H'mmm. That your name?'

'Yes, sir.'

'Editor. H'mmm. Editor. Editor. What of? Newspapers?'

'Yes, sir, newspapers.'

'Editor. Newspapers. H'mmm. Deal with messages at all? Cables? That sort of thing? Telephones?'

'Yes, sir.'

'Right. Royal Corps of Signals. My old lot.'

I was befriended on the train by another recruit, rather more unwilling than I, who said defensively that though his name was Jones he wasn't Welsh. He was a costing clerk in a Jewish dress factory in the East End which made, at cut-price wages, posh clothes which were sold to posh women at cut-throat prices in the West End. He made his real money as a sparring partner ('Look at my face') in a professional boxing gymnasium in the Old Kent Road. A punch-ball.

'You've got a black hat,' he said. 'Are you an undertaker?'

'No. A journalist.'

'A journalist. Do you know Peter Wilson?'

I shared a soggy seed cake his wife had given him on the station and, having praised it, had to go on sharing the weekly supply as long as we were at Catterick. He wrote to me for many years after the war, but owing to the death of his wife from cancer, didn't send my share of the seed cake. He was one of the nicest of the people I met during the war.

There was not, so far as I could see, and certainly not among the shower who joined us at Rugby, a Rupert Brooke among us.

> 'Blow out, you bugles, over the rich Dead!
>   There's none of these so lonely and poor of
>   old,
>   But, dying, has made us rarer gifts than gold.
> These laid the world away; poured out the red
> Sweet wine of youth; gave up the years to be
>   Of work and joy, and that unhoped serene,
>   That men call age; and those who would have
>   been,
>   Their sons, they gave, their immortality.'

Talk about immortality. One of the recruits on the train asked me how long the war would last.

'Three years.'

'How do you know?'

'Neville Chamberlain told me in Downing Street the day it began.'

He thought I was screwy.

During the journey, when I was not sizing up the others or guzzling the seed cake, or nipping out to get bottles of beer from the station bars, I read the mail my secretary had stuffed in my pocket as I dashed out to catch the train. The first I opened contained the threat of a writ for libel which I posted back to my wartime successor Stuart Campbell with my compliments.

There was a letter from the sacked War Minister Hore-Belisha welcoming me to his (former) Army. 'A great public will suffer through the lack of your stimulus,' said he, 'and I doubt whether this will be compensated by the accession of strength which the Army is about to gain.' It was scarcely a testimonial I could show to my Commanding Officer.

There was a letter from Major-General J. F. C. Fuller, containing a list of books I should read in idle moments—of which, he warned me, there would be many. One of the books was Oswald Spengler's *The Decline of the West*, with its gloomy historical but true doctrine that every culture expands and flourishes and matures and then decays. It was a philosophy much favoured by the Nazis.

The only urgent matter was the proof of an article by Basil Liddell Hart to appear in the *Pictorial* that week-end. It severely criticised the conduct of the war and Liddell Hart was insistent that I phoned him in Devon that night, however late, to discuss whether he had been too frank. He had heard the paper had been in trouble with Winston Churchill.

When we arrived at Richmond late on Friday night there were three or four brisk men in khaki barking and marshalling us in groups like sheepdogs. The sergeant who was barking louder than the others drove the tenderfoots towards the Army transport. I explained my problem to him and asked if I might find a phone box in Richmond, phone Liddell Hart, and arrive at the barracks by taxi. Would he be good enough to tell me exactly the location of Catterick Camp?

His eyes roved over me from feet to head and focused on my Hannen Swaffer black felt hat and cigar.

'Get,' said the sergeant, 'into that ———— truck.'

In his letter General Fuller said, 'Outside the Tank Mess at Catterick you will find a tree planted by my humble self.' He also said, 'You will find the Army a strange change after an Editor's office.'

When the rookies were packed off to bed on the second night somebody had his portable radio on at full blast.

'Hey—listen! It's about us. It's Godfrey Winn. Christ Almighty! And he mentioned Codlip.'

To my dismay it *was* Mr Winn, and when the initial guffaws died down he was saying, 'He is now in a Nissen hut somewhere in Yorkshire. I know that his new friends will love him as much as we loved him in Fleet Street. He made me a star.'

The heroes were laughing themselves to sleep.

'Godfrey Winn's a poof, isn't he?'

'Codlip created him, he said.'

'Did he do you—or did you do him?'

Cassandra visited me in Yorkshire early in 1941 to consult me about the libel snares in a book he was writing called *The English at War*. He told me the curious story of the trouble *he* was involved in with Winston Churchill. The following item appeared in his column in the *Daily Mirror*:

> I am indebted to the magazine *Life* for this apocryphal story of Churchill's continued war on wordiness in official documents.

Shortly after returning from his tour of the Near East, Anthony Eden submitted a long-winded report to the Prime Minister on his experiences and impressions. Churchill returned it to his War Minister with a note saying:

'As far as I can see, you have used every cliché except "God is Love" and "Please adjust your dress before leaving."'

The correspondence which followed between Churchill and Cecil King concerned Cassandra's irreverence:

From Mr Churchill's Private Secretary, 10 Downing Street, to Cecil King:

January 23 1941

Dear Sir,

The Prime Minister has had his attention drawn to the enclosed cutting from the *Daily Mirror* of January 1. He desires me to inform you that this offensive story is totally devoid of foundation. No such report was ever made by Mr Eden, nor any such comment by the Prime Minister . . .

Yours truly,
Kathleen Hill
Personal Private Secretary

From Cecil H. King to Churchill:

January 24 1941

Dear Prime Minister,

Thank you for your letter of yesterday's date. The story printed in our issue of January 1 was taken from the very well-known American paper *Life* and was described by Cassandra as 'apocryphal' . . .

From Churchill to Cecil H. King:

January 25 1941

Dear Mr King,

I don't think the mere adding of the word 'apocryphal' is any justification for foisting upon the British public an absolutely untruthful story, which is of course extremely offensive both to me and to Mr Eden . . .

Yours sincerely,
Winston S. Churchill

Why should I worry? It was snowing in Catterick Camp and I had to get on with the job of delivering the coal. The officers' wives were shivering in the Married Quarters.

———— ◆◆◆◆ ————

10

Newspapers, Always Bloody Newspapers

Punch last year asked a number of people including me how life might have turned out differently on a second time around. Some took the question seriously. I regarded it as an opportunity for some light-hearted rumination, for there is, after all, a touch of the Walter Mitty in us all.

The fact that I began my journalistic marathon as a child reporter below the age of consent and ended up as chairman of what we modestly referred to as the world's largest publishing corporation should not be taken as proof that I would have been a dolt at anything else. Oh, no; indeed I had some difficulty in deciding whether to be a world-famous conductor (orchestra, not bus), a general (military, not manager) or a lawyer (of the silver-tongued advocate variety, Old Bailey and all that, not specialising in patents and taxation like Margaret Thatcher).

I pursued the possibility of becoming a general with some thoroughness. Any fool (well, any fool like Winston Churchill and me) could see war was inevitable as soon as Adolf Hitler started throwing his weight about on the Continent. I embarked upon a study of military science and strategy, starting with the three volumes of *Vom Kriege* by Karl von Clausewitz; you have to start somewhere. Karl had concluded that strategy should concentrate on three main targets–the enemy's forces, resources, and will to do battle; I had taken the same view long before I had heard of von Clausewitz. His doctrine that war was nothing but a continuation of political intercourse with the admixture of different means was also old hat to me, and who, anyway, would pretend that war is an end of itself? I never understood why he had to write three books to prove the point. I was, nevertheless, encouraged by our identity of view, and the fact that he was a Prussian indicated I was on the right lines.

One would expect the reverse, but the dream of generalship progressively faded as soon as I joined the Army. They spent about six months teaching me high-speed morse with a machine that buzzed into my ear all day and gave me sos nightmares in the

Nissen hut, then changed their mind and trained me as an infantry officer at Sandhurst (after all, the *cradle* of generals).

The crammed wartime cadet course at Sandhurst was in itself a gruelling affair. I found that running, jumping, night marching, and bayoneting straw bags while shouting 'You filthy Hun' and making blood-curdling yells did not come as easily to a former Editor of twenty-eight as to the younger material who had learnt it all in the OTCs at public schools. I yelled my best. Unfortunately for me Brigadier Mike Wardell, one of Beaverbrook's inner circle, had rejoined the Army, and—worse—was instructing at the Royal Military College while I was there. In my off-duty hours, non-existent, he ordered me to produce two issues of the *Sandhurst Magazine*, a highbrow and snobbish affair for which I had neither time nor taste. Rewriting the regimental history of the 5th Battalion, Royal Sussex, while we were preventing the Nazis from landing at Margate was more to my liking.

My first experience of official journalism, self-induced, was on the good ship *Santa Rosa* sailing in convoy from Liverpool to Suez in 1942. It threatened two months (two months!) of weapon drill, PT, map reading and 'cleanest platoon' competitions unless . . .

Brigadier Lee was the imaginative commander of the troops on board. When we were bobbing about in the Mersey waiting for the convoy to assemble, he told me of his problems: (a) how to keep the heroes in cramped conditions occupied and fit for immediate military action at the unknown point of disembarkation; (b) how to maintain their interest in the war without any information of any sort for a prolonged period. I was appointed Entertainments Officer to put on cabaret shows in the dining-hall. Then a better idea occurred to me.

There was a civilian on board, only one, a furtive character rarely seen, but seen once by me taking a breather on the deck. He told me in his cabin that the *Santa Rosa*, now a trooper, was recently an American cruise-ship plying the Caribbean; he was a custodian on board for the duration because he had been the purser. The dialogue was interesting:

'You know this is an American convoy,' said the purser.

'Yes, sure.'

'And you know that liquor is not allowed on any ship in an American convoy?'

'Sure, yes.'

'BUT,' he said, 'don't tell a soul. Can I trust you?'

148

He could. It was going to be a long journey. Over the first nip I asked him about the *Santa Rosa* in peacetime and discovered that it was a well-found ship that printed its own menus. I expressed a professional interest in the printing arrangements and he took me down to the bowels of the ship and unlocked a steel door. There was movable type—the stuff you select by hand, letter by letter assembled side by side in a metal hand-held container and laid out line by line in a steel frame. And a small flatbed printing machine worked on a switch. The hell-hole was steeped in dust but to me it was Aladdin's Cave.

We returned to the purser's cabin for another drink to hear his bawdy reminiscences of Caribbean cruising. 'Spinsters, most of them were. Or widows. From Seattle or New England. From everywhere, almost. As the weather got warmer I had to install a turnstile on the door of my cabin.'

'There wouldn't be any paper on board, would there?'

'God only knows, but we'll find out,' said the purser. 'I've got all the keys. Only me. Nobody else has—or will.'

The following night, after another confidential sip in his cabin, he took me on a second journey downstairs with his ring of keys. In the meantime I had visited the ship's wireless officer to inquire if I could scribble down the news as it came over the radio. Why not, sir, why not?

'Brigadier,' I said at the ship's concert, 'may I see you for a moment in your cabin? I have a suggestion, sir, that may help.'

I told him that if there were four compositors on board or even three or possibly two or even one, I could produce a daily one-page newspaper throughout the whole journey if I could be relieved of some of my regimental duties. There were half a dozen compositors on board and *Ocean News, No. 1* appeared the next day. The creaky menu machine had never produced anything more meaningful than the menus, but by the time we reached Freetown, our first brief stop, *Ocean News* was a two-page daily. Before we reached our second stop at Cape Town we were supplying our captive customers with a four-page special on Sunday *in colour*. I had discovered a mass of old travel brochures. The comps and I cut out the coloured pictures of beautiful cruising girls with a razor blade and stuck them with paste (flour and water from the Army cooks) into the white spaces we arranged in *Ocean News*.

It was a morale job. We were going to be the best-informed shipload of soldiers to arrive at wherever the hell we were going to.

Ocean News reported the truth so far as it could discover the truth, good or bad. It was 1942, and all the news was uniformly depressing. During our sea journey from the end of May to the end of July Rommel drove the British out of Libya. The Japs occupied the Aleutian Islands. The Russians were rolled back on the Don. The Nazis entered Egypt and split the Eighth Army in two. Tobruk fell while Churchill was negotiating in Canada with President Roosevelt. From Britain news came of mounting public uneasiness on the midnight and early morning radio despatches.

Ocean News had no time or staff or inclination to deal in investigative journalism. In the two months of its existence it unearthed, inadvertently, only one transgressor, a Private Zwillenberg. He was the winner of 'The Cape of Good Hope Poetry Contest' for original work written on board ship. It was the only entry that rhymed and scanned. I announced him as the winner and read out his mini-masterpiece at the next ship's concert.

After the formal presentation of the prize to the bard, a book of poetry by Swinburne which I had eased from the cruising ship's library with the connivance of the purser with the keys, I led him aside.

'Private Zwillenberg,' I said, 'your secret is safe with me. For ever. Somewhere in your pocket is a coffee-coloured cutting from the *Daily Mirror*. The winner of the contest is Patience Strong. But have no fear. I do not want to expose the gullibility of *Ocean News* and fortunately there is no rival newspaper on board the *Santa Rosa* able to do so.'

As we were sailing from the Gulf of Aden to the Red Sea the news improved. The last issue of *Ocean News* was distributed by hand to the troops as they disembarked on July 1 1942 at Suez: 'Rommel Halted at El Alamein. Special Edition.' It was God's answer to the prayer of a propagandist who had neglected weapon drill and deck sports. I omitted the other item of news that day. 'Nazis Capture Sevastopol': we had enough on our minds.

The worthy comps and I had a small price to pay for our diligence. As the convoy had zig-zagged its way, blowing the hooters or sounding the sirens on each ship at each turning-point to outwit the German submarines, turning left around the Cape of Good Hope into the Indian Ocean, we had happily laboured in the stomach of the *Santa Rosa* in our underpants, trying to select an *i* from a *j* and an *m* from an *n* in the flickering light. There was no fan in the tiny hold where the menus had been printed in better days. Our faces were waxen and our bodies were covered with the rash of prickly heat. The smiles of the luscious athletic white South African girls in Cape Town were directed at the bronzed gods of the upper deck.

There was a further problem for me. When I arrived, late and dishevelled, at the head of my platoon in the shambles of the marshalling yard at Suez about to 'entrain' for Cairo, I discovered to my horror that they were guzzling slices of water melon bought for a song or a grin from the happy but unwashed Egyptian kids who roamed the docks. Typhoid!

I heard a certain amount of noise as a platoon commander with the 5th Battalion, Royal Sussex, during the defence of the El Alamein Line in the summer of 1942, but missed the shattering bombardment and the start of the forward push in October. They had changed their minds about Lieutenant Cudlipp again. I was *ordered to report* to Cairo immediately, was equipped with a driver, a truck, a typewriter and a set of maps and *ordered to report* to Major-General Harding (now Field-Marshal Lord Harding, GCB, CBE, DSO, MC) somewhere in the Western Desert, of no known address. He was then streaking westwards with the Desert Rats in pursuit of Rommel and his Afrika Korps. I caught up with the great soldier on the east side of Tripoli and was informed that he was out on a personal recce in a tank. His ADC was not available because he had recently been killed by an enemy missile while standing at the General's side. I remember knocking on the 'door' of the tank with a stone and feeling rather silly.

This was another assignment that did not last long. A few journalists then serving in the Army were scratched together to be on the spot and to send back to Britain the story of what the Desert Rats were actually doing: the best among us was 'Mac' McClellan, a fine writer of steely courage who considered he was slacking unless he managed to locate himself near the target where the shells from our own tanks were expected to land, trajectory projection allowing. But it was a propaganda mission. The only occasion on which I was blown up by a Teller mine was when I was returning with 'copy', not when patrolling as an infantry officer until I could see the whites of the enemy's eyes at Alamein.

The Walter Mitty generalship finally faded when I was *ordered to report* to Allied Forces Headquarters, North Africa, and later to contact Mr Harold Macmillan, British Resident Minister at General

Eisenhower's court. I flew to Algiers from Tripoli via Marrakesh in Morocco, a service which linked the Allied troops until they joined together from east and west in Tunisia.

The cause of the bother had occurred during Winston Churchill's visit to Casablanca for the summit conference of January 1943, the occasion when Roosevelt produced his terms for ending the war, 'Unconditional Surrender'. The deliberations lasted ten days and Winston noticed that every morning on his breakfast table there was a copy of the daily American Services newspaper *Stars and Stripes*. It was a commendable production, fat in paging, but where was the British newspaper? The landings in Morocco and Algeria two months earlier were under the command of General Eisenhower, but it was an Anglo-American expedition. No British newspaper? Action this day! The British officers were rather busy at AFHQ when I arrived late in February and were relieved when I said, hopefully, that I could solve the problem.

'Well, Cudlipp, what shall we call it?'

I replied, saluting sharply, '*Union Jack.*' Orders is orders. It was newspapers again, always bloody newspapers.

The concept was of major significance. What was incredible was that it had taken three years for anybody in the War Cabinet to realise that an official service of information in the form of newspapers produced on the spot for fighting men serving overseas is as essential as the supply of ammunition and boots and beer and mail from home. Divisions and even battalions had already produced their own amateur magazines or news sheets, but the pioneer in Army newspapers as such was Warwick Charlton, miraculously producing one-page copies of *Eighth Army News* on mobile printing presses miraculously provided and maintained by Major Edward Budd in the Western Desert and in calmer times in Tripoli and Bari. Warwick was a maverick, erratic and mischievous, but a man of sustained inventiveness and maniacal energy. Montgomery knew and understood. Nobody was in any doubt at all that Monty was running the Eighth Army so long as *Eighth Army News* was alive, and it certainly wasn't Warwick Charlton's fault that Montgomery and the Eighth Army were not invited to run the country when the war was over.

Warwick's best headline, I thought, was:

BENITO FINITO

Churchill was the instigator of *Union Jack*, and therefore the urgency of the exercise was impressed upon me several times, happily over a drink or two in the officers' mess at AFHQ. They said my arrival in Algiers had already been reported to 'Adam' in London. Adam? It sounded like a code, but I was in the public not the secret service: 'Adam' was General Sir Ronald Adam, Adjutant-General to the Forces, a wise and understanding soldier and philosopher who materialised later in the game. I undertook to deliver a report at 10.00 hours at AFHQ the next morning, and sat up all night typing it on faded, war-bedraggled mauve notepaper in a small bedroom in a hotel in the company of some indigestible salami sandwiches, a bottle of tepid *vin rosé*, and some black dried-out cigars I had picked up in Marrakesh. They burnt with a crackle and exuded the stench of saltpetre.

The strategic plan of AFHQ was totally unkown to me and at that time known only hazily by AFHQ. I had to make assumptions:

1. Any idea of producing one daily newspaper for the Services at a single production centre to cover what within a year or two will be a vast area embracing three or four countries is unrealistic. We require a series of small units leapfrogging forward, each capable of publishing a complete daily newspaper swiftly and if necessary unaided, backed up by a supply of features and cartoons from the British Army Newspaper Unit's HQ, which will always be sited with a newspaper-producing unit but will also be leapfrogging forward. Geography and distribution problems are the keynote of the operation.

2. The priority must be to produce the maximum information at the most forward sphere of military operation where men have neither the time nor the will nor the equipment to tune in to the BBC overseas service.

3. The first newspaper should be published in Constantine, half-way between Algiers and Tunis, the second in Tunis when it falls, and the third in Catania (Sicily) or in Algiers if the invasion of Sicily is delayed. One of the two or three North African newspapers will leapfrog to Rome or Bari or Athens according to military needs and timing.

4. The Services newspapers must be manned by soldiers, later perhaps augmented by the RAF and the Navy and probably by indigenous technical operators—Algerians, Tunisians, Italians and Greeks—employed as 'civilian labour', but on no account by

civilians exported from the UK. It must be a Services operation, subject to military discipline.

5. We must charge the soldiers one penny for the paper. News-papers voluntarily bought would be believed whereas give-away sheets would not be.

This righteous notion of mine caused us some trouble. We had £20,000 or more after a year or so sitting idle in an account at the Bank of Algeria and couldn't get rid of it. 'Nothing to do with us, old boy,' said the Command Paymaster, 'try somebody else.'

There was further thinking of a nature I knew would be instantly acceptable to AFHQ. The Commanding Officer of the British Army Newspaper Unit (i.e. me) would be solely responsible for the contents and policies of the newspapers, delegating power as he thought fit. He would be accountable direct to AFHQ, to which he would have access on the highest level at all times. The Editors of the individual newspapers, though their units would be self-contained, would not *repeat not* be responsible to the Divisional Commands where their newspapers were published.

Well, the rest of it, from an organisational aspect, wrote itself. Obviously each unit would need equipment and one operator from the Royal Corps of Signals to monitor the news from London.

I had no newsprint, no ink, no machinery, no staff, no news. It was a bold plan and it was not regarded as foolish or impracticable. I was instructed, after cabled exchanges between AFHQ and London, to draw up the establishment. Throughout the command the word went out that journalists, linotype operators, compositors, etc. were ordered to disclose their qualifications to the Company HQ. I imagined the stalwarts of the NUJ, and the printing unions now known as NATSOPA, SOGAT and SLADE, then disguised in khaki, frustrated and disgruntled in a vast variety of military units, studying the notice boards with a glint in their eyes. Could it be true?

It occurred to me, soonish, that running official newspapers without any meaningful official information would be no sinecure. The Americans and the French (my God, de Gaulle!) were already involved, and before long we'd have the North African Arabs, the Greeks and the Italians. And the Pope, issuing encyclicals after press time. And the Polish Division. The scope for disputed news, contentious views, and unintended innuendo was awesome. I decided not to worry AFHQ about these minor matters and to cross the mental minefields when we met them.

They had taught me at the Royal Military College in Sandhurst (the wartime quickie course) that no military plan should be formulated before reconnaissance.

The first move was a journey in a borrowed jeep from Algiers to Constantine to confirm that it was the right site for our first production. Geographically perfect, not on AFHQ's doorstep and as near as possible to the sharp end, linked by rail (newsprint supplies) with Algiers and Tunis and the port of Philippeville fifty miles north. It was a city of just over 100,000 souls in racial and religious conflict.

Constantine was not an idle choice picked out on the map with a pin. It had a newspaper plant publishing the *Dépêche de Constantine* in Rue Georges Clemenceau, a narrow road leading from the bustling city square and sloping steeply down to the squalid Arab quarter with its twisting lanes and mosques, flanked on each side by Jewish jewellery and tailors' shops and relatively well-to-do apartments filled with warm-hearted people. I demolished the front window of one of the tailors' shops on a later occasion when the brakes failed on our one and only car, a 1931 Ford.

The walled city, dating from Roman times, is built on a majestic rock plateau, divided from the terrain around it by a gorge in some parts 1,000 feet deep. On my journey across the Western Desert to catch up with General Harding my companion, apart from Private Jones, the amiable driver, had been the five volumes of *The History of the Decline and Fall of the Roman Empire*, compactly published in the Everyman pocket-size series. I had been impressed by Gibbon's account of the Siege of Constantine and the reason he described for its failure. At its narrowest point the ravine surrounding Constantine was merely fifteen feet wide and the young matrons of the town aroused their menfolk and demoralised the invaders by lifting their skirts and wriggling their thighs in a regular 'Come and get it' ballet every evening.

Constantine, rather than Algiers, was obviously the propitious birthplace for the first newspaper of the official, anointed and established British Army Newspaper Unit.

A half-hour consultation with the British Resident Minister, Mr Harold Macmillan, who had troubles enough of his own, indicated the problems in store for me. France, so far as its possessions in Africa were concerned, was now on *our* side. Nothing could be requisitioned, including newspaper offices. All dealings must be on a commercial basis. The supply of newsprint was essentially a shipping problem. French newspapers must survive. 'Psychological Warfare', the American propaganda exercise to which Richard Crossman had been seconded, imported its own newsprint and I would be lucky indeed if they syphoned off any of that. Summarised, the message was, Good luck, old man, but conveyed with charm.

I was able to borrow some newsprint from the proprietor of *Dépêche de Constantine* on my undertaking that the stocks would be replaced as soon as our own supplies from the UK arrived. This was a promise I freely gave, though I was far from certain when our stocks would arrive, if any, or from where, or how regularly. I was a believer in the theory that once you produce an essential newspaper it somehow or other survives, and that on the whole luck is on the side of those who deserve it.

The first manifestation of luck was the arrival of Sergeant Ralph S. Thackeray.

Sitting in Constantine, alone, I appraised the qualifications of the men who had reported at their Company offices for this unlikely duty, and the one who mattered urgently was Mr Thackeray. A *Manchester Guardian* man. Sub-editor on their foreign desk, French-speaking, but I had to apply some pressure through AFHQ to expedite his release. His major insisted that he was indispensable. He was. He was the only soldier on the strength who could translate the major's weekly laundry list into French and talk with the natives about other matters of lower military priority.

Sergeant Thackeray, who rapidly became Lieutenant Thackeray, then Captain, then Major, was surprised at his first assignment with his new commanding officer.

'Ralph,' I said in our room at the *Dépêche de Constantine*, 'can you get some big and robust cardboard labels printed quickly— simply saying 'Union Jack, Constantine'. Better print two dozen. And a stapling gadget that can fix them on the side of railway trucks. And a flashlamp. And can you be ready with them at 04.00 hours when the train from Algiers comes in?'

I had heard that a mighty pile of newsprint was arriving at dawn at Constantine station, assigned to 'Psychological Warfare' and *Dépêche de Constantine*. It seemed to me that the morale of our own troops was at least as important as the demoralisation of the enemy. A daily newspaper in English—or a hundred thousand pamphlets in German and Italian scattered by an aeroplane over the ruins of Carthage? Ralph and I neatly and convincingly readdressed half of the newsprint consignment in the railway trucks and were away from the scene of the crime well before dawn. I called this sort of exercise 'improvisation'. A lot of it was necessary to get the newspapers off the ground and a great deal more to keep them in the air.

Others have written, and I confirm, that Churchill's enmities were not usually of a permanent nature. Sir James Grigg, then War Minister, told me on his visit to the Central Mediterranean Forces that my appointment as Commanding Officer and Editor-in-Chief of the official Services newspapers was made with Churchill's personal approval. A further indication of the official forgiveness occurred when I flew to London for a week after *Union Jack* was launched to organise the right to lift any material from the British newspapers free of charge and to lay on news and picture services. During the quick visit the Minister of Information asked me to write a 3,000-word piece about Montgomery for the Canadian magazine *Liberty*. The BBC asked me to broadcast on the triumphant desert campaign of the Eighth Army. Beaverbrook, then Minister of Aircraft Production, phoned me the next morning with a message: 'Do you know who this is? The Prime Minister and I listened to your Eighth Army broadcast last night and Winston thought it was great stuff. Good-bye to you.'

No newspaper merely appears; there's always a last-minute drama. A little imagination had solved the technical problems and I ticked my list as a final check:

✓ Newsprint: pinched.

✓ Crude Arab ink: thin with petrol.

✓ Iodine and chemicals for picture blocks: get from British Military Hospital.

✓ Local news: daily from France Afrique Newsagency to office by pigeon link.

March 24 1943 was to be publishing day, but I advanced it three days when Churchill announced the plan for the Britain of the future on the evening of March 21. The first issue was sold at three a.m. to a sleepy, tipsy sapper making his way back to his billet. *Union Jack*'s second and third productions appeared in Algiers and Tunis in September, and the peak was reached in the first half of 1945 with five separate editions, plus *Eighth Army News* which came under my wing in April 1944, plus a twelve-page weekly magazine titled *Crusader*. In addition, improvised Battle Editions were published for short periods during swift advances by the Army. In Catania the Royal Engineers constructed a water pipeline to drive the plant hydraulically. In Florence the roof of the office was in use as the HQ of the partisan snipers. In Rovigo, where 56 Division had temporarily halted before the next push, we drove the printing plant by a belt attached to the wheel of my jeep: the town's electricity works had been blown sky-high.

Editorially, the management of the General Election of 1945 in the non-political Army newspapers was probably our most important and exacting achievement. We were even able to distribute complete results twenty-four hours after the declaration.

I had the good fortune to gather together a team of first-class professionals and technicians, all serving soldiers already in the Mediterranean or sent out by the War Office. General Adam sent me Cassandra, then Captain W. Connor of the Royal Artillery: it was the War Office's idea, not mine. General Oliver Leese was so horrified when I took Cassandra with me to one of his briefing conferences that he banned him from the whole of the area occupied by the Eighth Army–quite a slice of Italy: Leese had been told of Captain Connor's rambunctious record as a critic of some of the Army's cherished traditions.

Peter Wilson arrived, and a Welsh Guards officer named Lieutenant John Philpin Jones. He became famous as 'Jon' for his Two Types cartoon and joined the *Daily Mail* after the war. Robb was doing something or other in Italy and I persuaded him to draw beautiful ladies for our newspapers.

The indispensable Ralph Thackeray, now Assistant Editor of the *Sunday Telegraph*, always edited the *Union Jack* in the publishing location nearest AFHQ–Algiers, and then Naples. That had to be the most respectable and reliable edition of the lot, and I could always rely on Thackeray to defuse the bombs. 'I get the idea,' said Ralph. 'I wag my tail in the rear while you're barking at the front.'

Cassandra was an eager and inventive volunteer when I was opening up new editions or producing highly improvised issues in a town that had just been taken. He was the man who drove the jeep, elevated on railway sleepers, that drove the belt that motivated the plant at Rovigo: the back wheel of the car was included in the circuit of the belt, a Heath Robinson device that caused the town's traffic to be diverted. He was at his best as a forger of Army orders. Rome was American territory but it was essential to get there quickly to grab a newspaper office. AFHQ had warned that authority could only be granted by US Army Command, a process which would have lost essential time. Cassandra drove me there with certain equipment I always carried, a typewriter, official notepaper, carbons, and a battery of rubber stamps collected in Italian newspaper offices, saying nothing in particular but impressive to soldiers who couldn't read Italian.

The road to Rome was manned by 'snowballs', i.e. US military police, at a series of check-points, and when we encountered the first hurdle we drove off the road to a secluded spot to implement the old routine.

'Bill, the typewriter.'

Captain Connor would concoct a suitable Movement Order written in terse unyielding military language. Lieutenant-Colonel Cudlipp, H., and Captain Connor, W., were under immediate orders issued by AFHQ to report urgently to General Mark Clark. Any measures that could facilitate their mission must be granted by Allied personnel and any impediment in their transit instantly reported by Signals to CO, BANU, AAI. I, of course, was the Commanding Officer of the British Army Newspaper Unit, Allied Armies in Italy. By the time I had written an indecipherable signature on the document and Cassandra had used two of his Italian rubber stamps the Movement Order would have got us past Hitler's personal bodyguard. This one certainly got us to Rome with the victorious American troops.

There was something intriguing about the titles of the newspapers into whose offices we squeezed ourselves by fair means or foul in the chaos of war. *Dépêche de Tunis, La Gazzetta del Mezzogiorno* in Bari, *Il Mattino* in the bustling, noisy Galleria Umberto in Naples, *Il Popolo di Roma* in Via del Tritone. Our entry was achieved pleasantly as a rule, sometimes threateningly, but always successfully, decisively and quickly.

When a country is conquered, 'unconditional surrender', there is no problem. You simply *requisition* anything you need or want or covet–transport, houses, newspaper plants, newsprint, the lot. It is easier to twist the arm of a co-belligerent than an ally, but in Italy, weary of war and not over-anxious to provoke the liberators, a uniform and a revolver on the belt worked wonders in speeding up negotiations.

I recollect no single newspaper office in Italy which was not totally staffed from proprietor to doorman by members of the intrepid and populous Italian Resistance Movement. With armbands, hastily sewn on, to prove it the moment the Germans retreated. No one seemed to have been a Fascist except Mussolini. We perfected the dialogue with experience, but it was usually along the following lines:

'I am going to produce a daily British newspaper called *Union Jack* in this office. Beginning now.'

'We would like to welcome you, but it is unfortunately impossible.'

'Why?'

'We already produce our own newspaper in this office. There is room only for one.'

'You may be right. In that case I will stop the production of your newspaper tonight.'

I ignored the voluble protestations and demanded to see the files of the previous month's issues of the Italian newspaper concerned, turning over the pages one by one, gravely pointing to the headlines and occasionally fixing the eye of the proprietor with mounting revulsion. I did not go out of my way to tell my adversary that I could not read Italian, but it was reasonable to assume that their political philosophy had undergone a timely change as the Germans withdrew and the British bombs and shells landed uncomfortably nearer. I remember an American naval officer telling me of a huge painted sign draped across a dockside building in Tokyo when the wartime American Fleet approached: 'The Tokyo Forgive-and-Forget Engineering Company'. There was a good deal to forgive and forget in Italy.

After studying the files of the offending newspaper I would explode in a manner designed to impress the Italian audience that I meant business, and then would say quietly and reasonably to my interpreter, 'Please tell Signor Macaroni that I will wait five minutes more here in his room while he consults his technical colleagues. If he returns in five minutes, or preferably sooner, to tell me that two newspapers *can* be produced in this office I will have no need to stop the publication of his own newspaper tonight. Otherwise . . .'

I would then look, so far as I could without grease-paint, like Tito Gobbi playing Scarpia in *Tosca*. And within a short time we were, of course, the best of friends.

HARRY GUY BARTHOLOMEW:
'He punished me for the unpremeditated crime of being
his only visible editorial successor.'

CECIL KING: 'Aloof and lonely,
but seeking no one's company.'
Pictured when our partnership
began in 1937.

The *Daily Mirror* enters the abdication crisis, breaking the
news on December 3, 1936, and demanding the disclosure
of the facts a few days later.

In the Constantine, North Africa, office of the
chain of wartime Services newspapers.

At Rovigo in Italy. Handing out a 'rush edition'
of *Union Jack* to the advancing 56 Division.

'Please tell Signor Macaroni that I understand that he had to publish all that flattery about the occupying Nazi Army. From now on he will be free to publish kind thoughts about the British and the Americans. *Union Jack* wishes him well and will help him with his problems.'

The conference usually ended with a coffee and a glass of strega. As for the censorship or 'guidance' of the indigenous newspapers, that was not our department.

The Mediterranean was a sensitive theatre of war in which to conduct a chain of newspapers spread over several countries and rarely in communication with each other by telephone.

True, the Allied forces were more 'allied' than in any other sphere of operation throughout the war. The Supreme Commander, General Eisenhower, directed the massed sea, land, and air forces, and General Alexander was the effective Commander of all the Allied armies. Ike and Alex were on splendid terms, so were the commanders of all the Services, so were Harold Macmillan (UK) and Robert Murphy (US) on the diplomatic and international side. But the course of the campaign itself was the subject of persistent disputation between the White House and Downing Street and also between the chiefs of staff on both sides of the Atlantic.

The African Expedition in West Africa in 1942 was a British not an American conception. The attack on Sicily was only reluctantly endorsed. It was the hugest joint operation ever launched in military and naval history: 160,000 men, 14,000 vehicles, 600 tanks and 1,800 guns transported in nearly 3,000 vessels of all shapes and sizes in the initial assault alone. Costly and time-consuming. The capture of Southern Italy, useful principally because of its airfields, was also rated by the Americans as a dubious exercise.

How far was it all necessary? At what stage should it stop? Was it, in its massive consumption of manpower and fire-power, delaying the Second Front in Northern France? Was Churchill's grand design of an assault upon the soft underbelly of Europe a spectacular sideshow to exploit the success (principally British) in North Africa? 'New Gallipolis lay tantalisingly upon the horizon.'[1] There was distrust. In America there was the suspicion of a flavour of post-war Imperialism in Churchill's thinking, and in the Kremlin it was suspected that the rescue in Northern Europe was being delayed

[1] A. J. P. Taylor in *English History 1914-1945*.

until Communist Russia was permanently crippled or even obliterated by the Nazis.

The result was a compromise. Eisenhower and Alexander did not have at their command when it was needed the overwhelming striking power in planes and landing craft for a series of fearsome crocodile bites, greater Salernos and greater Anzios, that would have broken the back of the Italian peninsula in two or three more places, forcing a swift retreat by the German occupying forces along defined routes which could be mercilessly strafed. The result was a crawl with bitter fighting, assaulting one after another the classically natural defensive positions provided by the mountainous backbone of the country, God's gift to Field-Marshal Albert Kesselring.

The decisive year in Italy was 1944. The Allied landing at Anzio, north of the Cassino line, took place on January 22. The British Eighth Army's battle for Monte Cassino lasted from February 1 until May 18. The American Fifth Army's triumphant surge into Rome was therefore delayed until June 4. The Eternal City, the most beautiful of all, dominated by St Peter's Basilica and the Vatican, the Roman Catholic centre of the world, the religious headquarters of the Pope, Vicar of Christ, successor of St Peter, prince of the apostles, was liberated a year later than had been hoped and anticipated. The glittering prize went solely to General Mark Clark and his American Army, a suitable and just reward for President Roosevelt's support for a protracted campaign in which his advisers had limited faith. The world, as well as America and Britain, was moved and thrilled by the news. And a significant by-product was that the headlines in thousands of newspapers across the United States, 'US Liberates Rome', would stimulate even further the interest of the new world for the old.

The fall of Rome might also have resulted in an event of somewhat lesser significance, the fall of Lieutenant-Colonel Cudlipp, H. The ancient ruins of the city were augmented by two bricks of disturbing size and weight dropped by the Rome edition of *Union Jack*, each causing alarm in the High Command.

I was responsible to Alexander's right-hand man, General Sir Brian Robertson, with whom I had good relations. Macmillan described him as the most efficient 'Q' officer since Marlborough's Cadogan: he was certainly the distinguished soldier son of a distinguished soldier father, Sir William Robertson of World War One, the original private who really did find a Field-Marshal's baton in his knapsack. There were times when I was of great value to Sir Brian, and other occasions when I fear I caused him some distress. He kept me in the picture so far as he could during the edgy crises, but it was a swiftly changing picture and we met more frequently after than before *Union Jack*'s blunders or indiscretions. Our crime, as a rule, was telling the truth; the old trouble.

America's Roman feast had all been stage-managed with diplomacy and taste by Alexander. And then some damn-fool war correspondent, regrettably British, blew the gaff. Philip Jordan cabled to the *News Chronicle* in London, handing a copy of his story to one of our Editors, that 'Owing to the valour of the British Eighth Army, fighting against grim odds in the Apennines, the American Fifth Army were able today to sweep nonchalantly into Rome, unopposed by the retreating Nazi troops.' Worse, our official weekly newspaper *Crusader* printed Jordan's despatch word for word on its front page.

General Robertson sent for me with some acerbity. It was resolved, on my suggestion, that the *amende honorable* could only be achieved if I was ordered by Alexander to journey to General Mark's forward HQ, now scurrying further north, to apologise in person for this gross misinterpretation of military history–i.e. the facts.

Major Ralph Innes–the famous Hammond Innes who wrote *Wreckers Must Breathe, Attack Alarm, The Lonely Skier, The Angry Mountain, Atlantic Fury*, and many other world best-sellers (rather appropriate titles in the light of our mission)–accompanied me on the journey. Cool in a crisis, Ralph Hammond Innes was a great asset in the unit.

Union Jack was responsible for the second ruin we added to Rome's impressive collection. During that period we lived in a villa on the Aventine Hill, and a sharp knock on the door at six a.m. one morning disclosed the presence of an excitable staff officer under orders to convey me instantly to General Robertson some miles away. He was white-faced, agitated, and momentarily speechless, stabbing the front page of the newspaper with his forefinger. I trust that the brevity of my description of the situation will not disguise the enormity of the indiscretion.

There had been a secret discussion in the Vatican between His Holiness the Pope and General Alexander.

The Pope disclosed to him that a number of British soldiers, escaped from German prison camps, were hidden within the walls of the Holy City.

The protection they had enjoyed was in direct contravention of the tradition of diplomatic immunity affecting the Vatican. Participation in the war, even in the role of saintly succour, might have invited the bombing of the Holy City.

It was agreed that the soldiers would depart from the Vatican under cover of darkness, and be whisked away by transport secluded near an inconspicuous side door, reporting back to the British Army.

In absolute secrecy.

General Alexander gave the Pope his word as an officer and gentleman that not one whiff of information would appear in the Press of the world about this clandestine manœuvre.

Indeed, all precautions (or nearly all) were taken. It was decided that rather than risk the possibility of *one* war correspondent discovering the facts by chance, *all* correspondents should be told and pledged to confidence. There was a hastily summoned press conference announcing total censorship on the story. One correspondent contrived a version which would hopefully be passed by the censors and handed a copy to *Union Jack*, his normal practice.

His story was instantly suppressed for publication in Britain but appeared in *Union Jack* the next morning. As large as life. In Rome.

'Here it is, in General Alexander's *own* newspaper. Look at it,' Robertson said to me. And then, after a pause for breath: 'Why? How? What can I tell him? I cannot keep *Union Jack* from him–he is reading it *now* at breakfast, in the next room. What can I say to him? How did it happen? What can he say to the Pope? What can anybody say to anybody?' The man was distraught.

I offered, interspersed with a battery of 'sirs', my rational explanation of what had happened. The man in charge of military censorship had obviously invited to the most important conference in his life every newspaper in the world except the official newspaper published on his own doorstep.

'*That* bloody fool,' said the General.

'Yes, sir, that bloody fool. One of his military censors is working every night at my request in our publishing office. He didn't tell him either.'

Official dialogue, especially in the Services, tends to become a simulated conversation between two ventriloquists' dolls in the absence of the ventriloquists. The facts in this case amounted merely to an orthodox military balls-up in which the only innocent party was *that* particular newspaper published at that particular time in that particular place. But I was there to be helpful. My apology to General Mark Clark over Brick Number One had been successful, and I needed a bright idea to get over Brick Number Two.

'Sir,' I said, 'why not say to General Alexander that you have sent me back to the infantry?'

Robertson said, politely, 'No. That won't help at all.'

What he meant was: 'No. We might get a bigger fool than you as your successor.'

What I meant, but could not say in a dialogue between ventriloquists' dolls, was this: 'My dear Brian, you honest soldiers should relax. The word of an officer and a gentleman is illusory once war has begun. There is no gentlemanly way in which civilians and their children can be bombed, but it is often necessary to do just that. His Holiness the Pope was in the Vatican long before the Allied Armies came to Italy and he or his successor will be here long after we have left. He is the same Pope who condoned Italian Fascism and reached a concordat with Mussolini. Nor did he denounce Franco's Spain—another Catholic country—or Hitler's Germany. Alexander's word has been broken, but the Pope may well come to the conclusion that his own word has been spoken. This particular copy of *Union Jack* may even be filed in the Vatican archives, not under D for "deceit" but P for "propaganda". To take under the wing of the Vatican the British prisoners who escaped from the Germans was a gesture he would wish to conceal from the Germans while they occupied the Eternal City. It is not necessarily a gesture he would wish to conceal from the Allies now that the Allies occupy the city and the Germans are facing defeat throughout Europe. The Vicar of Christ may well be winking today as he says his morning prayers in his private chapel. What if there were a reverse in this campaign? What if Rome were re-liberated by the Nazis? Maybe the Pope would invite Field-Marshal Kesselring to a similar conclave in the Vatican to tell him in confidence that a number of German soldiers who escaped from British prison camps would be leaving under the cover of darkness that night at the same side door providing that Kesselring, as a German officer and gentleman, would give his pledge of secrecy. Alex should on no account apologise. He should issue an encyclical of his own to the Pope questioning the security arrangements at the Vatican.'

The ventriloquists' dolls were unable to be so frank. But I heard no more about that particular Roman scandal. The next time I saw Brian was in a private room in the railway hotel at Paddington. The future Baron Robertson of Oakridge was appointed Chairman of the British Transport Commission in 1953 and was meeting the national Press. We both had the good taste not to mention the Pope or General Mark Clark. He did confide, however, that he found soldiers a more amenable lot than railwaymen.

Then some other bloody fool declared peace.

The roundabout suddenly stopped and all the lights went out in the fairground. The victors crammed money into the pockets of the vanquished, fed their sickly babies with orange concentrate, helped them restore their smashed cities and factories and railways and get the plumbing working. Europe joined the Forgive-and-Forget Engineering Company. British troops stayed on in Germany to rebuild the bridges they had blown up or the RAF had bombed.

Men with tanned faces and bristling moustaches who had been tearing across the desert in armoured cars reported for duty at the Midland Bank branch in Sidcup, Kent, looking curiously like the Two Types and telling the typists they preferred sand instead of sugar with their office coffee. Devil-may-care Wing Commanders came down from the sky to worry about the price of Rank Org Ord, Dunlop Hldgs, or bullion and catch the 5.12 from London Bridge to Horsham. Instead of 'Aye, aye, sir' on the bridge of a destroyer on the cruel sea it was 'Yes, madam, it *does* suit you' from behind the counter of a departmental store. The bucks with roving eyes, accustomed to spotting talent packaged in the uniforms of Wrens, Waafs and Ats and among the luscious natives of Italy, France and Germany, returned to their domestic duties and petulant children in semi-detached suburbia. Elderly men and women, retired colonels and policemen and schoolmistresses who had worked all night doing their duty as air-raid wardens, held hands and said good-bye in derelict houses, the headquarters where they shared their giggles and coffee and sandwiches brought from home. Hitler was the cupid who had launched a million extra-marital affections in wartime England, and the end of hostilities was the end of romance. The house where I lived in Chelsea after the war had been a wardens' post. It became, in the less stimulating years of peace, a *poste restante* for parted lovers where letters arrived which were never collected; I could only put them on the fire, unread.

New names were engraved on the blank and less sunny sides of the cenotaphs in the towns and villages.

They demobbed me the day before my birthday in 1946. A

pleasant and considerate gesture by the Army Council, I thought. And General Alexander sent me a charming letter remembering the mortar and forgetting the bricks. I did not hear from General Mark Clark or the Pope.

IV

THE
STORMS BEFORE
THE STORM

11

Sword of Damocles

This chapter begins with 'Hello, Bart' and ends with 'Good-bye, Cudlipp'. Harry Guy Bartholomew celebrated the end of the war by producing a sumptuous leather-bound book for the employees of the *Daily Mirror* entitled *The Call and the Answer*. No doubt other companies did the same, but Bart's tribute was typically different. He had the sort of convoluted mind that could attribute evil and devious motives to a bee-keeper offering him a pot of home-produced honey as a gift. Those who remained in the office for one reason or another during the war were mentioned first and those who joined the Services were listed at the back of the book as 'They Also Served', in smaller type. Just to make them feel at home when they returned.

The death of John Cowley in 1944 was unmourned in the office. The important point was that Bart was now the Chairman, supremo of both newspapers, the one he created and the one he hated. His scope for malevolence was now limitless, and it was not an opportunity he was likely to ignore. I received a letter from him when I was preparing to pack up in Rome, planning the future of the Army newspapers with Ralph Thackeray, my successor as 'the Colonel'. I read Bart's letter several times and held it up to the light.

I knew he didn't want me back in the office and had said so to his toadies. If he could have ended there and then the King-Cudlipp axis he would have done so with relish. His antipathy to Stuart Campbell, Editor of the *Pictorial* in my absence, was unabated, but there was the compensating factor, if my reincarnation could be aborted, of forcing King and Campbell, who despised each other, to continue to work in harness. Very tempting to Bart. It was only the Act of Parliament, obliging employers to reinstate employees returning from the Services, which prevented him from firing me before I returned.

The letter seemed innocent enough:

March 12 1946

My dear Cudlipp,

Glad to get your letter, also your date; had hoped it would be earlier. There is much to be done to the *Pictorial*; your criticisms in a letter to C.H.K. are sound, and I am sure he agrees.

I do not think there are any long-term commitments on the *Pictorial*, or any long contract. I am afraid you will have to try out most of the people there for quite a time; any mass changes would be out of order and would cause a lot of trouble. This doesn't mean that in the course of time there can be no changes—or that additions cannot be made—but it is a point you will have to watch very carefully.

Yours sincerely,
Guy Bartholomew

Sweet reasonableness, but also sweet intrigue. There was a pungent PS: 'When you reach England, see me before you see anybody, even if you have to wait.' It was not hard to guess the identity of 'anybody'.

I heard from Cecil King the same month: 'I cannot find any two opinions about the need for a shake-up on the "Pic", but everything is being left unaltered until your return. I shall be so glad to welcome you.'

The natural urge was to rejoin the newspaper I had helped to save in 1937 when its circulation was a falling 1,300,000 and now to bring it up to a robust 5,000,000; also to continue the collaboration with King.

A future with Bartholomew as head man, or head executioner, would be uneasy and uncertain: the greater the success of the *Pictorial* the greater the wrath. He would never appoint me Editor of the *Daily Mirror*.

I was therefore happy to receive two direct approaches before I was demobbed, from Lord Rothermere (Esmond succeeded Harold in 1940 and was in total control of the vast *Daily Mail* empire, financially the most substantial in the industry), and from Arthur Christiansen, Editor of the *Daily Express*, as emissary of Lord Beaverbrook. When I mentioned to Esmond Rothermere that I was morally obliged to return to the Mirror Group because they paid their staff, including me, a proportion of their civilian salaries while they were in the Services, he smiled. 'Oh, I shouldn't worry,' he said, 'we could send Bart a cheque to recompense him.' Christiansen had written: 'I don't know whether it would be asking too much of you not to enter into any firm commitments and not to make up your mind positively about your future until we have had an opportunity to talk.'

The brighter side of it all was picking up the *Sunday Pictorial* where I had left off in December 1940. Newspapers in the early post-war years were severely rationed for newsprint and the maximum size for a tabloid was still twelve pages. After we had accommodated sport, pictures, show business and all the other furniture, plus news, there wasn't much room for manœuvre, for much personal impact. In 1976 the same newspaper, now the *Sunday Mirror*, frequently luxuriates in forty-four or forty-eight pages. But there was the precious *rapport* with the readers, the link with the 'ordinary' people of the day which Stuart Campbell, the wartime Editor, had preserved.

The newspaper reflected the issues of the time: it was a crusading newspaper. We'd won the war, yet there was still austerity, rationing, shortages, delays in housing and replanning programmes. Thousands of men in uniform were still awaiting demob and their families were still awaiting their return. Labour was in power, assisted by the *Mirror*'s 'Vote for Him'–the husband or boyfriend in uniform– campaign in the election of July 5 1945, and it was too soon to attack the hesitations and deficiencies of the new central government. The nation was suffering from nervous and physical exhaustion.

The *Pictorial* appointed its own Vigilance Council, chaired by War Correspondent Rex North. It demanded justice for Army pensioners. It dealt sympathetically with the problem of marriages broken by the war. Mervyn Stockwood, then the Vicar of St Matthew's, Bristol, a friend of Stafford Cripps, wrote an article called 'Cut Out the Humbug'. The message, which still needs to be heard, was that without social justice Britain can never become a really Christian land. He was still campaigning in the same cause nearly thirty years later as the Bishop of Southwark.

I launched an experiment in assessing public opinion, a pioneer effort at a national referendum. We selected on a scientific basis One Hundred Families to Speak for Britain, and their first demands were a salutary challenge to the politicians. Forty-three families out of one hundred were waiting for a new home; they needed more fats, tea and clothing. The *Pictorial* regularly consulted the Hundred Families on the problems that were making their lives less joyful than they need be because the Labour Government was loath to jettison the easy social justice of rationing.

To some Editors the principal purpose of a newspaper is to print news. If the death toll in a pit disaster or a rail crash is more accurate or enormous in their final edition than in the rival's, that makes their week. The spur of efficiency in this particular school of journalism is to be first into Birmingham with the news of a murder, or Kent with a rape, or everywhere with the final score. Their god is the news scoop and the boast 'Exclusive' justifies their existence. Arthur Christiansen, the best Editor the *Daily Express* ever had, was the patron saint of urgency, but Christiansen's greatest contribution to popular journalism was presentation and perfection, word-economy, stiletto sub-editing.

I felt that 'first with the news' was a drug. What newspapers were about, to me, was controversy. Stimulating thought. Destroying the taboos. Taking on the complicated subjects like economics, national health and production, and explaining them in language all could understand. The paper worthwhile to me was an Open University, and this meant presenting the news and views in a sensational manner in the new days of mass readership and democratic responsibility. A pioneer in this sort of valuable public service was Silvester Bolam, a graduate in economics at Durham University who edited the *Mirror* from 1948 to 1953 at the time when the paper took the prize of the world's biggest daily sale from the *Daily Express*.

'We shall go on being sensational to the best of our ability,' he wrote. 'Sensationalism does not mean distorting the truth. It means the vivid and dramatic presentation of events so as to give them a forceful impact on the mind of the reader. It means big headlines, vigorous writing, simplification into familiar every-day language, and the wide use of illustration by cartoons and photographs. Every great problem facing us—the world economic crisis, diminishing food supplies, the population puzzle, the Iron Curtain and a host of others—will only be understood by the ordinary man busy with his daily tasks if he is hit hard and hit often with the facts. Sensational treatment is the answer, whatever the sober and "superior" readers of some other journals may prefer. No doubt we shall make mistakes, but we are at least alive.'

I became involved in the immediate post-war years in two controversies which are interesting in retrospect. One concerned the aftermath of the war, the other centred around a challenge by a bishop to orthodox views on religion.

The German war leaders, those who had not already despatched themselves like Adolf Hitler, were arraigned at Nuremberg on charges of war crimes. Twenty-one were tried, three were acquitted, and twelve were sentenced to be hanged, including Goering and Ribbentrop. An American sergeant and a lance corporal hanged eleven of them on two gallows erected in the gymnasium of Nuremberg Prison. The evidence of their death, in a set of photographs, was passed from hand to hand in the diplomatic centres of the world. Politicians and journalists saw them, but not the public. The surviving relatives of the millions who had died from bombing in the cities or on the battlefields, the masses of people of all nations—including the Germans—who had been duped or deprived by the Nazi thugs were considered to be too fragile, or sensitive, or impressionable to see that retribution had been exacted. Justice had been done, but should it have been seen to have been done? Was the picture of a dead war criminal more disturbing than the picture of a live war criminal?

Mr Clement Attlee, the new Prime Minister, was in no doubt at all. He told the House of Commons:

'The Allied Control Commission, on which His Majesty's Government are represented, decided last week that no cinematograph film or photograph should be taken of the execution. Photographs of the bodies will be taken after death by an official photographer . . . for record purposes . . . There has been no decision of the Central Council on the question of the publication of these photographs. For my part, I should be strongly opposed to their publication.'

It was a view with which most reasonable people would agree. But Hermann Goering, the most notorious of the Nazi leaders in the dock at Nuremberg, had escaped the final punishment after the verdict of Guilty by committing suicide with a phial of poison concealed in his clothes or smuggled to him through the gaolers. The myth was spreading in Germany that Goering had been spared; worse, that the Allies had lost their nerve in this particular case because his execution might have caused resentment among *some* of the German people.

A picture of Goering, dead, appeared in the *Sunday Pictorial* of October 26 1946, and I wrote the words underneath:

HERMANN GOERING: THE END ...

We print below the final picture of Hermann Goering–the Nazi leader–whose cunning enabled him in his last hours to cheat the verdict of the Allied Judges. It is an ugly picture but it is no uglier than pictures the Press of the world published as evidence of the crimes of this man. Remember the photographs of our own air-raid victims? Remember the photographs of Belsen? Those were Goering's crimes: this is his retribution.

If the ends of justice had been served and Goering had died on the scaffold, this photograph would not have been necessary. But already in Germany the myth has grown up that the Allies 'funked' the hanging of Goering for fear of its reaction on the German people. Such beliefs are dangerous.

The British Government decided last week that no official sources in this country should circulate the pictures of the executed Nazis. This was a wise decision, which could safely have been left to the discretion of the British Press. Though France and America have published the pictures of the executed Nazis we do not believe that such a course is either necessary or desirable. The testimony of the Allied witnesses at the officially conducted hangings is sufficient. But Goering's death occurred under very different circumstances. It was an escape from orthodox justice–just as was the death of Himmler, the hanging of Mussolini, and the suicide of Admiral-General von Freidburg. Newspapers then accepted their responsibility and published the pictures as evidence. So with this–the last picture of Hermann Goering.

Right or wrong?

Clement Attlee was asked another question in the Commons two days after publication. Could he explain how a picture got into one of the Sunday papers? What was the good of taking these decisions if they were not carried out? The Prime Minister replied: 'I explained to the Hon. and gallant Member that I could express a wish but that I have no control over the Press in these times.' 1942 was a long time ago.

Right or wrong? In *Union Jack* and *Crusader*, the official Service newspapers, I had published the distressing pictures of the piles of Jewish bodies stacked at Belsen, pictures taken when the Allied armies reached the Nazi prison camp and freed the emaciated fragments of human life still hobbling and breathing. The pictures were sent to me in Italy by the British Government of which Mr Attlee was a prominent member as head of the Labour Party in the Coalition Government. I saw every reason to publish in the *Sunday Pictorial* the irrefutable evidence that one at least of the perpetrators of genocide was no longer a member of the human race. I recall no protests from our readers.

The second controversy was less grim, though certainly not less important. This time there were undertones of humour, or at any rate irreverence.

The practice of newspapers was—and still is, with many of them—to genuflect with or without sincerity in the direction of established religion. The worse perpetrator among the media of religious mumbo-jumbo of the classical brand is the BBC with its monotonously regular programmes, not only on Sundays but every day. The unctuous Lord Reith began it all, and it continues unabated in spite of the revelation in his own diaries that he was a most unchristian and uncharitable gentleman. A pocket adding-machine, and there are now plenty of them around, could quickly prove to the BBC that the time they devote on the air and the TV screen to religion is out of proportion to public interest. Successive Directors-General continue to pay lip service to Lambeth Palace to distract attention from their progressiveness or backsliding in other directions. They know religion is no longer the opium of the people, but they also know that ersatz public worship 'on camera' in scheduled slots is a useful antidote to sex, crime and violence at peak hours. Commercial television genuflects even lower on the knee to demonstrate that its interests are wider than its critics suppose.

The student of *The Origin of Species* and *The Descent of Man* at the age of ten observed at thirty-three an earnest discussion in highbrow places of a book published by Longmans. It was by Dr Barnes, Bishop of Birmingham. It probed the authenticity of the Miracles. Even the resurrection of the crucified Christ from the sealed sepulchre was approached by the Bishop in a rational mood.

I read the book and arranged for its serialisation in the *Sunday Pictorial*. Had the tempest been stilled? Was it conceivable that

Lazarus was raised from the dead? And was the miracle of the loaves and fishes a likely story? Dr Barnes was asking the questions I had asked Mr Francis, Mr Massey and Mr Hussey in Sunday School at the Wesleyan Church in Cardiff. I presented the doubts of the Bishop to the millions. There was surely no reason in heaven or earth why the doubts of Dr Barnes should be confined to a desultory chat among intellectuals in the cloisters.

A phone call received after the third instalment ('Water into Wine at Cana', I think) indicated that Dr Barnes was no longer *persona grata* at Lambeth Palace. In 1927 he had written *Should Such a Faith Offend?*, followed by *Scientific Theory and Religion* in 1933. He was already the unloved provoker of dissension in his own profession. *The Rise of Christianity*, published in 1947, would not have given cause for forgiveness in the hierarchy even if it had passed by unknown to the public as a book: serialisation in a newspaper, a popular newspaper, was a different matter. The thoughts of the unfaithful were now being transmitted to the faithful. The verger and his relatives were invited to share the heresy of the man in the pulpit.

The phone call was intriguing:

'This is Prebendary Stanley Eley.'

'Yes, Prebendary.'

'I am speaking from Lambeth Palace, and I am bidden by the Archbishop to seek a meeting with you. I am His Grace's private chaplain.'

The meeting took place at five p.m. that day because I needed a little time to rearrange the décor in the office. I removed some of the more flamboyant newspaper placards from the wall in my room. It occurred to me, as an example, that 'FIVE IN A BED: SHOCKING PICTURE' might suggest a sexual orgy rather than a housing problem in a slum. But I left the poster proclaiming: 'SUNDAY PICTORIAL—6,000,000 readers'.

'Mr Cudlipp,' said Prebendary Eley over the cup of tea, 'you must have upwards of 2,000,000 readers.'

His speech was measured, his demeanour grave, and the tone was Stage Ecclesiastical. When I casually nodded towards the poster Mr Eley, unperturbed, said: 'Then my mission, if I may say so, is trebly important.'

The Archbishop was displeased with Dr Barnes and later rebuked him before the Convocation of Canterbury. That was an intellectual exercise His Grace could conduct at leisure: a more urgent matter was that the vulgar readers of the vulgar Press were being nobbled by Barnes.

The message from the Archbishop was a request that the newspaper would publish the other side of the case by some other bishop, a divine of equivalent rank and standing.

'I am also bidden to say,' said Prebendary Eley, 'that His Grace will be content if you, as Editor, freely choose that bishop yourself.'

It seemed too good to be true.

'Of course, Prebendary,' I replied. 'I would like Bishop Alfred Blunt of Bradford.' Who was it, on the eve of the Abdication crisis in 1935, who had said in a solemn sermon that the King was in urgent need of God's grace? Dr Blunt was then unaware of the monarch's love for Mrs Simpson, and was referring in general terms to Edward's easy mode of life and circle of friends. But the remark was considered at the time to be a warning from the Established Church, and the obscure bishop became renowned throughout the world. Everybody knew his name: verily Dr Blunt was my man.

On Sunday, November 30 1947, I made the announcement on the front page:

THE CHURCH AND THE PICTORIAL
a request from the Primate.

The *Sunday Pictorial* is able to announce today that the Archbishop of Canterbury has chosen Dr Alfred Blunt, Bishop of Bradford, to reply on behalf of the Church to the widely-discussed articles from the pen of Dr Barnes which have been appearing in this newspaper.

He will deal point by point with the Bishop of Birmingham's attitude to the Resurrection, the Crucifixion, the Miracles and the Gospels.

Dr Blunt's outspoken reply will be written with the full authority of the leader of the Established Church.

And the consequence, as Mr Francis used to say in Sunday School, was that the sensational *Sunday Pictorial* became for three or four weeks the pulpit from which, officially, the Church of England restated to the multitude its attitude to the miraculous and supernatural elements in the Christian faith. I might well have considered invoicing Lambeth Palace for the space at our usual advertising rates, but the sequel was more ironical than that. Dr

Barnes refused to accept the offered payment from the newspaper for exposing the Miracles. Dr Alfred Blunt expected and received a fat fee for refurbishing the ancient legends on the orders of his Archbishop. God moves in a mysterious way his wonders to perform. I remembered my favourite hymn.

A recurring topic was the Royal Family, and the *Pictorial* never hesitated to join the advisers at Buckingham Palace. It was more than light-hearted impudence, it was a reflection of the new healthy public mood of questioning authority, especially the Establishment. The mood was no longer docile acceptance and silent reverence.

A piece called 'The Prince, the Palace, and the Rumours' was followed a month later by a public poll on January 5 1947:

SHOULD OUR FUTURE QUEEN MARRY PRINCE PHILIP?

A. J. Cummings, the distinguished political columnist of the Liberal *News Chronicle*, had written: 'The King and Queen, it cannot be doubted, are fully conscious of the wisdom of learning in due course what is the public sentiment on the proposal of the Heiress Presumptive.' He considered the moment was approaching when the public should be given some explicit information. The *Manchester Guardian* also intervened: 'It is essentially a matter in which "the voice of the people must be heard".'

The *Pictorial* page-one story began:

> In spite of denials from the Palace, the conviction is strongly held in informed circles that an announcement is contemplated sooner or later of the engagement of Princess Elizabeth and the young Prince Philip of Greece, who is shortly to become a British subject. The *Pictorial* has therefore decided to conduct–in advance–a test of public opinion on this important issue. Many people believe that if the Princess and the Prince are in love, then nothing should be allowed to stand in the way of their marriage. Others are concerned with the political consequences of so strong a link between the British and Greek Royal Houses at this stage.

I had no doubt at all about what the attitude of the majority of readers would be–love, and the happiness of the Princess, should be the deciding factor.

After one week the Poll showed:

55 per cent in favour (if they are in love);
40 per cent against a marriage with Prince Philip of Greece.

The full count, given a week later, showed:

64 per cent in favour;
32 per cent against.

In both figures the missing percentages represented people who said, 'Yes–if they're in love. But the Princess should renounce her right to the throne.' I was told at the time by a friend of Prince Philip's that he had followed the voting with some interest.

The same year there were criticisms that the projected world tour of the King and Queen was 'Empire propaganda', too lavish, and that the refitting of the *Vanguard* was extravagant. The paper never took a Little England or penny-pinching attitude on such matters. It concluded that 'The Royal Family are fulfilling an important public duty which can have only one result, a strengthening of the bonds of the Commonwealth in a world where unity is sorely needed.' But the paper did not hesitate to make a thundering complaint that Princess Elizabeth's programme of public engagements at that time was 'hopelessly inadequate for the training of the Heir Presumptive to the Throne of the Commonwealth'.

What interested, or captivated, or shocked the readers of newspapers in the three years that followed the war is of some sociological interest; the moral stance of the *Pictorial* at that time might still appeal to Lord Longford but to few others in this permissive age.

The paper exposed vice in Soho and in the principal cities of the provinces, apparently not successfully or with any permanence. Vice is still being exposed in 1976 when the vice is more vicious. The Editor fell off his chair in moral indignation because of the public exhibition of 'the most disgraceful film ever made in Britain'. It must be banned, and quickly, said the *Pictorial*, and Dr Summerskill joined in the denunciation. The film was *No Orchids for Miss Blandish*, a harmless romp for Wolf Cubs and Brownies compared with *Last Tango in Paris* and *A Clockwork Orange* and most forms of public entertainment in the 1970s.

The readers were asked, 'Would you *ban* or *pass* this outspoken play if *you* were *the Censor?*' The theme of the play, tut tut, was artificial insemination, and it was described as 'the most outspoken play of our times'. There was another searching question: 'Is

Princess Margaret setting a good example to teenagers?' The lady was enjoying 'late-night parties'. The moralists among the (privately) immoral late Victorians decried Sunday trains, so maybe some progress in the direction of a more liberal attitude was being achieved.

The *Pictorial* also took the first timorous journalistic steps in sex education. In 1946 it published *The Miracle of Children* by Grantly Dick Read, and the next year rather more daringly published *How a Baby is Born*. The secrets were unveiled with biological exactitude, and with charm and understanding, but I was nervous or shrewd enough to send a copy of the book before publication in the paper to the *Pictorial*'s One Hundred Families for their approval. I have not the slightest doubt that any eight-year-old today would regard that delicate series as positively old hat.

By the end of 1949 the *Sunday Pictorial* was poised to achieve a circulation of 5,000,000 and pass its immediate rival *The People*. It had already long exceeded the sale of the *Daily Mirror*, but instead of the Chairman's vote of thanks that one usually receives on such achievements I was awarded the Order of the Boot. On this occasion Damocles was not a sycophant of Dionysius the Elder, which was the basis of the trouble. Nor did Dionysius the Elder invite Damocles to a sumptuous banquet in Syracuse to demonstrate his power before the other sycophants. Damocles knew that the sword was directly above his head, suspended by a single hair: what he did not know, and could not know, and was not intended to know, was when the hair would break.

Harry Guy Bartholomew chose the moment with commendable cunning. He was as patient, in his own fashion, as Cecil King. When he said to me in 1937, 'I'll tell you this, you'll not get any help from me—no help at all. That's all,' he meant what he said. He also meant what he had said to King, that he would do his best to ruin any *Mirror* executive who accepted King's invitation to be Editor of the *Pictorial*. A period of twelve years, which included the Second World War, divided the threat and the fulfilment, and the occasion he chose was classically Bartian.

Cecil King was in Eastern Nigeria, investigating the possibility of expanding the sales of our African newspaper, the *Daily Times*, published in Lagos. (It already sounds like one of the duller stories of the Travellers' Club bore.) He drove around the more populated areas at Enugu and was surprised by the crowds gathering in the roads through the villages. There was a strike in the mines, and when Cecil returned to the rest house, the equivalent of a government staging post, one of the waiters was standing on the steps with a carving knife in his hand. Cecil tells the story in *Strictly Personal*:

'I asked him why. He said, "Your people have been killing mine." The conversation then terminated as I found a scorpion within a few inches of my foot.'

More than a dozen African miners had been killed in a riot, and Cecil recognised that it was 'obviously a big story'. His first instinct was to move into the angry African town to find out what really happened. Cecil never lacked personal courage, but he was informed that if he did so he would not live to tell the tale. He therefore reconstructed the story from eye-witnesses and, with difficulty, prised open the public cable office to despatch it to London.

'I was rather pleased with my efforts,' he recorded, 'but when I got back to Lagos I found a cable from Bart asking why I had said nothing about the Enugu riots. It then came out that the cable had arrived in good time for publication (on Saturday night) and had not been used, though the story supplied the lead in the London papers on the following Monday, Tuesday and Wednesday. Hugh Cudlipp was on duty that night, and was not one in the ordinary way to miss a world scoop, but for reasons never explained spiked the story. I lost my one bid for a world scoop and Cudlipp was fired.'

Bart's first manoeuvre, in which he failed, was to disconcert King for not cabling a story and then to disconcert me for not printing it or passing it on to the *Daily Mirror*, in which he succeeded. As I wrote at the time, 'Had I omitted the story of the Boxer Rebellion, the Black Hole of Calcutta or the South Sea Bubble the mercurial Bart wouldn't have cared two hoots, but here was the opportunity to embarrass both King and Cudlipp in one fell swoop.'

On that particular Saturday night we were publishing a spectacular issue of the *Pictorial* and were running late. Nigeria, as Neville Chamberlain said of Czechoslovakia, was a country far away and Enugu was not close to our readers' hearts or to mine. Harold Barkworth, my Assistant Editor, didn't rate the Cecil scoop of world-shattering importance, nor did I. It wouldn't have sold a copy and nobody knew that better than Bartholomew. If I had published a story saying 'Cecil King Scoops the World' he would have been in trouble with Bart–and so would I–for different reasons. That was not the point.

The tone of a note from Bartholomew, obviously written on his behalf by a stooge, indicated clearly the shape of things to come. He enjoyed himself for a few days sharpening the axe and awaiting the return of King from Nigeria. Christmas was coming and there were few things which appealed to him more than a pre-Christmas firing squad. What sort of fight, if any, Cecil put up for his Editor is unknown; Bart wouldn't have listened to him, anyway. I would find it hard to believe that Cecil acquiesced in the execution without a murmur, and he sent me a pleasant letter within a day or two. Regretting that we should no more be working together, referring to 'the lot of fun we had', hoping I would be 'happier in the new job than latterly at Geraldine House', and proposing that we forgathered from time to time (which we didn't).

My mood is apparent in the reply. At least I wasn't as hypocritical as the politicians who write such chummy letters when they have been chopped by the Prime Minister:

11 Dec. '49

My dear Cecil,

Thanks for your note.

There is nothing I can say about Bartholomew's appalling behaviour that hasn't already been said by almost everybody who matters in Fleet Street. I have never had such a fan mail, and I doubt if any other Editor has. This at least was some comfort.

Bartholomew fires me with all the subtlety accorded to a tenth-rate sub-editor who turns up late on the first morning of a month's trial.

However, now that there is only one cockerel in the barnyard I suppose Bart's hens on the *Mirror* will all know even more clearly when, and how often, and to whom to lift up their skirts.

We have, as you say, had a great deal of fun with the *Pictorial* together–and we *did* pass *The People*.

Hugh

I reproduce this letter from the other Cecil, Cecil Thomas, not to prolong the agony but because it gives an insight into his relationship with Bartholomew. Thomas worked as Editor of the *Daily Mirror* under Bart for fifteen years and had happily retired the year before I was fired. I am unaware of any other single occasion on which he expressed any view at all about his tormentor:

December 23 1949

My dear Hugh,

I was shocked and disgusted to read in the newspapers about your leaving, for I had always assumed and hoped you were happily bedded-down there. I know few details, but I know enough of you to realise there are some things you won't stand for.

One thing I am certain of is that Bart has done himself no good at all, as last Sunday's issue showed pretty clearly. He has so few there of real calibre, that he simply cannot afford to lose talents like yours. And—well—after you had put the circulation up as you did without any help there just aren't words to express what I feel.

I am writing to say sincerely how I hope you will find success and happiness, as I have no doubt at all that you will, in your new job.

For the first time in my life I have just had a Christmas card from Bart inscribed, oddly I think, 'May this Christmas and the coming year leave an imprint of achievement, happiness and success.' I can only assume he thinks I have got to get down to it again—after forty years in Fleet Street.

Can it be that the little man is becoming something more than odd? I shouldn't be surprised.

With all good wishes,
Yours sincerely,
Cecil Thomas

Bart appointed as my successor Philip Zec, the brilliant wartime cartoonist who was now a Bright Ideas Man and director but who had never been a journalist.

12

The Demon Beaver

I phoned Arthur Christiansen, the Editor of the *Daily Express*. Chris phoned Lord Beaverbrook at his retreat in the Caribbean, a house called *Cromarty* in Montego Bay, Jamaica. Within two hours I had joined the *Express* organisation and within six hours a cable reached me from the Beaver: 'It is with enthusiasm that I welcome you to our house where you will be happy and contented. I have sought your companionship for long. Beaverbrook.' It was not necessary to draw the dole from the Labour Exchange even for one week.

Chris also wrote as soon as the deal was completed: 'As you know, I have been trying to tempt you to our side of the Street for years and years, and I take it as a high compliment to our friendship that you made contact with me. I will do everything possible to make your life in the *Express* outfit happy.' The welcome could not have been warmer.

Beaverbrook settled in England from Canada in 1910, acquired the *Daily Express* in 1913 and raised its circulation from 300,000 to 4,200,000 by 1950. He founded the *Sunday Express* in 1918. Of course, I relished the opportunity to observe first-hand the greatest operator since Northcliffe at work and play.

He was always the proprietor, or the chief shareholder as he preferred to call himself, but more significantly he was also the Editor-in-Chief, forever talking to his recording machine about his newspapers and bombarding his Editors and executives with memos, bristling with ideas, scathing criticisms and probing questions. His son Max Aitken has thirty thousand of these missiles which I hope he will publish—the lot, including the cruellest. Beaverbrook was ruthless, capricious, a born political intriguer, essentially a man of mischief who would use his newspapers to wound and when possible annihilate his opponents without pity or remorse; he was all of that and more. He did not differ or quarrel, he conducted vendettas. But the redeeming factors were his bubbling sense of fun, his engaging whimsicality and his unexpected compassion for those in trouble on his staff or in politics. His personality created and dominated his newspapers. They were gay and tantalising and therefore entertaining and effervescent: it was his gaiety that enabled him to have and to hold a large slice of the top talent in the profession.

Beaverbrook's intention was that I would eventually follow John Gordon as Editor of the *Sunday Express*; I began as John's personal assistant and a little later became the Managing Editor of the paper. Beaver twice appointed me Editor but omitted to tell John Gordon. I had the sense merely to mention the appointments in confidence to my wife Eileen Ascroft, then Woman's Editor of Beaverbrook's London *Evening Standard*.

The Fleet Street taverns were always alive with stories about Beaverbrook and I was soon telling them myself, joining the host of raconteurs like my brother Percy, Chris and George Malcolm Thomson who were already well established.

An audience of one was sufficient for the Beaver to put on his act; probably no audience was necessary at all. When I arrived on my first visit to his top-floor apartment in Arlington House, above the *Caprice* restaurant and near the *Ritz Hotel*, overlooking Green Park, he was bawling into the telephone: 'No. No. No. No. No. No. No. No. No.'

He replaced the handset and walked slowly around the room, his hands on his hips. He then returned to the instrument, picked up the handset and, as he jumped six inches into the air, delivered one final thunderous '*No!*' That was the end of the matter. It wasn't on. He was agin' it. And that was final.

On two occasions, when a searching question was under discussion, he said, 'Hugh, bring your chair over here. Not there–here!' We sat immediately opposite each other, with knees touching, and Lord Beaverbrook peering silently into my eyes. It was the loyalty test, or was it mesmerism? I peered silently back; there was no alternative.

It was prudent as a newcomer in the Beaverbrook organisation to discover precisely how the policies of the newspapers were decided, but the research occupied only one second of my time. The Editors of the *Daily Express*, the *Sunday Express*, the London *Evening Standard* and the Glasgow *Citizen* enjoyed absolute freedom to agree wholeheartedly with their master's voice. They were entitled to take the view, untrammelled, that Empire Free Trade was the solution to Britain's economic problems (which it wasn't), that the traditions of the British Empire were inviolable and immortal (which they weren't), that British troops should leave Germany (which would have been disastrous), that the activities of the British Council abroad were a

wanton waste of public money (a myopic concept). His friend Aneurin
Bevan could be chided in the newspaper but not savaged. Earl
Mountbatten could be savaged but not chided. Nehru was a man of
straw, and Sir John Ellerman–more about Ellerman later.

The Editors were also entitled to advocate high wages, to be kind
to the Labour Party between but not during elections, and to be civil
to any public personality whose birthday was mentioned in the
'Londoner's Diary' of the *Evening Standard*.

There was the Policy Committee, and I was invited by Lord
Beaverbrook to join it shortly after my arrival. That was real fun,
much enjoyed by the old timers and by me, usually ending in a drink
all round from the Electric Rum-cocktail Mixer (Jamaican rum and
West Indian limes, 'absolutely paramount'). The Committee, after
due consideration, endorsed the view that Empire Free Trade was the
solution to Britain's economic problems, that British troops should
leave Germany, and that the British Council was a waste of public
money.

A good deal has been written about his vendettas, especially his
feud against Lord Mountbatten. He once sent Eileen Ascroft a cable
congratulating her on an *Evening Standard* article of no particular
merit, and she was puzzled. 'Let me read it,' I said. 'Ah-ha, here it is.
It criticises the hats and hemlines of a certain Countess, and the lady
is Dickie Mountbatten's wife.'

My own experience of the vendetta mood concerned the unhappy
Sir John Reeves Ellerman, second baronet since 1933, director of
Ellerman Lines Ltd, a millionaire many times over with no heir, a
man whose only publicly known address was 19–21, Moorgate, EC 2,
the offices of his company in the City. He was the subject of biannual
scrutiny in the Beaverbrook Press. Every movement of John Ellerman's was recorded in one of the three newspapers, and the fact that
he never spoke or appeared in public did not deter the Beaver from
stimulating news or gossip about him. How wealthy was he? What
were his business activities and his hobbies? Why was he a recluse?
Who were his friends? Why could nobody succeed in writing an
article about his beautiful wife Esther, the daughter of the late
Clarence de Sola of Montreal?

Nobody on the *Express* organisation had succeeded in getting near
to the shy Sir John until I arrived on the scene, and the meeting six
months later was not of my seeking. My memo to Lord Beaverbrook
gave a factual report of what occurred:

London
June 21 1950

'These facts about Sir John Ellerman may interest you as background.

'Our first article by Bernard Harris appeared June 11; the second June 18.

'Half-way through that week I had a visit from Sir Ian Fraser, MP, on an "errand of mercy". Would we please never publish anything about Ellerman again? Why did the Beaverbrook Press persecute him?

'I told him that a second article was to appear within a few days.

'Then he said: "Will you lunch with Sir John Ellerman and myself?"

'I agreed, stipulating that if the intention of the lunch was to persuade me to agree to "no more Ellerman articles" he was wasting his own time and Ellerman's; apart from that I should be delighted to meet him.

'The lunch was in the *Dorchester*, where Ellerman now lives. Present: Ellerman and wife, Fraser and wife, myself.

'Ellerman smiled when we were introduced. And then for three-quarters of an hour he said not one word. The women (both versatile and friendly) did most of the talking. Lady Ellerman comes from Canada: still has a Canadian accent.

'Ellerman is unquestionably a haunted man. Sick, emotionally and physically. He was, throughout the meeting, on the verge of collapse, and his wife frequently looked at him with a maternal concern. (She is uninhibited, and has a sense of humour: he has none.)

'The meal was a light one—fresh salmon. Ellerman could eat only half of it. He drank water. An obvious case of stomach trouble, created by his nervous condition.

'After three-quarters of an hour, he turned to me abruptly and said: "Now, Mr Cudlipp, about this terrible persecution." Then, smoking a four-inch cigarette, he spoke disjointedly, but without stopping.

' "Why am I plagued by the Press? Why am I persecuted by you? I don't mean you—I mean whoever it is. I am followed. Driven from house to house. Every hiding place is discovered. Last week you had reporters and cameramen outside this hotel. Why—why—why? I had to lock myself in my room for three days. I couldn't eat—couldn't work. And always it is the Beaverbrook Press—just because he quarrelled with my father. Nobody is interested in me. Whenever you mention me I get thousands of begging letters . . ."

'Fraser told me in an aside that at the last moment Ellerman had wanted to cancel the meeting. The venue had in fact been changed three times in three days: *Savoy*, *Connaught Rooms*, *Dorchester*.

'Ellerman then simply and rather pathetically asked for advice. Here are extracts from our subsequent conversation:

'*E*: How can I end it all–this abominable persecution?
'*C*: There is only one certain way. Give away your forty million pounds. Every newspaper will then publish an immense story about you–and probably ignore you for the rest of your life.
'*E*: Do you really think so? If I could only believe that I would do it now. But how can I know? What if the persecution goes on? How can I do my work–important work, too. (He meant his scientific studies into rodents.)
'*Fraser*: I have advised Sir John to hire a public relations officer to talk to the Press.
'*C*: If you employ an energetic but stupid one there is of course the possibility that he will so inundate newspapers with uninteresting nonsense that we should be obliged to ban Sir John Ellerman as a publicity-seeker.

'(This was the first time Ellerman nervously smiled.)
'*E*: This is no laughing matter. You don't understand what it is like. All those millions, and this persecution of the Press, are driving me crazy. I can't stand it any more.
'*C*: Other people also have their problems, Sir John. Millions for instance, have the problem of unending, day-in-day-out poverty and privation. However, about the PRO.
'*E*: Yes–there's another problem. Good Lord, he wouldn't have enough to do. Am I expected to pay him all the year round?
'*C*: Now seriously, Sir John. With forty millions you cannot pretend to be concerned about paying £600 a year to a PRO and £500 a year to a secretary to tear up all the begging letters?

'I told him that no newspaper would consider excluding his name for one second. Here was Sir John Ellerman frightened about his money and the notoriety it brought him–yet thousands of other people, less well-breeched, were terrified of mice–the very mice he calmly dissected in his laboratories at two in the morning.

'"After all," I said to Ellerman, "you could risk ten or fifteen millions and start your own newspaper. You could make sure you were never mentioned in it–and then read that paper alone."

'But this idea didn't appeal to him. "I didn't even read the articles the *Sunday Express* published about me. I daren't. All I know is that they were printed."

'He then took me aside and clutched my arm. In fairness, I repeated my assurance that so long as he was Britain's wealthiest man, so long he would remain of interest. I talked to him as a sort of combined Dutch uncle, mother and psychiatrist. And he finished by pleading:

' "Do see me again. Will you come again? I am persecuted and I cannot stand it."

'In my opinion his fear of public limelight is genuine: he is a sick man.'

A message from Lord Beaverbrook for 'Hugh Cudlipp of the *Sunday Express*' arrived quickly. He had received the memo and found it 'a most interesting communication'. What a wonderful story Ellerman would make for the newspaper 'before long' (the fact that two articles by Bernard Harris were currently appearing was not mentioned). Of course, said the Beaver, Ellerman felt badly about the publicity he got if he didn't like it. How many of the public characters analysed by the *Daily Mirror* objected to the publicity? Sir John was 'one of the principal, in fact the principal, shareholder of the *Daily Mirror*,' so what he gave in one direction he appeared to get in another. Beaver then stated that he had never known Ellerman's father, never had business conversation with him or any relation with him whatsoever. He merely had the pleasure of his acquaintance, nothing more. He was 'a short stout little Jew. He didn't attract anybody, or please those he came in contact with.'

I hoped that my description of the hounded man would have persuaded Beaverbrook to call off the vendetta, I did not know then that it was impossible to loosen the talons from the prey.

Another message arrived just before the General Election of 1951. It reminded me it was time the *Sunday Express* were doing an article on Sir John Ellerman, the multi-millionaire. He had crossed the Channel quite recently to appoint a successor to a dead man. Also his interest in newspapers, wasn't that of importance at the present time? The siege ended when Beaverbrook died, but I am sure

Ellerman did not feel safe and secure from the Demon Beaver until he died himself.

Curiously, though no longer associated in any way with the Mirror Group, I knew that Winston Churchill was suing the *Daily Mirror* for libel because of its election-day front page in October 1951 before the Editor knew himself. It was the famous front-page 'Whose Finger?', bearing the obvious implication to a war-weary nation that Churchill would be more likely to pull the trigger, or encourage America to do so, than Clem Attlee: the message was vote for peace and détente. I was with Beaverbrook at Arlington House when Churchill phoned. The question was simply, 'Shall I sue?' and the answer was simply, 'Yes. Issue a writ, Winston.'

What made Max Beaverbrook the supreme journalist was his ferocious energy and his inquiring mind. I worked in his gymnasium for merely two years but I have a fat file of the memos with which he bombarded his editorial executives, only the merest sample of his gigantic output. The themes changed, but the supply was inexhaustible and the style unchanging. Virile. Penetrating. Infuriating.

A paragraph about the Derby in the William Hardcastle gossip column was 'old stuff', but John Gordon's article was 'good stuff'. He noticed in the *Sunday Express* that 1,400 children were waiting to have their tonsils removed: were we aware (this message from New York) that it was probably an unnecessary operation and that in a few years the British would be looked upon as barbarians for having carried out such savagery? The answer was the new drugs, and the nose and throat specialists in England were merely enjoying a good livelihood. Hardcastle must be a column of praise, not one word of criticism about anybody. Logan Gourlay (the entertainments writer) must apologise in his next column for his paragraph about Bob Hope's reference to Danny Kaye walking on the water. His lordship decided it was one of the coarsest jokes, one of the most brutal jokes, made upon the London stage in a long time. There were to be no jokes under any circumstances or any attacks upon organised religion in all its manifestations, including spiritualism and especially Presbyterianism. Why didn't the film story in *The People* appear in the *Express*? Would Mr Robertson investigate how that joke about Jesus got through the Editors; Gordon knew nothing about it, Cudlipp must have seen it.

Lord Beaverbrook's verbal offensive was ceaseless, from Montego

Meeting [some of] the people in the headlines: *Above*, with
the delectable Elizabeth Taylor in 1958. *Below*, with Norman
Hartnell, Eileen Cudlipp and Raymond.

'There's a Mr Cecil King and a Mr Hugh Cudlipp to see you, sir?'

Two Bernard Hollowood cartoons from *Punch*. The second appeared in 1961 during the Mirror's Group's period of rapid expansion.

Bay, or Cap d'Antibes in the South of France, or Arlington House in London, or from Cherkley Court, his house near Leatherhead. The only respite occurred during travelling time, between the bases, which gave the dictaphone time to cool off.

John Gordon, Editor of the *Sunday Express*, was urged to ration the space devoted to his own articles just the same as he rationed space generally. Had Nathaniel Gubbins seen the adulation of Lord Mountbatten poured out in the *Sunday Despatch* by Godfrey Winn? Why publish a letter from a reader of seventy claiming that he still worked? Beaver himself was seventy-two, still working; there was nothing remarkable in that. The paper should reserve its fire on the Socialists: it would be more effective if they were left alone for most of the year. He had seen the suggestion in the *Sunday Express* that the Duke of Edinburgh should be given the title of King and recommended very strongly that the subject should be dropped altogether. Why was the newspaper so fascinated with Laurence Olivier? Was *Time and Tide* right when it said the *Sunday Express* had departed from good taste? He was not getting satisfactory replies to his complaints, satisfactory explanations. He had a feeling that some things were being held back. 'I must know, please.'

King had decided in December of 1951 that the time had come for the Bartholomew regime to be erased. Bart, nearly seventy, was increasingly irascible, grotesquely unjust and was hitting the bottle. He was occasionally incoherent and frequently unreliable. Cecil set about his task with his usual patience and calculated ruthlessness. As a furniture remover, once his mind was made up, he was without equal even in an industry accustomed to furniture removal. The Cecilian Chant was heard again. Were they to wait, at their peril, until Bartholomew did something monumentally stupid? Wasn't it in Bart's own interest that he should go now, before his reputation lay in tatters? There was no question about who should tell Bart the news: King volunteered. One, two, and then three directors agreed with him, which totalled four. He lunched with Philip Zec whose support was numerically essential. There were only seven directors, but if Bartholomew could muster one vote he could defeat the palace revolution. Zec? Phil Zec agreed with King that the time had come. Silvester Bolam, the Editor? Bolam had already sided with King.

It was, in fact, Zec, not King who broke the news to Guy Bartholomew. Bart still believed he had a majority in his favour and knew, or hoped, that Bolam would never vote against him. When Phil Zec told the old man the facts, he broke down and wept, saying, 'Bolam? Judas! How could Bolam do this to me? I made him.'

I was forgiven for having 'spiked' Cecil's one and only scoop—the fate of those unhappy miners in Enugu—and was invited to return to the fold. Max Beaverbrook understood, and we remained friends. I know of no reason why I should not draw my sword in his defence. In 1963 he sent me a copy of his book, *The Decline and Fall of Lloyd George—and Great was the Fall Thereof*, with an inscription in rather shaky handwriting on the title page: 'To Hugh Cudlipp. He has seized my mantle. This book is from his friend and admirer, Max Beaverbrook. The end of October 1963.' He died on June 9 the following year, taking his mantle with him.

There I was again, back in Geraldine House in 1952, editing the *Sunday Pictorial* for the third time. I felt I had won it outright, but before the year ended my responsibilities vastly expanded when I was appointed Editorial Director (I preferred this title to Editor-in-Chief) of the *Daily Mirror* as well as the *Pictorial*. An additional assignment emerged, something to do in my spare time. Bart had bequeathed to his successor, King, a mammoth problem in Australia. I had been there before, indeed when the Big Idea was germinating in Bartholomew's mind.

13

Australia Rediscovered

Australia is the only country in the world where, in a gentlemen's urinal, I was offered two jobs which would have earned me far more than a decent living at the style to which Editors are accustomed. The blandishments were offered on separate occasions, I should add, and by different gentlemen in different establishments. The first came from Sir Frank Packer, proprietor of the Sydney *Daily Telegraph* and the second from Ezra Norton, proprietor of the weekly paper *Truth*, published in three or four different cities, and also of the Sydney evening paper the *Daily Mirror*. Ezra, while adjusting his dress before leaving, nudged my arm and added, 'Of course, if you say Yes there'll be a big block of shares for you and you'll run the show when I pack in. I'm getting more interested in horses than bloody news.'

If Australia Fair was the sort of place where one was casually offered, in the loo, a job ('Name your price') plus a free house overlooking Sydney Harbour, there was no knowing what other tempting titbits and perks might be thrown in upstairs in the bar or the dining-room.

I was in at the beginning of 'Captain' Bartholomew's rediscovery of Australia, accompanying him on his first abortive voyage. When the deal was eventually reached to buy a newspaper there I was away on my enforced sabbatical on Beaverbrook's *Sunday Express*. I later helped in Australia to conduct the struggle for survival and was a prominent mourner when the funeral took place in 1957.

In 1948 Bart had heard that the roughneck Ezra Norton was negotiating for the sale of his properties to an American publisher. He therefore swiftly organised a posse consisting of himself (one of the world's worst negotiators), James Cooke (then Financial Director and one of the world's best negotiators), and me (no doubt earmarked to run *Truth* and the Sydney *Mirror* if our bid succeeded). It was a Bartian mission in the classical style, conducted in an atmosphere of extravagant secrecy with false names and coded cables. Cooke and I were instructed to call him 'Guy' during the 12,000-mile journey to Sydney in a Sunderland flying boat. And all I saw of Australia on that visit was the four walls of a bedroom because Bart insisted on appearing to be alone and conducting the talks with Norton on his own. Cooke and I were not to be 'seen'.

The Mirror Company, or rather Bart and one or two other directors, had decided to expand overseas because expansion at home, owing to newsprint rationing in the post-war years, had offered no opportunities. I also suspected that somebody had figured out, the way things were going in Europe in the Cold War, that it would be shrewd to spread some of the assets and interests far beyond the shores of Britain. And you can't take your 'funk' money further than Australia unless you are planning to launch the *Antarctic Explorers' Advocate* or the *Arctic Whalers' and Sealers' Midnight Sun*.

During the first visit I occupied my days and nights of seclusion in the hotel room by studying the Australian continent and its people, including the aborigines, as they were reflected in the newspapers and magazines. Vast piles of this literature arrived every morning and evening. I tuned in to the commercial radio stations from which Sydney had more than its share of ceaseless punishment, and sneaked out to buy some books about the recent past.

With the exceptions at that time of the *Sydney Morning Herald*, dominated by the shrewd and worldly-wise Rupert Henderson on behalf of his opaque proprietors, the Fairfax family, and of the Melbourne *Age*, the newspapers were eccentrically xenophobic. The boundaries of the world were Darwin in the Northern Territory, Perth in Western Australia, Brisbane in Queensland in the northeast, and Melbourne in Victoria in the south. In the papers in New South Wales events in Adelaide in South Australia seemed to me in my bedroom cell to be reported by 'our own foreign correspondent'. *Truth*, the weekly we were seeking to buy, was overflowing with lurid sex, fabrication and innuendo: in comparison the *News of the World* in Britain was a sedate parish magazine. I formed the impression, without meeting anybody or seeing anything or going anywhere, of a strongly but self-consciously masculine society where the women were expected to be, and didn't object to being, gabby and decorative, fashion-wise, efficient and charming hostesses, vivacious, sun-bronzed, noticeably pulchritudinous. Horse-racing was clearly the national pastime, and judging by the pictures in *Women's Weekly* and in the ample social pages of the newspapers all the men in the grandstands wore large-brimmed trilbies at a jaunty, sock-me-on-the-jaw-if-you-dare angle and all the women were bedecked in floral dresses, floppy hats and elbow-length gloves. It was forever Ascot.

The finance pages indicated a strident money-making urge. It was a materialistic society paying lip service to organised religion, gambling on Saturday, God or yachting on Sunday, chasing rainbows in the expectation that there would be a pot of gold at the end. The Symphony Orchestra performances were reported more as social occasions than cultural events. Famous but faded English and American actors were arriving or just leaving after playing in the chosen cities at the fag-end of their careers, squeezing their last rounds of applause. Visitors who extolled the virtues of Australia in extravagant terms in their radio interviews at the airport or quayside were acclaimed by the Press for their perception: those who were foolish enough to hesitate or quibble, or used the banned word 'provincialism', or implied a lack of culture, or criticised the service in the hotels, which was excruciating even in my brief experience, were lacerated. There was a pack of columnists, with pens poised like bayonets, waiting to fall upon them. Condescension to Australia was an indictable offence, more serious than rape. Those who carped were dissected without an anaesthetic and their bodies disposed of.

The nation in 1948 had a chip on its shoulder even larger than the Irishman traditionally wears on his. They were anxious to forget their boisterous past, especially in New South Wales at the turn of the century and beyond, of roguery, racketeering politicians, two-up schools, corruption, of scoundrels regarded as men of esteem by lesser mortals who were equally manly but less successful. The age of the larrikin, Australia's equivalent in the 1890s of the modern mugger or the motor-cycle thugs, the vicious gangs who put the boot in or slashed a copper or a queer in Merrie England, were recalled in the 'Fifty Years Ago' pieces I read in some of the popular newspapers with adjectival distaste but a whiff of nostalgia. There was still a resentment against Authority; knighthoods and other awards from the Mother Country were regarded seriously by the recipients and their wives and (at any rate in their presence) by their friends, but no joke was more popular than a figure of the Establishment slipping on a banana skin.

Australia had squeezed itself into the corsets of twentieth-century social respectability, overdoing it a little, but Ned Kelly was still the patron saint. An unprincipled rogue and murderer was invested with the halo of Robin Hood.

There were other aspects about life in Australia I gleaned in my monastic studies. The magazines and books displayed the natural beauty and challenge of the continent and the harsh reality of its deserts. The immigration of a million Chinese, Japanese, Malayans and Indonesians would have solved the problems of the hotel waiters and other more important matters in a jiffy, but it was White (or nearly white, or off-white) Australia: the unwelcome had to pass the 'dictation test', in Japanese for the Chinese and in Chinese for the Indonesians, or so some wit'was saying in the papers. Labour was therefore scarce, and the White Australian, aggressive and independent, was not a servile animal in search of a visitor's tip. The national mood was 'Stuff it'.

I enjoyed the virility of the newspapers, reflecting the pugnacious restlessness of a young nation half-way through the century of opportunity. The columnists were frustrated Cassandras to a man and the Antipodes was the breeding ground for cartoonists–David Low, Keith Waite, Rigby, and then some. The politics, judging by the reported speeches, were pragmatic and expedient, but frankly so and not necessarily the worse for that; the political philosophy of the three-line whip in Westminster was not the only way of life. I formed the view in my dungeon that if I were to be left behind as a hostage it would not be an intolerable sacrifice: when, on later visits, I knew the Australians who were enjoying the life of Reilly outside the four walls of my bedroom I learned how the chip on the shoulder could be sand-papered and varnished. The answer to 'The same to you' was simply 'With knobs on'. I liked the Aussie bastards and I was not a Pom they despised.

Bart returned rather late one night from the *Malmaison* restaurant after a farewell or *au revoir* supper with Ezra Norton. Oysters and champagne. No deal. Ezra didn't want to sell his newspapers no more. For Chrissake, why should he? Who did the Pommies think they were? To hell with it, and us.

'We're off tomorrow,' said Bart. 'Ezra's ulcers are better. Let's pack.'

I should perhaps decode this piece of intelligence. Ezra was a lone wolf who deserved and relished his unpopularity. In almost every aspect of his personality he was a four-letter man, but he liked to attribute his isolation from the human race to his forthright journalism–the truth in *Truth*, without fear or favour. Whatever pain he inflicted on others, he suffered from pain himself in the epigastrium. Ulcers. It was at these times that he wanted to sell his newspapers, but he was now feeling better. The alkalis had worked wonders and Bart's 12,000-mile journey from London had proved to be unnecessary. Bart, however, was not a man to accept defeat with grace.

In 1949 Ezra again developed the symptoms. Indigestion lasting several weeks. Pain for two or three hours after a meal. Vomiting. *Truth* was up for sale again and Bartholomew made his second voyage to New South Wales with a different crew, only to discover that Mr Norton had once more recovered. Who did the Pommies think they were?

Bart would not return to London a second time without achieving something. He bought for Daily Mirror Newspapers Ltd., London, the controlling interest in the *Argus*, Melbourne. The paper had once enjoyed world fame and prosperity, but was now visibly staggering. It was a disastrous deal. Wrong paper, wrong city. The weakest of three papers in a place that could sustain only two. The *Argus* had foolishly jettisoned its classified ads during the war and the monopoly in that market was grasped by the *Age*. The giant was the *Sun Pictorial* group managed and editorially directed with sagacity by Sir Keith Murdoch and after his time by Sir John Williams. Nobody had much faith in the secret weapon of the *Argus*, already ordered at great cost and being installed in the plant. Colour printing 'on the run' on offset presses. Colour printing that would attract world advertising and send the circulation soaring ever upwards. It did neither, but it delayed production every night.

By 1951 a million pounds had gone down the drain, and the drain was waiting for the second million and possibly the third. One, but only one, of the reasons why Cecil King organised the insurrection against Bartholomew's chairmanship was his concern over the company's investment in the Australian newspaper industry; no return on the money, no sign there ever would be. The gloom was relieved only by a highly profitable entry into commercial radio, including the number one station in Sydney.

When I returned to the Mirror Group in 1952 King told me his principal worry was the Australian Misadventure. I was despatched to Melbourne to give a second opinion on the size of the problem. I suppose that over a period of five years I visited the continent seven or eight times, so did Cecil King. His knowledge of the world newspaper industry was an asset in the situation we inherited from Bart, but his knowledge and my ideas and energy were not enough to reverse the facts of life. The team on the spot were first class, notably John Patience, Alex McKay, now managing director of the News of the World Organisation in London, Bill Horniblow, a former Editor of the London *Daily Mail*, and Bob Nelson. We had as columnists Clive Turnbull, the most wittily readable of the Australian sociological historians, and Peter Russo, the best-informed expert on Chinese and Japanese affairs I ever met. All that, and colour.

The Australian newspaper proprietors, a rum lot, hugely enjoyed the London *Mirror*'s failure to pull it off, and why shouldn't they? I wrote to King from Melbourne saying that the only hope was to 'heighten the challenge', to leak out massive plans for the future, to prepare quite noisily to produce an evening newspaper in direct competition to the *Melbourne Herald*, the *Sun Pictorial*'s companion publication. I advocated buying the church next door to our office, up for sale because of a dwindling congregation, and buy it we did. The extended premises would have made the production of an evening newspaper a feasible project.

John Patience was our Australian chairman, an extremely able lawyer and financial negotiator. He conducted the obsequies with calm and skill. He sold the *Argus* to the *Melbourne Herald*, which welcomed our departure, and King later sold the radio stations to Associated Television. 'Captain' Bartholomew's rediscovery of Australia ended, miraculously, with the piddling profit of the order, as they say, of £80,000 or £90,000, but we averted a loss of £3,000,000.

In the course of our business journeys, belting along from Melbourne to Adelaide or to Sydney in our custom-built Ford, flying to Canberra and Brisbane and Perth, John Patience showed me more of Australia than most Aussies have seen themselves. I quickly developed an affection for the people which resulted in many permanent friendships. Even for Ezra Norton, and Ezra for me.

'I'm a bastard,' he said to me over the champagne and oysters in the *Malmaison* dinerie. It was his favourite diet, not normally prescribed for ulcers.

'Ezra, I know you're a bastard,' I replied. 'Everybody says so. They can't all be wrong.'

'No, you don't understand. I really am a bastard.' I believe he was only boasting.

After a dinner-table chat about his piles, he told me a touching story about his father, John Norton, generally accepted as the greatest rogue unhanged in the present century's history of Australia. Dad used his newspaper *Truth* to garrotte those who incurred his disfavour, specialising in a form of demagoguery and political skulduggery which deluded the poor and humble into accepting him as their saviour. Measured against the evil stature of Norton, senior, our very own Horatio Bottomley was a pious petty con-man. Cyril Pearl, a splendid writer who devoted some years to assessing the lack of character of the man he described as a power-drunk megalomaniac, gave the considered view that Jung's description of Hitler might serve as Norton's epitaph: 'An irresponsible, ranting psychopath cursed with the keen intuition of a rat or a guttersnipe.'[1]

A few headlines will suffice to indicate the flavour of Norton the Elder's *Truth*:

THREE PESTILENT PEES
Parliament, Press and Pulpit
or
Parlipests, Presspests and Pulpests

HORRIBLE HIGGINS
Diabolical Doings with His Daughter

DIMINUTIVE DAMSEL DEFILED AND DEBAUCHED

'Don't believe everything you read or hear about my old man,' said Ezra. 'Mind you, he knocked me about a bit, but at heart he was sentimental.' Time, and the second bottle of champagne, had dimmed the son's memory, but when I pressed him for an example of the softer side of John Norton's nature he obliged with this romantic vignette:

'When I was a boy, I remember sitting with my father on the balcony of our house in Pitt Street. It was a Sunday and the people strolling along the road were returning from the morning service. "Come over here, son," he said, and he put his arm around my shoulder.' There was a tear in Ezra's eye as he continued. '"Look at them," said father, "look at them in all their Sunday finery, the bloody hypocrites. Never forget this, my son. When you carry on my great work in *Truth*, keeping up its traditions, without fear or favour, you will be in the same position of trust as me, always able to pour a bucket of —— over the lot of them."'

'You'll like Frank Packer,' said Cecil King. 'When I first met him and we exchanged a handshake, Frank said, "I'm interested in women and horses. What are you interested in?"' Frank, as a young man, was also interested in boxing. He became Australia's amateur heavyweight champion, a useful background for a newspaper proprietor in that country. Yachting also appealed to him; he formed the syndicate which backed Australia's entry for the America's Cup,

---

[1] *Wild Men of Sydney* by Cyril Pearl, W. H. Allen, 1966.

Gretel, named in honour of his first wife, a lady of exuberant charm and personality.

I looked forward to my meetings with Sir Frank Packer and was happy when he always called on me in London years after the Mirror Company's retreat from Australia Fair. He was a massive bear of a man with a twinkle in his eye and a permanent half-smile, talking like Humphrey Bogart or Edward G. Robinson in short bursts of verbal machine-gun fire, a mighty tough guy with shoulders as broad as a double-page spread on a tabloid paper who sent red roses and bunches of black grapes to the girls on his staff when they were ill.

We were walking together down the steps of the Sydney *Telegraph* office one Christmas Eve and encountered his best advertising representative trying to walk up.

'Sir,' said the rep, 'sir, it's Christmas. Christmas! We've had a great year—can I buy you a Christmas drink, sir?'

'No,' said Packer. 'I can't afford it.' He knew the item would appear on the rep's expenses sheet.

When we were lunching in the *Savoy* in London he asked me who was 'the bloke who keeps looking at me three tables away'. Frank had a severe eye affliction and hadn't yet noticed that the bloke was now coming towards him. I rapidly explained that he was one of the two television tycoons King had arranged for Packer to meet at an expensive dinner on his previous visit to the UK: the other guest that evening was Lew Grade, whom nobody ever forgets.

Tycoon No. 2 told Frank that a friend of his, an especially talented writer, was shortly leaving for Sydney; if Tycoon No. 2 gave the young man a letter of introduction, would Packer be good enough to see him?

'Oh,' said Frank, not too pleased. 'What's so special about him?'

'Well, he's a hunchback,' said the tycoon.

'We've got plenty of writers. I eat them for breakfast,' said Frank. 'In your letter stress the hunchback bit—I haven't got any hunchbacks.'

The doyen in the Australian newspaper field was Sir Keith Murdoch, a man of great ability and studied charm. He won his fame as a reporter at Gallipoli, and Northcliffe helped with finance when the ambitious Keith decided to go into newspaper production in Melbourne. The *Sun Pictorial* and *Herald* group, conspicuously successful, was his creation: why Bartholomew decided to confront that formidable organisation in the city where the *Mirror* technique would be most likely not to be welcomed is a mystery that won't be solved until Bart's reincarnation, an event I hope will not coincide with mine.

The day after our first meeting in Melbourne, Australia's financial centre and most mannered metropolis, Sir Keith took me to the war memorial, an imposing edifice affording a view of the city itself. He was wearing a cloak, like Northcliffe's cloak and like Northcliffe's nephew's cloak. He affected the style and speech of the cultured English gentleman of standing; the corset of Australia's twentieth-century respectability fitted him perfectly.

'I am worried about my son Rupert,' he said. 'He's at Oxford and he's developing the most alarming Left-wing views.'

He needn't have worried. Young Rupert became the capitalist businessman *par excellence*, a newspaper operator as formidable as his father but on a world-wide scale. The music of the cash-register now dominates his life more than the disturbing thoughts of Karl Marx. His natural habitat is the merchant bank. He moves restlessly from capital to capital, from Australia to Britain, from Britain to the United States, in search of the Holy Grail. The radicalism of his Oxford days was a fashionable veneer, not a lifelong conviction. He shed all that nonsense, left it behind in the cloisters for the next year's intake of innocent undergraduates.

Cecil and I visited Australia alternately. He usually went during the English winter and I during the English summer. It took me some time to figure out why those long journeys always left him looking bronzed and healthy, whereas I became increasingly pallid.

Then I rumbled it. He was having two summers every year and I two winters. Wykehamists!

With the good fortune that usually, but not always, fell my way, I was able to make a final journey to Australia in 1972 to visit the activities of Reed International in that continent. The election was on, the one that made Gough Whitlam Prime Minister.

Aussie reporters are intrepid cross-examiners, and they waylaid me at odd hours of the day and night when I arrived at the principal State airports, maybe hoping that I would let slip an incautious remark on the hustings. I considered the Press coverage of the election was outstandingly fair and said so. What surprised me, and I also said so, was that the political battle was being conducted in so gentle-manly a fashion, in fact with kid gloves. 'This is the softest election

I've seen in the world. For my taste there should be more fire and brimstone.'

After my first visit to the USSR, the worldly-wise Cecil King told me I probably would not find it necessary to go there for another ten years: 'The changes evolve so slowly that you do not notice any change has taken place.' No one would say that about Australia. Since my last visit I observed that even the ludicrous tradition of the men guests gathering at one end of a social party to talk sport and money and the women at the other end of the room to chat about fashion, hair-do's and gossip had broken down. There were no longer two nations, male and female. Sex apartheid was at any rate abating. Xenophobia was no longer regarded, in the cities, as proof of patriotism. A visitor who did not acclaim as evidence of Australia's uniqueness all that he saw and heard was not automatically proscribed. The searching question, 'What do you think of Australia?' followed by the deeper probe, 'What do you *really* think of Australia?' is not asked so frequently. The proof of national maturity is now apparent in the confidence and social performance of the people who are fortunate to live in a continent whose potential abundance equals only that of Canada. The self-conscious jokes about 'us old ignorant colonials' are no longer heard.

I was even able to make a small jest in a broadcast about Canberra, the capital of Australia built in the tiny Federal territory of the Commonwealth, the seat of the Australian Government since 1927, the home of the Australian National University since 1946. Before 1913 there was nothing there that mattered except the view. Like all ersatz cities concerned exclusively with administration, foreign representation, and nothing else, it exudes an atmosphere of soulless efficiency and moral rectitude. One misses the smells of Naples, the sins of Rome, the seamy side of New York. There is no equivalent to London's Soho, no hint of Montmartre or Montparnasse. There are no bearded artists or impecunious composers but many bearded and well-to-do economists and researchers.

'What do you think of Canberra?' the radio interviewer asked me after I had been there half an hour.

'It is a beautifully laid-out city,' I replied. 'A very beautiful city indeed. City planning at its noblest. But it is full of diplomats and civil servants and foreign diplomats—all professionally on their best behaviour. It's like being in heaven before you're dead.'

And I was not rebuked at that night's splendid dinner party in the University.

When I arrived in 1972 the first people I spotted, lunching cosily at the Wentworth Hotel, Sydney, were Rupert Murdoch and Rupert Henderson. The last people I saw, just before leaving Australia, were the journalists of the Melbourne Press Club who had assembled together to put on a lunch with me as their guest. The plane from Canberra was delayed an hour and I had to make the hop from the airport to the centre of Melbourne in a hired helicopter, arriving as the third course was being served. It was a gay and warm occasion in a city where I had failed to save a newspaper.

During the brisk and hilarious question-and-answer session, which I enjoyed as much as the Australians, somebody said, 'We're just coming up to the sixteenth anniversary of the closure of the *Argus*. Could you throw some light on it?'

'I had no idea its burial was celebrated annually,' I said. 'Well, some newspapers succeed and others fail. I've had other flops since then. Let's start with why the *Daily Mirror* of London came to Melbourne to buy the *Argus*. It was because an irascible old gentleman called Harry Guy Bartholomew travelled 12,000 miles on his first journey out of England since the First World War, for a meeting with Ezra Norton to relieve him of telling the truth any longer. But unfortunately Ezra's ulcers got better . . .'

14

Fighting the Elections

The great decade in the history of the *Daily Mirror* can be accurately charted. It began in 1954 and it preceded the era when Cecil King, who had succeeded Guy Bartholomew as Chairman, faltered in his judgement and wandered towards personal intervention in national affairs. A newspaper which achieves power and influence is entitled to exert its influence. It is in peril of losing its power and its influence if used by an individual as a power-base.

In the great decade the newspaper enjoyed the maximum of approbation and obloquy, a healthy state of affairs. It also achieved a sale of 5,000,000 copies a day at the end of it, a suitable reward. Tabloid journalism stretched its wings and they were not singed. At the heart of it all was the King-Cudlipp collaboration at its best, backed by an editorial phalanx of rare energy, enthusiasm and ingenuity. The newspaper, already acknowledged as audacious and irreverent, elbowed its way into national and international affairs at an exciting time with a panache that avoided pomposity and punditry.

In 1954 Churchill was in the third year of his second Premiership, the oldest PM since Gladstone. After thirteen years of Tory power the Labour Party won with a tiny majority in 1964 and Harold Wilson became at forty-eight the youngest Prime Minister of the century. The decade included the Suez War of 1956, the Premierships of Anthony Eden, Harold Macmillan and Alec Douglas-Home, and the untimely deaths of Hugh Gaitskell and Aneurin Bevan. There were also political high-jinks of a curious variety. Cecil King was Chairman of IPC and I was Editorial Director in charge of all our newspapers through the time and for four years beyond.

The *Mirror* supported the Labour Party in the post-war elections, but not doggedly or blindly, indeed on occasions critically or conditionally. It gave all sides, published election appeals to its readers from the three Party leaders, and held its withering fire until the two or three days before polling day. Hugh Massingham of the *Observer* called it 'that chuckling innocent'. The Labour Party usually cried for help before we were prepared to give it, but the Tory leaders were never the most surprised men in the world when the shells fell among them.

'Vote for Him' in 1945, and 'Whose Finger on the Trigger?' in 1951, were followed by less subtle campaigning in more stridently political times. The issues that faced the nation then, as now, called for bold leadership rather than political dogma. The problems of obsolescent plant, low productivity, effete management and Luddite trade unionism, imperialistic nostalgia, unrealistic expenditure on defence East of Suez–in brief, the urgent task of evolving Britain's new and less dominant role in the post-war world–could not be solved by a simple conflict between free enterprise and nationalisation. The harsh economic facts tended to produce similar economic solutions. The policies of the two principal Parties were rhetorically divergent in the election manifestos but noticeably similar in practice.

I had been fortunate in luring Vicky, the cartoon genius, to the *Mirror* from the *News Chronicle* when that newspaper feebly refused to publish one of his satirical works. His character 'Butskell' summed up the political aridity of the times.

The attitude of the newspaper with overwhelmingly the largest readership was of national significance during the years of Tory power and during the Socialist dominance, interrupted for only four years, which followed. It was quoted, praised and criticised more than any of its contemporaries.

The advancing senility of Churchill during his final two years in Downing Street again brought him into conflict with the *Mirror* and again I was the culprit. In June 1953, then aged seventy-eight, he was ordered to rest for at least a month by his doctors. We had reason to suspect that the illness was more severe than the public were being allowed to know.

We asked the question, 'Should Churchill Retire?', and returned to the subject two months later. I am indebted to the late Lord Moran, Churchill's personal physician and friend, for some glimpses into the great man's anger toward the *Mirror* at this time.[1] Here is Moran's entry in his diary for August 17 1953:

'"Have you read the *Daily Mirror*?" he asked, and rang for a secretary.

---

[1] *Winston Churchill: the Struggle for Survival, 1940–1965* by Lord Moran, Constable, 1966.

'As it was handed to me, I read the big headlines on the front page: "What is the Truth about Churchill's Illness?"

'"Five million people read that," the PM said grimly. "It's rubbish, of course, but it won't help at Margate" (the Tory Party Conference).'

Churchill returned to the attack on November 24 1953. Moran wrote:

'As I entered the PM's room this morning he threw away the *Daily Mirror* with a gesture of disgust.

'"They want Prince Charles to mix with working people. I suppose they would have a ballot, and each day the successful twelve would come to the Palace. I wish we could buy the rag; it is doing so much harm."

'I picked up the *Mirror* while he got on with his breakfast. "Why not Open the Palace to the People?" was the heading. It was this that raised his ire–there was nothing about Prince Charles.'

On January 26, 1954, Charles Moran wrote:

'Winston is very subdued this morning.

'"I wish, Charles, I had more energy. Can't you do anything for me? I must do something for my living. The *Mirror* is suggesting I am past it and that I ought to resign. Read it," he growled, passing me the paper. "Why do I waste my time over this rag? I am being bloody tame. I defer too much to other people's opinions."'

Lord Moran quoted Churchill on the eve of his eightieth birthday when the *Mirror* produced a souvenir issue to celebrate the event:

'"Take my pulse, Charles." It was 82. When I had reassured him, he brightened up a little. "The *Daily Mirror* has declared a truce for tomorrow. They have sent £1,000 to my birthday fund. I am to be given a cheque for £140,000 tomorrow. All this leaves me very humble: it is more than I deserve."'

There was, of course, a most serious aspect to the hoodwinking of the public over Churchill's true state of health, particularly in June of 1953. His thrombosis was spreading. His hand was clumsy and feeble. He had difficulty in turning over in bed. He could hardly stand. He couldn't take a Cabinet meeting. He had to cancel a summit with President Eisenhower in Bermuda. He was saying he was not afraid of death but thought it would be inconvenient to a lot of people.

All studiously concealed from the British people. There was no answer at No. 10 Downing Street. The Prime Minister was in residence either there or at Chartwell, but physically and mentally he was not at home in either place over considerable periods.

Churchill clung on to power until 1955, using one international event after another as the excuse for postponing his departure. He infuriated his heir apparent, Anthony Eden, and exasperated his principal colleagues in the Cabinet by refusing to name a date, or by naming a date and then capriciously extending it. The tragedy was that when he did resign on April 5 the whole of the British national Press was on strike, unable to publish—for the joy of the greatest Englishman of all time, and for the pleasure of the British public—the tributes cabled to London from all over the world. Nor was the British Press able to salute the man who was a great journalist as well as a great war leader.

Churchill resigned on April 5 1955, succeeded by Eden, fighting the 1955 election less than two months later. The *Daily Telegraph* nervously raised the curtain on the scene with this comment:

> Remembering 'Whose Finger on the Trigger?' Conservative campaigners have been watching the *Daily Mirror* with all the uneasiness of so many people locked in a room with a time-bomb.

Polling day was May 26, but the chuckling innocent kept them guessing for several weeks. The battlefield was over-populated, it seemed to me, with warriors bedecked with long-service ribbons. A front-page piece asked a simple question:

THE ELECTION:
ARE THE OLD MEN
AGAIN GOING TO TELL US
WHAT TO DO?

The question was more damaging to Labour than to the Tories.

The Tories, the *Mirror* said, had 'reduced the average age of their Cabinet Ministers. They have promoted some youngsters and shed some oldsters. They are steps in the right direction. There are *nearly* as many stupid young men as there are stupid old men, but YOUTH is adaptable and can learn. AGE is peevish, obstinate and past learning. If the Tories have accepted this fact, the *Mirror* applauds their realism.'

There was nothing to please Labour in the next sentence: 'The average age of Labour's present Shadow Cabinet is about sixty. If Attlee wins the Election is he going to bring the Old Brigade back or bring the New Boys forward?'

Mr Attlee, seventy-two, was reminded that Labour was 'building a moat around the very old'. He never liked the Press and had no reason to.

The centre pages were given over to 'Young Labour–This is What the Under-45's are Fighting For and Against.' The paper was talking sense, and I can prove it: of the eleven young Labour politicians we selected to express their views in 1955 only one was not in Harold Wilson's first Government, the rebel Woodrow Wyatt. Christopher Mayhew had been appointed but had resigned as Navy Minister.

Kingsley Martin wrote in the *New Statesman*:

> I am told that Tory headquarters are terrified lest the *Mirror* front page, on the day before the poll, displays a baby with four heads (or, more likely, a woman with four bosoms) accompanied by a headline telling you this is what you will have to expect if you vote Tory.

A week before polling day the *Mirror* put everyone's mind at rest:

THE ELECTION AND THE H-BOMB

> The *Mirror* does NOT believe that the H-Bomb should be allowed to become a scare issue in the General Election. It will take no part in scare campaigns by one side or the other.

On the same page was the following announcement: 'Which way will you vote? The *Mirror*'s advice to its readers will appear in its issue of May 24.' The advice, described by the *Economist* as 'superbly clever', appeared dead on time:

KEEP THE TORIES TAME

> We do not have to pretend that Labour's chances of victory are rosy. We know that the Tories are cock-a-hoop and that Labour is anxious. But we urge YOU to VOTE LABOUR on Thursday. The return to power of the Tory Party WITH A BLOATED MAJORITY would be a national disaster. It would be an open invitation to the

most sinister and reactionary section of the Tory Party to grab power and to attack and destroy the Welfare State.

The *Guardian* commented:

The Tories are said to have been awaiting the *Mirror*'s contribution to the election with some anxiety. They will not relish the form it has taken.

There were still two days to go. On the eve of polling the front page was filled with pictures of 'MILES and MILES of EDEN SMILES'. 'But will *YOU* be *SMILING* if the Tories get back with a BIG MAJORITY???' the *Mirror* asked. 'Which is the true face of Toryism? Is it Eden's smooth smile? OR is it the hard face of the Old Gang?'

The *Guardian* was again moved to comment:

The *Mirror*'s suggestion that Labour voters must do their best today to keep the Tories in check may be more successful, and technically more skilful, than anything the Party could have done itself. A newspaper can afford to envisage defeat as well as victory. A Party cannot.

On election morning Eden was again featured on the front page. He was pictured, aged thirteen, in his Eton attire. Alongside him was a picture of Alan Smith, aged thirteen, pupil of a State secondary school. 'Who will help him most?' the paper asked. 'The Tories–or Labour? Labour built a better Britain for us all. DON'T let the TORIES cheat our CHILDREN.' On the back page Vicky's cartoon showed Eden, Butler and Macmillan tiptoeing past a sleeping worker, labelled 'Labour's full voting strength', on their way to the poll. The caption read: 'Sssh! Let's hope he doesn't wake up in time . . .'

Tribune, the Left-wing weekly, reported a curious incident:

Mr Julian Ridsdale, who called himself the Conservative-Liberal-Unionist candidate for North-East Essex, has solved the problem that has defeated many politicians. The problem: how to silence the *Mirror*.

A team of his helpers bought up every spare copy in the constituency on polling day. By 10 a.m. 500 copies were piled in the election agent's office. I hope Mr Ridsdale didn't burn the papers in the street. That might have given people unpleasant thoughts about his political tendencies.

When the Tories were returned with an increased overall majority of 58, we conducted a front-page inquest on Labour's defeat:

Labour lost–

Because its leaders are TOO OLD, TOO TIRED, TOO WEAK.

Because the Labour movement has been BAFFLED, BEWILDERED and BETRAYED by internal feuds.

Because its organisation is RUSTY, INEFFICIENT, pathetically INFERIOR to the slick Tory machine.

The prescription was drastic. Attlee, the chief architect of defeat, had to go, but Aneurin Bevan was not fit to take over the leadership. He was too arrogant, too obstinate, too undisciplined. Maybe Labour needed more money, but it also needed more brains, more zest.

The brains and the zest were supplied by Hugh Gaitskell. He succeeded the aged Attlee at the end of that election year, becoming at forty-nine the youngest leader of any British Party for sixty years, and a closer relationship between Labour and its most useful supporter in the Press was inevitable. Or almost.

Hugh Gaitskell did not understand the *Mirror*. He assumed, rather imprudently, its automatic support as if it were a popular version of the unpopular *Daily Herald*. His relationship with King was as cold as any other relationship between two suspicious Wykehamist intellectuals, and the divergence of views over the major issue of Britain entering the Common Market was an additional barrier. From 1961 the Mirror Group vociferously advocated British entry: it was among the pioneers, but Gaitskell set up a battery of conditions which the EEC would clearly not swallow.

I was on excellent personal terms with him and so was our Political Editor, Sydney Jacobson. He consulted us about some of his speeches before the annual conferences of the Party, and for one of his performances at Blackpool Sydney and I had been consulted separately. We stood together at the back of the hall, neither knowing that the other had contributed to the speech but each recognising the style when the passages were intoned from the platform with suitable gestures.

Gaitskell dealt at some length with education in the middle of his speech.

'Very good,' I said to Sydney.

Then Gaitskell came to his conclusion, an all-out parody of the Tory Government for 'absentee landlordism', delivered with unusual gusto and humour. It happened that in that particular week nearly every Tory Minister was abroad and I handed the words to Gaitskell instead of using them in an editorial.

'Nice peroration, Hugh,' said Jacobson.

Sydney Jacobson (Military Cross, 1944) and I enjoyed a lively liaison for twenty-one years; we called it the collaboration between the minorities, the Welsh and the Jews. I first met up with him when I returned to the *Pictorial* in 1952. His variegated background as an Assistant Editor with Malcolm Muggeridge on the *Statesman* in India, then on Edward Hulton's publications *Lilliput Magazine* and *Picture Post*, as a special correspondent, and finally as Editor of the *Leader Magazine*, had fortified his high intelligence with judgement and experience. As soon as I was Editorial Director, in charge of the *Daily Mirror* as well as the *Pictorial* and our other newspapers at the end of 1952, I made Sydney the Political Editor of the *Mirror* for ten years. And the variegation didn't stop there. He later edited the *Daily Herald* and initially IPC's *Sun*, and succeeded me as Editorial Director of all our newspapers when I became Chairman in 1968.

We talked politics every day of our professional lives together, eventually joined by John Beavan. Sydney shared with me the ability and desire to communicate what we knew to those who didn't, and in straightforward language all could comprehend. He also believed, as I did, in the philosophy of Josh Billings, the American humorist whose real name was Henry Wheeler Shaw: 'It is better to know nothing than to know what ain't so.'

It was a period of change in the leadership of both Parties; indeed, the changes were bewildering to the people who had to put their 'X' on the ballot papers. In 1957, half-way through that Tory administration, Anthony Eden resigned his Premiership on doctor's orders, disillusioned and mentally exhausted by the fiasco of the Suez invasion of 1956, and, more decisively, a physically sick man. Harold Macmillan patched together a shattered Party and by the sheer force of his effervescent personality bounced into the 1959 election with the buoyant boast—'You've never had it so good.'

Once again the voice of youth was the springboard to the paper's campaign. Labour's Youth Commission (Gerald Gardiner was its chairman and my wife Eileen a member) had recommended votes at eighteen. The result of a *Mirror* poll gave an overall majority of two to one in favour of reducing the voting age. How could the *Mirror* make its greatest contribution to this general election, the paper asked. Answer: 'By letting YOUTH SHOUT ITS HEAD OFF.'

Do the Under-25s think that Macmillan (aged 65) is a dehydrated mothball? Or that Gaitskell (aged 53) is a desiccated calculating machine? What do they think of Bevan? He's 61. Or of Butler? He's 56. Does Youth think there is any real difference between the political parties?

Readers under twenty-five were invited to send in their observations. The politicians were invited to have their say, too. In the 'most important series of election articles which has appeared in any newspaper', I gave a page each to Jo Grimond, Gaitskell and Macmillan, Bevan, and Butler.

Premier Macmillan wrote:

Think of all the families getting a car, owning a house, buying all those luxuries of yesterday–things like washing machines and refrigerators–which have become necessities of today. Life is good. Our policy is to see it stays good.

The front page of the same issue carried a different message:

THE TIME HAS COME
FOR THE TORIES TO GO!

WHY? See Monday's *Mirror*. WHY? See Tuesday's *Mirror*. WHY? See Wednesday's *Mirror*. WHY? See Thursday's *Mirror*.

One Tory, Lord Hailsham, prepared to face the worst. 'Hailsham is Worried about "Secret Weapons,"' the front page reported the following day. Above was a picture of the Tory Party Chairman, his face cradled apprehensively in his hands, his head cowering in anticipation of the blow. Hailsham had been asked about the secret weapon Labour had promised. 'I think it is one of two things,' he replied. 'Either the purchase tax pledge was the secret weapon, or their secret weapon is the campaign going to be started by the Mirror Group.'

The campaign was aimed at one specific section of the electorate– 'The Vital Don't-Knows'. The opinion polls reported that eighteen and a half per cent of the voters had not yet made up their minds, so we published six points every day to help the six and a half million 'don't-knows' to decide. 'Only DOPES will be Don't-Knows on Thursday,' was the daily slogan until polling day.

Readers were reminded that the choice between Hugh Gaitskell or Macmillan was only half the question. Voters also had to choose between Bevan or Selwyn Lloyd for Foreign Secretary. 'Here is your guide to Selwyn Lloyd–EVEN HIS BEST FRIENDS TELL HIM.' The paper reprinted critical assessments of Lloyd by his best friends, the Tory Press.

Where the voters of 1935 had been urged not to dine until they had voted, the *Mirror* carried a slogan more in keeping with the affluence of 1959:

TO HELL WITH THE TELLY UNTIL WE'VE ALL VOTED.

On the TV page the list of programmes was left blank until nine p.m. 'The normal service will be resumed at 9 o'clock when the ballot boxes are sealed,' viewers were informed.

Votes were cast by 78·8 per cent of the electorate–two per cent more than in 1955. The following day a leader headed 'Good Luck!' declared:

> No sour grapes. The *Mirror* batted for the losing side.
> Mr Harold Macmillan, leader of the Conservative Party,
> will lead Britain and speak for Britain at the Summit.
> That is the nation's verdict.
> Democracy is good enough for this newspaper.

The fourteenth Earl of Home, alias Sir Alec Douglas-Home, alias the fourteenth (or did that make him the fifteenth?) Earl of Home–he returned to the Lords after his walkabout among the common people–is now acclaimed among his friends, and indeed accepted by the public and the *Sunday Express*, as an elder statesman of established sagacity. Mr John Junor, the Editor of the *Sunday Express*, to which Alec contributes at the age of seventy-three, has conveniently forgotten what it said about him in July 1960 when he was appointed by Macmillan as his Foreign Secretary, replacing Selwyn Lloyd. It called him 'this unknown and faceless earl . . . this obscure man . . . the eyes are mild, the chin is weakish.' The *Sunday Express* told its Tory readers in 1960 that the only one real and distinctive achievement of the fourteenth Earl was to have been born the heir to the thirteenth.

I found the theme irresistible. 'Why choose a stooge? Why Home, aged fifty-seven? Why not Iain Macleod, forty-six, or Duncan Sandys, fifty-two, or Reginald Maudling, forty-three?' asked the *Mirror*.

The appointment of a pleasant but dim aristocrat to the most vital office of all will raise a guffaw in the Kremlin and a chuckle in Peking. We cannot possibly have the spokesman for Britain's foreign policy in the House of Lords. It would be the most reckless appointment since the Roman Emperor Caligula made his favourite horse a Consul. It is reported that Mr Ted Heath, at present Minister of Labour, will relinquish his important post in order to act as Foreign Affairs spokesman for Lord Home in the Commons. To instruct the intelligent Heath to wag his tail as a stooge's stooge would be an insult.

On July 28 the newspaper announced the Cabinet changes, a piece I was able to write with the mirth it merited:

Government changes–OFFICIAL
JOLLY OLD PALS
CABINET
Headmaster Macmillan
hands out the prizes

The page was delightfully illustrated with a picture taken only one month before of Mr Macmillan after he had received a prize himself, the Chancellorship of Oxford University. His sixteen-year-old grandson, Alexander (an Etonian), was holding the train of the Chancellor's gown and Supermac was nonchalantly waving his mortar-board. I began the story:

No. 10 Downing Street has spoken. The rumoured Government changes are now OFFICIAL.

Mr Macmillan (an OLD ETONIAN) announced last night that:

The Earl of Home (an OLD ETONIAN) is now Foreign Secretary.

Mr Duncan Sandys (an OLD ETONIAN) follows Lord Home as Commonwealth Secretary.

Mr Peter Thorneycroft (an OLD ETONIAN) follows Mr Sandys as Aviation Minister.

Mr John Hare (an OLD ETONIAN) becomes Minister of Labour.

Mr Christopher Soames (an OLD ETONIAN) becomes Minister of Agriculture in place of Mr John Hare.

Viscount Hailsham (an OLD ETONIAN) is also handed a prize. He is now Minister for Science AND Lord President of the Council AND Tory Leader in the House of Lords.

Mr Selwyn Lloyd ends his long spell at the Foreign Office, where he has 'fagged' for two OLD ETONIANS (Eden and Macmillan), and now becomes Chancellor.

The ETONIANS have never had it so good.

Mr Edward Heath leaves the Ministry of Labour to become Lord Privy Seal–with responsibility for answering Foreign Office questions from MPs. Fielding in the Commons while Lord Home is batting in the Lords.

An OLD HARROVIAN has taken over the War Office–Mr John Profumo.

Macmillan was, and remains so at eighty-two, a major world personality, not only politically. I shall always be grateful to him for manoeuvring, from his sick-bed in a London hospital in 1963, his succession by Douglas-Home. It was a gift beyond price for the election campaigning the following year. I again invoked the Horse in the editorial commenting on this droll apotheosis:

'BRAND X'
IS THE BOSS

A man without a face has been smuggled into No 10 Downing Street and juggled into position as Premier-designate of Great Britain.

The long-suffering public is invited to go into battle led by a cipher–a man existing solely in the imagination of the posher members of the Tory hierarchy and a handful of aristocratic, knicker-bockered, pheasant-shooting cronies.

A nice chap and a polite peer.

But Caligula's appointment of his horse as a consul was an act of prudent statesmanship compared with this gesture of sickbed levity by Mr Macmillan.

'Brand X' is now The Boss and you can like it or lump it until the election. Alec (not Smart Alec–just Alec) is playing chess with a Cabinet containing at least four members of greater stature, brain-power, personality and potential than himself.

Butler has been betrayed, Maudling insulted, Macleod ignored, Heath treated with contempt, and Hailsham giggled out of court by the jester in hospital . . .

In one mighty bound self-effacement and amiability are proclaimed the cardinal virtues, and men of solid achievement and promise are cast aside.

Alec Home was always affable when we met at Foreign Office receptions or dinners for visiting statesmen, and once at Downing Street for a private talk during his brief premiership. I could only conclude that he never read the *Daily Mirror* and that his secretary politely diverted any cuttings from that obstreperous newspaper to the w.p.b. I may have been wrong. I had reason to know, because of a television documentary about him in later years in which I was invited to speak, that Lady Home lovingly collected *all* the Press references to him and stuck them in a family album, including my equestrian allusions to Caligula.

The climacteric was the election of 1964, Wilson versus Home, a watershed in British political history. King always took a passionate interest in these campaigns, goading my team on with daily enthusiasm, delighted with my slogans and angles and stunts. The purpose was serious, but the team—Sydney Jacobson, John Beavan, Alan Fairclough, myself and eventually Deryck Winterton—hugely enjoyed ourselves at the hustings. Our front pages had more power on one morning than a million pamphlets or a hundred speeches in the drill halls, parks or schools in the provinces. The newspaper, flexing its muscles, announced that it was going to wake up the politicians so that this would become the toughest-fought election of the century.

When the dust had settled, leaving Harold Wilson with his wafer majority of five, psephologists D. E. Butler and Anthony King wrote in their book *The British General Election of 1964*: 'It was the *Mirror* rather than Mr Wilson which sustained the Labour campaign to a polling day climax.'

Two weeks before polling day, adapting the question that had dominated the election thirteen years earlier, the front page asked:

WHOSE FINGER ON THE TRANQUILLISER?

Certainly not the *Mirror*'s. It was exposing the 'Tory Plot' to keep the election quiet. In the film *Goldfinger*, which opened in London that week, Pussy Galore used a tranquilliser gun to put James Bond to sleep for twelve hours. Operation Apathy Galore–the Tory plan 'designed to send us all to sleep until after the election'–had been rumbled:

> The *Mirror* is going into the election right now with all guns firing. We're going to make it our business to alert the British public to the peril of 'leaving things as they are'.

The paper promptly announced where it stood:

> WE BELIEVE Britain desperately needs new men at the top with new ideas.
> WE BELIEVE a fourth term of office for Westminster's weary willies, with the diehards even more firmly in the saddle, would not only be BAD for the country but fatal for the Tory Party itself.
> WE BELIEVE a victory for Labour will not only be GOOD for the country but essential if we are to maintain in Britain the basis of a two-Party democracy with an alternative Government.

The theme was the thirteen wasted years of the Tories in office. The guns opened up. First salvo: 'The Deathbed Repentance'. Subject: The Tories' election promises. Second salvo: 'The End of the Dynasties?' Subject: Macmillan and his Top Tory relatives.

> The BEST qualification for a job in the Tory Government is to be related, however distantly, to Mr Harold Macmillan, the former Tory Prime Minister.
> As surely as the knee bone is connected to the thigh bone, the Soames are connected to the Churchills, the Churchills are connected to the Cavendishes, the Cavendishes are connected to the Macmillans, the Macmillans are connected to the Devonshires, and the Amerys and the Dilhornes and the Homes–and old Supermac is everybody's flippin' uncle.

Once again Lord Hailsham, then commoner Quintin Hogg, provided a provocative interlude during the campaign, eight days before polling. When a heckler shouted, 'What about Profumo?' at a Plymouth election meeting, Hogg retorted angrily: 'Profumo! I would say just one thing. If you can tell me there are no adulterers on the Front Bench of the Labour Party you can talk about Profumo. If you can't tell me that, you had better keep your mouths shut.'

Later that night I was in conference with Ted Heath at the Albany, Piccadilly, in his elegant apartment dominated, not surprisingly, by a grand piano. Some music of Johann Sebastian Bach, opened, was resting on the rack. We had met to discuss the article he was engaged upon for the *Mirror* expounding 'The Tory Case'. A knock at the door, unexpected, revealed the presence of an excited John Beavan, and Mr Heath was good enough to retire to another room while we talked. John was hotfoot from the office, bearing the news of Mr Hogg's outburst. I telephoned the Editor from Ted Heath's flat and dictated the page one headlines:

HOGG BLOWS HIS TOP
He makes a fantastic smear
against Labour's Front Bench

Date, October 7. On October 8 the headline was: 'Home Must Rebuke Hogg, Says Attlee,' but Mr Hogg had also returned to the affray in a speech at Dulwich. On the day the *Mirror* published Edward Heath's case for the Tory Party, Mr Hogg complained that the *Mirror* headline had suggested 'exactly the opposite of what they knew I was intending to say'.

He counter-attacked: 'If they say I am smearing people, which I am not, let them publish on their front page tomorrow the numbers of thousands of pounds they have had to pay for either satisfying the verdicts of a libel against them or buying off libel actions. Then their readers can judge fairly between them and me—and how much weight they can place on that headline.'

The *Mirror* promptly obliged. In the previous five years, apart from two instances of Liberace and Lord Boothby already mentioned by Hogg in his speech, the paper had not been involved in a single libel action in any court. In the same period it had paid less than a trifling £1,000 in settling out of court.

Hogg ended the affair with characteristic good humour. 'Shall we call it a day?' he suggested in a letter to the Editor. 'There are more important issues to discuss. Anyhow, it's my birthday.' The *Mirror* printed his letter in full, wished him a happy fifty-seventh birthday and returned to dealing with the 'more important issues'. One of them:

On the very day the Tory blood-and-thunder brigade
(they're the same confused, weary Cabinet Ministers

you've seen on TV) set off on their tour of the country to try to scarify the voters, the *Mirror* publishes the Tories' own BLACK RECORD.

The centre pages presented a mass of newspaper headlines concerned with Rachmanism, defence muddles, the economic stop-go policy, Tory Party purges and the neglect of schools and hospitals.

Another 'important issue': the predominance of Old Etonians in the Cabinet. The black uniform of Eton, readers were reminded, was worn in mourning for George III.

WHY SHOULD BRITAIN BE RUN BY 'CHAPS'
MOURNING FOR GEORGE THE THIRD?
HE DIED (MAD AS A HATTER) IN 1820, AGED 81,
FIVE YEARS AFTER WATERLOO

It is insane that the corridors of power in Westminster should forever be bolted and barred against scientists and engineers and intelligent grammar-school boys who are demonstrably more in touch with the aspirations of the millions of people whose fate is merely to be governed.

I did not go out of my way to mention that two of Cecil King's sons were Etonians.

On the day before polling we published an eight-page shock issue: 'Is This the Promised Land?' It was a national portrait of slums, ramshackle schools, soaring prices, disillusioned teachers and poverty-line pensioners. The election day slogan was: Let's *All* Vote Today and Vote for *Our* Future.' On the front page, Harold Wilson (aged forty-eight) looked steady-eyed and confident. On the back page Wilson (aged eight) stood on the steps of No. 10 Downing Street, photographed there on a No. 2 Brownie camera in 1924 by Herbert Wilson of Huddersfield, his father. 'The Most Prophetic Family Snap of all Time?' asked the *Mirror*. It was right again.

The public, who were no doubt surprised to read the ferocious altercation between Hogg and Cudlipp would no doubt be even more surprised to know that Quintin and I became, and have remained, the best of friends. He has the liveliest of minds and strength of character, and one of my current pleasures is to hear him speak in the House of Lords.

As soon as the row about the alleged adulterers on the Labour Front Bench faded, and the Tories lost the election, I asked Phillip

Levy, then head of the *Mirror* legal department, to retain the services of Mr Hogg as our leading Queen's Counsel in any libel actions during the coming year.

'Your idea?' asked Quintin with his usual roguish smile the next time we met.

'Yes,' I said. But there wasn't a single case, settled in or out of court, during the year. It was one way of proving him wrong.

Politics was only a sector of the spectrum of life which fascinated the *Mirror*, but a significant ingredient, handled with a collective knowledge which made an aggressively popular newspaper 'must' reading among the opinion-forming elite of the Establishment. An asset was King's foresight and grasp of international affairs; in military terms (I hope this does not sound too immodest) he was the Alexander and I the Montgomery in our campaigns. Because we were more often right than wrong, and were proved by events to be so, we irritated those who took a blinkered view of Britain's position and prospects in the world. Our constant demands for trade union reform, our persistent lecturing and hectoring of the prominent in public life, did not (surprisingly) make us many enemies. I made a point every year of going to the annual conferences of the Labour Party, the TUC, and the Conservative Party to face the music, but there were usually more handshakes and cosy talks over a drink in the *Mirror* salon than rebukes or cold shoulders.

The attitudes, whether expressed as the paper's official stance or by individual writers, were designed to be mentally stimulating, usually progressive, provoking the readers to think. The columnists, like Cassandra and his successors, were free to differ from 'the policy' and frequently enjoyed doing so. Vicky moved in his own orbit, but the victims of his cartoons, including successive Prime Ministers, often begged me for the originals to frame in their studies or reproduce in their memoirs. I had to decide whether Gaitskell or Rab Butler should have the first 'Butskell' drawing.

I indoctrinated the redoubtable Dick Crossman into the gentle art of tabloid journalism in 1949 when he began to write a weekly column for me on the *Pictorial*. He was the most formidable of the intellectuals in Aneurin Bevan's Keep Left faction of the Labour Party, a former New College don and lecturer to the Workers' Educational Association, accustomed to the exposition of heavy subjects but then operating as a journalist in the more rarefied precincts of the *New Statesman*. King had noticed a piece by Dick in another magazine and thought he might be useful as an occasional contributor: my enthusiasm when I met him went much further. The dialogue between us was as brisk as I was hoping the column would be:

'How long? How many words?'

'Eight hundred and fifty.'

'Good God. How many subjects?'

'Four normally, three in a lively week, one alone in a tumultuous week of national crisis or international confrontation. Eight hundred and fifty words in all, war or peace, government or dissolution, Second Coming or Judgment Day.'

'Good God. Can it be done?'

'If it's twice as long, half as many people will read it. Fatal.'

'Well,' said Dick, 'we don't want that to happen, do we?'

The only question he didn't ask—as Clem Attlee, who couldn't communicate with anybody, always did—was 'How much?' though Dick, MP, wasn't offended when I told him the fee.

I caused Crossman some embarrassment among his Keep Left buddies when I wrote, as Editor of the *Pictorial*, a piece about Aneurin Bevan. Michael Foot took me severely to task for this heresy:

'The Bevanites were accused of every form of machination . . . The final touch was supplied, on the eve of the [Labour] Conference itself, by Hugh Cudlipp of the *Sunday Pictorial*—quite unknown to Crossman—in a full front-page article. "END THE BEVAN MYTH" was the screaming headline and every twist of the typographer's black art was used to present the maniacal voice of a man whose "arrogance, vanity and spleen" threatened the whole future of the Labour Party.' [1]

Michael Foot did not quote in his book even the gist of the article, but his assessment was uncompromising:

'It was the nearest the Britain of the 1950s saw to a McCarthyite essay in character assassination.'

I had committed sacrilege. I had questioned the motives of his god, and Michael's wrath was as fearsome as that of Moses when the Israelites, in their apostasy, worshipped other idols.

In 1954, at the beginning of the great decade, I switched Dick

---

[1] *Aneurin Bevan, 1945–1960* by Michael Foot, MacGibbon of Kee, 1962.

Crossman's column to the *Daily Mirror*, and it became the spur of many controversies.

Was it all sweetness and sunshine on the even-more turbulent newspaper during the 1954–1964 decade? Was there universal accord about everything? Were there no demarcation disputes about the policy? And how was policy decreed? Lord Shawcross, as Chairman of the Royal Commission on the Press in 1961, probed this question with Cecil King and me. A misunderstanding had arisen from a memorandum submitted to the Commission by the Company:

> *Shawcross*: You say there is a committee to discuss strategy?
> *King*: There is no committee; there are only two of us–Cudlipp and myself.

King told the Commission that he met the Editors of the daily and Sunday papers 'very, very occasionally'. He then explained: 'I would say that on editorial policy Hugh Cudlipp and I, who have been directors together for very many years, work closely and are in general agreement on what sort of line we are going to take. I suppose I see him nearly every day, and if anything fresh crops up we decide what we are going to do, but I rarely see the Editors. He sees the Editors and the Editors are responsible to him.'

Lord Shawcross wished to know more. How, for example, did the *Mirror* formulate policy on issues like the Common Market or the death penalty? Were the Editors, he asked, instructed as to the line they should follow? Cecil felt that he had dealt with the question, so I took over to help Lord Shawcross and his Commissioners a little further:

> 'A fortnight ago–the Common Market is a very good example–Mr King thought it was time we began to explain the Common Market to the British public, which I set about doing with enormous zeal, as I am greatly in favour of the Common Market. Hence it is being explained, beginning last Thursday in the *Daily Herald*, and tomorrow in the *Daily Mirror*. From then on we do not have long conferences about it, because Cecil King has some faith in my intelligence, which I hope is justified, and he leaves it to me to carry on. I enthuse the Editors on this issue, and they also by a happy coincidence are in favour of the Common Market. That is how it works in practice. But I should add this, that if the policy of the papers is, shall we say, pro-Common Market, and a writer

like Cassandra passionately felt that the Common Market would be disastrous for this country, he would not hesitate to say so.

'When Vicky drew cartoons for us, I can't remember a single occasion on which he agreed with the policy of the paper, and Cassandra might be miles away from it, but both are given freedom of action.'

The policy and timing of the newspaper's interventions were customarily the end-product of the discussions between King and myself. When Tom Matthews, the former Editor of Luce's *Time*, wrote his book[1] on what he considered in 1957 to be Britain's two most significant newspapers, the *Mirror* and the *Guardian*, he spent three months wandering around our office chatting up the inmates from King to the doorman. Like others before and after him, he gave his assessment of the partnership:

> 'Hugh Cudlipp is a very pure example of the new kind of editor evolved by mass-circulation journalism . . . Belligerent and quick-tempered, with the assured arrogance of earned and precocious success, he would never submit now (though earlier in his career he might have endured it) to a subordinate position in which he merely carried out orders . . . King is the boss; he can say No to Cudlipp; but if he said No too often, Cudlipp would leave.'

Cecil never discussed these vulgar intrusions into our partnership; that is not the Cecilian way of life. The questions between us at that time were *when* we should say it and *how* we should say it, rather than *what* we should say: on the vital issues there was accord or compromise. The problems which arose from his *personal* interventions in national affairs did not surface until the Labour Party was back in power in 1964.

King's Law did not always prevail. The newspaper campaigned consistently against hanging, eventually abolished by a free vote in Parliament in 1965. It denounced the ultimate deterrent as an archaic survival, a degrading legalised re-enactment of the original crime, and questioned its efficacy in reducing the frequency of murder. The Chairman of the *Daily Mirror* and its readers were in the other camp. I did not personally hold a deep conviction on this issue, but those who did so, including Sydney Jacobson and Cassandra, created the anti-hanging policy. Not always, but occasionally, King respected views sincerely held by others in opposition to his own.

[1] *The Sugar Pill* by T. S. Matthews, Victor Gollancz, 1957.

A frontal clash of opinion was provoked by the Suez Crisis of 1956. In the initial stage Cecil and I were diametrically opposed on the question of a British military initiative but the problem was resolved in a civilised manner.

Suez is a well-tilled field, or a well-swum canal, already the subject of many a convoluted chapter in the memoirs of the committed politicians. How far there was collusion between the Governments of Britain and France, and France and Israel, and Britain and Israel has still to be definitively resolved, but here I deal briefly with the *Mirror*'s role on the home front in the affair.

On July 26 1956 President Nasser of Egypt abruptly announced the nationalisation of the Suez Canal, and his clear contravention of international treaties was the start of the most tormented period in British politics since World War Two. On July 31 came the first concrete evidence that Eden was contemplating the use of force. The Admiralty and War Office announced 'precautionary measures' to strengthen British positions in the Eastern Mediterranean, and re-serves were recalled to the colours. The stage was set for a long hot summer.

What was said at the policy conference in the office was set down by Sydney Jacobson for the archives while the events were still fresh in his mind:

'At the end of July Cudlipp and Jacobson went together to Paris. They met the editors of *France Soir* and a number of other French journalists and politicians. This was also an opportunity to discuss the line the *Mirror* would take if Eden used force against Nasser.

'They returned to London on a night flight and early the next morning went to see Cecil H. King to discuss Suez policy.

'King opened the debate. He said that if Eden resorted to force, the *Mirror* should support him. He thought Eden was "a weak man trying to act like a strong one", but Nasser was a danger to world peace, the Suez Canal was essential to Britain's economy, the Egyptians could not run it, and we should no longer stand for international treaties being pushed aside at the whim of a dictator. Nasser could be toppled, and a more reasonable man put in his place. Force against Egypt would be popular in this country, and if we could get it settled quickly, the Americans might criticise in public but would be secretly on our side. Some of the Labour movement, particularly on the trade union side–mindful of the

226

economic consequences of a closure of the Canal–would also favour force. In short, if international pressure failed to shift Nasser, Britain should use force and the *Mirror* should support the use of force.

'As King spoke, Cudlipp and Jacobson grew more morose. When he stopped speaking, King looked from one to the other, and bleakly commented: "Well, I don't seem to have made much impression on my audience."

'Hugh Cudlipp said: "No. And the reason is that Sydney and I take the completely opposite point of view."

'He told Cecil King that we had been in Paris, and had discussed the problem with contacts there. It was true that the French Socialist government and much of the Press were violently anti-Nasser, partly due to the fact that France was then fighting a colonial war in Algeria (a war which the *Mirror* had condemned) and hated Egypt for helping the Algerian nationalists. As for Britain, the only context in which the *Mirror* should possibly support the use of force was if it was sanctioned by the United Nations, supported by the Commonwealth and by the United States. These conditions were most unlikely to arise. The *Mirror* had for many years spoken out against gunboat diplomacy. Were we now to condone it? We had spoken out against colonial wars and in support of the independence movements in Asia and Africa. Were we now to crash into reverse? A war of this kind could conceivably succeed only if the whole country were united. A war against Egypt would split Britain into two.

'Jacobson said the *Mirror* was a Left-wing paper. The whole of the Left in Britain–Labour, Liberal, progressive Toryism–would be against force. It was true that Gaitskell's first reaction had been cautious, but since then the Labour Party had been taking a much stronger line. A big campaign, led by Bevan but supported by all shades of opinion inside the Party, was being mounted. Gaitskell had told Jacobson that he would denounce the use of force outside the UN. The *Mirror* must not get into a position where it was out of sympathy with all progressive opinion.

'It was agreed to adjourn the discussion. Hugh Cudlipp saw Cecil King later the same day. The upshot was that it was decided that the *Mirror* should support international action to keep the Canal free for all navigation and to set up an international agency to run the Canal. The *Mirror* did not support aggression by Britain.

'The first fruit of this decision was a leader in the *Mirror* on August 10: "*The Suez Crisis: A Sane Policy for Britain.*" And it said: "If Nasser blocks the Suez Canal or endangers British lives in Egypt, then Britain must use force against him. Short of such an emergency, it is folly for Britain to think of 'going it alone' in the face of world opinion . . . Britain must stick to the policy of collective international action."

'Four days later, August 14, the *Mirror* came out with a front-page leading article headed: "The message to Eden. NO WAR OVER EGYPT!"

'Written just before a 22-power conference of maritime nations opened in London, the *Mirror* leader was the bluntest warning yet to Eden. It contained this prophetic sentence: "If he allows himself to be goaded into rash deeds by his own bold words, by the din from the sabre-rattlers and gunboat diplomats, or by applause from France, he will find himself in a position that could be resolved in one way only—HIS OWN RESIGNATION AS PRIME MINISTER."'

There was no ambiguity in the policy of the *Mirror*. In successive editorials it criticised Mr Eden's 'double-talk', warned that a war against Egypt meant war against all the Arab states, a prolonged, bloody and costly affair. The policing of the Suez Canal meant the occupation of all Egypt, a job not for one brigade but for many divisions, saddling Britain with a crushing burden. We urged diplomacy at which (we reminded him) Eden excelled. But throughout August the ominous military build-up continued, and the holiday-makers on English roads became accustomed to crawling along behind Army convoys.

Would Eden risk his political career on the sort of gamble that the use of force would involve? Late in August Krishna Menon, on his way to the United Nations, urgently telephoned Jacobson to exchange information, and they met over an ascetic cup of China tea in Menon's suite at Claridges. Jacobson spoke of the doubts then prevalent in Britain about Eden using force. 'They are living in a fool's paradise,' said Krishna Menon. 'Eden means to have his war.'

Parliament met on September 12 and the day before the front page consisted of a photograph of the Prime Minister, with these words:

The *Mirror*'s message to Eden today:

SI SIT
PRUDENTIA

This is the first headline ever to
appear in the *Mirror* in LATIN
(and we hope the last!)
What do these three Latin words mean?
We'll tell you. They mean:

'If there be
but *prudence*'

SI SIT PRUDENTIA is the motto
of Sir Anthony Eden's family. The words
appear on the Eden coat of arms.
Today the *Mirror* reminds the Prime
Minister that PRUDENCE is precisely what is
needed as the Suez crisis reaches its climax.

The rest of the story can be told in diary dates:

1956

October 29: Israeli forces crossed the Egyptian frontier in Sinai, overwhelmed the Egyptian forces and headed for the Suez Canal.

October 30: An Anglo-French ultimatum demanded that Egypt and Israel stopped the fighting and withdrew ten miles from the Canal. It requested the Egyptian Government to agree that Anglo-French forces should move temporarily into key positions at Port Said, Ismailia and Suez to protect the Canal. Israel accepted. Egypt predictably did not.

October 31: The British bombed Egyptian airfields.

November 5: Britain and France invaded Port Said.

December 22: The last of the British troops withdrew from Port Said.

1957

January 10: Anthony Eden resigned as Prime Minister and was succeeded by Harold Macmillan.

April 9: The Suez Canal was reopened to shipping.

Postscript I:

When the Suez crisis began the Minister of Defence was Walter Monckton, high on my list of the most civilised of men who modestly trode through public life in my time. Early in October 1956 he phoned me to arrange a private talk in his apartment in the Inner

Temple. He told me that he was opposed to the use of British force in Egypt without United Nations approval. He was agonised by the question of should he resign, and I urged him not to resign on that issue. No doubt others gave the same advice. At midnight on October 18 Sir Anthony Eden announced that Walter Monckton had been replaced as Minister of Defence by Anthony Head. Walter became the Paymaster General. The British bombed Egyptian airfields thirteen days later.

Postscript II:

Anthony Eden was indeed grievously ill, obliged to embark upon a series of cliff-hanger operations. In January 1966, in the care of his wife Clarissa, Winston Churchill's niece, he was recuperating in the sunshine of Barbados. I was visiting our newspaper, the *Barbados Advocate*, accompanied by Jodi Hyland, the former Editor of *Woman's Mirror*, who had been good enough to marry me in 1963 after the tragic death the year before of Eileen Ascroft.

The four of us met for lunch on a Sunday at Lord Avon's villa. It was called *Nova* ('Avon in reverse,' said Clarissa), and it was on a hillside, hidden among mahogany trees with pendants of wild orchids growing from their aerial roots in the bark of the branches.

Anthony produced a cutting, rather faded, of a *Mirror* editorial–not about Suez, but a graceful tribute to his services to the country over many years and in many crises.

'It was a great comfort to me when I read it in the hospital in America before the operation,' he said. 'Did you write it?'

Postscript III:

The Mirror lost 70,000 circulation over its advocacy of negotiation rather than invasion. *Si sit prudentia*, or whatever, the readers were all for bashing the Wogs.

15

In Court. In Prison

The most secure position in a court of law is a seat in the public gallery, observing the affray between the leading counsel, assessing the character of the accused and anticipating the verdict. It was one of my many pursuits when I first came to London. The dock should be avoided at all costs and the witness-box avoided whenever possible. So far as Her Majesty's Prisons are concerned it is obviously wiser to be a visitor than an inmate.

I have never occupied the least desirable position in either of these establishments, but as a witness in court in a Famous Case in 1956 and a visitor to Wormwood Scrubs on a curious occasion in 1961 I had my share of judicial and penal discomfort.

The Liberace libel suit against the *Daily Mirror* was a *cause célèbre* conducted before a distinguished judge, Mr Justice Salmon, now a Lord of Appeal, and fought by the leading Queen's Counsel of the time, Mr Gerald Gardiner, QC, for the *Mirror* and Mr Gilbert Beyfus, QC, for Mr Liberace. Mr Gardiner later became Lord Chancellor, but not as the result of losing this case.

The *Daily Telegraph* covered the sporting event with round-by-round accounts occupying six columns a day: there was a laugh a line. The *Guardian* called it the case of the year, observing that it wouldn't do any harm to newspaper circulations. It inspired leading articles. The *News Chronicle* pontificated that strong speech had its limits. Weak speech also had its limits: the *News Chronicle* expired.

Cassandra wrote a column about the glittering entertainer (that's not libellous) which did not appeal to Liberace in any sense at all. There was laughter in court when Mr Beyfus read one of the passages:

> I spoke to sad but kindly men on this newspaper who have met every celebrity arriving from the United States for the past thirty years. They all say that this deadly, winking, sniggering, snuggling, chromium-plated, scent-impregnated, luminous, quivering, giggling, fruit-flavoured, mincing, ice-covered heap of mother love has had the

biggest reception and impact on London since Charlie Chaplin arrived at the same station, Waterloo, on September 12 1921. This appalling man, and I use the word appalling in no other than its true sense of terrifying, has hit this country in a way that is as violent as Churchill receiving the cheers on VE Day. He reeks with emetic language that can only make grown men long for a quiet corner, an aspidistra, a handkerchief and the old heave-ho. Without doubt he is the biggest sentimental vomit of all time. Slobbering over his mother, winking at his brother and counting the cash at every second, this superb piece of calculating candy-floss has an answer for every situation.

Mr Liberace objected in particular to twenty-two words which proved to be the most expensive William Connor (Cassandra) ever penned. His defence was that he had not intended the imputation alleged. There were many moments when the Judge smiled, Cassandra smiled, and the Court guffawed without rebuke from the ushers; Mr Liberace was smiling as he always smiles. Especially when Gilbert Beyfus, in his final address to the jury parodied Bill Connor's style: 'He has put me on my mettle but I am afraid I cannot match him. If this in any way resembles the language of Cassandra, might I suggest,' said the QC, 'that this newspaper is vicious and violent, venomous and vindictive, salacious and sensational, ruthless and remorseless. I don't think that it is up to Cassandra's standard but it is the best I can do.' It was not up to Cassandra's standard: he scorned alliteration, but Beyfus did his best.

The star witness was Cassandra himself, curiously unconvincing in a court of law. The question which really concerned me was that he should not be left alone to face the Liberace music, with or without candelabra. Beyfus, QC, known as the Old Fox, was a dangerous advocate in a case custom-built for his offensive technique.

He was seventy-four, dying, and it was his last case but one. His cross-examination of me would clearly be lengthy, meticulous, and lethal. But there was one weapon I could and did deny him, the opportunity of drawing the jury's attention to the absence in the court of any director or executive to share responsibility with Cassandra, forlorn in his hour of peril. Mr Beyfus would have made a meal of the callous, absentee landlords, and I explained to Gerald Gardiner that I would prefer to be devoured in my presence.

Gardiner was already advising me that we were losing the case and would be wise to settle out of court. If I went into the witness-box, he warned me, I would be 'severely mauled', but it was my decision.

Beyfus was unaware that I would be called, but on the table in front of him was a copy of *Publish and Be Damned*, a book I had written about the *Mirror*. He had used it extensively in his cross-examination of Cassandra, and I had taken the precaution the night before of rereading any chapters that would provide the opposition with ammunition. The Old Fox, studying his brief in his lair, had already picked up my scent.

As soon as I had been sworn in, he said with a deep-throated chuckle, 'My desire is . . . that mine adversary had written a book.'

In the few moments of leisure I was allowed in my hours in the witness-box, usually when he was calmly turning over the pages of my book, I was able to gauge the technique of my tormentor. At one stage a cat, the next a hawk, and then a snake. A cat crouching low, creeping up on the mouse, pouncing with its claws outstretched, then releasing its victim to catch it again, more interested in the hunt than the kill, reviving it with playful pats when it is on the point of expiring through exhaustion. Circling like a hawk, sighting its prey, fluttering on its wings, choosing the moment to drop to the field and soar into the sky with the next snack struggling in its talons. A snake, its head reared, weaving from side to side, its eyes mesmerising its opponent, hissing, fangs bared, arched to strike.

Mr Beyfus: The tabloid revolution was turning what had previously been a gentlemanly and decorous newspaper into a sensational newspaper?

Mr Cudlipp: I think it would have been less decorous but not less gentlemanly.

Q: Shall we say, then, turning what had been a decorous newspaper into a sensational newspaper?

A: We were not living in a very decorous age in 1935, and the newspaper changed its form and its approach to life to keep up with the changes we thought were taking place in society.

Q: I am not sure whether you are agreeing with me or not. The tabloid revolution consisted in changing the paper from being a decorous newspaper into a sensational newspaper?

A: Yes; I would agree with that.

Q: I suggest that it is a paper which presents the news and its views in a sensational manner?

A: A vivid manner.

Q: In a sensational manner?

A: That is what the word 'sensational' means and the way in which it is defined in this book. There are many definitions of the word 'sensational', but the definition is clearly given in this book. May I draw attention to it?

Mr Justice Salmon: Just listen to the question. Your own counsel will have a chance of dealing with any particular point later.

The witness in a court quickly realises he cannot match insult with insult, or protest at innuendo, or even cry 'Foul'. He may only answer questions, as the Judge will coldly remind him, and indeed reminded me. Ribaldry or verbal brutality are permissible from counsel, but a strangulated joke from the nervous witness is instantly suppressed as levity, likely to excite the rebuke that 'This is a court of law, not a music hall.'

In the box, sworn to tell the truth, the whole truth and nothing but the truth, one is in fact confined to answering tendentious questions designed to disclose only those glimpses of the truth convenient to an advocate's client. It is difficult to avoid the impression that at the end of a case, or half-way through it, the QCs representing both sides, so passionately hostile to each other in court, will be sitting together on a *chaise-longue* in one of the Inns of Court with a Scotch in their hands welcoming newly qualified barristers-at-law to their black craft, laughing themselves silly. The assumption is that the witness is a shifty liar. The onus is on him to satisfy the court he is telling the truth, but he must do so quickly so that he does not, heaven forbid, waste the time of the wigged professionals.

Mr Beyfus had noticed the phrase 'living dangerously' in *Publish and Be Damned*.

Q: In order to bring about this tabloid revolution, to use your own words, I think, you had to live dangerously?

A: That is correct.

Q: 'Live dangerously' means taking the risk of unpleasant consequences as the result of your presentation of news and views in a sensational manner?

A: No. I wrote the phrase 'live dangerously'. May I explain what I meant by it? By 'living dangerously' in 1935 was meant challenging some of the orthodox ideas of the day. That is what I meant. I certainly did not mean challenging the law. No sane person would endeavour to do that. What I meant was challenging the conventions of the day. Britain was getting behind the times in the world, and I felt we had to go on to other ideas.

Q: I suggest that one of the instances of living dangerously is printing such an article as you printed about my client?

A: That remains to be seen. I have not heard the verdict.

Mr Beyfus savoured other examples of what he called 'living dangerously'.

Q: You were threatened by the Home Secretary in the course of the war with suppression?

A: When you say 'you', I do not know whom you mean. I was in the Western Desert at the time. I have read the whole evidence, and in this book I do give my verdict on it. I do not think the paper was guilty of anything. Though I was not there, I am extremely proud of the part it played during the war.

Q: I apologise for saying 'you'. The First Defendants, the Daily Mirror Newspapers Limited, were threatened with the suppression of the newspaper by the Home Secretary during the war?

A: That is quite correct.

Q: Owing to a cartoon, and in particular to the caption written for it by the Second Defendant [Cassandra]?

A: That is correct, in that Cassandra wrote the caption to that cartoon. I was not there, but he said so in the box.

Q: One of the excuses put forward was that the Second Defendant Mr Connor was a hard-hitting journalist with a vitriolic style?

A: No, you have misread this letter from Mr Churchill.

Q: Have I?

A: The letters referred to a quite different incident altogether. The letters with Mr Churchill do not refer to the cartoon.

Q: Very well.

A: They are about Mr Connor's column. They are nothing to do with the cartoon at all.

Q: I am not going into details with regard to it.

A: It is not a matter of detail; that is untrue.

Q: In order to excuse the behaviour of the newspaper the Editor wrote that the Second Defendant was a hard-hitting journalist with a vitriolic style?

It was Cecil King who had written the letter, not the Editor. There followed, at this point, a tedious inquiry into who did what, with Beyfus getting all the facts wrong. And then he moved to a profile I had written of Cassandra in the book, a humorous character study which had not been designed as a lawyer's brief.

Q: With regard to your association with the defendant Connor, you mentioned that when you were both in London you therefore attended the office, and you met daily? You may meet socially every day? Up to quite recently it would be a quite frequent sight to see both of you drinking in a Fleet Street bar?

Drinking! Mr Beyfus was insinuating a nightly carousal, and it was necessary for me to correct this impression in case there were any teetotallers on the jury.

A: Most certainly, in *El Vino*, where barristers meet after their cases and where we meet after our newspapers.

Mr Beyfus dropped the point. No dice.

Q: Since 1935 you would have had a very fair opportunity of judging Mr Connor as a journalist and his journalistic style?
A: Yes.
Q: You deal with him, and you describe him. You say this on page 132: 'He drifted into journalism and swiftly progressed in the only profession where big-scale incessant rudeness (skilfully written) is highly paid.' Is that your view of journalism?

The other profession in which big-scale incessant rudeness (skilfully spoken) was highly paid was obviously legal advocacy. When I said that Mr Connor, though a very rude man on occasions, was a very kind man on others, Mr Beyfus dismissed my irrelevance. 'I am talking of his writing,' he said. 'He may be an angel in his private life.' The cross-examination on this point–raillery to the Judge, Beyfus and me, but enjoyable character assassination to the jury and the public gallery–continued for a quarter of an hour. He then moved the scenery around.

Q: The whole of the *Daily Mirror*, when not devoted purely to sensationalism is devoted to dealing with sex, is it not?
A: I refute that entirely. I think that is a ridiculous suggestion which just is not true.

There followed a prim argy-bargy about why the first Lord Rothermere severed his financial relationship with the paper. Was it due to the attitude to sex as I had written on one page? Yes, but I explained that in another part of the book Mr Beyfus would find that it had been a good moment, skilfully but not honestly fabricated, for his lordship to get out financially.

'Ah–h–h–' The cat pounced. The hawk dropped from the sky. The snake hissed, fangs bared, arched to strike. '*Are you suggesting that what you wrote on one page is not true because of what you said on other pages?*'

The introduction of the name of the first Lord Rothermere, Cecil King's randy Uncle Harold, into a court-room discourse on sexual decorum was buffoonery. Beyfus knew it, and knew that I knew it, but the jury didn't. I was expecting that at any moment he would exhume and subpœna Jack the Ripper and Christie of Rillington Place to give their considered views on chastity and homecraft.

Gilbert Beyfus, no prude in his private life, affected to be shocked by the daily cartoon *Jane*. It began as 'The Diary of a Bright Young Thing' and was buried in the 1950s when she became, in changing standards, a dull old thing. At moments of stress her left nipple, or the right cheek of her bottom, sedately drawn in black and white, was occasionally visible to her audience. The jury were not impressed by this pretentious exercise to denigrate the *Mirror*, and Beyfus conceded the point. It faded beyond recall in the following Q and A:

Mr Beyfus: The whole appeal of the *Jane* cartoon is an appeal to sex?

Mr Cudlipp: Sex of a rather genteel type.

Q: Genteel?

A: You cannot be frightfully sexy in a cartoon twò inches deep.

This was the feline treatment. I was being revived by playful pats so that I could be caught again. Earlier in the case Mr Justice Salmon silenced me with the remark: 'Just listen to the question'. He did not rebuke Mr Beyfus when he departed from formal questioning and delivered the vicious innuendo that 'Nothing by a *Mirror* journalist would surprise me.' A similar broadside from the witness-box, on the lines of 'Nothing by a barrister of your notorious venom would surprise me,' would have provoked Mr Justice Salmon into a severe admonition. He did not say to Mr Beyfus, 'Just listen to the answer.' I was a witness in the Royal Courts of Justice in the Strand, the noble rambling edifice at the western end of Fleet Street, opposite the Church of St Clement Dane ('Oranges and lemons say the bells of St Clement's'), not a member of the freemasonry of the legal profession. My diet was lemons.

237

The Old Fox ended on a materialistic note. Mr Liberace was not short of the odd dollar, but his advocate wanted the jury to know that his detractor, the *Daily Mirror*, was also not on the dole queue.

I do not repeat here the twenty-two colourful words to which Mr Liberace especially objected. The case cost the *Daily Mirror* £8,000 in damages, plus £27,000 in legal costs, a grand total of £35,000, excluding the consumption of a gin and tonic by Cassandra and myself before our separate appearances in the witness-box.

Some interest was maintained for a while by the Press (the Press!) by an incident in court. Iain Adamson describes it in his biography of Gilbert Beyfus:

'The woman juror gave Liberace the news before Mr Justice Salmon was back on the bench. She winked, nodded then silently mouthed the words, "It's all right." When Liberace arrived at the Savoy Hotel she was already there and advanced smiling with a piece of paper for his autograph. David Jacobs (Liberace's solicitor) spotted her. "Quick, run for it," he told Liberace. "If she speaks to us it could mean a new trial." They fled along the corridor and bolted the door.

'"I wanted to end his suspense, to let him know everything was all right. Any woman of feelings would have done the same," she told a reporter. "I felt for him all the time. I never wavered for a minute from the second I sat down."'[1]

The Judge publicly congratulated Mr Beyfus on his brilliant advocacy in the case, but there wasn't a word of appreciation for his victims in the witness-box. Beyfus was, of course, great–ruthless, sensational, but great. He could have changed places with Cassandra as a columnist, but Bill Connor could not have changed places with him as an advocate. Cassandra did not have the voice for public appearances, in court or on TV.

All was forgiven and forgotten. When the case was over and done with Mr Liberace resumed his pleasant relationship with the *Daily Mirror*. He was genial enough to send me a cable to be read out at our farewell dinner to Mark Goodman, the head of the paper's legal department at the time of the case.

This year, 1976, I was serving as a member of Lord Salmon's Royal Commission on Standards of Conduct in Public Life, an

---

[1] *The Old Fox* by Iain Adamson, Frederick Muller, 1963.

inquiry ordered by the Government after the corruption scandals disclosed during the hearing of Mr Poulson's bankruptcy.

We move from crime to punishment, from the Law Courts in the Strand to the prison famed as Wormwood Scrubs.

In 1961 one of its sensitive inmates was 'Zeno', who pleaded guilty in 1958 to a charge of murder and was sentenced to 'life'. His book, briefly entitled *Life*, is a remarkable document on what happens to a man when he moves into a different society. Zeno won a Koestler Award with his collection of short stories in 1963 in a contest open to those serving in Her Majesty's Prisons: he also served with the British Airborne Division at Arnhem. He and I had met in the *Old Cock Tavern* in Fleet Street long before his trouble, and he lunched with me in the office when his prison days were over.

The link was that remarkable woman Xenia Field. He was one of the hundreds of thousands of men and women in gaol whose miserable existences she makes more bearable by organising concerts and talks on Wednesday evenings at six o'clock. A glimpse of the world outside the walls. Xenia also knows everything about roses, and she tells the readers of the *Daily Mirror* about gardening in her weekly article. I call her Dame Xenia, and so she should be known officially.

At one of the 'Field concerts' in Wormwood Scrubs I was performing one evening with a team of speakers, some of them Editors of our women's magazines. I was aware of an atmosphere, but didn't fathom what it was all about until Zeno wrote his book. [1] This was one of several visits I made to prisons with Xenia, but on this particular evening there were a number of wardens on parade with truncheons at the ready, evidently in anticipation of aggro. We had a sherry with the Governor, Gilbert Hair, before our small party was taken to the platform, unaware that some of the residents had chosen that night to upset him and that the Scrubs was on the verge of a sullen mutiny. Zeno tells the story:

'Big George and I are seated at a table, uncertain as to whether it is worth starting our game of bridge. Johnny and his partner, the pair we are playing, come up and join us. As a rule, at this time in the evening most of the men have settled to some occupation or another, but tonight they mill about, for although they know the concert is to be held they don't know what the conditions of

---

[1] *Life* by Zeno, Macmillan, 1968.

attendance or non-attendance will be. Johnny throws himself down on a chair and drums irritably on the table with his fingers, and then he says:

'"Well, what's it going to be, bang-up for those who don't go, or will we be able to stay out and play?"

'Johnny doesn't expect an answer, for we know no more than he does and he's aware of it.

'George turns to me. "Who is this fucking Cudlipp guy anyhow?"

'"He's the editorial director of the Mirror Group, and he's considered to be the best tabloid newspaper man in the world."

'"So what? So I'd sooner play bridge."'

The rules were not inflexible at Wormwood Scrubs. Sometimes, it was the concert or the early lock-up and punishment for those who refused to go. Other times, when they had mustered enough to make an audience, they let the rest carry on with their chosen pursuits. Nobody knew the form that evening until the bell rang and a screw announced from the desk, 'Form up for the concert at the centre gate.'

Zeno and his friends stayed where they were, watching 'the eager beavers, the men who will watch and listen to anything,' make their way to the gate, forming a queue. Other men still sat at the tables, and when a young screw walked up to Zeno's bridge table with a reminder, Big George announced the policy:

'"We don't have to go to any God-damned concert. The judge said nuthin' to me about listenin' t' Hughie Cudlipp while I was inside. Why can't we stay right here and play bridge?"'

Then the screw announced the Governor's policy: 'You've got to go. No. 1 Governor's orders. The whole Hall's to go—no exceptions.' They had to attend or take the consequences. It was an order.

The issue was debated. Bridge, or Cudlipp? The bang-up, or the concert? Zeno's contribution was philosophical: 'We can't play bridge. It's simply a matter of what each of us prefers. I'm going to bang-up.' The prison officer locked the gate, went to the desk, rang the bell and called the mutineers up to join him. Fourteen men had remained behind to give their prison numbers, cell numbers, and names. Seven of them were serving life sentences.

The fact that fourteen men in a prison, with no alternative entertainment except bridge, preferred the likely punishment of three days' bread and water, with nothing to smoke, in preference to putting questions to me for an hour was a salutary antidote to any pretensions I might have developed in the future about walking on the water.

16

Wooing the Readers

Opinion was the message, but it was the pulsating excitement of the paper day after day that attracted and held the audience. It had its own vivid personality, pathetically copied by the late *Daily Sketch* and more diligently by the current *Sun*. It had warmth and independence. And the brand of earthy cheek that its readers themselves possessed but did not have the nerve or words in their own humdrum lives to express.

The reporters were masters and mistresses at seeking out the human angle even in the most arid of subjects. The selection at night of the next morning's news diet, the terse sub-editing and headline-writing, and the choice and treatment of pictures were consistently more compelling than in the other popular papers. The customers were given not only what they needed, easily digestible information, but also what they wanted—entertainment and 'human interest'.

The Shock Issue on housing conditions in slum areas produced during the 1964 election was one of a series over the years that dynamically focused on a national issue in a single issue of the paper. I evolved the technique as an exercise in brutal mass education. One of them dealt with the problem of death on the roads:

> Today's Mirror WILL shock you.
> But it MAY save your life . . .
> SAVE YOUR
> LIFE!
> A Mirror Shock Issue to fight
> death on the roads.

The front page was dominated by the stark silhouette of a skeleton at the wheel of a car.

Another eye-opener was the *Mirror* which exposed the export of live horses under revolting conditions to become horse-meat on the Continent. I struggled for a while with King's concern that we should do something effective about the problems of old people, not a welcome assignment to a newspaper which prided itself on its youth-appeal. The Shock Issue on that occasion was entitled:

LONELINESS
The Mirror has more YOUNG READERS
than any paper in the world
THIS IS A FRANK REPORT about a
blot on our conscience

In 1976 the topless young model with two big blue eyes is obviously the essential daily aphrodisiac which differentiates the popular Press from *The Times*, the *Daily Telegraph* and the *Morning Star*. But that day the counters of the W. H. Smith bookstalls displayed the grey, world-weary face of Ada Timmins, time-etched by experience but tolerant and patient rather than sad or disillusioned. She was eighty-two, living alone in a flat in Balsall Heath, Birmingham. 'I am lucky,' she said, 'my neighbours look after me.' Were others so lucky? The women's magazines in the IPC publishing empire combined with the newspapers in the launching of Old Folks' Week to stimulate interest in the 'senior citizens' the Welfare State was neglecting.

A Shock Issue exposed the 'Scandal of our Youth Service: Dingy Clubs ... Not Enough Money ... Too Few Leaders.' Another dealt with child neglect. A photograph of a leather-jacketed Wild One speeding along on a powerful motor-cycle illustrated the front page of the 'Suicide Club' issue, warning the young of the perils on the roads. The message as always was unsparing in reality:

The Suicide Club
devours 130,000 members every year!!
100 MPH CAN GIVE A KICK!
... BUT
THERE
ARE NO
KICKS
IN A
CEMETERY

Guy Bartholomew had midwifed the rebirth of the *Mirror* in the pre-war years in a conspiracy of silence, but the objective now was a daily sale of 5,000,000 copies. It was essential to get the newspaper talked about. What could the *Mirror* do to create news about itself?

H. W. (Tommy) Atkins joined me from the *Sunday Express*. He became the Group's Publicity and Promotions Director, the Circulation Director, and later also the Chairman of Fleetway Magazines–a considerable publishing performance. He is an ideas germinator, and when he wasn't thinking up his own ideas he was brilliant at improving mine or anybody else's. I have never seen, anywhere in the world, promotions to equal his in presentation and public entertainment.

'Tommy,' I said, 'the *Mirror* could help the Exports Drive by staging a highly original dinner in the cities which are producing the best results. Let's call them the Boom Cities. I'll produce a Boom City *Mirror* in the same area on the day you're staging the banquet. What about the *Adelphi Hotel* in Liverpool for a start, with the PM as the Chief Guest? Harold has heard of Liverpool.'

'No,' said Tommy, 'let's have it on a ship.'

He chose the flagship of the Elder Dempster Line. Dinner was served by the ship's own sun-bronzed stewards in smart white tropical uniforms. The empty showcases were restocked, the Purser's Bureau staffed, and the ship dressed overall–not merely dressed overall but swung around by tugs so that the bows faced the guests when they arrived. Behind the Chief Guest, the Prime Minister, was mounted the emblem of the City of Liverpool, complete with a *real* liver bird borrowed from a zoo.

The other Boom City dinners were also startlingly original. A team of steel plate riveters transformed a Newcastle hotel banqueting room with the atmosphere and noise of their shipyard. A motor cycle burst through a screen before the audience in Birmingham. In a Bristol hotel the first big model of Concorde shimmered above the diners as the telephone rang, and over an 'open line' the top man in Toulouse discussed progress with his opposite number at the British Aircraft Corporation.

We staged a *Mirror* Pets' Club lunch at the *Café Royal* in London, all laid on by Atkins with chimps leaping from table to table, and goats, ducks and a bush baby roaming the Napoleon Room on their best behaviour, and George Cansdale's pet python gently winding itself around anyone who was willing to oblige him. An American tourist was surprised when the lift-man said: 'Other lift, please. This one is reserved for donkeys.'

When we were unable to lay our hands on Francis Chichester's *Gipsy Moth II*, Tommy built a full-size replica, including the cutlery, and moved it against a wall in the foyer of the Mirror

Building. He berthed Alec Rose's *Lively Lady*, the actual ship this time, on a lawn in Holborn Circus. Adventure, even simulated, is a significant part of men's dreams. A popular paper has to know this.

The *Mirror* not only succeeded in being talked about: it achieved the greatest circulation and the greatest commercial success of any newspaper in the Western world. On Tuesday, June 9 1964, it announced an average daily sale of 5,000,000. And that meant a readership of 14,000,000 for each issue.

17

The Sun that Didn't Rise

Well, go on. Very interesting. Tell us about the failures and the
flops. What about the *Sun*? Why did Rupert Murdoch make a go
of it when Cudlipp and King failed? (Cecil won't at all mind my
name preceding his on this occasion. Success has many fathers:
failure is a bastard.)

Why did Rupert the Bull, the brash young Australian, pull off
the only *new* success in newspaper publishing in Britain in the
past five or six years with the title IPC launched in 1964 and wished
by 1969 it had never heard of? Murdoch did not sire an editorial or
creative breakthrough. He produced a Woolworth edition of the
Marks and Spencer *Daily Mirror*, hi-jacking staff and ideas, but
it was a notable commercial triumph which provided a daily newspaper to print on the presses not fully exploited by his Sunday
News of the World. That's good business in any language, including
Strine.

Well, go on. Why couldn't or didn't IPC do what he did?

I'll tell you over the port and cigars now being served.

In November 1958 Cecil King acquired Amalgamated Press,
founded by Northcliffe. I learned the news from a cable when I was
journeying in Russia: '*Thinking of buying Uncle's old business in
Farringdon Street stop Cable your views but deal may have to be
completed swiftly warm regards Cecil King.*' The vast magazine
emporium, in a very poor state indeed, was bought from Michael
Berry. To achieve any sort of success the magazine market–including
the more lucrative end of the industry owned by Odhams Press
(*Woman, Woman's Own*)–urgently needed rationalisation, cover
price increases, and an order for 'controlled fire' on promotion, free
gift and publicity expenditure. There was not enough advertising
available for all, and some of the women's magazines would have
to go to the wall. So Cecil took over Odhams Press in 1961 after a
sharp affray with Roy Thomson to whom the Odhams directors,
quite shewdly, had run for protection. The purchase of Odhams
Press brought the *Daily Herald* into the *Mirror* Group.

We'll take a break here.

There were Parliamentary objections to the *Mirror* take-over of Odhams, and Hugh Gaitskell, Leader of the Labour Party, was far from keen on more power–particularly over Left-wing newspapers –going to Cecil King. Gaitskell wanted Thomson to win. It was for this reason that I came up with the bright idea that we should guarantee the *Daily Herald*'s existence for seven years. The move was necessary to match a similar, though vaguer, offer from the other side.

I know of no other occasion on which the man about to be hanged was given the privilege of selecting his own rope and specifying the time he should spend in the death cell before the definitive act.

There were other stipulations, freely entered into by us, indeed *conceived* by us, which conditioned our behaviour and decisions at a later stage. Cecil willingly signed a piece in the *Daily Mirror* which I had written. It gave two pledges:

1. The future of the *Herald* as a separate entity would be fought for with the utmost energy.
2. No amalgamation of the *Daily Herald* and *Daily Mirror* would ever take place during the period of the Mirror Group's control of Odhams.

When the defeated generals, Lord Thomson and Sir Christopher Chancellor, Chairman of Odhams, had retired from the battlefield and the dead and wounded were counted, Cecil accepted my hint that he should immediately meet the Editors and principal editorial staff of each publication at a series of evening social functions in his office suite. I knew that some of them, or most of them, or all of them were agitated at events which deeply concerned them but over which they had no control. It was not, because of my stage management, a mass baptism of the Meet Your New Boss variety. I was concerned that if first impressions were unfavourable it would be through no fault of King's or mine. Cecil graciously presided over the cocktail parties and invited any of his colleagues on the IPC board who were free to join him.

At the end of the marathon get-together was the *Daily Herald*'s night, with its Editor John Beavan and his principal editorial staff as the guests. Cecil wasn't there that evening, nor was I accompanied by any other IPC director of any particular importance in the eyes of the guests except Ellis Birk. I knew in that lonely moment that the *Daily Herald* was being baptised as 'Cudlipp's baby', not as

Cecil later called it 'King's Cross'. It was dumped firmly in my lap. The prospects of success were zero. I no doubt had everybody's best wishes, especially Cecil's, but no condolences.

Nobody sane in publishing would have paid a penny to acquire the *Herald*: it was part of 'the package'. It was the official Labour Party newspaper, owned by Odhams Press (51 per cent) and the TUC (49 per cent). The *Herald* was in a straitjacket. Despised as a costly chore by Odhams. Compelled to laud the official policy of the Labour Party on political matters, however confused, and of the Trade Union Congress, frequently disunited, on the industrial front. It had broken the hearts of a series of Editors who had been invited to shed their blood freely but not to dig too deeply into the Odhams coffer, which was replenished each week by *The People* and *Woman*. Somewhere or other their names are surely engraved on a plinth–William Mellor, W. H. Williamson, Francis Williams, Percy Cudlipp (my brother was among the unsung heroes), Sydney Elliott, Douglas Machray. And yet there were more volunteers, determined men fully aware of the overwhelming opposition that faced them outside and inside the office, and from the Labour Party itself. It was the Editors' Passchendaele.

John Beavan (Lord Ardwick) was facing the enemy fire from the *Express* and *Mirror* when I arrived on the unhappy scene. He was a close friend of mine since our days together as young reporters in Salford. He is a journalist with vast knowledge and energy, groomed in the *Guardian* school, but not by nature an Editor, a writer rather than an executive. During the lull that followed the take-over bombardment he told me an excellent story. He was unaware as Editor of the anxieties in the Odhams board-room. The directors were reasonably preoccupied with their own fate as well as with their duties to the shareholders. Were they going to be wooed by Roy Thomson or raped by Cecil King? John Beavan was celebrating the newspaper's fiftieth birthday in an expansive editorial. 'We look back with pride, we look forward with confidence'–you know the sort of thing. He wondered why the directors took so long in passing and applauding his panegyric. It contained the phrase: 'The *Daily Herald* is passing a DANGEROUS CORNER.'

Dick Dinsdale, Deputy Editor of the *Mirror*, was seconded to join the *Herald* as Editorial Adviser, a shrewd, outspoken Yorkshireman who had sat on Hannen Swaffer's black hat at a London first night and was prepared to sit or stamp on any piece of journalistic work he considered less than perfect. Then Sydney Jacobson,

Political Editor of the *Mirror, volunteered* in 1962 to be Editor of the *Herald*. I warned him that it was professional *hara-kiri* but he knew that already.

Brave men, but it didn't work. May we, in our comradely humility, give the last word to Brother Brown, that prominent newspaper expert now known as Lord George-Brown:

'I was certain that the *Herald*, which the Labour Party badly needed, would be better off in the hands of Cudlipp and King. This put me rather at loggerheads with Gaitskell, and as I was also having my own disagreements with King, there was a very tangled situation.

'He (King) did in fact keep it going for the seven years he promised, but nobody seemed to be able to make a go of it.

'Where I was wrong was over Cudlipp. I thought that Cudlipp could run the *Daily Herald* as it ought to have been run: and I'm still convinced that a popular Labour newspaper could be run successfully. But they weren't able to do it: maybe Cudlipp just lost his touch for running newspapers. We have now seen what the Australian Rupert Murdoch has done with the *Sun*. A few years ago we'd have said that just wasn't possible, but it has happened.'[1]

Good old George. And also good old Harry Rochez. Harry was the executive director in charge of *The People* and the *Herald*, and in that capacity he had organised more golden (or silver, or bronze, or copper) handshakes for Editors than he would care to remember. The importance of Mr Rochez on this occasion was that he came from a family of circus artists. A tight-rope walker was just what we needed.

'Why not start again?' said Harry. 'Launch a new title. Basil de Launay suggests the *Sun*?'

Now this was talking sense. The *Herald* had already masticated three years of its seven-year guarantee of life and liberty. It was a bloated, listless boa constrictor suffering from fatty degeneration of the heart, displaying the vital statistics of sudden death as they are known and feared by any student of newspaper mortality. It had the highest proportion of men among its readers of any 'national morning' (59 per cent). Only 33 per cent of its readers were housewives, compared with 38 per cent for the *Mirror*, 37 per cent for the

---

[1] *In My Way* by Lord George-Brown, Victor Gollancz, 1971.

Mail and 36 per cent for the *Express*. It had the highest C2 and DE readership. It suffered at that time from the same disease that afflicted the Labour Party, its biggest fall-out was among the younger generation.

So the *Sun* it would be, and it rose in 1964. Nobody could be fired and therefore very few hired. There were tortuous negotiations with the TUC to loosen their policy stranglehold. We couldn't change the physical shape of the newspaper, the surface size, because of the mechanical inflexibility of the Odhams rotary presses. All that–and more. But the blast-off was great: 'THE PAPER BORN IN THE AGE WE LIVE IN.' We splashed the money in publicity and promotion. Sidney Bernstein's Granada TV produced a documentary.

It worried Fleet Street, but not for long.

The new paper flopped. We couldn't play a new tune on the old *Herald* fiddle, not at any rate convincingly. Jacobson edited the new/old newspaper for its first year, followed by Dick Dinsdale when Sydney became Editorial Director of both the Odhams newspapers. The last struggle for survival was a part of my overall responsibilities, and I had no doubt at all that a final flat-out effort was vastly preferable to attending a protracted funeral with the *Herald*, because of its mounting losses, conducted on a 'care-and-maintenance' basis.

The facts and anxieties of these situations, now being faced by several national newspapers, are of far more than professional interest in a country acutely aware of the need for variety and freedom in its Press. By spring 1969 the combined losses on the *Herald* and *Sun* over a period of eight years had reached a total of £12,702,000. The sale of the *Sun* was falling below the million mark, advertisement revenue was declining and newsprint prices were due to go up again by at least £2 a ton in 1970.

The pledges to the unions to keep the *Herald* going for at least seven years and the *Sun* for two years over that period, in return for considerable reductions in manning, had been honoured. In the first half of 1969, I as Chairman of IPC and Frank Rogers as Managing Director instructed the Newspaper Division to put forward every conceivable proposal for a viable future for the newspaper. On July 15 the IPC board examined the plans and costings and unanimously resolved it was unable to continue publication of the *Sun* after the stipulated period expiring in January of 1970.

The newspaper had been vastly improved editorially. The public demand, stimulated by the scintillating publicity campaign, was initially cheering but swiftly fell away. There was no room in the market for another text-size newspaper of its type, and survival was impossible unless it had been twice as successful as it was.

Why didn't IPC turn the *Sun* into a tabloid-size newspaper?
Or amalgamate the *Sun* with the *Mirror*?
Or just close the *Sun* down instead of letting it go to a competitor?
The Sun *as a tabloid*: this was never feasible as a commercial, journalistic or technical venture.

Commercially, it would have been crazy to set up a competitor to the *Mirror* within IPC. Journalistically, it would have meant turning the *Sun* into a brash sex-mad tabloid aimed at the bottom end of the *Mirror* readership. This was against the whole trend and recent development of the *Mirror* as an intelligent tabloid. Technically, the *Sun* could not have been printed in true tabloid size because of the structure of the Odhams newspaper presses. It would have meant total replanting.

Amalgamating the Mirror *with the* Sun: to make any sense this would have meant closing the *Sun* with the device of amalgamating the title into the *Mirror*, in the hope of capturing more *Sun* readers and witholding the title and goodwill from a competitor.

When IPC took over Odhams in 1961 they undertook never to merge the *Herald* into the *Mirror*. It could be claimed that this pledge did not apply to the *Sun*, the successor of the *Herald*, but this would have been recognised as a shoddy evasion.

A merger would have been troublesome politically. IPC knew, from the then Prime Minister, that a *Mirror–Sun* merger would have been referred to the Monopolies Commission.

There were other considerations. Over forty per cent of *Sun* readers at that time already took the *Mirror*. The gain to the *Mirror* in sales would have been comparatively small, and of a type that would not have helped the *Mirror*'s advertisement profile–elderly, mainly men. They would have fallen away rapidly; it was the *Daily Mail–News Chronicle* dilemma, in a more acute form.

Amalgamation would not have appreciably reduced the redundancy problem.

Closing the Sun *instead of letting it go to a competitor*: the answer to this lies in the industrial problem. In November 1969 the number of people employed by the *Sun* in London and Manchester was

3,161. Had the paper been closed down, all–except for a handful of journalists and clerical staff–would have become redundant. In fact, total redundancies made by Odhams were 1,298. Had IPC refused to sell, the results would have been:

1. A further loss of 2,000 jobs directly attributable to IPC's fear of competition.
2. Great union resentment, which would probably have caused heavy production losses to the other IPC newspapers, in particular to the *Mirror*. The effect could well have been more damaging short term than anything Murdoch could achieve long term.
3. Had redundancies on that scale been created by refusal to sell the *Sun*, IPC in particular, and the national Press in all probability, could have said good-bye for many years to any hope of productivity deals with the unions.
4. In any case, if Murdoch had not been able to get the *Sun* he would have launched a new tabloid daily a few months later. The economics of the *News of the World* plant made it imperative for him to do so.

I would come to the same conclusions if confronted today by the same problem, and so I believe would my colleagues. The answer to our dilemma was the offer made by Robert Maxwell in April 1969– to take over the paper free in order to run it as a committed Labour daily, published only in London with a smaller staff, a non-profit-making venture printed on the *Evening Standard* presses and supervised by a Trust. I was certainly in a position to guarantee him the total fulfilment of the non-profit-making aspect of his plan. Journalists were sceptical. Maxwell offered the Editorship successively to Robert Edwards, then of *The People*, Geoffrey Pinnington of the *Mirror*, Michael Randall of the *Sunday Times*, and William Davis of *Punch*. They were all too busy that month. The printing unions were hostile, in particular SOGAT. On September 2 Robert Maxwell withdrew his bid.

IPC's *Sun* did not rise. Maxwell's *Sun* remained in total eclipse. Murdoch's *Sun* rose and shone. He inherited no labour problems by buying it. He was conditioned by no pledges from the past. His machines could produce a tabloid-size newspaper, and to produce a paper to compete with the *Mirror* was precisely what he planned to do. Nobody could say he has not been successful.

Rupert's originality as a journalist and publisher has still to be established, but who can doubt his business flair or nerve? In a

Guardian interview he was musing with Terry Coleman about his thoughts in 1968 to expand from the Antipodes and lay siege to Fleet Street:

> 'Coming here,' he said, 'you begin to think–is Cudlipp all that damned good? You know, they all think he's God. Or is Cecil King God, or something? Maybe one could mix it over here . . . it was almost bravado.'

Go on, then, Were there any more flops? Well . . . er . . . um, there was *Junior Mirror* (my idea), and there was *Mirror Magazine* (not my idea), a free insert in colour, principally red as things turned out, which appeared once a week with the newspaper or at any rate did so as long as we could afford it. But it's getting chilly in this graveyard.

The sad story of IPC's *Sun* did produce one tiny wry smile. The *Spectator* felt that the paper ought not to die without some memorial. In a competition it invited its readers to compose an epitaph or epigram upon its fate, and one of the winning entries came from Mr George van Schaick:

> O what a wond'rous thing
> Has mighty Cudlipp done!
> He who deposed a King
> Has now put out the Sun.

The deposing of Cecil King took place in 1968. He was in at the birth of the IPC *Sun* but not at the funeral.

The story of the remarkable conflicts and controversies which made his face familiar on the television screens and the front pages of the rival newspapers, and an account of the abrupt and unexpected climax to his career, are related in the concluding section of this book, 'A Man of Destiny'.

V

A MAN
OF DESTINY

18

Chaste Minerva

Cecil Harmsworth King has never achieved a relationship on equal terms with any human being of any generation; he is aware of this bleak incapacity and shields himself by avoiding the obligations of social intimacy. It has to be headmaster and pupil, father and wayward son, the mature and the immature, or, at its most inelegant, employer and employee with Cecil King holding the exclusive right to hire and fire or cosset or crumble. A few tried to penetrate the stratosphere, but they were sooner or later deep-frozen or shooed away, or ignored as if he hadn't heard what they had said. He avoided the intrusive by turning his back on them, physically.

The Harmsworths were rude to each other and mutually suspicious. The professional colleagues of all of them were with few exceptions regarded as visitors from the servants' hall. They were carrying on the arm's-length tradition of Northcliffe with his rule that he and his Editors should avoid friendship, especially family contact, with public personalities because of the embarrassment at a later stage when policies might clash. The creed of his nephew, Cecil King, was more exquisitely honed because he had been treated by his own family with scant courtesy. One must be seriously attached to nothing and nobody. A relationship that hasn't been allowed to flower is easier to uproot.

His *rapport* with me was therefore exceptional. I acquired the status of a favourite son, though subject on rare occasions to severe mental chastisement.

It was snowing on Christmas Day in 1955. My wife Eileen Ascroft and I were peering over the Thames from our first-storey window, sampling an early champagne cocktail, waiting for neighbours and friends to join us for drinks and turkey. Among them were two handfuls of Editors and writers of one sort or another, politicians stranded in London that day, an actor or two, a sprinkling of trade union leaders and their wives, and a detective from Scotland Yard–a Santa Holmes on overtime–who was keeping an eye on an unsavoury case in Cheyne Walk, Chelsea, where we lived. Cecil

King's house was Number 109, appropriately near World's End, a mile further away from the sea than No. 9, where we lived, and occasionally our mail criss-crossed. I remember Cecil chortling just before an election at a letter which arrived at 109 seeking his personal subscription to the Tory Fighting Fund. It was signed by Sir James Waterlow, Bt., the managing director of Amalgamated Press which the *Mirror* had just taken over, and mine arrived a few days later. The *Mirror* at that time was conducting a vociferous anti-Tory campaign.

'Cecil's in the front garden,' said Eileen, 'in the snow. Did you ask him to the party?'

'No. You don't invite Cecil to parties, especially a Christmas party.' There was no knock on the door. He had delivered a letter and was retreating into the blizzard, a gaunt and solitary figure with an undersized trilby perched uneasily on his head and his hands stuffed into the pockets of a shabby raincoat which made Harold Wilson's Gannex look like a mink.

Dec. 24 1955

My dear Hugh,

At this season of goodwill I feel impelled to write and say how happy I have been working with you this past year. Not only have we had great success and much added prestige, but certainly I have thoroughly enjoyed myself in the process. As you know, I am a rather inarticulate character about my feelings, but I should like you to know that I regard you with warm affection and great respect.

Yours ever,
Cecil King

It was a pleasing Christmas present, for I knew that communicating like this was agonising for him, even in a letter to a man with whom he worked in harmony for so long. For thirty years we wrote to each other around the globe, even during the war when I was in the Western Desert, and then in Italy and Greece and Austria, and he was on fire-fighting duty under the bombs on and around the *Mirror* office in London. It was a chore he performed with conspicuous courage. His wartime epistles, I might add, caused me some concern, especially when for a period at Alamein I was a fledgling infantry lieutenant. The letters from London were laden with gloom and prophecies of defeat; had they been steamed open by my commanding officer I would have been suspected at the least of being a fifth columnist though I was merely on the receiving end.

Because of public school surname protocol, which is silly, and Harmsworth hauteur, even sillier, the transition from 'Cudlipp' to 'Hugh' was a tedious process, and from 'King' to 'Cecil' took longer. It was like a *pas de deux* performed on cracking ice even when we had known and not disliked each other for more than a decade. Why did one care or try? The answer is that a friendship with Cecil King, however tenuous, is a rewarding experience. Yet he is a disturbing person to have in your life: when he remarked to me casually one day that he was rereading Machiavelli's *The Prince* I bought a copy and also reread it. Later on I wondered if it was one of Harold Wilson's bedside books.

Cecil sent me another personal letter after Guy Bartholomew had fired me and after King himself had fired Bartholomew as head man. 'Let's get together,' he wrote, 'and make a dent in the history of our times.'

Cecil's first impressions of me were not adjusted because of later events:

'It was really the triumvirate of Bartholomew, Nicholson and Cudlipp who created the new *Mirror*, while I supplied the ballast, the sense of direction and continuity which were very necessary. Cudlipp at that time had little education, no foresight, but a galaxy of journalistic gifts. He was a brilliant reporter and sub-editor; he had acquired a wonderful technique for lay-out from Drawbell [Editor of the *Sunday Chronicle*], and has a gift for timing which is quite beyond price in a daily paper. Over the years he has acquired an excellent education, and has picked up from me a habit of looking ahead which, once acquired, cannot be forgotten. Though there were no journalists in the family, the eldest brother Percy was the first to reach an editorship–that of the (London) *Evening Standard*, and Reg was the last–that of the *News of the World*. But Hugh was the youngest and by far the ablest. In the popular field in my day Hugh Cudlipp has been the outstanding editor anywhere in the world. In the more serious press you have figures like Beuve-Méry of *Le Monde*, with whom it is not possible to make a comparison. But the outstanding popular newspaper editors of my time might be Hearst, Beaverbrook and Springer, and the *Mirror* has certainly been a better and more successful popular newspaper than any put out by the three men I have named. It was, of course, an achievement of partners, but the man who put the words on the page throughout was Hugh Cudlipp.'

Strictly Personal, the book in which this over-generous testimonial was recorded, was a collection of think-pieces which appeared in 1969, a year after our noisy public parting. He showed me the manuscript before publication when we were still working together, and I knew he would change nothing in pique or anger after the palace revolution. There is more grandeur in Cecil King than pettiness or spite.

He deplored sycophantic obituaries. In his view the ultimate hypocrisy was to promote Tammany Hall politicians to statesmen of note, or quacks to distinguished physicians, and run-of-the-mill Sunday sermonisers to eminent divines solely on the evidence that the circulation of their blood had ceased, breathing had stopped, and rigor mortis had set in a few hours later. I write of King with the frankness with which he encouraged me to write of others, warts and all, and am happy that what I write appears in his lifetime.

My first reaction was that I, like others, felt ill at ease in his presence. The usual invitation on the office phone was 'Cecil King. Let us have a chat, shall we?' I didn't know much at the time about Wykehamists or Northcliffe's nephews or the dynasties who owned and ruled Fleet Street. I knew Bartholomew disliked him but I was not as ignorant or egocentric as Bart, or as offensively independent. I suppose the truth is that I recognised Cecil King's integrity and superior knowledge and experience, resented his apparent condescension (in retrospect I realise he was rarely condescending to me), but respected and liked the man. My contribution to the partnership was to introduce him gently to the human race, of which he was largely unaware; my extroversion and vulgar *bonhomie* somehow made him less inhibited. I encouraged him at the outset to say a few words in public by banging a tray and calling upon him, always with a persuasive warning beforehand. The stumbling 'Merry Christmas' speech at an office party was followed by a tonic talk to newspaper wholesalers at dinners on circulation tours in the provinces, usually delivered in hesitant and humourless phraseology. My elocution course for the tongue-tied was so successful that as the years went by he wouldn't refuse an interview to *Old Moore's Almanac*, or a schoolboys' magazine, or to some hirsute yobo from the States working for his Ph.D. on mass communication. And as soon as he was freed of his inarticulacy he appeared at the drop of a hat on every radio and television programme except 'Desert Island Discs' and the weather forecast, talking with ease and wit. He educated me and maybe I taught him how to use his education. I must have done something around the place.

King told me that whenever he read anything in a newspaper or magazine about himself he couldn't recognise the person portrayed; his assessment of himself is therefore admissible evidence, especially of his younger unhappy years. A tenth-rate psychiatrist could identify the symptoms while eating his cornflakes but would probably be wrong in his diagnosis. Mother played a sinister role, but Cecil King was not the most lovable of sons or fathers or mentors.

The patient himself has given us glimpses into the tender years of the man who was to be King and sought to be Kingmaker. No one is spared in his musings, especially himself; he was deep in the rites of self-pity and self-revelation long before the oleaginous Dr Buchman persuaded rich men that public confession was good for their soul, and good for his treasure chest. The curious paradox is that the introvert who sought solitude invites us all to come inside and share the agonising orgy.

The point that matters is that Cecil was the second son of Geraldine Adelaide Hamilton Harmsworth, a sister of Alfred Harmsworth, the first and only Lord Northcliffe. Without this quirk of birth he would probably have been a chemist, engaged in scientific research rather than dispensing cough mixture for Boots or rolling pills for Timothy White. Or he could have been an uncivil servant in the Foreign Office; his father was Sir Lucas White King, a senior civil servant of some repute in India.

The problem in writing about C. H. King, removing the tissues to get to the heart of the matter, dissecting his fears and vanities, assessing him in mortal terms, differentiating between what he thought of himself and what others thought of him, is essentially an exercise in where to begin. I opt for the cot.

There was no similitude between King and Northcliffe, no mental parallel, no identical facet in their characters. Cecil would have liked it otherwise and is a suspect witness in this matter: the subject recurs in his writing and conversation. He was so often told of his resemblance to Northcliffe that he thought there must be a considerable facial resemblance: 'I find it hard to take this in, as

Northcliffe was short and square whereas I am tall and rather droopy.' Certainly in Cecil's life the ghost of Northcliffe was never laid. He diverted business journeys in southern England to visit or revisit, several times in my presence, a house where Northcliffe had lived, knocking at the door and announcing, 'I'm Cecil King. Northcliffe lived here. May I come in?' I shared the embarrassment of the occupants.

He was fascinated to find at the Amalgamated Press offices in Farringdon Street a small mahogany desk at which Alfred Harmsworth had worked, and he stood before it in silence. He entertained me with monologues on the great man's weaknesses and strengths and with stories of his eccentricities and mistresses and illegitimate children. A portrait and a caricature of no artistic merit of Northcliffe were on view in his office. The link was essential to his self-confidence.

There was also no resemblance in the attitudes of Alfred Harmsworth and his nephew Cecil Harmsworth King to their respective mothers, Geraldine and her daughter Geraldine. Matriarchy was formidable in both cases, and the mares were spirited and tempestuous. Northcliffe succumbed in nauseous subservience, but the nephew resented and rebelled in his fashion.

Northcliffe caressed Geraldine the First physically with his arms. He was a mother-hugger, a mother-kisser, constantly in humble attendance, besieging her with gifts, lavishly sentimental or sentimentally lavish, sending his mother doting letters and childish cables which would have brought a blush to the cheeks of Oedipus. The building where the *Daily Mirror* was produced was named in her honour, Geraldine House. At the age of fifty-two, sent by Lloyd George to the United States to head a British mission (and to distract him from public affairs in London), he wrote to her: 'Wouldn't I like to start straight back to my darling Mum, submarines or not!' Mother's responses were less filial: 'Alfred, I cannot make up my mind which of your two principal papers is the more vulgar this morning.'

The nephew's attitude to his mother, Geraldine the Second, and hers to him, moulded and mildewed his character. We have only the son on the psychiatrist's couch, but he is candid enough to speak for both and I find no reason to doubt his veracity. I met the lady once only, and enough was enough. It was explained to me in advance by her son and his first wife, Margot, that Mother didn't approve of the newspaper I edited, the *Sunday Pictorial*. He advised that the prudent course was to listen and say little, preferably nothing, and I wondered why he wished to stage-manage such a potentially combustible confrontation. I inquired if there was any sort of Press photograph, any at all, which could conceivably appeal to her? Yes, I was informed, *horses*. During my brief encounter with Lady King at Cecil's house in Henley-on-Thames on a Sunday morning I steadfastly pointed to a picture of a rampant stallion I had sited on the centre pages of that day's issue, and none of the family heirlooms was shattered.

Cecil was never sure in his own mind whether his mother, Geraldine the Second, was an evil woman determined to destroy him, or a violent and selfish woman quite indifferent to the threat she presented to—his own description—a sensitive, emotional child. Yet he adds: 'Any hostility towards me was, of course, quite subconscious, as she regarded me as her favourite son.'

The sole evidence of this favouritism is that when his elder brother Luke was killed at Ypres in 1915 his mother, 'not a loving woman', was barely sane and was entirely dependent on Cecil's hourly presence. Was he the cherished son? Was the friendly Uncle Cecil Harmsworth, his godfather, 'very flattered' because Cecil was taken as his son? The evidence on this occasion is again Cecil King's, quoting his mother. Was he, as he often said, Northcliffe's chosen nephew? Other members of Cecil's generation in the Harmsworth family, including Esmond Rothermere and Geoffrey Harmsworth, have told me the claim is fanciful. He was not the only nephew to be presented with a golden sovereign when Northcliffe became a peer in 1905.

Mother is depicted as needing his constant company when Luke died, but he describes her ritual of cleaning his ears with a handkerchief and a hairpin—painful, and he thought at the time intended to be so—as a favourite ploy. She was Northcliffe's sister, and one of Alfred's relaxations when he was twenty-fivish was to keep in his bathroom an aquarium divided into two compartments by a sheet of glass, with a pike on one side and goldfish on the other. 'When it amused him,' says one of his biographers, Paul Ferris, 'he would lift the partition to study the results.' Apocryphal? Probably true, for one of his peccadilloes in later life was to appoint two people to virtually the same job and watch them fight to the death, putting his money on the pike. Cecil's godmother, Aunt Violet, another Northcliffe sister, also displayed the cruel streak that afflicted some of the Harmsworths: Cecil once told me that his mother had surprised

263

Vi in the garden as a young girl picking the eyes out of a live sparrow with a knitting needle.

Malevolence is not the normal manifestation of the maternal instinct, but I accept without reservation King's description of his mother and of this particular woman's effect upon this particular son. In all his writings there is but one fleeting romantic reference to her—imaginary, because he was not present. He pictures Geraldine falling in love at first sight with his father Lucas, she twenty-three and he thirty-three; she 'must have looked quite lovely with her excellent features, wonderful skin and dark gold hair'. He writes wistfully of her striking good looks being plainly visible in a photograph taken on her return from India: what is plainly visible in the picture to anybody who was not emotionally involved is that she was the right old bitch her son knew her to be, the woman, he says elsewhere, who devitalised her husband and squashed him flat.

Ten years after she died, when Cecil King himself was fifty-four, he dreamed she was still alive and woke up in a panic. 'I must have hated her. I have no wish to do anything with my hands and it has seemed to me over the years that this was because in early childhood I had wanted to strangle her with them.' I can recall, on reflection, no phrase more stark in a description of family life. Beside it *Oedipus Rex* is a Brian Rix comedy, *King Lear* a rapturous musical, and *Macbeth* a marital romp.

Lord Northcliffe's last wish was to be buried as close to his mother as possible. Cecil, I am sure, would wish to be buried as far away as possible from Geraldine II.

It is arguable to what degree, or whether at all, the character of an adult is prescribed by his early schooling. Cecil King's morose introspection over *alma mater*, another mother he thought neglected him, deserves some brief attention.

The family lived in Ireland, but Cecil was replanted into Rose Hill Prep School at Banstead, near Epsom, across the Irish Sea. He was shy, miserable, homesick and a bed-wetter; his thinness, he thought, may well have had a psychological cause and the family doctor in Ireland said he would die if he were left in that school. At Strangeways, his second school in Stephen's Green, Dublin, he found the boys a tough lot and the masters even tougher; the women teachers, two of them, were better. King was already weighing the human race in the balance and deciding that the standard of teaching seemed higher than at Rose Hill. At all events, with or without encouragement, he read Dickens, Thackeray, Jane Austen, George Eliot, 'even Scott', but not Trollope, and he could read French.

He hated almost every day at Winchester. It was England's oldest public school, founded by William of Wykeham in 1382 in that beautiful city among the chalk hills of Hampshire where England's monarchs were crowned until the end of the thirteenth century.

Cecil at fourteen or fifteen was a non-conformist in a conformist institution. He recalls with pride that he was an exasperating member of the house, disinterested in games, indifferent to Winchester 'notions', yet meticulously obeying the rules and customs including the ones he thought silly: 'A rebel is all very well, but a conformist suspect of despising what he conforms to is another matter.' The boy who was homesick at Rose Hill Prep was 'very' homesick at Winchester, self-conscious of his good looks, aloof, tall and ungainly.

He was desperately dependent on being alone part of every day, but at Winchester the tradition did not cater for such absurdities. He was rarely allowed to be alone; he had to be with another boy of his own seniority and in his own house, not with two other boys, certainly not with younger boys. I would regard the rule as an incitement to homosexuality rather than a deterrent, but the Headmaster's intention was to discourage. Old Boys like Dick Crossman, an energetic heterosexual, told me the ruse often failed. If there was a good deal of homosexuality, Cecil King duly noted that he was certainly unaware of it. The other sprigs called him 'Chaste Minerva', why he did not know: the goddess of wisdom, patroness of the arts and crafts, would not have sought solitude in an establishment where even the lavatories had no doors.

Dick Crossman classified Winchester's end-products into three categories. The third was 'the few–their minds sharpened by six years of mental struggle with the tradition but in lifelong reaction against it. . . . They are the radical throw-outs of the Public School system; and some of them even became "traitors to their class".'

Those were the Wykehamists, the traitors to their class, the radical throw-outs, who I met around the barricades of a changing society, notably Crossman, Hugh Gaitskell and King, and to a lesser degree Douglas Jay. Oswald Mosley, another Wykehamist, I deplored and avoided.

The frustrations of King's early years left permanent scars:

'Going through life has always seemed to me like walking in thick treacle up to your neck. You get along, but how slowly and with how much effort!' The pilgrim has recorded his progress with heart-rending precision, but his lot was less gruelling than the common lot. Self-analysis is the morbid hobby of this unhappy man. He shadows himself with the persistence of the police inspector-psychologist Porfiry Petrovich dogging the footsteps of Raskolnikov in *Crime and Punishment*, but in Cecil's life-story of himself there has been only punishment. His single recorded crime was driving a carriage, to wit a bicycle, on the public pathway near Dublin, for which he was fined sixpence.

He is a keen do-it-yourself psychoanalyst, forever probing the insecurity of his youth, dissecting his phobias and obsessions and depressions, brooding over his current uncertainties and mal-adjustments.

He was convalescing at home in Ireland in May 1915 when his brother Luke, six years older, was killed. The Germans were also responsible for the second sudden death in the family. In the autumn of 1918, when the Irish Sea was bristling with submarines, Mother was stupid enough to send her sons from Ireland to be educated in England but cautious enough to insist they travelled by ferry on different days. It was Cecil's turn to reach Winchester a day late, and merely to avoid a fuss with his housemaster, Bather, he swopped the trips with his brother Bobby, who was two years younger. Bobby's ship sank, torpedoed, and he was never heard of again.

The family misfortunes in World War One, and his front-line witness of the destruction of large areas of London in World War Two, would have justified a hatred of the Germans. Yet a recurrent theme of Cecil's in the 1960s was to urge a closer relationship between the two countries. King wanted our newspapers to help. Should we consult our mutual friend Axel Springer, the German publisher?

'I have no reason to love the Germans myself,' he said to me, 'but we must learn to understand them.' It was a magnanimous attitude for the Germans had also killed two of his cousins, the sons of Uncle Harold Rothermere. King's thinking, unclouded by personal emotion or self-interest, was characteristic of his breadth of view; it is a further example of the disparity between Northcliffe and his nephew. Northcliffe's hatred and fear of the Germans ('Hang the Kaiser') was one of the manifestations of his insanity when he lived in a shed on the roof of his Carlton Gardens mansion. He died with a Colt revolver in one hand, a Bible in the other, stalked by phantom Huns.

A stranger hearing for the first time Cecil King's observations about himself would tap his forehead, but the candour has persisted. Above all, he was determined not to be destroyed by his mother. 'As you are shy and frightened, you have to try to be invisible . . . sounds impossible and of course in any complete sense it is, but it is surprising to what an extent one can become invisible if one sets one's mind to it.' When he grew up he discovered that he could pass someone he knew on a narrow pavement without being seen, and he could get into and out of a party without being seen by anybody he wished to avoid.

The phantasy is ludicrous: in a person of lesser intellect it would be dismissed as an hallucination requiring treatment in Harley Street. A probable explanation is that when he was exercising his gift of delitescence or evanescence the intrusive voyager on the narrow pavement and the snubbed party-goer identified the Invisible Man ten yards away and took avoiding action by invoking their rival armour of anopsia. Two can play at this game, and the man who is six feet four inches tall doesn't necessarily win. Maybe the human race for reasons of its own is avoiding the Invisible Man. I observed him on one occasion invoking his gift of invisibility at a social function at Tower House, headquarters of Newnes Magazines. I was acutely out of favour at the time and he was exercising his talent for getting-into-and-out-of-a-party-without-being-seen-by-anybody-by-whom-he-did-not-wish-to-be-seen. That he did not wish to be seen by me was apparent, but there he was as large as life, not one inch of the six feet four missing or blurred, indeed in an advanced state of materialisation. No ectoplasm.

The Wykehamists, most of them, went on to New College in Oxford. King, relieved to see the end of them and they of him, went to Christ Church, where a Leicester Harmsworth cousin had died as an undergraduate. Christ Church was snobbish and King, unlike his mother, was no snob then or ever; what he got out of Oxford was an interest in history and three years in which he could be alone. 'I kept myself to myself.' The quest for solitude was the Holy Grail. There was no strong friendship with anybody of his own sex at Oxford but he was peeved when his tutors took little interest in him.

His cautious attitude subsides when he talks or writes about his own talents and virtues. He assesses his judgement as very good and over a wide range. He saw himself as the man behind the throne, the *éminence grise*, yet never found anyone to be *éminence grise* to, and so had to take the front seat himself. He supposes that if one knows far more about far more than anyone one meets, one tends to be a formidable and unattractive acquaintance; 'no one much has ever sought my company'. What makes him formidable and unattractive is the suspicion of acquaintances that only one-eighth of the iceberg is visible.

He concedes there are drawbacks about knowing far more, especially in such personal relationships as meeting women who attract him. Unlike other mortals he can see 'the course of the affair and how it would end' and finds the effect inhibiting. Well, yes, it could be: gifted with the same uneasy prescience others might have felt the same. Romeo and Juliet (two dead, one faked suicide, two genuine suicides, one by poison and one by stabbing); Abélard and Heloïse (the seduction was fun but Abélard was emasculated by the lady's testy uncle): Radames and Aïda (buried alive, the pair of 'em); Mark Antony and Cleopatra (he killed himself on hearing the false report of her death and she applied a poison asp to her bosom); Othello and the artless Desdemona (the Moor, insane with jealousy, strangled his bride and ended his life with the request that he be remembered as one who loved not wisely but too well); all would have had second thoughts if Cecil King had been around in Act One to tell them what would be the end of the affair when the curtain came down and the band played *God Save the Queen*.

He rates himself, and who would differ, as a rather complicated character. Yet he is unaware of the inconsistencies so obvious to others. The man who claims an intuitive grasp of the thoughts of millions—I recollect no single instance to substantiate this claim (that was my department)—jovially admits that if he were to edit the sort of newspaper he wants to read himself it would have a circulation of one. The clairvoyant who can see people before they notice him, and knows their mood, confesses to a difficulty in having any idea what the man he is talking to is thinking. The thoughts of millions he can comprehend; about individuals he can only generalise. The 'good judge of people' has no idea whether others like him or dislike him unless they make it obvious—presumably by some overt act such as dropping a banana skin in his path.

Like Narcissus, he exhibits the same neurotic obsession with his image and is gratified by an appreciation of his physical and mental attributes. Unlike Narcissus, he does not love all that he sees in the pool. No flower will be named after him.

Apart from a handful of tormented clues there is little fodder for the psychologist in his attitude to women and sex. Between five and eight he preferred the society of little girls to little boys and was rebuked by his nurse for such heresy at that age. His first flirtation at fifteen, yet another fractured experience, ended in a tragedy with the death of the girl from cancer of the brain. As an adult he still preferred the company of girls and women to that of boys and men, but not necessarily for the same reason as the rest of his sex: he found women 'on the whole easier to understand'. He was aware in his youth of being mildly attractive to homosexuals. There was no reciprocation; he is 'entirely heterosexual, but in some ways very feminine, far more maternal than some women'.

A complicated character? He confessed, even as he was approaching his seventies, that he still frequently and strongly felt the lack of a mother. And at no single stage of his life, except in his marriage to another complicated character, Ruth Railton, is there a discernible trace of adjustment, acceptance or serenity.

On the subject of sex he is forthcoming for an introvert. He finds the teaching of Christianity on sex and marriage ambiguous and materialistic, and that the 'guilty feeling' which permeates Christianity does not extend to other religions. 'Why deplore and decry sex, or teach that it only exists for the procreation of the species?' He regards this as a sour view, and his enthusiasm goes further. 'Sex is not only the source of the most intense physical pleasure available to mankind'—i.e. sex is fun—'but under favourable conditions can be the source of great spiritual experience.'

People were puzzled that the austere Cecil and the gregarious Hugh were ever able to achieve a fruitful relationship. 'You couldn't get two more different people than Hugh and me,' said King.

The loner, to his surprise and initially to his embarrassment, found himself linked with the activities of another member of the human race. Cast in the same enterprise like Swan and Edgar, Bourne and Hollingsworth, Barnum and Bailey, but reserving the right to end the partnership if he so wished. Appearing in the same opera house on the same night like *Cavalleria Rusticana* and *I Pagliacci*, but free to lower the curtain and declare that the comedy was over.

When King was at Rose Hill in Surrey, pining for home and hating home, Cudlipp was unborn; when he was duly delivered in 1913 in Wales, King was a twelve-year-old day pupil in Dublin, complaining that the boys were a rough lot and the masters even rougher. In January 1915 when King began the unhappiest days of his life at England's oldest public school, seeking solitude in a world of doorless water-closets, Cudlipp was wetting his diapers in the family pram in Cardiff. When King was studying constitutional history at Oxford, with currency, finance and banking as his special subjects, wandering around Northcliffe's newspaper empire during the vacations, Cudlipp was at Gladstone Elementary School.

I exploded in confusion and tears at the age of ten, frightened, I guess, when my mother told me I had passed the examination (just) for the Howard Gardens Secondary School in Cardiff. The same year King, aged twenty-two, married Agnes Margaret, whom I knew and liked later, much later, as Margot. She was the daughter of the Reverend Canon G. A. Cooke, Doctor of Divinity, Regius Professor of Hebrew, Oxford, and Canon of Christ Church. King's rooms in Canterbury Quad were 'dark and damp', but from the top of his sitting-room window he enjoyed 'a worm's eye view' of the Deanery garden and presumably, therefore, of Miss Cooke at a sedate Deanery tea-party.

When I became at fourteen a reporter on the impecunious *Penarth News*, King was twenty-six, employed on the Harmsworth news-papers, dabbling in reporting (for which he was, by personality and temperament, utterly unsuited) and advertising. He became a director of the *Daily Mirror* in 1929: I was a reporter in Salford where my friend Walter Greenwood was learning about life as a milk-roundsman's boy, a pawnbroker's clerk, a stable-boy at a millionaire's stable, a packing-case maker, a song-writer, car driver, warehouse-man, with periods on the dole until he wrote his book *Love on the Dole*. Walter died last year in the Isle of Man, the Bahamas of the lesser authors.

When we first met in 1935 King was the Advertisement Director of an ailing newspaper, as determined as anybody else to play his part in putting it right, and recognising that Guy Bartholomew was the only man in the shaky hierarchy who, given a free hand (and advice and pressure whether he liked it or not in the areas where he was notoriously weak), could visualise the new roaring tabloid that was to become the world's most successful newspaper.

For Cecil King some but not all of the frustrations and ignominies were behind him. I came to the view, observing his mode of operation, that unobtrusively he was packing a punch he would deliver without mercy or remorse in middle age at anyone who stood in his way. Beneath the cultivated shy exterior, but not far beneath, there was a repressed pride, an expectation of deference from others, a smooth superiority and an urge for revenge I have not witnessed in other men. He was a social misfit in any stratum of society. He complained that life had always been difficult because 'this is not my world . . . what has made it harder was that until well into middle life no one believed in me, my family near and far were hostile.' He knew that he was fairly unapproachable but he had learned something from Bather, the housemaster he despised at Winchester: the brand of intellectual arrogance was apparent, but without the blend of conventional good manners that Dick Crossman mentioned was also high on the curriculum.

19

The Humble Seeker after Knowledge

Cecil King presided over the world's largest publishing enterprise in a suite on the ninth floor of the *Daily Mirror* building in Holborn Circus, London, EC1. There is an orchestra of rotary presses at subterranean level that gives one the eerie feeling of being in a technological cathedral. It all cost £11,000,000, available in cash without raising a sou from the banks because of the success of the *Mirror*. I used to tell the taxi-drivers it was 'opposite Gamages' until Gamages bled and fled.

Sir Owen Williams, who played the major role in its construction, was sitting at my side at the official opening. 'Owen,' I whispered, 'do you think there's any danger of the whole bloody edifice falling down on our heads as soon as we start up the presses?' He replied: 'Curious thing you mention that. I built Wembley Stadium and had a chilling experience when that was unveiled. I had worked out the stresses and strains for every eventuality among a crowd of soccer fans–elation, dismay, victory, defeat, the lot, based on the crowd being divided in their emotions. Or so I thought. Then I saw the first item on the programme–simple enough, *God Save the King*. The one eventuality I had not figured out was the effect in stress and strain of 80,000 patriotic citizens suddenly standing to attention. I was greatly relieved when they reached

> Happy and Glorious,
> Long to reign over us,
> G–o–d S–a–v–e t–h–e K–i–n–g.

Then I realised I hadn't worked out the stresses and strains for what happens when 80,000 patriotic citizens suddenly sit down.'

Cecil King's number on the private internal office circuit was 00.
The suite was furnished to his taste, and it contained the only coal fire in that smokeless zone. Conversation languished as he revived the embers with a poker and added coal from the scuttle, an eighteenth-century wine cellarette. The ritual seemed to be of significance, like Sir Thomas Beecham sitting down ceremoniously,

slowly and pompously in the orchestral pit at Covent Garden after the national anthem. The other open-fire addicts in London at the time were John Lennon and the Beatles in the Apple headquarters in Savile Row, WI. They favoured a grate set in a Regency green surround. Cecil chose Adam, but all that is left now is the chimney-pot jutting incongruously above the skyline.

The walls were lined with shelves housing his rare books on Africa. Somewhere in the suite was a safe containing his latest private purchases of Georgian silver. An investment or a cultural pursuit, or both? There was more silver in the strong room than on view, and certainly the investment paid off in later years.

Citizen Kane would have envied the spectacular piece of the set, the octagonal desk about eight feet wide consisting of a pair of William Kent mahogany writing tables, placed together, worth £8,000 when purchased in 1959, £12,500 in 1965 and in 1968 estimated by Christie's to bring in £30,000 on a good day later on. The room was graced by two Ghordies Anatolian family prayer mats, one antique Kermanshah carpet with a tree, bird and foliage design in gold and green, some Chippendale mahogany armchairs, a Hepplewhite wing chair with carved scroll legs upholstered in green silk damask, and a Stuart period oak-panelled sideboard. The *objets d'art* included an eighteenth-century bracket clock, and gilded and gold-splashed bronze bowls.

When the relics came under the hammer after Cecil's departure John Gordon described it as 'a picture of mogul-like splendour, tables set together to form a desk fit not merely for a King but for an emperor, this potentate setting'. Anthony Howard wondered how many other company chairmen fancied themselves as some kind of reincarnation of the Turkish sultan Suleiman the Magnificent. (Howard was wrong here: Cecil has stated quite emphatically that his special liking for rice, though not rice pudding, and other more intellectual evidence has made him ponder whether in his last incarnation he was a Chinese—'not an aristocrat but more probably a scavenger'.)

A visitor hijacked to the place would assume at first glance that he was at the country retreat of a cultured aristocrat, a former Viceroy. What the room did not in any way resemble was the power-house of a world-wide publishing empire responsible not only for *Country Life* and *Halsbury's Laws of England* and other impeccable tomes but for popular newspapers and mass magazines regarded by highbrows like King himself as sensational or vulgar. His most priggish description of the *Daily Mirror*, without whose success he would have languished in academic oblivion, ran as follows:

'The success of the *Mirror* was due to the fact that it appealed to people who wanted something simpler than the *Daily Express*. But there comes a time when each paper has reached a lower level than the previous one, until you get down to bedrock. You can't publish a paper which appeals to people less educated and less intellectual than the *Daily Mirror*.'

He entertained the BBC's television viewers with this estimate of his principal product though he despised such snobbishness from his relatives, especially his mother.

'Like all the Harmsworths,' he wrote, 'she deplored my connection with the *Mirror*. Popular newspapers were the source of their wealth, their power and their titles, but they did not want to be reminded of this any more than they wished to be reminded of Brondesbury.' A house called *Fairlight*, in Salisbury Road, Brondesbury was the place Cecil's mother left to be married, and it was in the same meek district that Northcliffe met and wooed his wife Molly. Yet Brondesbury did not exist in the family archives and was taboo in conversation.

Since his first appearance before the public as a Grain of Mustard Seed, a one-word part which he muffed in a school play in the parish hall at Dundrum, near Dublin, he regarded himself as misunderstood. 'Fleet Street,' he said, 'is a jungle. I shall survive. A man of my ability will keep his head above water.' Quizzed about his future after the take-over of Odhams, a rival publishing group, he pointed out that if you were a boa constrictor and had just swallowed an elephant you wouldn't be worried about your next meal. He is not the prototype of Santa Claus or the Good Samaritan. When he considered that ruthlessness was the only means to achieve the desirable end, he was ruthless.

Newsweek called him 'a tall, massive man, with cool, accusative eyes, a beaky nose, a heavy jaw, a bull neck, and a charming boyish smile. He is a muscular Sidney Greenstreet, a magnanimous John D. Rockefeller, an intellectual Captain Bligh.' This is the sort of word-portrait in which he does not discern much resemblance: not, at any rate, to himself as he sees himself and hopes that posterity will see him.

I worked for and with him with much excitement and anxiety for more years than most and was regarded by others as the leading authority, unhanged, on the subject. Whether I knew much more than anybody else is dubious. Even when in disarming asides he was helping me with my inquiries he camouflaged the clues and would strive to become at any rate mentally invisible. The exception was an occasion in 1966 when a book called *Fleet Street* was published to raise funds for the restoration of the London Press Club, which he never visited. I was shown the foreword written by Prince Philip, with its provocative thoughts:

'I am afraid that I have a reputation for living in what might be described as a state of armed neutrality with the Press; a state which is sometimes supposed to descend into open warfare. Certain apocryphal stories circulate and these have gained the authority and acceptance of holy writ. In consequence, people tend to think that I never have a good word to say for the papers or the Press as an institution. If this had really been the case, I would never have become a member of the Press Club. Exasperating as I sometimes find the newspapers . . .'

He cooled off after this curtain-raiser and acknowledged that genuine democracy could only flourish if it was exposed to the scrutiny of a free and uncensored Press, etc. By comparison the material for the book contributed by somebody else about C. H. King was turgid, a sort of *Who's Who* entry.

'This won't do,' I said to Cecil. 'I will write a 3,000-word profile of you instead. Let's get nearer the truth this time. You are always telling me you can't recognise yourself in anything written about you. Will you write a page or two about yourself? In other words, explain yourself to me?'

'Very well,' he said, 'I'll try. If you don't like it you can throw it in the wastepaper basket.'

The exercise produced the following gem. This is the first time Cecil King's Guide to Cecil King has been published in sequence and in full, naked and unadorned, comma-perfect, without explanatory notes. If only Marshal Ney had goaded Napoleon to speak or write so frankly about himself. The two hundred and sixty words were simply headed 'For Press Club Book':

'People expect me to be a business tycoon keen to enrich myself or to impress other people. But I am essentially a shy introvert: not good at human relations, hence better in a large organisation than a small one. I am not interested in money but am interested in politics and using my publications to exert influence in directions that seem to me important. This influence has never been used for personal ends and often others have been allowed to take the credit that really belongs to our publications. My success is due to the fact that I have good intuitive judgement over a wide area of people, finance, editorial quality for instance—and that I am a good organiser very ready to delegate and anxious to bring on young men of promise. I have never been a conformist and run into trouble because I tend to see things with a fresh eye regardless of the accepted point of view. I think the essential qualities of a publisher are courage and integrity and I feel I have developed a fair measure of both.

'I am *Irish*. This is overlooked because I have no Irish accent and am not a Catholic. But my kind of conversation and sense of humour are essentially Irish and I am far more at home in Dublin than anywhere else.

'Finally I have a very large fund of general knowledge—covering more ground than anyone I have ever met. So my good judgement is based on a solid foundation of knowledge quite unusually wide in its way.'

I still possess this intriguing document, occupying the back and front of a foolscap sheet in his own scrawling handwriting. It is artless and arrogant. Not the blustering arrogance of the short but the insidious arrogance of the tall. It has the innocence of a schoolboy's essay on 'How I enjoyed my holidays', honest, frank and truthful. It is also the prospectus of a take-over bid for the world. It was written in 1966, and behind the scenes at private political lunches over the next few years and eventually in public, the shy introvert was expressing the same thoughts more stridently. 'Exerting influence' developed into exercising power.

He read my profile of him, which contained a number of outspoken and irreverent remarks, with good humour until he came to the last two paragraphs:

'A Fleet Street acquaintance of King's expressed to me his puzzlement at hearing him say on television that he believed in the Almighty: this did not seem consistent with his intellectual, logical and scientific approach to life's problems.

'"Don't you see," I explained, "if Cecil did not believe in the Almighty he would be admitting that the chairmanship of IPC is a dead-end job."'

King didn't like it, didn't see the point. I invoked his Irish sense of humour, but with no success. I tried to explain the joke, always an unhappy exercise. 'But you don't understand,' he said, 'I *do* believe in the Almighty.'

He was not exposed to public scrutiny as many hours of the day as most men. He left his office at 5.30 p.m. and retired to bed at 9.30 p.m. in *The Pavilion*, the riverside house at Hampton Court to which he moved from Chelsea.

King didn't claim to run, singlehanded, the 12 United Kingdom newspapers, 11 overseas newspapers, 75 consumer periodicals, 132 trade, technical and specialised journals, 20 printeries, and extensive book-publishing companies which at that time constituted the International Publishing Corporation Ltd.; indeed he publicly admitted he was not familiar with every item in each issue of *Cage and Aviary Birds*. Nor could he supervise alone the interests in newsprint, television, relay wireless, exhibitions, books and news-agents' shops. He was the head man, no doubt about that, and he prided himself on picking able directors to run the King Empire. He usually left them alone to get on with the job assigned. He felt that his IPC board could rival or surpass man for man any comparable operation in the world, and staked the claim that he could produce from his team a Cabinet better than Harold Wilson's or Ted Heath's: when I prodded him at a private board dinner to allot the Cabinet portfolios he declined. This was no laughing matter.

He personally owned a tiny proportion of the shares in the companies he dominated, and the Nephew of Northcliffe status had little to do with the chair he filled with massive ability for many years. He was unanimously appointed Chairman of the Daily Mirror and Sunday Pictorial companies in succession to Harry Guy Bartholomew in 1951, and Chairman of IPC and the Reed Paper Group in 1963. With the same unanimity in 1968 he was asked, sadly, to resign. And refused.

King was not interested in money, but he did not subsist on the breadline; nor could the houses where he lived at various times be rated as pull-ups for carmen, or as lean and mean garrets. The Georgian mansion on the Thameside at Henley: the wartime apartment in the legal quarters of New Square, Lincoln's Inn, conveniently near the office; the five-storey home in Cheyne Walk,

Chelsea, where a silk rug on which a Persian emperor's throne once stood served as his bedside mat; *The Pavilion* at Hampton Court, designed by Christopher Wren—they had grandeur or history or individuality, or all three. His jumbo Rolls Royce was hardly a second-hand jalopy. Yet nobody who had seen him at work at close quarters during the growth of the company would doubt that he could have been a millionaire times over if the whim had been there.

Money meant nothing or little to him (apart from collecting silver and later coins, another promising investment) because his uncles, God bless them, were rolling in the stuff and almost without exception were unhappy to a degree of misery. King did not wish to emulate the first Lord Rothermere who, if he cared to spare the time, could have counted out £25,000,000 of his own in the 1920s. Cecil told me of a visit to pay his respects to Uncle Harold during the Wall Street slump when his lordship, after answering a transatlantic phone call, casually poured himself a drink and mentioned that he had just lost five million pounds. Cecil had no desire to leave behind him wealthy sons. Michael, Francis and Colin all laboured somewhere in their father's vineyard—one on the *Mirror*, one in West Africa and then in magazines, the youngest in newsprint—but none was favoured beyond his abilities and zeal. I felt they would have prospered sooner elsewhere, beyond the range of Father's vigilance.

He is as candid about his own qualities and problems as about other people's. When he says that he is not good at human relations he and others can prove it. Personal friendships and physical proximity embarass him; sycophants and yes-men were, until the end of the story, non-starters at the court.

The world outside the office caught some curious glimpses of Cecil Harmsworth King and I became accustomed to the question 'What is he really like?'

If a social function bored him he left before or between the speeches; I saw him at a Newspaper Press Fund dinner dozing peacefully through the speech of another newspaper chairman until awakened by the sound of polite applause in which he joined.

At the Odhams dinner to celebrate Hannen Swaffer's eightieth birthday some years before Odhams and the *Mirror* merged, Sir Beverley Baxter delivered himself of a highly polished benediction extolling Swaff's virtues one by one. His phrases were rotund, his voice melodious, but King left his seat at the top table before

Swaff replied, and whispered to me as he passed: 'Home, sweet bloody home.'

He is outspoken, often regally so, specialising in distilled condescension. At a reception at the Hurlingham Club for the Soviet trade fair King spotted Sheila Black, then Women's editor of the *Financial Times*. In the presence of her Editor, Gordon Newton, he expressed views about Mr Newton's newspaper, and when she telephoned him the following morning to express her surprise at his ribaldry, King said, 'Was I rude? Good heavens, isn't that what social functions are for?' At an election-night dinner King was sitting next to the wife of a former British colonial governor, and the lady insisted on entertaining the company by questioning the integrity of the head men of the newspaper industry. King asked mildly whether she thought her strictures could be applied, for instance, to Laurence Scott, chairman of the *Guardian*, and the climax of the script was:

The Lady: All newspaper proprietors are crooks.
King: All governors' wives are tarts.

At an Academy dinner a retired general sitting opposite stood up, purple with anger, and said, 'Sir, you are insulting my medals.' King had obliged another guest with a description of what the medals stood for: more for defence, deference and devotion than for offence.

At the same function there was an incident involving Christopher Mayhew, a Member of Parliament later of ministerial rank, who was sitting on one side of King. Cecil told me next morning that there had been a verbal blow-up about commercial television; he thought there might be some reverberations from the Labour Party or the Commons (threatening an MP?) and wanted me to know the facts in advance. During the controversy over King's diaries in which–to the dismay of his former colleagues and the horror of his lunch-time guests–he offered the public a cornucopia of confidence, Mayhew recalled the confrontation in a letter to *The Times* in 1972:

Sir,
Those who have been traduced by Mr Cecil King should not issue disclaimers. Instead, I feel, we should record for posterity our own impressions of Mr King, and the conversations we have had with him which do not appear in his book.
My first meeting with Mr King was at a Royal Academy

banquet in the late Fifties. We were seated next to each other, and Mr King opened the conversation, as the soup was being served, by asking me how my campaign against commercial television was going. I told him. He then said that if, which he doubted, my views ever carried weight with my party leaders, it would be necessary to start a 'Mayhew must go' campaign in the *Mirror*. I replied that he could say what he liked about me in his bloody papers.

From then on, we sat in silence, while the fish, meat, sweet and savoury course were served; and I have never spoken to Mr King again—wisely, as I now think. He made a most unfavourable impression on me, an arrogant and stupid man, I thought, quite unfit for power in a civilised society.

In Toronto in 1965 Cecil cut Lord Thomson down to size, or the size he wished and hoped he was; what more suitable place than Roy's own backyard in Canada? 'Thomson,' said King, knowing that the local newspapers not owned by Thomson would make a meal of it, 'has made a minus contribution to Britain. The only contribution is to his own bank balance. Why did he get a title? Oh, no one is known to have gone knocking on the door of No. 10 Downing Street more often.' King wished to make it clear that he had no harsh feelings towards Roy Thomson, 'in fact I rather like him.' No one who saw Thomson posing for a picture arm-in-arm with King in London a few weeks later would have thought otherwise, except Roy.

King has his own explanation of this brand of off-the-cuff interview. 'I start my studies at rock bottom. If I meet His Grace the Archbishop of Canterbury I don't automatically assume he is the most erudite and pious churchman in England.'

He did not expect this sort of frankness to make friends, and it didn't, but he hoped it would influence people. Was the Newspaper Proprietors' Association influenced when King described it to the Royal Press Commission in 1961 as 'a helpless jellyfish washed up on a dry shore. Rather than standing upright they would prefer to lie on the floor and invite people to come and kick them.' In the same year he was appointed Chairman of that body, curator of the jellyfish. When the Press Council was formed in the 1950s as a self-disciplinary committee in which the Press was prisoner, prosecutor and judge, King described it as an unacceptable compromise, 'doomed to futility'. He believed the Press Council should have an independent chairman of legal standing recognised as such by Parliament and people.

In his judgement of people and events the shy introvert becomes the brash extrovert.

When he reviewed a biography of William Randolph Hearst, he wrote: 'In this interesting, detailed and most readable book, Hearst emerges as the most odious character of all time.' Addressing the National Press Club in Washington, he said: 'I'm at the top of the heap or the end of the road, so I don't see why I should waste your time and mine with clichés.' King ruminated on the naïvety of the New World. 'It is astonishing to a visitor that this country, far ahead of the rest of the world in technology and certainly in the front row of scientific research, should be so backward politically. You are still in the horse and buggy stage, and that is dangerous not only to you but to all of us,' he told them. 'The Russians are ignorant, clumsy and bloody-minded, but contemporary.' Wasn't the Kennedy Administration giving America the contemporary look King said it lacked? 'Certainly not,' he replied. 'He is trying to get you from about 1885 up to about 1895 and in about four years he'll have got you into the twentieth century.'

It was vintage Ceciliana. The US pressmen, with unusual politeness, presented their guest with the National Press Club's customary certificate of appreciation. 'King of Kings', said *Time* in a headline. *Newsweek* settled for 'King of England'.

The monarch told me that he had enjoyed or endured the best education money could buy, a Wykehamist ('Manners Makyth Man') who moved on to Christ Church, Oxford, to read modern history. But he had no hidebound views about a university background for the newspaperman; a better academic education, he believed, would have spoiled Northcliffe for journalism. He thought that if I had gone to Oxford or Cambridge I would have emerged as an advocate, 'and there are plenty of those'.

The developing arrogance led him to say to Jocelyn Stevens, 'People tend to come round a corner and find me sitting there.' The confidence was generated in a lifetime of travel and evenings of reading. He avoided being too close to the job or to the people who did it. He was a critic, not an activist, the strategist not the tactician.

Business meetings with King in his office ended when he glanced at the eighteenth-century bracket clock above the Adam fireplace surround, and the nearest he wished to get to any human being was the other side of the William Kent desks. Yet there was scarcely a newspaper, a magazine, a trade and technical publication company, a printery, a newsprint mill, a television studio, a paint factory or a wallpaper operation in the world-wide group which did not catch a glimpse of him at least once a year. His commercial diligence, until his mind was dominated by the affairs of state, was prodigious.

The business expanded so swiftly under his zest for hugeness that when I published *At Your Peril* I was able to write the chapter on Northcliffe's early days in the periodical world in his old room at Fleetway House, Farringdon Street, the chapter on Lord South-wood, the tender tycoon, in his own office at Odhams Press, and the preface in a temperature of 85 degrees at the Colony Club, Barbados, where we had acquired the *Barbados Advocate*.

It was the *Daily Mirror* of which Cecil was proudest, and to which he was closest in spite of his low view of the clientele. He regarded it as 'easily the most powerful paper in this country'. His early ambition, come what may, was to be the *Mirror*'s Chairman, and he said to me–years before Bartholomew's sudden exit through the stage trapdoor–'I am a very patient man.' With reluctance he passed the title on to me when he became head of I P C; a gesture, I recognised, of some warmth. Earlier in this book I have written of Cecil's special contribution to the *Daily Mirror*.

To a *Star* reporter in Toronto he said: 'I'm just a humble seeker after knowledge.' Elsewhere the seeker said: 'I see nothing wrong with power as long as I am the fellow who has it.'

The sensible company rule, set by King himself, was that all directors would retire at sixty-five; he was remembering the dotage of Bartholomew and the elderly vanities of too many of the politicians, notably Churchill. It was a concept I applauded and fulfilled myself five years in advance of sixty-five, for good measure.

In 1964, shortly after the thirteen years of Tory government ended in Harold Wilson's victory at the election, Cecil quietly informed his colleagues at a board meeting–without consultation with a soul in advance–that he would continue as I P C Chairman until seventy. Nobody made a comment because there was, come to think of it, nothing to say: at any rate nobody made any comment during the meeting. Yet the announcement was more significant than anyone realised at the time.

He had sensed an exciting fresh dawn in the twilight of his career, a limitless opportunity for influence and more than influence. By 1967 and 1968, but no longer than 1968 (for reasons then beyond his control), the humility of the seeker after knowledge was engulfed by the searing personal ambition of the man at the top of the heap who saw nothing wrong with power so long as he was the fellow who had it.

The ugly face of Cecil King's personality had been apparent to me in his dealings with politicians over the years, with men and women who had been elected to exercise power. He now directed his attention to the new Prime Minister and Cabinet Ministers of the first Labour administration for more than a decade. It was a disturbing resurgence of the times when Northcliffe was nearing the peak of his influence and, in Churchill's words, 'the sun of newspaper power began to glow with unprecedented heat'.

King was aware of his own unattractiveness, but it didn't bother him enough to offer much in compensation. His contempt for all, or almost all, in high office can only be diagnosed as chronic self-exaltation. The frequent public charge of megalomania merely produced the private comment to me, 'I won't waste much sleep over that. Why should I?'

He devoted a part of each day to recording on paper his views on other men caught up in the events of our time, and gossip about them. It was a kind of daily doomsday of his own, preserved in a series of diaries 'written out of interest and with no thought of publication' until, whimsically or wantonly, most people thought outrageously, he decided in a final gesture of scorn to publish the lot and be damned.

Public personalities were felled while still alive like rotten oak trees. Aspiring politicians were weighed in the balance over a single lunch or several, found wanting, and trampled underfoot like field mice. Brave and sincere men, though not great or posturing as great, were summarily dismissed as charlatans or fools. It is hard to recollect over a span of thirty-three years of conversation or correspondence with Cecil King more than half a dozen public figures who would have been wise to ask him for a testimonial. I take my share of the blame, for he mentions that it was an interview between Hugh Cudlipp and Leslie Hore-Belisha on the Minister's dismissal from the War Office in 1940 that gave him the nudge to start writing his own diary during the war.

Cecil's diaries specialise in the obnoxious practice of recording and later publishing remarks made by others in confidence about their superiors, colleagues or friends who were absent and therefore had no opportunity of reply or refutation. I have always found it hard to explain this deplorable blemish in a man of Cecil King's character. Harder still to understand his exultation at the shock he provoked in those who had respected him. Perhaps the explanation was given by Bather, his housemaster at Winchester, whose final report on the non-conformist read: 'There is still much of the child about him.' Writing in his sixties about his schooldays King remarks that he took the criticism, meant as a severe condemnation, as something of a compliment. Even in his seventies he is still stamping in puddles, raiding birds' nests, ringing doorbells, hitting over piles of toy bricks, riding his bicycle on the pavement, chasing cats and dogs and breaking windows.

His most mischievous book covers the life and death of Harold Wilson's Labour administration from 1964 to 1970. Its characteristic is that, with the notable exception of the diarist himself and of half a dozen other lesser deities, the Government and Opposition and men in the corridors of power in Whitehall and in diplomacy are dismissed as merely futile.

There is some consolation for the dim, dull, silly, immature, vain, weak, useless, unstable, insignificant, superficial, woolly-minded, colourless, dreary and disastrous lightweights and failures who in King's estimation infested Westminster in the second half of the 1960s. They had their counterparts during the Second World War, laid naked and pilloried by the same remorseless executioner. King's disdain for his fellow men embraces seven decades and persisted through peace and war, boom and bust, office and opposition. He used the same yardsticks of opprobrium or approbation for the lot. He once explained what he meant by his constant use of the dull-as-dishwater word 'nice'; he meant somebody who put more into life than he took out.

Cecil King's wartime judgements were not confined, at any rate, to the luncheon table. His first sight of Herbert Morrison was standing beside him in a public lavatory–not, King concedes, the best setting: none the less he was unimpressed by the urinating wartime Home Secretary. It was like removing Venus from her plinth in the Louvre and assessing her pulchritude astride a bidet. Later on, in a different place and closer to (how closer can you get?), King thought Morrison was a much more convincing personality. Our 'Erb was the only man I recollect who was vouchsafed a second hearing.

There are too many corpses to count. Was Cecil Harmsworth
King alone the hope of mankind and civilisation? Well, yes, though
there were a few promising aspirants in the wartime scene shrewd
enough not to stay too long in the range of his eye lest they, too, be
found wanting. One spotted a familiar haggard face or two among the
walking wounded–Walter Monckton, Maynard Keynes, Basil
Liddell Hart, Stafford Cripps, Emanuel Shinwell, Professor Patrick
Blackett, Beveridge. Barbara Ward–ah, Barbara Ward: 'A most
charming and admirable person, assistant editor of *The Economist*
and a leading Catholic propagandist. She is about thirty (February
17 1945), very feminine, very nice-looking and exceedingly intelligent.' Of no person of either sex did I hear Cecil consistently
speak more warmly and approvingly through the years than of this
estimable lady. Charm, beauty and intelligence–thrice-blessed
Barbara radiantly blooming in a garden of obnoxious weeds.

God knows how we won the war, even with the timely aid of
the USSR and the United States. King had unbounded faith in
himself, but no hope and little charity towards others; he believed
in the Almighty, but his personal philosophy was the quintessence of
gloom and foreboding.

One of the enigmas I failed to unravel was Cecil King's loathing
for Lord Beaverbrook. He could scarcely dismiss the volatile
Canadian as weak or insignificant, colourless or immature. For him
he reserved a special award–*evil*.

There was no relationship between them, and King as Chairman
of IPC certainly had no cause to be envious of the proprietor of the
Daily Express and the founder of the *Sunday Express*. They met a
dozen or so times at semi-official functions in the presence of others
but only once alone in Beaverbrook's apartment at Arlington
House. King's attitude puzzled his colleagues, some of whom had
worked for Beaverbrook, as much as it infuriated Beaverbrook's
friends and family. There was certainly no incident in which Cecil
was upstaged, snubbed or double-crossed by the Beaver.

The first meeting was at a dinner in London given by Joe Kennedy,
the hostile US Ambassador in 1938, when, amiably enough, Beaver
shook Cecil's hand and said, 'Well, young man, you have made your
mark in Fleet Street.' He was surprised but evidently gratified,
recalling the remark even thirty years later: it was scarcely insulting
or condescending.

King's vendetta was conducted in private conversation in the post-war years. The name of Beaverbrook could not be mentioned without a display of repugnance. It was the cause of the anger Max Aitken, the Beaver's son and heir, felt towards King, and was the spur of the many snide remarks about him in John Gordon's column in the *Sunday Express*.

Max and I had understood each other for many years, and I could scarcely hold any animosity towards Beaverbrook, who had rescued me from the breadline within an hour of my theatrical dismissal as Editor of the *Sunday Pictorial* by Bartholomew. The tender spot was Max's ferocious loyalty to the memory of his father. When Cecil decided sometime in 1966 or 1967 that the newspaper industry would benefit from a closer collaboration between the *Mirror* and the *Express*, rival newspapers, in tackling the commercial and union problems, the notion was that I should have a preliminary talk with Max. 'How,' he said, 'can I work with a man who calls my father evil?' But we agreed to hammer out that problem first before we faced the problems of the industry. Max said he would come to a meeting with King if I were present.

Max put his cards on the table, and King listened with his usual patience and courtesy; it seemed possible, at last, that the axe would be buried. Then King, after due consideration, replied: 'There is no malice in what I say or think. Beaverbrook was an evil man.' It was clear that Fleet Street's problems, if they ever were to be solved (and they weren't), would have to be solved without any collaboration between the *Express* and the *Mirror*.

Lord Weidenfeld published King's first book in 1969, less than a year after he departed from the newspaper industry. An uncorrected proof copy of *Strictly Personal* was available to any newspaper which cared to inquire a month or so before it reached the bookstalls and one of these copies, not surprisingly, reached Max Aitken. In a chapter on Fleet Street, King related his first brief encounter with Beaverbrook ('Well, young man, you have made your mark in Fleet Street') and then proceeded to denounce him as positively, actively evil, moreover as a person who enjoyed destroying young men.

Max wrote to him vehemently in February 1969, and later showed me the letter:

'I have seen the references to my father in your Autobiography.
'It would be easy to say that I do not believe that they will damage the reputation of my father, but I think this would be

feeble and facile. Few people alive today knew my father intimately and his reputation must depend on public report.

'Your description of him therefore will be accepted by a large
number of people who do not know better. It is, if I may use
simple words, wickedly false. He was not an evil man and he did
not destroy young men. He was a man who held strong views of
his own and went about his business in his own inimitable way.
Many people disliked him because he was successful and because
he would not tolerate inefficiency, woolly-mindedness and
humbug, the three commodities which procure easy popularity.

'We are becoming increasingly conscious–and here Herr
Hochhuth has rendered a public service–that there is some need
to protect the reputation of recently dead people who cannot
protect themselves from malice and falsehood and people who
inflate their own reputations by a professed acquaintance with
the great. I do not believe your knowledge of my father entitled
you for one moment to make any kind of assessment, let alone a
just one. I do not believe that you could list any evil acts that he
performed. I am certain you could not list the young men he is
supposed to have destroyed since there were not any. I could
list–and it would be a long document–the young men he has
assisted unobtrusively and undemonstratively throughout the
years. It is significant that what you are prepared to say now you
would never have dared to say in my father's lifetime.

'I am inviting you to withdraw these observations. I do not
wish to quarrel with you. We have had a long and friendly
association but if you publish these statements I shall be compelled
to take every possible step to vindicate my father's reputation,
and you may be surprised to find how many other people feel
as I do.'

King capitulated, a gesture I have not known him make before
or since. The passages about Lord Beaverbrook did not appear in
the published version of King's first book. His second book was
published one year later, *With Malice Toward None: a War Diary*.
Had he forgotten the deletion in the earlier book? Or was there
malice towards some? The capitulation was short-lived.

In his war diary he quotes a private reference of Churchill's in
1940 to Beaver's 'demoniac energy'. When Beaverbrook as a
Cabinet Minister sent for him the same year the praise is glowing;
the Minister of Aircraft Production is described as a man of real

ability, head and shoulders above most of the governmental figures he had met, past his best but still full of energy and drive. In 1941 he is still extolling Beaverbrook as one of the two or three of Britain's wartime leaders who seemed to have some guts. In 1942 King is telling Stafford Cripps that the main danger with Beaverbrook was that he was fundamentally mischievous. Fair enough and true enough, but then the dirk comes out of the scabbard. 'Cripps quite agreed, and said that the way he turned his bright young men into drunkards was done out of sheer sadism. Beaverbrook certainly had an intentionally demoralising effect on his young men and young women.'

Any notion that the resurrection of this charge was due to inadvertence is dispelled by what follows. Once removed from the scabbard, the dirk is plunged between the shoulder-blades. A year after deleting the savage reference to Beaverbrook from the published version of his first book, King included it in the Afterword he wrote in June 1970 to his war diary. The man is ignominiously exhumed and then reburied as the most unattractive member of the wartime Government, a failure as a Minister, a backstairs intriguer whose personality and money gave him malevolent influence through and over such diverse Prime Ministers as Bonar Law and Churchill. The indictment is as ferocious and all-embracing as the passage he earlier expunged. The dirk is twisted, as it is designed as a weapon to be twisted, in King's definitive denunciation which occupies one sentence:

> 'Looking back over my lifetime I suppose the most dominant figures in the public life of the country were Joe Chamberlain and Max Beaverbrook, both men whose influence has been evil.'

It was an uncharitable view. Beaverbrook was a success in the early stages of his wartime Ministry; arguably, he failed as a Minister as time went on, and unarguably ended up as a thorough nuisance to most of his Cabinet colleagues. Beaverbrook's attempts at political influence through his newspapers were a failure. The Empire Crusade was economic trash. His debilitating campaign 'There Will Be No War' collapsed with World War Two, his Keep-Out-of-Europe capers were a dangerous joke at the expense of history. His vendettas against Mountbatten and John Ellerman and other men and causes were despicable. Like Northcliffe he liked playing pikes-and-goldfish and like Cecil he was ruthless, but he had the balancing virtues of generosity, humour, a zest for life, friendship,

Some of the front pages that kept the
Daily Mirror itself in the news.

THE LIGHTER SIDE OF JOURNALISM

Lee Howard, Editor of the *Daily Mirror* for ten years, with
friend. The Editor is on the right.

Myself, cartoonist Vicky and Michael Foot, at a party to
celebrate Vicky's exclusion from *El Vino*, the famous Fleet
Street wine bar. He was 'banned' for wearing, without formal
permission, the manager's bowler hat.

and no one would doubt his patriotism. I would not, if I were Madame Tussaud, place him in the same evil chamber as Richard the Third, Rasputin and Jack the Ripper.

What is impossible to substantiate is King's repeated assertion that Max Beaverbrook enjoyed destroying young men. Who were they and where are their early graves? The testimony of the austere Stafford Cripps and the unsociable Cecil King, who can scarcely have taken part in these drunken orgies themselves or even observed them, is unimpressive. Cripps's further allegation, assuming that Cecil was quoting what he heard rather than what he wanted to hear, that Beaverbrook turned his bright young men into drunkards *out of sheer sadism* has none of the supporting evidence that Cripps himself would have required as a lawyer to make the prosecuting case stand up in court.

I knew most of the eaglets in or around the Beaverbrook aviary when they had grown into downy birds, a generation or half in front of me. Aneurin Bevan was one of them, a close friend of Beaverbrook for many years; 'occasionally exchanging political advice offered and accepted with mutual caution, agreed politically about nothing—except the right of free speech.' The words are Michael Foot's, Bevan's biographer and disciple. Bevan 'dined with Beelzebub in person; many grave eyebrows were raised and many whisperers were ready to mock him as a hypocrite.' Can it seriously be suggested that Beaverbrook corrupted Bevan? Michael Foot was also in the Beaverbrook *ménage*, editing his London *Evening Standard* and living for some years in a cottage on the boss's estate near Leatherhead. Who can establish that Michael was seduced from his political course, or socially suborned, or morally enfeebled, or intellectually impoverished, or reduced to delirium tremens? When Peter Howard joined Beaverbrook as a political writer he was an agnostic; when he left he was a Christian activist, a pillar of the Moral Rearmament movement. My brother Percy, a Beaverbrook Editor for years, and Arthur Christiansen, the best Editor the *Daily Express* ever had, thrived on the mental conflict. Frank Owen was looking hale and hearty on his seventieth birthday last year. George Malcolm Thomson, who spent the best years of his life as a leader writer trying to make sense out of Beaverbrook's political fantasies, is the most mentally agile member of the Garrick Club at over seventy-five, still writing brilliant books. And who would describe Edward Pickering, the cool individualist from the North Riding of Yorkshire who worked for Beaverbrook for thirteen years in top-echelon posts as a crushed lush or a zombie reduced to garrulous subnormality to excite the sadistic pleasure of a millionaire? I did not sense the imminent danger of decay during the two years I worked for Beaverbrook. Who were the young men who were ruined and exploited beyond their own willingness? Lord Castlerosse?

The accusation is spurious. The weak who fell by the wayside fell because they were weak and not because they were weakened: you can lead a thirsty man to a bottle of Bollinger but you can't make him drink. Yet Cecil could not be dislodged from his calumny.

When Reg Payne, as Editor of the *Sunday Pictorial*, was obliged one Saturday morning when I was overseas to run the gauntlet of an hour's exchange with Cecil on national and world affairs–a less congenial exercise for him than me–he diverted the conversation to easier pastures.

'What do you think, sir,' he asked, 'of Lord Beaverbrook? As you know, I worked for him for several years.'

And King replied: 'If I saw him approaching my house I would set my dog on him.'

20

The Duel

Harold Wilson barely had time to hang up his Gannex in Downing Street on October 16 1964, say good morning to Marcia and light up his briar before Cecil King began to monitor his shortcomings as Prime Minister. The scrutiny was relentless, and I doubt whether any other politician has endured the like: the honeymoon was the briefest in the history of political compatibility.

On October 5 1965 King was telling a senior civil servant that he thought Wilson rather rashly assumed the support of the *Mirror*. 'He thinks your readership prevents you doing otherwise,' said the scs, but King confided to his diary that the Prime Minister was in for some rude shocks, adding a menacing exclamation mark. When he saw Wilson on February 17 1966 he expressed a low opinion of many of his Ministers and the need for introducing new blood. By March 20 1966 he was stating his aim to break loose from any close connection with the Labour Party because he thought that both on balance of payments and on Rhodesia Mr Wilson was going to run into horrible trouble before the end of the year.

It was full frontal political nudity with Wilson as the reluctant stripteaser and Cecil King, in a soft and cultured voice, chanting, 'Get 'em orf.' By June 26 1966 King could not see Wilson surviving his five years in office and was astonished how much the prestige of the PM had dropped in the short time since the March election the same year. Vanished so soon were the memories of the reckless wooing of 1964 when Cecil's view of Harold the Thruster was of a new young leader who had put on such a wonderful performance in Opposition. In that election he had moved around London in his Rolls with a red flag on the bonnet saying 'Vote Labour'. The spectacle of a Labourite owning this exquisite machine would have puzzled the late Mr Rolls; Herr Karl Marx, living in retirement at Highgate Cemetery, must have turned in his grave at the thought of the proletariat putting on such airs. The boys in the backroom at the *Mirror* regarded the flamboyance with amusement: they did not know that Cecil occasionally appeared at the theatre or a social affair in a red-lined cloak, as Northcliffe did.

As early as June 25 1966, three months after Labour's second election victory, Cecil was canvassing me to think in terms of an all-out attack on Wilson in the newspaper. Soon, or when? Of course, the timing must be right. The diary records that Cudlipp thought it might be an idea if he wrote Wilson a long letter, not in any hope that it would bring about a change of heart but to have his (King's) position on record. My object was to delay the attack as long as possible, in Cecil's interest as much as in anyone else's.

He wrote to Wilson as a friendly outsider who wanted him to emerge as a great Prime Minister; the urgent need was for him to become the man of the hour. What followed was an energetic indictment of the administration which I read before it was de-spatched. I wanted the demolition at that stage to be in a confidential letter rather than in a published editorial. It was an engaging example of the sport of battledore and shuttlecock which those engaged in the cut and thrust of newspaper policy must, if they are to survive, play with consummate skill. Cecil was a master, I was at any rate a promising pupil.

He reminded Wilson his government would stand or fall by its ability to control wages, and so inflation; the *Mirror* had given all the support in its power to the prices and incomes policy, but this had not so far had any success in the control of incomes and only limited success in the control of prices. Cecil urged that the time had come for Wilson to put his personal prestige and that of his office behind the campaign. The Common Market was not the best British foreign policy, it was the only one. Our continued presence in Arabia and South-East Asia was an anachronism we could not afford; the run-down was too slow in view of the alarming state of our balance of payments. He should not try to be Foreign Secretary as well as Prime Minister.

The administrative abilities of his Cabinet team were also ceremoniously embalmed. Michael Stewart, Douglas Jay, Frank Cousins, Barbara Castle and Arthur Bottomley held offices far beyond their capacities; above all, what the country needed was leadership, a clear account of what sacrifices the Prime Minister demanded of the country. 'We at IPC can be a great help and are very willing to be just that, but you are the conductor of the orchestra: we are only one of the players.'

In his earlier years Cecil was tone-deaf, singing 'very out of tune' when auditioned for the choir at his first school, Rose Hill; he was the extraordinary noise coming from the rear. The musical analogies (there were more to come) emerged only after his marriage in 1962 to Dr Ruth Railton, the founder and musical director of the National Youth Orchestra. In her own sphere her brilliance and tense dedication as a musician and organiser of music amounted to genius; I know of no woman more fascinating to observe in creating and maintaining high artistic standards, guiding people of unusual talent with authority and yet compassion, and especially in blazing her trail through bureaucratic indifference or incompetence. Cecil refers to her endearingly in his public writing as 'my dear wife' and 'my much beloved wife': others find her less consistent and easy to comprehend when the music stops and she turns her mind to other subjects.

The letter from King to Wilson explained why 'you may think we have been drifting apart and that the support you have been having in our papers is less enthusiastic than it used to be.' It was despatched with Cecil's good wishes but was predictably received at No. 10 Downing Street with the same enthusiasm with which a guest at an early sixteenth-century Italian feast would accept a chocolate meringue from Lucrezia Borgia. The document was sincere, disinterested, patriotic, politically sound and logically unassailable, Cecil King *par excellence*, the candid critic in the role he relished, an encyclical, power in search of responsibility. Harold replied that he was most grateful to Cecil for writing so fully on the problems as he saw them, and suggested a meeting.

The meeting took place, a lunch at No. 10 five days later, but it merely served to widen the divide. King dismissed the consultation contemptuously as a gesture to keep him quiet.

They lunched together at No. 10 again and alone on January 13 1967, and King again concluded that the purpose of the meeting was to flatter him: apart from a point about the Common Market he was asked no questions nor was his opinion on anything invited. Cecil told me about the meetings as soon as they occurred and kept anyone who happened to be passing by fully informed.

At this particular stage of the duel his egomania was in no need of sustenance, but the paragraphs which appeared in the *Daily Telegraph* of July 14 1966 between those two abortive lunches at Downing Street caused him no visible distress:

Mr Cecil King's outspoken observations in London yesterday on the prices and incomes policy, and the effect it will achieve, represent something of a landmark in this intensely interesting career.

Since Mr Wilson took office Mr King has been steadily gaining eminence in the world outside his own of publishing, as witness his appointments to the Bank of England and the National Coal Board, to name only two.

Thus Mr Wilson has secured Mr King's talents in fields where they are of value. And Mr King has achieved a position as candid counsellor to Prime Ministers in his own right, to which he has long aspired and which in earlier regimes he faintly missed.

Both Mr King and Mr Wilson gain by this, but it looks just possible that Mr King is going to gain more than Mr Wilson.

The headline was: KINGMAKER.

During the two years before the final split between the two men in 1968 King was the deathwatch beetle in Wilson's power-house, ceaselessly expressing his misgivings to Wilson's own Cabinet Ministers, overtly encouraging disloyalty and disillusion among the Prime Minister's entourage, stopping short only of advocating open revolt. Throughout the whole of this period, whenever he saw Wilson alone, or at a public reception, or on television, he described to me with some relish what he imagined to be the Prime Minister's physical and mental deterioration and exhaustion. He was successively older and slower, or less buoyant, or dwindling, or obviously out of his depth. For a man who was so frequently buried it must be said the Prime Minister displayed remarkable ability in leaping from the grave.

On June 10 1966 Cecil was lunching with Denis Healey, Minister of Defence, noting that though Denis was scrupulous in making no criticism himself of the Prime Minister some of King's more critical remarks passed unchallenged: in King's mind an embarrassed silence implied endorsement. Similar remarks did not pass unchallenged on March 3 1967: on that occasion, when King said he thought Wilson an even worse Prime Minister than Alec Home ('Difficult as that was!') Healey entirely disagreed.

On February 22 1967 he was nagging Roy Jenkins, then Home Secretary, with his view that the Government was too bad, Wilson was no PM, and that at some point the *Mirror* would have to move into open attack. The same Minister, when Chancellor of the Exchequer, was told on January 2 1968 that Britain would get no real return of confidence without the displacement of Wilson as Prime Minister.

It was vintage political wine for these younger men to sip, and it is to their credit that it did not go to their heads. The message to Wilson's subordinates, most or all of them, was that Harold Wilson had neither the drive, the personality, the conviction nor the administrative ability to pull off the approach he was planning to the Common Market via Italy and France, furthermore that Wilson was such a bad PM he could not be expected to last. When Jim Callaghan asked King on September 18 1967 why the *Mirror* was so hostile to Wilson the reply was 'Because he is a failure.' Callaghan loyally said he could not agree: he was standing by Wilson who was doing his best. It was a crusade of intellectual sedition, conducted with such zeal and steadfastness that Iago by comparison was a bumbling novice. The stage had been reached in Cecil's Wilphobia in which anyone who did not share his contempt of the man was discarded as a sycophant or a victim of self-deception.

There were other occasions when King did not have an easy passage in denigrating politicians to their colleagues, and a notable clash had occurred during the previous Tory Government.

When I invited Iain Macleod to lunch with Cecil and Sydney Jacobson at the riverside club near the Mermaid Theatre, Iain was Chancellor of the Duchy of Lancaster, Leader of the Commons, and Conservative Party Chairman. 'I've got the lot,' he told his friends. He was at the zenith of his political promise during the last three years of Macmillan's Premiership. During the first course of the lunch Cecil breezily commented upon 'What a sorry lot the Tory Cabinet are,' and ignoring or not sensing (which is more likely) the rising anger of our guest, proceeded to run through the top team with deprecatory and even rude remarks about each one. Macleod neatly folded his napkin, finished his drink, and stood up. 'I'm sorry, Hugh,' he said, 'but I'm damned if I'm going to listen to King any more. What kind of a Minister does he think I am?' He left abruptly, and Sydney accompanied him to his car on the bomb-site outside. I joined them briefly, merely to say that I understood. When Sydney and I returned to the restaurant to join King and complete the fragmented meal, Cecil, who was eating heartily, said, 'Well, well! What an odd fellow. I was telling the truth. I had heard he could be moody.'

I wrote to Cecil at the *Madison*, Washington, from London on September 9 1966, two months after the July financial crisis, mentioning an hour's off-the-record talk with Wilson at Downing Street. We had discussed the balance of payments crisis, the wage freeze, his determination to speak frankly at the TUC annual conference (whether the vote there would be for or against the Government), George Brown's appointment to the Foreign Office, the future of the Department of Economic Affairs and Rhodesia. I made the comment: 'Wilson was, as always, full of confidence, but I got the impression this time that the confidence was more solidly based.' I suspected that my mild heresy would not pass unnoticed in Washington, nor did it. The rebuke was airmailed: 'I think you respond too easily to Wilson's spell-binding. He usually *says* the right things. His problem is that he does nothing and his judgement of his team is very poor–I think you have done a great deal to propel Wilson in the right direction but don't let's be starry-eyed about him.' In Cecil's absence, without the daily brainwash, he feared I was backsliding, a hapless victim of Harold's magic.

My self-appointed role through the fourteen months which preceded Cecil's 'Enough is Enough' front-page article of May 10 1968 was to avert or at worst delay a public cleavage between him and the Labour Prime Minister and above all to prevent an overt and acrimonious dissociation between the *Mirror* and the Labour movement, stranding the newspaper high and dry with no committed policy or political direction other than an impotent anti-Tory stance. That is why I urged them both to continue to meet and exchange views, however sterile the meetings might be; that is why I set down my own views at some length, here greatly condensed, to King on Sunday March 19 1967.

Jodi typed the letter on the sunny balcony of the *Oceanic Hotel* in Madras as I watched the crows swoop down in a ceaseless bombing raid to steal the sugar and the sticky cakes from the tea-table. We were more than half-way through a journey which began in Japan and ended in Siberia. Cecil had said that Madras was quite different from other parts of India and that I should know it: it did not occur to me at the time that his father, Sir Lucas White King, had been born in Madras.

Dear Cecil,

In Madras, a reasonable distance from immediate office problems, I have been mulling over the wider factors involved in any attack the *Mirror* may have to make in the autumn upon the Government record with particular reference to Harold Wilson.

I argued that the central issue in timing was Britain's position *vis-à-vis* the Common Market. An attack on Wilson as leader or on the Government's record would be singularly inappropriate at the moment of entry, if that stage had been reached, and would achieve nothing but harm to the country. If by the autumn Wilson was still genuinely trying to get into the Market, an attack on a Prime Minister who was pursuing our own policy in the paramount sphere would be equally damaging and inappropriate, a gift to the anti-Marketeers. If in the autumn he had tried and failed, our approach should be a no-holds-barred reappraisal of Britain's position in the world. It was essential to keep the paper's political record straight and avoid any counter-charge along the lines of 'They foisted Wilson on the country and now they stab him in the back when things go wrong.' Our indictment would have to establish beyond dispute that the Government had not conscientiously tried to carry out the programme the *Mirror* stipulated as the basis of its support (in the March 1966 election we asked for 'Government Without Alibis') and appeared to be incapable of doing so.

The letter continued:

'(i) The most hazardous line to take would be "Wilson must go". I am well up to date with the current disenchantment of the UK papers and periodicals, but I doubt whether Wilson would allow this low-ebb to go on too long. A frontal attack on Wilson may well pull the whole Party together behind him. Michael Foot would not hesitate to assail the perfidy of the *Mirror* . . .

'(ii) If the *Mirror* advocated a government which, in effect, would not be based upon the present realities of Parliamentary rival power we would surely be accused by all Parties of usurping the power and privilege of Parliament itself . . . The charge would be Fascism, to which the reply of "patriotism" would sound reedy. The [political] periodicals would recall the first Rothermere's dabbling with similar notions, and the harm to the *Mirror* could be irreparable for many years. To attack Wilson is one thing: to be denounced by him and the Labour Party is another.

'The standing of the Press is not so high as for us to assume that it is the *Mirror* which would be believed. A stand-up public battle between politicians and the Press, particularly Left-wing politicians and the Left-wing Press, might remove even more of the gloss from each other.

'The wiser line would be to advocate that since the necessary talent demonstrably does not exist inside Parliament, the Government should call in talent from outside . . .

'This leaves us with two possible lines; the advocacy of a National Efficiency Government with outside patriotic aid, or a Labour Government with outside patriotic aid. Neither of these lines of attack would be taking the dangerous course of allowing our motives to be misconstrued as the usurping or side-stepping of Parliament itself . . .'

I analysed the virtues and failings of Wilson's probable successors in Labour leadership, and among the practical suggestions mentioned the possibility of articles signed by Cecil King at the appropriate time. But his crusade against Wilson had reached the obsessional point of no return. On July 20 1967 he wrote to me: 'It is quite obvious that the Government is disintegrating.'

On October 23 1967 Wilson was telling King at a Downing Street dinner for Kiesinger, from Bonn, that they had not seen each other for some time. No doubt, King wrote to him next day, the Prime Minister might think they were drifting further apart, and he committed to paper again the basic reasons for the *Mirror*'s critical attitude. There was generous praise for Wilson's supremacy as a Parliamentary tactician, but reiterated condemnation of the Government's administrative abilities. Cousins and Snow had done nothing to improve the situation; better men were available. 'It is because I feel it is so vital to Britain's future that your Government succeeds that I am so critical.'

I met the Prime Minister and his wife, accompanied by his kitchen cabinet, Mrs Marcia Williams (now Lady Falkender) and Trevor Lloyd-Hughes, that night at a reception given by Desmond Hirshfield in the Orchid Room at the *Dorchester*. We stepped aside and discussed the new letter from Cecil; again I urged that contact should be maintained and Wilson should invite Cecil to No. 10.

Cecil told Edward Heath on October 3 that he and Heath knew Labour wouldn't make good, and told Wilson on October 24 that it was vital Labour did succeed. When King and Wilson met again

on November 27 1967 'any approach to reality was brushed aside';
it was a desultory chat.

With his education and family background, the self-pitying
trials of his schooling, his tortuous relationship with his mother,
his Garbo-like yearning for being alone, his belief in his invisibility,
Cecil King might be expected to behave conversationally with the
chattiness of an uncooked clam. The reverse was now the truth:
the lips, once unsealed, were rarely closed. He regarded indiscretion
as a cardinal virtue and public service. Guests left his dining-table
like racing pigeons with messages of foreboding. His opposition
to the Official Secrets Act, frequently expressed in public speeches,
was not a legal quibble but an act of faith. The assumption of
confidentiality by others was regarded by him as a licence to blab.
It occurred to me that the Almighty would be ill advised to confide
in Northcliffe's nephew the date of Judgement Day; the human
race of all creeds and colours would know in a jiffy and be jostling
in the queue before the Pearly Gates were open.

Cecil was also in his spare time a mighty gossip, repeating tittle-
tattle that on the barest scrutiny was unlikely to be true, and relaying
without reservation what anybody said about anybody else, however
prejudiced, however callous, however tainted by their own self-
interest. I was not the only person who was privy to these 'confidences'; they were available to all. The number of people he
mentioned to me over the years as homosexuals led me to ponder
whether *homo sapiens* could be relied upon any longer to propagate the
species. He regarded his gossip as humorous rather than malicious,
a whimsical example of his Irish sense of humour, yet in serious
matters, especially political, his regard for the truth was exemplary
and his reportage on a dialogue at which one was not present could
be relied upon to the veracity of the last comma. That is why when
his standard work on indiscretion, his *magnum opus*, was published
in 1972 as *The Cecil King Diary*[1] there were wails of remorse and
cries of 'Foul' in high places but no writs.

His honesty and sincerity were of the highest order: he simply
could not understand why anything said to him should be regarded
as confidential. 'It would not occur to me to say anything to anybody
I wished to keep secret,' he said to me; and on another occasion,
'But I did not tell him I was *listening in confidence.*' He was the man
who bugged everybody including himself. I knew he had kept a

---

[1] *The Cecil King Diary 1965–1970*, Jonathan Cape, 1972.

diary during the war, and he had supplied me with useful and important extracts when I was writing in *Publish and Be Damned* of the Cabinet threat to close down the *Mirror*. I did not know that the quill pen was quivering again in the second half of the 1960s.

Peter Jenkins wrote in the *Guardian*:

> . . . other Ministers find Mr King somewhat tedious. Those who attend his *tête-à-tête* lunches have grown tired of the three-band gramophone record which, they say, consists of running down the Government and the Prime Minister in particular; complaining about the trade unions; and griping about the poorness of British management by comparison with the International Publishing Corporation.

Cecil developed his theme, with no variations, among a wide assortment of politicians, civil servants and business tycoons with whom he lunched daily in his private dining-room on the ninth floor of the *Mirror* building and with people he casually met at functions. Occasionally I would be present, usually not: I would be lunching elsewhere with similar people. Exchanging our information, we were thus able to have a clear idea of what was, and what was not, going on in the country. What I did not know at the time, and what his guests had no reason to suspect, was that their views, however incautiously critical of their ministerial colleagues or of the Prime Minister himself, were recorded in the host's diary that afternoon or evening before he settled down to supper by candlelight after a relaxing bath. My conversations, dutifully reported to Cecil, and my memos to him as Chairman after private talks with Harold Wilson, Edward Heath or whoever, were also set down and many of them later published.

Professionally I was closer to him than anyone else, certainly in so far as the political and editorial scene was concerned. He saw me or phoned me nearly every day after his working lunches to tell me what had been said about whom and by whom. When either of us was abroad on business we exchanged frequent letters. I was always within audible range of the forebodings.

Cecil's attitude towards the human race was 'non-fraternisation': it was relaxed or shelved in his dealings with me, particularly at this time. The letter he delivered on Christmas Day of 1955–'I should like you to know that I regard you with warm affection and great respect'—was not a permanent passport to familiarity or uninhibited friendship. I knew that the warmth of the affection and the greatness of the respect were expendable at any moment it might be convenient to kick the recipient down the stairs. Good-bye affection, farewell respect: the passport had to be renewed, annually. In the rarefied world inhabited alone by Cecil there would be a vacancy for another puppet on a string. Svengali would mould or create another person, or Frankenstein another monster.

It was, to him, a marriage of convenience, yet the day-to-day contact was close. His views on the popular appeal of the newspapers, on which their success rather than their significance was based, had to be treated with circumspection. The ugly significance of films like *Bonnie and Clyde* eluded him. Rock music was a nightmare. He regarded himself as the sole arbiter of the sincerity of our principal writers and never understood the world of 'pop' or Mary Quant. He wanted me to sack Felicity Green, who was first on the scene in national newspapers with off-beat fashion. 'Really, Hugh, can you imagine the wife of a Sheffield bus-driver wearing *that*?' Felicity tells this story:

'A year after I joined the *Mirror* from the *Pictorial* the so-called Swinging Sixties were at their height and Mary Quant had become a fashion force to be reckoned with or so *I* thought. Our Chairman, Mr King, wasn't so sure.

'One morning when the *Mirror* had published a strong fashion feature showing the latest in Quant ideas—mini skirts and *boots*, no less—I met Mr King coming round a corner in Geraldine House.

'"Why," he asked, peering down from his great height to my five feet one and a quarter, "do you put those *extraordinary* things in the newspaper? Surely you don't think anyone is actually going to *wear* them?"

'I said yes, I did think so. In fact, I was even thinking about wearing them myself. To the office.

'"What do you think might happen to me if I did?" I asked, hoping to get a joky reply about being chased round the News Room by impassioned sub-editors.

'A very unimpassioned Mr King looked down at me.

'"What might happen," he said, "is that you might get fired."'

The diminutive Miss Green wore her mini skirts and *boots*, no less, to the office and Miss Green wasn't fired: indeed, she later became the first working woman director on the board of any Fleet Street newspaper and was among the first of the *Mirror* talent Rupert Murdoch sought to kidnap when he bought the *Sun*.

There were occasions when it was necessary for me to be spontaneously deaf, or stupid, or uncomprehending, but the day-to-day contact between Cecil and me on the major issues was a different matter in a different league. The vacuity of ministerial speeches, the camouflaged but imminent financial crises, the awakening of the British people to the true character of their peril, these were the recurrent themes of our morning and evening talks and week-end phone calls. On these issues King's influence was prescient and potent, the basis of wide agreement between us and the cause of no conflict until King convinced himself in 1968 that nothing would be achieved without his personal intervention in national affairs.

In his personal life he was austere, but there was certainly no austerity in his dealings with me. He usually conveyed his kindnesses through my wife Eileen and later Jodi at a dinner where they would be sitting together.

'I have told de Launay that Hugh must have a large suite in the new building, with everything he wants.'

'I think I should get him a Rolls Bentley, don't you?'

'Where shall I send him this year–South America, China? He can pop over to Europe any time. Would you like to go with him?'

'He ought to have a radio-telephone on that boat of his so we can always be in touch. Will you find out the best one available?'

At the beginning of 1967 Cecil added a new dimension to our collaboration. He invited me to devote Saturday mornings, so that there would be a minimum of disturbance from others in the office, to a mutual review of world and home affairs on the recurring theme of national bankruptcy and the crumbling of British society as we knew it. I enjoyed these sessions not only because of my respect for King's integrity and knowledge. It is, however, fair to say that anybody less inured than I to his encircling gloom would have jumped from the ninth floor in desperation after any average session. Schopenhauer, who depressed successive generations of young intellectuals with *The World as Will and Idea*, would have cut his throat on the Ghordies Anatolian prayer mat to relieve the tension.

At these sombre seminars we discussed what would happen, and how soon, and who in various activities in the land could be of any use at all when the fabric of the British Way of Life broke down. I recount the state of the nation as Cecil Harmsworth King saw it in his last year with the newspapers.

Parliament would be further discredited and the political parties would drift in disillusion and disarray. Politicians had earned the contempt in which they were held by the public, and with a few exceptions were a sorry lot. Cabinet Ministers, the same tired familiar faces, had merely played musical chairs. After twenty-five years of lacklustre leadership and a decline in the standards of public life the nation had fallen behind in every quantifiable sphere. Ministerial ineptitude, political cynicism and double-talk were the norm. The moderate union mandarins had lost their grip and were stripped of their authority by irresponsible and unofficial usurpers. The intransigence of the unions under the domination of the militant Left had become too ominous for a one-party government to face and control. In the financial holocaust which was about to engulf us Wilson's Labour administration would disintegrate in confusion and panic and its leader would remove himself from the darkling scene, or be forcibly removed, in ignominy.

Before, during, or after this *debâcle* there would be violence and bloodshed in the streets, the docks and the factories beyond the strength or patience of the police to subdue or contain. Cecil King had never taken the complacent view that it could never happen here, and with some reason. He had told me of his experience of the Easter Rebellion in Ireland in 1916 when he was fifteen and living four miles out of Dublin. If civil war could break out in Dublin in 1916 why couldn't it flare up in Liverpool or Birmingham or London in 1967 or 1968?

A new administration would be urgently required, perhaps a new regime if only for a limited period, dominated by new men or at any rate not by political hacks. Parliament, which had dug its own grave, would temporarily lie in it until national dignity and morale were restored. Parliament would remain the legislative chamber but it was futile to look solely to Parliament for the leadership required. What would be the role of the Royal Family, and who among those on or near the throne would occupy the centre of the stage? Who would be the titular head of the new regime? What was required was a man of courage and impartiality, widely known to the public and accepted as a leader; a Royal Connection would clearly be no disadvantage. Earl Mountbatten? (Hence the significance of the entry in Cecil King's diary for Saturday, August 12 1967:

'Cudlipp had some talk a few weeks ago with Mountbatten at some dinner. Hugh asked him if it had been suggested to him that our present style of government might be in for a change. He said it had. Hugh then asked if it had been suggested that he might have some part to play in such a new regime. Mountbatten said it had been suggested, but that he was far too old. Sixty-seven, I think.')

We did not waste much time discussing the policy of the 'new regime': that was all too obvious. Public expenditure would be reduced to suit the country's purse. Britain would no longer squander money it hadn't earned; there would be a realistic wages policy, the rat-race would solemnly be declared null and void, reward would be assessed by productivity. The final trappings of bygone Imperial power and pomp would be swept away and Britain would spend no more on defence East of Suez or on diplomatic representation overseas than she could afford or needed. The nation would live within its means and, by its own energies and genius and within the European Community, would raise itself to the standards now enjoyed by the countries it had helped to defeat in the first and second world wars.

There was a great deal in the shopping list which would have appealed to many people, including me, and most of the policy reforms Cecil King urged were the bare minimum for national survival then and now. The nagging question was what new men, or old men refurbished, would come to the fore, available and eager and acceptable and effective at the crucial moment. We were short of potential saviours, and though the list was frequently amended on Saturday mornings a recurring saviour was Lord Robens. Was Hartley Shawcross too old? Would Arnold Weinstock be useful? Jo Grimond, of course. Joe Hyman, of Viyella, had political ambitions but was too naïve. Lord Beeching? It was all rather difficult, but the list was kept in the top left-hand drawer of one of the William Kent mahogany tables.

There was no need to search for the *éminence grise*, and he had no doubt at all that the *Daily Mirror* would have a massive part to play during the constitutional upheaval. What was uncertain was whether the new regime would send for Cecil Harmsworth King or King send for the new regime; what was certain was that the moment was near at hand. Cecil's World in the last half of 1967 and the first half of 1968 was sincere, patriotic, exciting, but also whimsical and hallucinatory: it was the closest exercise to walking on the water in the history of aquatic sport.

Early in 1968 he surprised one of our directors, Frank Rogers, by casually remarking that he expected to be playing some part in the running of the country, adding: 'Of course I shall be taking Hugh with me.'

There was another occasion early in 1968 to which Cecil, pre-occupied by more historical affairs, accorded little attention. It was a conference not about the future of the country or at what precise moment Wilson should be dismissed, but about the future of the International Publishing Corporation.

Cecil King's style of management had always been paternalistic and aloof; the irregular fireside pow-wow rather than the monthly board meeting with minutes and matters arising and individual accountability; oral accounts of his visits and decisions abroad rather than memoranda. The ambience appealed to me but not to all. It did not appeal, especially, to those directors of a younger generation who had heard the siren call of cybernetics and the jargon of modern management expounded at week-end seminars in country houses and hotels. The notion that a computer is the answer to a shareholder's prayer, which it isn't, did not appeal to a man rising seventy. The dictatorship of a commercial Salazar, though benevolent, became increasingly irksome in an operation too complex to be directed by personal judgement, selection, and patronage. It did not appeal at the level of restless but not con-spicuously inspired or proven middle-management. A young bull, as any farmer or vet will affirm, is not necessarily worth a higher servicing fee than an old bull.

During the twelve months before Cecil's dismissal a number of directors had come to me to say: 'Don't you think the time has come for Cecil to go?' This was not in any sense pleasant news. Our partnership had been remarkable and profitable. We might not have succeeded in making a dent in the history of our times but we had made a few dents in something or other. There were others in the corporation, and important others, who were not able to enjoy the distraction or stimulus of daily journalism.

I would nominate February 1968 as the month when it became acknowledged as possible within the Corporation that the close of King's reign might have to be timed by a reluctant palace revolt against his will rather than by a gracious abdication. It was the month of a three-day conference of directors and senior management organised by Frank Rogers, the Managing Director of IPC, to review the progress of divisionalisation, to establish the way in which the 'centre' and the operating groups could best work together, and to consider the part that the central resources of the Corporation might play in its development during the coming five years. The exercise was entitled 'IPC '73' and it was held in a London hotel.

Cecil attended for one evening only, tonelessly reading a ghosted after-dinner speech, and amusingly answering earnest questions. He dealt at some length with the State of the Nation, a subject close to his heart, and then more perfunctorily with the current state of IPC and its future. He thought that in no circumstance could IPC ever be taken over, and regarded books–certainly not newspapers–as the growth opportunity. Whether he was right about books is debatable. He was unquestionably right about newspapers. The regal manner in which he spoke, rather than what he said or didn't say, seemed to be remote and unreal. His established colleagues were patient, but he made no impression at all upon the young: it was also clear that the young, perhaps justifiably on this occasion, made no impression on him.

Frank Rogers had invited Mr Harry Stieglitz, of the United States Industrial Conference Board, to sit in at the seminar during the three days and give his comments and impressions at the closing lunch. When he referred to the 'Old Man' who came one evening to dinner, merely meaning 'the Boss', there were some signs of uneasy, semi-suppressed mirth. Stieglitz had in no sense intended any discourtesy to Cecil King, but it was embarrassingly apparent that at any rate among some sections of the assembly Cecil King was no longer regarded with awe or even reverence.

At the end of that conference in February 1968, three months before 'Enough is Enough', one director, Veere Sherren, predicted to a few of his colleagues on the IPC board that the Chairman would not be with us at the end of the year. There was surprise at his frankness, but nobody demurred; there was no protestation of undying loyalty. Suddenly in the free-thinking and self-critical atmosphere of that conference, King's autocratic style of management seemed uncomfortably irrelevant, out-moded. There was scarcely a single person there who had not at some time or other, or on many occasions, been harangued by the Chairman on the iniquities of the Prime Minister and the incompetence and indolence of his lieutenants; they were more concerned, immediately, about problems nearer home.

King had created the International Publishing Corporation, the largest in the world, from the tightly knit and highly profitable nucleus of two successful national newspapers, an investment in newsprint, a problem in Australia and a foothold in Africa, reluctantly bequeathed to him by Bartholomew. The purchase of Amalgamated Press, which the *Telegraph* was happy to shed, led to the take-over battle with Lord Thomson for Odhams–Newnes and for the best of the women's magazines, *Woman* and *Woman's Own*, with the *Daily Herald* involved in the package for penance. Kemsley's Scottish outpost, the *Daily Record* and the *Sunday Mail*, was also absorbed and King made a tremendously successful company investment in what became Lord Grade's ATV, then in its pram and urgently needing more milk. In the publishing expansion, breathtaking in its speed, there was conquest without consolidation, and we became unenviably the world's biggest printers in an industry strangled by restrictive practices. The massive mantle was King-size. It fitted Cecil perfectly, but the shareholders would have been much, much better off with the more modest set-up in Bartholomew's will. In financial terms the *Daily Mirror*, the perennial Derby-winning racehorse, became a cruelly overburdened moke, deprived of oats because of other hungry animals in the stable.

Publishing was Cecil King's profession and career, but not his life. His personal contribution had been vast and he had hugely enjoyed himself once he was the man on the top of the heap and had overcome, but not forgotten, the earlier humiliations. Travel and reading were recreations, but the passport to the new horizon was politics.

At one of the Saturday morning private sessions Cecil told me the curious story of a telephone call the evening before at his home, *The Pavilion*. He was reading a book in French and Dame Ruth, who was tidying up things around the house, answered the intruder. 'When I finished the book I asked who had phoned. Ruth told me it was an anonymous caller, a man who spoke in a cultured accent. He would not give his name, but he said to Ruth, "You are married to a man of destiny, do look after him," and then rang off.'

Cecil told me the story unsmilingly.

21

Coalition–or a New Regime?

Never has any Prime Minister endured a more critical Press than Harold Wilson at the dawn of 1968: all he had to do to confirm the fact was to pick up the nearest newspaper, any paper, any morning, any evening, any Sunday.

Writing later in *The Labour Government, 1964–1970* of his return from Moscow on January 24 1968 after talks with Mr Kosygin, Mr Wilson says that though things were 'quieter' in London:

'. . . substantial sections of the press were engaged again on a "Wilson-must-go" campaign. It was not a view supported in the PLP [Parliamentary Labour Party] or in the public opinion polls, though it had the enthusiastic backing of Lord Shawcross. In no time at all the other members of the trinity, Lord Robens and Mr Cecil King, were joining in with demands for a coalition of all the talents–Great Britain Limited–though there were some signs that its leading proponents might not agree on whom the Queen would be advised to send for as Prime Talent.'

Wilson's buoyancy and rugged humour are retrospective: they do not reflect his dismay at the time. Early 1968 was the nadir of his reputation as a statesman and even as a politician, and nothing he experienced later approached that measure of unpopularity and rejection. The public opinion polls viewed him with favour because the public were not really aware of the problems that threatened to overwhelm his Party and the nation. Dr Gallup is accustomed to genuflection from the politicians when he comes up with the reassuring answer, but it is only in the bleakest moments of doubt and isolation that a Prime Minister seeks solace in the results of the doorstep quiz and street interview. The avowed loyalty of the Parliamentary Labour Party was also a fickle barometer.

Those closest to him in the Cabinet and in his kitchen cabinet knew, and told me, that he was desperately in need of some approbation, some applause, or at the least of some respite in the clamour of criticism and contempt from the Opposition and the opposition Press. Dick Crossman took me aside as we were leaving a pleasant party at Pamela Berry's house in Cowley Street–she is Lady Hartwell, the wife of the Chairman and Editor-in-Chief of the *Daily Telegraph* and *Sunday Telegraph*–and mentioned the depth of Wilson's misery: couldn't the Press, for God's sake, lay off, and couldn't the *Mirror* do something to help? He was concerned about the Prime Minister's mood and peace of mind. I was moved by what he said and by what Elwyn Jones, then the Attorney-General, also said, but when I repeated their pleas the following morning to Cecil it was received with the indifference he reserved for remarks about the inclement weather. It was like importuning a Master of Foxhounds with an injunction on behalf of the quarry when the hunt was in full cry and the hounds were baying, or expecting Muhammad Ali to feel sorry for Joe Frazier in the fourteenth round. A Wykehamist, even a non-conforming Wykehamist, does not shed tears on the eve of victory; a physical or even a mental breakdown in his adversary would not have aroused a modicum of compassion. The arrangements for a floral tribute would be delegated to his personal assistant.

The intervention of the Lord Chancellor, Gerald Gardiner, on January 24 was well intentioned: he shared the concern of Crossman and Elwyn Jones. He attacked the newspapers for their 'vicious vilification and denigration of the Prime Minister which has really passed all the bounds of public decency':

> 'One can understand it in a way because it is clear, whether the Government were popular or not, the people had great confidence in the Prime Minister. One can understand the Conservative Press feeling they were not going to do any good unless they could break that confidence. There comes a point where personal degradation really affects adversely politicians of all parties.'

What had happened was simply this. Mr Wilson had been given a fair wind in the initial period of his power in 1964 by most of the Press, but events had eroded their goodwill. It was a simplification to pretend that the whole of the Press had been for him and was now agin' him. The applause from the *Telegraph* newspapers had never been deafening, nor had the *Daily* or *Sunday Express*, apart from one or two lapses into tepid neutrality, relaxed their jaundiced attitude to the sayings and doings of Harold Wilson. What irked the Prime Minister was the disenchantment of *The Times* and *Sunday Times*, previously encouraging, and the disillusion of the *Daily*

Mirror in public and the icy insurrection of its chairman in private.

There was unquestionably a revolt by the professionally docile lobby correspondents at Westminster. They do not conduct vendettas or write their newspapers' campaigns or policy pieces. Their attitude at the end of January was correctly described by David Watts in the *Financial Times*:

> The cynicism or contempt with which political correspondents at Westminster are at present apt to regard the Prime Minister derives at least to some extent from the fact that they regard him as having abused the system and themselves. It is partly that they have been steered in the wrong direction too often by the No. 10 machine.

I had no doubt at the time, from what I was told by Mr Wilson's colleagues and from my own observations of the Prime Minister himself, that either the 'vicious vilification' of some of the Press or the dimensions of the problems he was facing, and inadequately facing, in early 1968 came near to breaking his spirit and piercing his armour-plated confidence. Only a man with his supernatural resilience and comforting self-delusion could have bounced back after the defeat of his government in 1970 to preside from No. 10 Downing Street over two further administrations.

The newspapers, sooner or later, usually sooner, get to know that something is going on, especially when a political mutiny is conducted in the open, but it was the *Guardian* in a solemn front-page piece and not *Private Eye* in a scurrilous paragraph that turned on the searchlight.

On Wednesday, February 14 1968–another incident in the year of the Man of Destiny–Cecil arrived at Nice by BEA shortly after lunch for the first sitting for the Graham Sutherland portrait. I had first met the artist at an elegant dinner party given by Hans and Elsbeth Juda at their penthouse in Palace Gate, and Graham's was naturally the name that sprang to my mind when the idea was mooted to me by Cecil himself of doing King in oils. What would our colleagues think of the idea, and wouldn't it be better, anyway, if the idea came spontaneously from them? This was the second visible sign of self-imposed apotheosis: the first was when Cecil struck a bronze medallion to commemorate in 1963 the first fifty years of the *Daily Mirror* with his impressive profile on one side.

He was anxious to have Northcliffe on the other side, but Tommy Atkins and I persuaded him, with some difficulty, that the Mirror Building would be more appropriate with some symbolic figures reading in the foreground.

Cecil was not the first in the publishing world to beckon history; Northcliffe named the first *Mirror* building in Fetter Lane after his mother, Geraldine; Roy Thomson named the home of the *Sunday Times* after himself, Thomson House. Lord Kemsley engraved the drinking glasses in his board rooms with a vulgar 'K' one inch deep. Cecil, thankfully, did not call the *Mirror* building King's Palace.

I thought it would amuse Graham at the dinner party to hear the story of his portrait of Lord Beaverbrook, but he was unhappy at what I related. I told him that I was a part-owner of this painting, or at any rate a contributor to the fee, and could prove it by producing a miniature reproduction in full colour autographed not by the artist but by the sitter. The explanation was that Beaver's right-hand man, E. J. Robertson, had coerced executives of Beaverbrook Newspapers—I was happy to be one of them at the time, having been fired from the Mirror Group—to enjoy the honour of contributing to this tribute to their benefactor: there was no embarrassment about what sum one should contribute—it was all computed in advance on a salary-percentage basis so that only a cad, a foolish one with no regard for his future, would wish to refuse. The artist had assumed that Beaverbrook had paid for it himself, though why he should worry I never understood.

Graham Sutherland doesn't like painting portraits. His 'Winston Churchill' had displeased the subject and, ridiculously, had been relegated to the cellar: where is it now? I was entranced to learn in my correspondence with him that his fee was at that time £5,000 from the waist up but £10,000 for a full-length portrait: who wants to paint pants, anyway, and who wanted to preserve Cecil's for posterity? We settled for 'waist up'.

Cecil stayed at the *Royal Westminster* in Menton, an old-fashioned but comfortable hotel then only open from the beginning of December until April; he had learned from family gossip in his youth that it was *the* place to stay at on the Riviera. Sutherland lives in a concrete blockhaus fifteen minutes drive into the lower Alps behind Menton and his studio is down two flights of garden steps from the house. Graham and Cecil got on well, and after the second sitting Kathleen Sutherland confided to Peter Stephens, the head of the *Mirror*'s Paris bureau who accompanied Cecil, that the painting was going to be a great success. There were daily one-hour sessions at eleven a.m. until Monday, February 19. The artist made sketches, chose his colours, principally grey, made notes and took colour photographs of the sitter.

Cecil was not prepared to be isolated from world events even for a Sutherland painting. At one lunch in Nice he met Raymond Comboul, the deputy chairman of the *Nice-Matin* newspaper group, with Cecil expounding on Mr Wilson and the economic situation in Britain, prophesying a second devaluation. At another lunch with the British Consul General, Mr Paulson, at his villa at St-Jean-Cap-Ferrat, Cecil met a distinguished group of mayors and members of the French Parliament, a university vice-chancellor and the US Consul General, and again expounded his views on Mr Wilson and the economic situation in Britain.

On Saturday, February 17, when he returned to the *Royal Westminster* there was an invitation to lunch as guest of honour with Prince Rainier and Princess Grace on Tuesday, February 20. The invitation was declined; there was no point in expounding on Harold Wilson and devaluation to minor royalty. He caught the train from Nice to Marseilles on Monday, February 19, after the final sitting.

Meanwhile, back at the power-house . . .

A telephone call from me awaited King at his hotel and he arrived just in time, a little breathlessly, to take it. Several newspapers and the BBC were pressing for a statement. I explained to him that the *Guardian* had devoted a large space on the front page to a story by its political correspondent, Francis Boyd:

Making a new start with a
Coalition Government?
MR CECIL KING
LEADING THE
SOUNDINGS

Coalition rumours are familiar enough during critical periods, but on this occasion there were unusual and even sinister undertones. Individual members of the three major Parties in the Commons, and, Boyd believed, a few Ministers, had been asked how they would view a coalition on certain assumptions: first, that to make a new start Mr Wilson and Mr Heath would be bypassed; second, that a dominant role would be given to Lord Robens, Chairman of the Coal Board; third, that a leading part would be played by Mr Cecil King. The *Guardian* story continued:

The leading figure in all this seems to be Mr King himself and the proposal is that if an embryonic coalition were found to exist, a number of people and newspapers would, at a given signal, all announce simultaneously their separate convictions that the Wilson Government should be superseded by a radical coalition pledged, among other things, to reduce waste by cutting the swollen Civil Service and abandoning, for example, the Land Commission.

A newspaper plot is one thing; a plot by newspapers quite another. An alliance to achieve such a purpose, or any purpose, was not feasible between Cecil King and his cousin Lord Rothermere, who viewed each other with disdain. Or between Sir Max Aitken, head of the Beaverbrook newspapers, and Cecil King. Or between the *Mirror* and Lord Hartwell's *Daily Telegraph*, which rarely mentioned the *Mirror* except in terms of irony or in a manner it hoped would be to the Mirror Company's financial embarrassment. Cecil King's popularity in Fleet Street was never such that he could command allegiance from the rival Press barons who, almost without exception, regarded him with disfavour.

As the *Guardian* warmed to its theme, the Identikit picture of Cecil King emerged more clearly as the ogre. Did not Lord Northcliffe and his brothers, who were Mr King's uncles, all itch to get into politics or to manage events? We were reminded that Northcliffe, through his ownership of *The Times*, helped Beaverbrook to push Asquith out and put Lloyd George in during the First World War.

The implication of the story was that Cecil Harmsworth King regarded himself as a power outside Parliament which was greater or potentially greater than that which existed within. I found the notion disturbing, but Cecil was pleased with the story and its prominence and was irritated when I urged a denial. I reminded him that only six days ago he had said, in a reported speech, that a coalition at this moment was 'just not on'. 'Oh,' said King, 'that was something John Beavan wrote and I read out,' and the speech was in fact written by Beavan. Nevertheless the denial duly appeared:

'My attention has been drawn to the story on the front page of the *Guardian* this morning, and a statement is called for.
'One paragraph said: "Mr King's role in this search for a new

political formula is patent. He is eager for office, which, I understand, was offered to him by the Wilson Government of 1964
on terms which he rejected and which was refused by the Wilson
Government of 1966 when he wanted it."

'I have never at any time sought office from either of Mr
Wilson's two administrations.

'The *Guardian* talks about the possibilities of a Coalition
Government bypassing Mr Wilson and Mr Heath yet including
Mr Grimond and suggests that I am "the leading figure" in
advocating this political dog's breakfast. This is also untrue.

'It is quite untrue to say that I have been "leading the soundings".
I have certainly been sounding the leaders—it is a publisher's duty
to know what is happening.

'My personal views on the notion of a coalition at this precise
time were clearly stated in my talk to the Foreign Press Association
in London on February 13 last week.

'I said: "The electoral system in Britain makes it impossible
to have several parties of Left, Right or Centre and so we can
never have a coalition except in times of direst emergency. And
yet there are other times in the history of our nation when the
situation is less than disastrous and when a coalition of men in the
Centre might form the most effective Government."

'In other words, a coalition at this moment is just not on, and
will not become so unless the political situation deteriorates
still further, which it may.'

It is true that King never at any time sought office as such from
Mr Wilson's administrations. The facts about such two-way wooing
as did take place are as follows.

On August 5 1965 the Prime Minister asked the publisher if he
would accept a peerage and a post as Minister of State in the Board
of Trade in charge of the export drive. Understrapper to Douglas
Jay? King told his diary that he would have regarded the offer as a
bitter insult if he had been of a vindictive nature, and to me he
expressed his reaction more volubly. He wrote to Harold Wilson
on August 7, 'flattered' that the PM should have thought of him in
this connection but not feeling this was a sphere in which he could
deploy his talents to the best advantage. 'With regret, yours very
sincerely.' Wilson replied to King on August 7 from his holiday
retreat in the Scilly Isles. He regretted the rejection of a ministerial
post, and added: 'This does not mean I might not approach you

when your help is needed in a different, i.e. not ministerial, capacity.' The Prime Minister mentioned, in passing, that he thought that the Tuesday and Wednesday issues of the *Mirror* that week were 'terrific'.

On September 18 1967 King was invited to lunch by Jim Callaghan at No. 11, and the question again arose would King join the Government? He said that when the Government was formed he thought that Robens, Sainsbury and possibly himself were inevitable as they had experience of administration and so few others had. He had been asked before they took office by Jim and George Brown if he would be prepared to help and he had said yes. The sequel was a directorship of the Bank, a membership of the Coal Board and of the National Parks Commission. Was this really the best use to which they could put his experience and ability? King told Callaghan that if the Government offered him a place he would consider it, but he did not take back what he had said earlier in their talk about the Government being a 'sinking ship'.

There was a further meeting with Harold Wilson in the Cabinet Room at Downing Street on the evening of November 28 1967. King recorded that the summons seemed to be to offer him a peerage and a Privy Councillorship. Mr Wilson told him that he had intended to offer him the Paris Embassy but that de Gaulle's decision in the afternoon to blackball Britain from the Common Market invalidated the idea.

King remained an observer on the sidelines because no offer of pleasing magnitude was made to him. But he was not forever content merely to observe.

The London *Evening Standard* hugely enjoyed itself with the coalition rumours: 'It provoked the first horselaughs of the week at Westminster ... If we are to have government by the *Daily Mirror* the two Party leaders will presumably have to fight each other for the job of Leader of the Opposition.' Cyril Osborne MP recalled what happened to Horatio Bottomley, the last person who advocated a businessmen's government in Britain.

Four days after his last sitting in Menton for Graham Sutherland ('He thinks his best portrait was of Adenauer, but is very pleased with the way mine is going'), Cecil was 'at the Bank', absorbing the financial intelligence about Doomsday. His private reaction to the noisy hint that he was leading the soundings or sounding the leaders (the joke was supplied to Nice from London for the denial statement as part of our usual service) was confided to the diary. 'While I was away,' he mentions nonchalantly, 'The *Guardian* had a big piece on the front page suggesting' (God forbid) 'that I was trying to organise a coalition . . . Politicians seem incapable of understanding that when I talk of coalition I am talking of the future not of the present. The whole episode is interesting as it would not have been given the prominence it was unless people are thinking in terms of a National Government. *The Times* gave me a cartoon yesterday.'

Harold Wilson reproduced the Mahood cartoon in his book. The Prime Minister was depicted as a confused little man walking hesitantly up the steps of an imposing State building; the formidable Cecil, labelled 'Coalition Government', was standing in his way and there was a 'thinks' balloon above Harold's head saying:

> As I was going up the stair
> I met a man who wasn't there.
> He wasn't there again today.
> I wish, I wish he'd stay away.

The issue was of some significance in a democracy. What was in question now was the divine right of King.

It wasn't the end of the affair. Peter Jenkins in the *Guardian* returned to the subject, analysing King's 'power politics'.

> Hugh Gaitskell saw dangers in the power and influence of Mr Cecil Harmsworth King which Mr Wilson may wish he had himself perceived earlier. Gaitskell was most strongly opposed to the *Daily Mirror*'s acquisition of the *Daily Herald*. Already in 1961 he saw in Mr King too much of his Uncle Alfred, Lord Northcliffe; he did not wish to see a monopoly of the pro-Labour popular press placed in his hands.

Peter Jenkins' version of the Wilson-King honeymoon was that when Wilson became Leader of the Opposition in 1963 they began by getting along very well; 'Mr Wilson started with the advantage of not being Hugh Gaitskell.' He detected a number of manifestations of the togetherness, but the reason for King's getting along well with Wilson was more mundane, disclosed by King with his usual frankness: '*Wilson was disposed to listen to advice as Gaitskell was not.*' The reason for the frigidity between the two Wykehamists, Gaitskell and King, was not that King resented Gaitskell's intervention against the Mirror Group in the Odhams take-over (King won, and victors rarely waste their energies on resentment) but that Gaitskell distrusted King before the Odhams take-over, during it, and for ever after, and told me so on more than one occasion. Wilson might well have been, or appeared to have been, disposed to listen to advice in 1965. In 1966 King sadly records 'I didn't feel I got through to him at all.' Wilson no longer listened and therefore Wilson no longer mattered and therefore Wilson must go.

Peter Jenkins was on surer ground in the remainder of his perceptive analysis. He said that by the end of 1967 the *Mirror* may have been near to a 'Wilson Must Go' campaign, but that King may have been persuaded against this—'so members of the Government think'— by his editorial confidant, Hugh Cudlipp. Instead, the *Mirror* at the beginning of January had launched an editorial campaign to build up the new Chancellor, Roy Jenkins. Public references to differences of opinion between newspaper barons and their chief editorial executive usually result in the demise of the chief editorial executive, but I survived.

Cecil was unduly sensitive to criticism in his youth, impervious to it in middle age, and relished it in his vain maturity. The disapproval of little and ignorant men was merely a spur, irrelevant or amusing. He noted that a more detailed attack had been made on him on the back page of the *Guardian*; the general theme he thought a bit confused, mainly on the lines that King was too powerful; they wanted no Northcliffes here. He wrote off the *Guardian*, as he was always ready to do with people or newspapers who said the wrong things (i.e. disagreed), as not an influential paper any longer, and if it came to open warfare he considered he had all the guns in both verbal dexterity and coverage. As the principal gunner in the King's Royal Artillery and the captain of the Prætorian Guard I was in fact apprehensive: the political thinkers on the editorial staff, two or three of whom were of high calibre, were as concerned as the *Guardian* about the robust manifestation of Northcliffe's ghost. So was I.

King wrote to Harold Wilson in October 1967: 'As you said last night we have not seen each other for some time and no doubt you think we are drifting further apart.' Was Cecil Harmsworth King himself also drifting apart from the *Mirror*, or the *Mirror* from him? Was the newspaper founded by Northcliffe, and subsequently ruled by his brother, the first Rothermere, now receiving visitations?

There is a fundamental difference between a newspaper exercising influence over politicians and seeking to exert power over politicians, and in the ultimate seeking personal power. The previous generation of Harmsworths, sons of an impecunious and tipsy barrister who hinted quite fancifully at royal lineage, had either not understood this democratic subtlety or wantonly ignored it. Northcliffe attempted to dictate Cabinet appointments in the First World War and threatened to 'break' Lloyd George; he rejoiced in the title of 'Napoleon of Fleet Street'. Harold Rothermere signed an article anointing Baldwin as 'one of the greatest Prime Ministers who ever held office'; four years later, when Rothermere insisted on being told in advance the names of the next Tory Cabinet and Baldwin rejected his 'preposterous and insolent demand', Rothermere denounced the same Prime Minister in his newspapers. 'Mr Baldwin is a completely incompetent person who got into high office by an accident of post-war politics.'

The bad old days were here again.

I always passed on King's Law to our political thinkers and to the Editors of our newspapers, adding my own misgivings on the rare but major occasions when they occurred. When they expressed over the years any positive policy lines or misgivings of their own I relayed them to Chairman King.

There was now the whiff of cordite in the air. I knew that King would soon be pressuring again to express in public the opposition he was lavishly expounding to all who would listen in private, not least to Wilson's principal Cabinet colleagues. I felt it was time for the Editors and political writers to hear the oracle at first hand, put their questions and express their own feelings. King agreed and the dinner took place in his office dining-room on March 5 1968. There were no flies on the wall so early in the spring; a pity, because they would have enjoyed themselves more than the guests.

Cecil opened the batting with his familiar demolition of Wilson, the promise of national financial bankruptcy around the corner and the social upheaval that would assuredly follow.

Sydney Jacobson, then Editorial Director of the *Sun*, at that time an IPC newspaper, and of *The People*, wrote this exposition of where he stood before the feast and emphasised the same points during the discussion:

'1. *A "Wilson Must Go" campaign*? I am against it, at any rate until there is another economic crisis caused by Govt. mishandling.

'I admit Wilson has so far failed. But I think such a campaign now would be a blunder, since it will not succeed. If we were to attack him all out now, we would only strengthen his position inside the parliamentary party—where his real power lies at present—and make it even more difficult for a credible challenger to emerge inside the Cabinet. And we would be inviting a counter-attack—on the lines of "power without responsibility"—which would be vastly popular inside and outside Parliament and might undermine the political stature of our papers.

'Once we had launched such a campaign we would be bound to oppose any government of which Wilson is the head. If he were still there at the next election, we would therefore be unable to support Labour. We would either have to sit on the fence or support the Tories. Either course would mean a complete break with the papers' radical outlook and tradition of outspokenness.

'2. *Alternatives to Wilson*: the realistic alternatives just now to Wilson are:

'(a) One of the present top Cabinet Ministers—Jenkins, Callaghan, Crossman, Castle. Except for Jenkins—where everything depends on the Budget and subsequent recovery or failure—they would all be caretaker Premiers designed to take Labour through its remaining years of office and into a certain election defeat. Can we honestly back any of them at present—even Jenkins?

'(b) Heath and the Tories? Do we believe that, even if given the chance, Heath is ready to take over and would make a better job of it?

'(c) A Coalition or National Govt: we certainly cannot rule this out; it might come about if there were a second devaluation. But I believe its base would have to be political rather than business ... I cannot see a basically businessmen's government being formed, nor do I believe we should press for one. I believe that if the Labour Govt. comes apart at the seams as the result of another financial crisis, the Government would be defeated through a split in the Parliamentary Labour Party, and there would be a general election and the Conservatives would romp home without having to go through a Coalition stage first.

'3. *How closely should we seek to become involved in the political scene?*

'I think we are in danger of becoming too involved on the inside of politics. Obviously we must know what is going on, and must try to influence the big decisions. But if we get too involved, if we tell the Prime Minister to sack George Brown, for example, we often make it more difficult for him to do so . . .

'There are a lot of people around who want, for one reason or another, to foster the impression that the Mirror Group want to run the country and Parliament and the Cabinet. (It might be a good thing if we did, but that's not what we are in business for.) I don't know what we can do about it, but I think it has dangers to our papers, and is worth discussing.'

John Beavan, Political Editor of the *Daily* and *Sunday Mirror* (now Lord Ardwick) expressed similarly independent views. He didn't go all the way with C.H.K. He didn't believe a crash was inevitable, but he did think it was horribly possible. Was it better for us to be on the inside of government or on the outside looking in? Beavan preferred the latter stance. He said that on a number of occasions he had been dismayed about the *Mirror*'s policy towards the Labour Government, but he felt retrospectively that the paper had been right and just. A government was not always free politically to do the right thing. Beavan summarised his attitude:

'We are in an old dilemma. The Government is about to ask the electors to accept heavy taxation and an incomes freeze. We cannot say we are (*a*) governed by an inept government and (*b*) people should accept the sacrifices this government demands.'

This is Beavan's recollection of the evening:

'We met the Apocalyptic mood of Cecil with an embarrassed and amused scepticism. When he told us before we sat down to the table that money would lose its value and we should have to live by barter, I said he would be able to live for years on his fabulous collection of old silver. I got a brush-off for this sally.'

John was seeing King every day and was telling him that the advice he was getting from 'a good source at the Treasury' did not support the information King was getting from the Bank of England.

Leon Alexander Lee Howard, DFC, was also on parade in the sixth year of his decade as Editor of the *Daily Mirror*. Lee was not a political animal, at any rate overtly. He observed rather than participated in the proceedings that night. He knew that it was news that sold the *Mirror* not views, entertainment not policies. A schism

Prime Minister Sir Anthony Eden, after his TV grilling by
Press Editors during the 1955 election.

Chancellor of the Exchequer Harold Macmillan at his Budget
broadcast with Paul Bareau and myself in 1956.

At the Newspaper Press Fund Centenary Dinner, 1964, with
Prime Minister Sir Alec Douglas-Home and his successor at
No. 10 Downing Street, Harold Wilson.

Welcoming Prime Minister Edward Heath as guest of honour
to the London Press Club.

between the pundits or a chasm between the *Mirror* and the Labour Party wouldn't have lost him a wink of sleep. On that particular occasion I enjoyed his smile and mock seriousness when people differed. He always welcomed my madder tabloid ideas more than my saner editorials.

Bob Edwards, then Editor of *The People* and now Editor of the *Sunday Mirror*, was there. He had made up his own mind: he thought a businessmen's government would be a catastrophe but was not able in the atmosphere that prevailed to put his point as decisively as he had hoped.

I was the convener. There was nothing for me to say that everybody hadn't heard before, and the object of the meeting was that the Editors could hear and question Cecil King first hand and state their views. But Cecil had made a mistake.

He had asked me, unwisely I thought, to invite the unpredictable George Gale, then occupying the space on the *Mirror* left vacant by the death of Cassandra. The mutual dislike between King and Gale was instantaneous. It was silly to expect George to concern himself seriously with the agonies of Labour in power and even sillier to expect him to be polite to King. When he had left the *Mirror* and was writing for the *Spectator* he recalled the evening rather grumpily in his review of King's 1965–1970 diary:

> He outlined his views about setting up a government of businessmen and he asked us for our views. I recall launching into a strong attack, saying that the idea was foolish, that a government required the ability to sustain a Parliamentary majority and so on–elementary stuff, but apparently necessary–and I ended up by asking King how he proposed to engineer his *coup d'état*, and did he propose collecting Alf Robens, Lord Beeching, Old Uncle Tom Cobbley and all into a charabanc and driving to the Palace and saying to the Queen, 'Ma'am, here we are, your new Government of National Reconstruction'? My contribution to the discussion was received rather coolly, King finally snubbing and silencing me with: 'Well, now that we have heard all that from Mr Gale, what has our political adviser got to say?' Whereupon up spoke stout John Beavan now Lord Ardwick saying nothing much. Nobody said much. King was surrounded by yes-men; and this was his trouble.

I do not recollect the shrill cries of 'Yes'; certainly not from stout John Beavan or from the wiry Sydney Jacobson, but George Gale is entitled to his dreams.

Cecil did not rate the dinner a success. He was not impressed by the cautionary tales of his colleagues: they had wasted their time and King evidently thought they had wasted his. The effect of their opposition was nil. He recorded an interview with Robin Day to be released on BBC television on Sunday March 31, three weeks after the dinner, and what he would say was liberally dispensed in advance to the Press the night before:

CAMPAIGN TO OUST
WILSON GROWS:
CECIL KING JOINS IN
(*Sunday Times*)

WILSON MUST GO,
SAYS CECIL KING
(*Observer*)

The indictment was familiar, but now public. And still nobody from the crowd, including Mr Day, asked the simple question, *Who in bloody hell does Cecil King think he is*? It was now accepted or assumed, especially by Cecil, that he occupied some undefined, unelected but absolute position of authority and responsibility in the country, indeed in the Western world, which few people challenged. His knowledge, knowing far more about far more than anyone he had met, his commanding height, his soft voice, his benign patience with the frailties of others, combined to give him the mystique of a twentieth-century Delphic oracle, dispensing like Apollo or like Zeus at Olympus the answers to inquiries about current public events. Rebuking Prime Ministers and encouraging their potential successors. Adjudicating on the merits or failings of industrial tycoons and indicating to such Secretaries of State as cared to listen the course of economic salvation. Adjusting foreign policy. Gently jostling Britain into its next niche in history. Walking in thick treacle up to his neck, getting along, but oh! how slowly and with how much effort. It was either a performance of unparalleled statesmanship or the greatest con trick of our political era.

The media rolled over on its back and gave time on the air, or space in rival newspapers, to propagate his views because they were sincere, uninhibited, different, provocative. Oswald Mosley a few decades before enjoyed, and Enoch Powell now enjoys, the same dangerous privilege. And Cecil was compelling television; he said what he believed to be true, however outrageous the view might be, and the audience liked the avuncular, effortless, world-weary style in which he specialised. Here, surely, was a disinterested pundit with no axe to grind.

The scenario for 'The Fall of Harold Wilson' was perfected in King's mind during 1967. In the first four months of 1968 his principal concern—indeed preoccupation—was casting the characters for the sequel, 'The New Regime'. We frequently discussed what the administration should be called: national governments and coalition governments were familiar devices of the past and no longer conveyed immediacy or instant national peril.

'What about *Emergency* Government?'

Cecil liked the idea, and Emergency Government took its place naturally in our crisis vocabulary. I was not at all surprised to hear later that others stumbled upon the same notion.

It was necessary at this time to make my own cool assessment of the gathering storm, away from the obsessive excitement of the man on the bridge. I was accustomed to his all-pervading gloom. Churchill had lived much *longer*, and American Man had landed on the moon (that Christmas) much *sooner*, than he had conclusively proved to be possible, but King had been uncomfortably accurate in the past in prophesying economic disasters. And the constant whisper of 'what they are saying at the Bank' added a new thrust of authenticity: no fooling, it was the Bank of England and he was a director.

The outside view of how the *Mirror* was run was no doubt that the headstrong Cudlipp and his Editors and experts, all talented in their different ways, were kept in check by the discerning Cecil King, tightening the reins, prescribing caution, tempering the undisciplined enthusiasms of younger men with sage advice. The reverse was now the truth. There was not a single soul on the editorial staff who had not doubted the wisdom of a 'Wilson Must Go' declaration, first me in writing from Madras and then independently others. But they were now regarded as uncomprehending men of goodwill but small stature and uncertain spirit who could not expect to measure up to the ultimate and fiery test of leadership. Omega was for him alone and he was deaf to any warning.

Cecil drew my attention with some amusement to a piece in *The Director* placing him as Minister for Education and Science in an imaginary Businessmen's Government of fifteen premiered by Lord Robens, but our conversations at this time were of sterner stuff. He told me that Wilson would be out of Downing Street probably within three months. King was pressing prominent men in the Labour Party to choose Wilson's successor as PM in an all-Party government. A financial crash and another devaluation, leading to the swift collapse of Labour in power, was inevitable. In March he thought that the real crisis was on–here at last, triggering the series of momentous events he had foreseen for so long. It was in fact delayed by another huge loan from overseas. Postponed again, he said, but not resolved.

There was nothing confidential so far as he was concerned about our talks. Other directors and Editors and visitors were sharing the same harangue. Had he been as mad as a hatter none of it would have mattered at all. It would have been a case for humouring; I would have produced a one-copy fake edition of the *Daily Mirror* reporting in big bold type that all of his baleful prophecies had come true, and that he was now in charge. I would have presented the special issue to him ceremoniously as he was taken gently away and then made sure that the type and the stereo plates were quickly melted in the pots. The disturbing fact was that Cecil Harmsworth King was conspicuously sane and might have been proved to be right.

I could no longer deflect him from his mission, nor could anyone else. I still, however, had influence upon the timing of the exercise. The 'when' of it all would be dictated by events, but everything would fall into place at or near the right time: he enjoyed the advantage of intuitive judgement, seeing things with a fresh eye, and the gift of foresight.

The illustrious name of Mountbatten of Burma now recurred in the Saturday morning thinking sessions. In an era when the reputation of politicians had sunk so abysmally low, when nothing short of a revival of national pride led by disinterested men of power and action would change the course of events, it occurred to King that this legendary personality in the history of our times was surely the man for the hour as the titular head of the Emergency Government.

Mountbatten. Lord Louis, the gallant sea-dog who served on battleships and submarines in World War One and commanded a destroyer flotilla at the outbreak of World War Two; his ship was torpedoed twice and sunk by dive-bombers. Chief of Combined Operations. Supreme Allied Commander, South-East Asia. Reconquered Burma from the Japanese. The man to whom the Japs surrendered in Singapore. Viceroy of India in 1947, transferring power to the Indians and Pakistanis. Requested by the Indians themselves to be their first Governor-General. And then dutifully returning to service in the British Navy.

'The trouble,' said Cecil, 'is that he is not the sort of person I know.'

By a coincidence I had heard from Lord Mountbatten that morning and phoned my secretary to bring the letter up to King's room. 'My dear Hugh . . . yours ever, Dickie.' Cecil did not pause to read the contents; it was merely a pleasant thank-you letter for something I had done. But I mentioned that, like many others, I had been on friendly terms with Lord Mountbatten for some years. Among his other attributes he was a fan of Cassandra who had interviewed him as Allied Commander-in-Chief Mediterranean in 1952, and he liked the manner in which the *Mirror* faced the realities of the world we lived in.

Cecil decided that a meeting with Earl Mountbatten at that crucial stage might be advisable, even propitious, and there occurred that week-end another of those coincidences familiar to people who run newspapers. On the Saturday evening Edward Pickering was standing in for me at the Burma Star Association annual reunion at the Albert Hall (the *Mirror* helped them in putting together their programme, gathering advertisements) and had a good deal of conversation with the star of the evening, their wartime Supremo. When 'Pick' mentioned that I was on the Solent that week-end Lord Mountbatten said he particularly wanted to see me—could we meet at the Royal Squadron at Cowes on Sunday evening (on my ship one isn't dressed for meetings at the Squad) or at Broadlands in Romsey, his country house where the Queen and Prince Philip honeymooned in 1947.

The meeting took place at Broadlands on Monday morning, over a glass of sherry. As we strolled down the long corridors, lined each side with glass cases preserving hundreds of silver polo cups, he remarked with a chuckle, 'You can see why they called me a playboy.'

He was as deeply concerned about the morale and problems of the nation as anyone else, and more than most, but whereas Cecil King's approach to the 'forthcoming crisis' was essentially political (chopping down the Rt. Hon. Harold Wilson) and economic (sweeping measures under a new regime in which he would himself be playing a leading part), Lord Mountbatten's approach was more circumspect and philosophical. Political manœuvre, in favour of whatever person or persons or faction, however lofty and disinterested the motives, was none of the business of the man who was 'Uncle Dickie' to both the Queen and her husband and Personal ADC to Her Majesty since 1953. What he was hoping for was a massive resurgence of the British spirit.

I arranged a meeting between King and Mountbatten and myself for 4.30, Wednesday, May 8 1968 at his London residence, No. 2 Kinnerton Street, SW I. He phoned on the day to mention he would be accompanied by Sir Solly (now Lord) Zuckerman, then Chief Scientific Adviser to HM Government; there had been no sort of conversation with King on any previous occasion and the move was obviously a precaution. Cecil and I had known Solly for a number of years and the choice seemed felicitous from King's point of view.

Cecil had given me no indication in advance of how far he proposed to go at the meeting; he always gave great thought to what he would say on important occasions, but did not on this occasion rehearse the part with me. He awaited the arrival of Sir Solly and then at once expounded his views on the gravity of the national situation, the urgency for action, and then embarked upon a shopping-list of the Prime Minister's shortcomings. He spoke with his accustomed candour. He did the talking and I sat back in my chair to observe the reactions, detecting an increasing concern on the part of the two listeners. He explained that in the crisis he foresaw as being just around the corner the Government would disintegrate, there would be bloodshed in the streets, the armed forces would be involved. The people would be looking to somebody like Lord Mountbatten as the titular head of a new administration, somebody renowned as a leader of men who would be capable, backed by the best brains and administrators in the land, to restore public confidence. He ended with a question to Mountbatten—would he agree to be the titular head of a new administration in such circumstances?

Mountbatten turned to his friend: 'Solly, you haven't said a word so far. What do you think of all this?'

treason? Sir Solly rose, walked to the door, opened it, and then made this statement: 'This is rank treachery. All this talk of machine guns at street corners is appalling. I am a public servant and will have nothing to do with it. Nor should you, Dickie.' Mountbatten expressed his agreement and Sir Solly departed.

Only a minute or two elapsed between Zuckerman's departure and King's. Lord Mountbatten was, as always in my experience, courteous but firm: he explained explicitly but briefly that he entirely agreed with Solly and that that sort of role, so far as he was concerned, was 'simply not on'.

His Private Secretary, John Barratt, accompanied Cecil and me to our car.

Two days later Cecil King announced on the front page of the *Daily Mirror* that Mr Wilson and his Government had lost all credibility, all authority, and demanded a fresh start under a new leader. On the night of May 9, when the presses were rolling (as they used to say in *Late Night Final*) Cecil was billed to appear in a television programme entitled *Famous Last Words*; the item was postponed to make way for an analysis of the borough election results and, as it transpired, an analysis of King's Farewell to Wilson, then available in the first editions. It so happened that on the day the piece appeared I was lunching with Edward Heath at his apartment in the Albany. Twenty-one days later King himself was dismissed as Chairman of IPC, and thirty days later I was sitting next to Mountbatten at a dinner at Brunel University. IPC had awarded a cybernetics fellowship and he had some months earlier agreed to speak on the occasion: Cecil was to have chaired the meeting, but in the circumstances I stood in for him.

------•◆◆◆◆•------

22

'Enough is Enough'

'Well,' said Winston Churchill to Cecil King in Downing Street in 1941, when the motives of the *Daily Mirror*'s wartime policy were suspected of being sinister or worse, '*you* look innocent enough.' Nobody assessed him with such condescension at the present stage of his progress.

Wilson-Day was Friday, May 10 1968, and it was a coincidence that on precisely the same day twenty-eight years back, May 10 1940, King had written in his diary about the fall of Neville Chamberlain as Prime Minister: 'So at last my campaign to get rid of the old menace has come off. I consider this the best bit of news since war was declared.'

Here is the piece which appeared on the front page of the *Mirror* side by side with the night's results, humiliating for Labour, of the borough council elections. The election news story was headlined: 'LABOUR PLUNGE TO ELECTION DISASTER, 21 KEY TOWNS FALL TO THE TORIES.' The moment could not have been more ominous for what King desired to say:

ENOUGH
IS ENOUGH

By Cecil H. King,
Chairman of the International
Publishing Corporation.

The results of the local elections are fully confirming the verdicts of the opinion polls and of the Dudley by-election.

Mr Wilson and his Government have lost all credibility: all authority.

The Government which was voted into office with so much goodwill only three and a half years ago has revealed itself as lacking in foresight, in administrative ability, in political sensitivity, and in integrity. Mr Wilson is seen to be a brilliant Parliamentary tactician and nothing more.

If these disastrous years only marked the decline of Mr Wilson and the Labour Party, the damage to our political self-confidence would be serious enough, but the Labour Party came into power with such high hopes from its supporters because it took office after thirteen years of dismal Tory administrations.

We can now look back nearly twenty-five years to the end of the war and see that this country under both Tory and Labour administrations has not made the recovery or the progress made by others, notably the defeated Japanese, Germans and Italians.

We have suffered from a lack of leadership and from an unwillingness by successive Prime Ministers to make any serious attempt to mobilise the talent that is available in this once great country of ours.

Frequent Government shuffles mean that in any case very few Ministers are long enough in any office to master their subject.

Since 1964 we have had three Ministers responsible for the vast area of our economy covered by the Ministry of Fuel and Power. In the same period, we have had four Ministers of Education, which means that, effectively, Mr Wilson has had no Minister of Education. And the same applies to other Ministries.

We are now threatened with the greatest financial crisis in our history. It is not to be removed by lies about our reserves, but only by a fresh start under a fresh leader.

It is up to the Parliamentary Labour Party to give us that leader–and soon.

The piece was written by King, even the headline, and was predictably repeated in the other two daily newspapers in the group, the *Sun* and the *Daily Record*. He suggested to Edward Pickering and me that we should take full-page advertisements in all the other national newspapers to reproduce the article and further the campaign: I indicated, I'm not sure how, that that would be over-doing it.

Most if not all of his public speeches and lectures, broadly based on his own philosophy, had been composed by John Beavan and before that by one or other of his successive personal assistants.

They wrote the variations on the original theme. The summary dismissal of a Prime Minister was a moment in his life he wished to share with no one except the historians. My 'pepper-pot of commas and colons and Thesaurus of potent words and wounding phrases,' as Cassandra used to call it, was not called into service. During the fourteen months and more in which his intention had been delayed or diverted by one debating device or another, I had said that when it did appear, and appear it would, the article or articles should be signed by him. The more the broadside was personalised the less the potential damage to the newspapers, and the event however cataclysmic would find its level as an episode rather than as policy sculptured in granite. There was no resistance from Cecil to this notion. I was not the first to have visualised the by-line 'Cecil H. King' on page one, but what Cecil and I did not know when we discussed it as a future event was that his first article and headline for the *Daily Mirror* were to be, for other reasons, his last.

I had neither the power to suppress nor the ammunition to negotiate yet another postponement. More importantly, I had neither the inclination nor the desire to try to stifle his political views or his personal views on politicians: it was a freedom I enjoyed and a responsibility I exercised myself. Our area of agreement on most matters had been wide over two or three decades, but he was the Man With The Last Word.

William Hardcastle: What is your process of working with your Editors and ensuring that they express the views you are in favour of?

Cecil King: Well, the Editor-in-Chief of the group is Hugh Cudlipp. I see him every day and we have in general the same sort of political views. I tell him what I think, he tells me what he thinks, and when we agree he sees that the respective Editors carry out the policy agreed upon.

Hardcastle: You said when we agree. What happens if we disagree?

King: I'm the Chairman.

BBC *Radio, 1966*

I could not dissuade a bull from entering a china shop by standing between the bull and the china; a more fruitful tactic was to try to save some of the more valuable crockery and as far as possible

330

subdue the bull. I reflected that politicians under duress are adept at pricking the pomp of overbearing Press tycoons. If Baldwin, scripted by his cousin Kipling, could rise to the occasion and castigate Beaverbrook and the first Rothermere for 'aiming at power, and power without responsibility, the prerogative of the harlot through the ages', no doubt Harold Wilson, with another poet at his side at No. 10, would not shiver or wither in silence.

I certainly did not assume that the Prime Minister would neatly fold his papers, collect his pipe-cleaners and saunter obediently out of Downing Street with Mary on his arm and Marcia humping her private files at the whim of a newspaper chairman, even Cecil. One outcome of the onslaught could surely be that, if Wilson shrugged it off, the *Mirror* and its associate papers would pre-empt their position in the next election and be obliged to support Ted Heath and the Tories, leaving no newspaper of any popular influence or validity to expound the Labour cause. That would certainly have been the case had the article not been personally signed. Yet it was the financial rather than the political aspect of 'Enough is Enough' that disturbed me before publication and others after publication. Among them was Ellis Birk, the prominent City solicitor who had been a director of our newspapers since 1952 and a legal adviser for many years before.

King was sworn in as a director of the Bank of England in 1965, one of eighteen in the full Court. He regarded the new appointment 'as more of a job than an honour. I have no interest in honours and titles as such.' He became a member of the Bank's Committee of Treasury (three of the executive directors and four non-executive) on March 7 1968. The power of a Bank director *per se* is negligible, even non-existent, but he is close to information about the precise financial state of the nation at any given time, and, in the case of a man with an eager ear, a busy tongue, a keen brain and wide international experience, close to a fount of inside knowledge and informed gossip. He was a part-time gnome at £500 a year, and those aware of King's frankness were uneasy at the appointment. Among them was the Earl of Cromer, Governor of the Bank at the time and later Ambassador to Washington, who was married to Cecil's cousin, Esme Harmsworth. Outwardly Cecil regarded the invitation as a natural progression, but inwardly was surprised and gratified.

An incident in September 1967 is interesting in view of later developments. King recorded after a lunch with Chancellor Callaghan, who had insisted upon his appointment, that the Bank ('i.e. presumably O'Brien,' then Governor), had complained of his hostile talk of the Prime Minister. 'This is amusing,' wrote King, 'as my views are to be found on the front page of the *Mirror* whether I utter them in person or not. Presumably I must now be more discreet at the Bank.'

One month before his elevation to the Committee of Treasury The *Guardian* named him as the principal promoter of a coalition government. King thought that Governor O'Brien wanted him to say again that if he got personally embroiled in political controversy he would resign from the Court as, under such circumstances, his continuance might embarrass the Bank. They cleared the point in a talk together.

Now, in May 1968, still a director of the Bank of England, he was proposing to tell the world, and on the front page of a newspaper, that Britain faced the greatest financial crisis in its history, not to be removed by *monthly* lies about our reserves but only by a fresh start under a fresh leader. I failed, twice, to persuade him to omit the phrase about the reserves, but did succeed in persuading him to delete the word 'monthly' in relation to the lies.

'It's true. We *are* threatened with the greatest financial crisis in our history, and we *are* lying about our reserves.'

'Yes, but on this occasion a director of the Bank of England is saying it's true and publicly saying it's true.'

'Time somebody did.'

'You will obviously be resigning from the Bank's Committee of Treasury. The only question seems to me to be when.'

'Of course. I shall resign just before the article is published.'

'That means before ten o'clock tonight.'

'I will write now to the Chancellor and to O'Brien at the Bank.'

'I'll arrange the delivery of the letters at the right time.'

The letters, written on his imposing deckle-edged notepaper, were read to me by Cecil, signed and licked into their envelopes and marked 'Urgent and Personal' in his own hand. It seemed inappropriate, *lèse-majesté*, for them to be delivered at some imprecise time by a *Daily Mirror* despatch rider in a snow-ball crash helmet, throttling noisily into Downing Street, the heart of Westminster, and Threadneedle Street, the soul of the City, on a vulgar farting motor-bike. One needed a sense of history and a regard for security; I therefore rejected the possibility of these particular letters being tucked in a saddlebag with half a dozen folders containing news messages about horse-racing and murders and pin-up pictures of semi-naked models, wedged between the cyclist's supper sandwiches and an apple and a change of socks.

I phoned Bryan Parker, the Deputy Editor of the newspaper. 'Bryan,' I said, 'I don't normally ask the top executives to deliver letters. If you look at the addresses you will know they aren't Valentines. One is for the Chancellor of the Exchequer, the other for the Governor of the Bank of England. I hope you'll agree to this chore, but don't use an office car. Please hire something from outside. Security. The time for delivery at No. 11 is seven p.m.'

Bryan Parker's report on his assignment was amusing. By the time he left the office he had caught a glimpse on the Editor's desk of the piece to appear on the front page that night:

'Outside the *Mirror* building a black Daimler Double-Six limousine, the type favoured by the higher-class firms of undertakers, was waiting. First destination was Downing Street, No. 11, the official residence of the Chancellor. A policeman, standing stolidly outside, took no notice as I knocked on the door. Almost immediately it opened about six inches and a dark, saturnine face peered out. I explained I had a most urgent letter for the Chancellor from Mr Cecil King and that it was imperative for him to receive it without delay. He said that the Chancellor would receive it as soon as humanly possible and closed the door. Twelve minutes later the Daimler was gliding through the deserted streets of the City. The Bank of England was as silent as a tomb; not a soul was in sight, even a policeman. There is no letter-box, bell or knocker on the main doors of the Bank, but two small side doors bearing the legend, "Night service for the delivery of letters". There was a bell and a speaking tube, but I did not think it necessary to talk to the Old Lady of Threadneedle Street herself. The door opened slightly and a bank official in full regalia, pink tail-coat and all, appeared with a sepulchral "Good evening". He took the letter and promised that it would be conveyed to the Governor as speedily as possible. He closed his eyes as though offering up a silent prayer and shut the door. On the way back to the *Mirror* I felt I should have worn a black tie for the occasion.'

King had been appointed by Chancellor Callaghan but the letter was to his successor Roy Jenkins; the devaluation of the pound had been the reason for the change of Chancellors. The note was laconic, for Wykehamists (Manners Makyth Man) wastyth no words:

Dear Chancellor,

As I am becoming more and more involved in political controversy, I think it will be more convenient for the Bank of England if I resign from the Court.

This is, therefore, to tender my resignation, effective forthwith.

Yours sincerely,
Cecil H. King

Roy Jenkins was weary that evening after working half-way through the previous night. He read the letter, went to bed, and did not think it necessary to inform the Prime Minister with any speed; he had no knowledge of the bomb that was timed to explode in the *Mirror* within a few hours and divined no immediate significance in the communication. Harold Wilson lived next door but was in Bristol that night.

Cecil performed on schedule. He handed over the letters to me, left the office as usual at 5.30, drove to *The Pavilion* at Hampton Court in the Rolls, entered the events of the day briefly in his diary, read a little, suppered by candlelight, and disappeared as usual at 9.30. He didn't wait up for the first edition and didn't want to know until next day how the other newspapers had reacted: ignite blue touch-paper and retire immediately. I have always been intrigued by the leisurely fashion in which unarmed combat is conducted in the political arena. Spines are broken and eyes gouged and opponents disembowelled with a fastidiousness that rarely interrupts the flow of conversation.

The article appeared in the issue of Friday, May 10, timed for comment by Miss Beloff, Mr Margach, Mr Hutber, Mr Waller and the leader writers in the unpopular Sunday Press.

That night Cecil invited some of our Editors and political sages to dinner in his office and said in his diary: 'Cudlipp, on his own initiative, had asked each editor whether he approved the line taken—and the answer was yes.' There is a difference between refusal to publish and approval of content, and the diary records the dialogue over-enthusiastically, indeed whimsically. What I sought and invited, to break the silence and tension of the occasion, was the reaction of the Editors to the Chairman's front-page piece. I was relieved that the climax had been reached, though not passed. I wanted to hear, and thought King should hear, what others thought.

Sydney Jacobson's account of the occasion does not concur with Cecil's diary:

'Cecil claims that you asked all the Editors whether they agreed with "Enough is Enough" and that they did. I do not think this is true, certainly not so far as I was concerned. I came back from holiday the day before publication, and you asked me over from Odhams and showed me the copy. You asked what I thought of it, and what impact it would have, and I said it would create a terrible rumpus but that I realised we could postpone it no longer and that it was a good thing Cecil had signed it. Later, when the first edition of the *Sun* was printing, I saw Keith Davenport, the Managing Director of Odhams newspapers, and said to him, "The Old Man has finally cooked his goose with that piece." At the dinner the next night Cecil asked me what the effect would be on Wilson's future, and I said it would rally the ranks around him, at any rate for the time being.'

The editorial chiefs had grown up with the problem for some time, and to most of them the occasion in Cecil's room was the ball *after* Waterloo.

Ellis Birk had been closer to King than the other directors and had achieved a rapport with him on business journeys abroad together. It was from Birk that I received the first explosive reaction to Cecil's essay in page-one journalism. He phoned me from Newcastle to say that he was 'hopping mad', and he was speaking as a member of the board, not in any sense as legal adviser to the company. 'This is the end of Cecil so far as I am concerned. I am returning to London immediately. Can we meet as soon as I am there?' I wanted him to be under no misapprehension, and told him that I had delayed but not opposed the publication. What principally concerned him was that it would appear that King was speaking for the board as a whole.

We met when Ellis Birk arrived in London. As a member of the Labour Party he disliked the whole article, but his very strong reaction to it was based not upon the attack on Harold Wilson 'but on my financial and industrial experience and knowledge of the City of London'. He continued: 'The references to the Bank of England and the reserves are outrageous and it is unforgivable that a director

335

of the Bank should make statements which could only have an immediate deleterious effect upon sterling.' The fact that Cecil King had signed the article as Chairman of the International Publishing Corporation could easily have made people assume that he was expounding views which had been approved by his board. Indeed it could, and indeed the price of sterling *did* slump.

On Saturday, May 11, in the environment of *The Pavilion*, King blandly recorded that the big blast had gone off the day before with a greater impact than he expected, due to his references to lies about the reserves. 'The pound had a bad day and I am blamed.' Then came the admission that as he knew the Governor had been very worried about the previous month's published figures he felt he was on safe ground; in view of the probable collapse of the pound in the fairly near future he had to say something on Britain's finances.

Why? Was he entitled, or was it his duty, as a director of the Bank of England and a member of the Bank's Committee of Treasury (which he was when the article was written) to disclose in a newspaper what he knew as a result of his confidential office to be the private worries of the Governor? Why was the impact greater than he had expected? What did he expect the impact to be? Was he surprised that 'the pound had a bad day', and could he conceivably be surprised he was blamed? Why did he feel, striding across a well-defined minefield, that he was on safe ground? With Cecil King in the witness-box on that particular day a moderately competent and sober barrister still wet behind the ears would have enjoyed a field day and won his spurs.

May 10 was also a field day for the financial journalists. The pound drooped to its lowest level since the March 1968 gold crisis and a wave of nervous selling swept Ordinary share prices down. The Labour Left, vigilantly led on this occasion by Mr Michael Foot and Mr Ian Mikardo, drafted a motion calling for King's removal from his directorship of the Bank. They did not know until later in the day when Roy Jenkins disclosed King's letter of resignation that the director had already removed himself the night before, a matter of hours before this massive involvement in political controversy. Jenkins' reply was no more effusive than the letter he received:

Dear Mr King,
  I have received your letter of May 9 and note that you have
resigned as a director of the Bank of England.
Yours sincerely,
Roy Jenkins

The Prime Minister was speaking that evening, May 10, at
Bristol, opening a new zinc smelter and discussing regional problems.
He made no reference to the prerogative of harlots throughout the
ages but counselled his audience, in a Wilsonian aside, not to believe
all they read in the newspapers that morning, adding cryptically:
'You would not buy them if you did.' When he was quizzed later
at a Press conference, he said: 'It's not for me to comment on what
Mr King said. It's a free country, it's a free Press, long may it
remain so. I hope that newspaper proprietors will always be as free
to find as much space in their newspapers as other citizens.' It was
not the comment of a man who was physically and mentally exhausted,
less buoyant, or dwindling, or out of his depth. I saw to it that the
Mirror gave the same prominence to Wilson's reply as had been
given the day before to its head man. The Prime Minister set down his
considered views on the King attack in his book *The Labour Government* and I quote him on pages 345–7.
  Cecil obliged the media by stretching his customary bed-at-nine-
thirty rule so that he could appear on the BBC's *24 Hours* and
ITV's *News at Ten* to emphasise that it was not his job to nominate
a successor to Harold Wilson—that was the Labour Party's; the
parlous condition of the nation was due to the incompetence of the
Government and its predecessors.
  On the same day Richard Crossman, Lord President of the
Council, who never hesitated himself to denigrate Wilson in private
conversation, predictably and loyally described King's statement as
character assassination. 'Mr King should take warning from the
fate that attended his uncle Lord Rothermere's attempt to dictate
Cabinet changes from the newspaper proprietor's office over thirty
years ago.' Edward Short, Minister of Education and Science,
extolled Mr Wilson as probably (probably? Watch your step, Short)
the best Prime Minister in this century in peacetime. Gallup Poll
figures published the same day rated Mr Wilson as the most unpopular Prime Minister of the generation; a week is a long time in
politics, but sometimes not so long as a day.

The Oscars for rudeness, and why not, went to Randolph Churchill and Emanuel Shinwell.

Mr Churchill, in the BBC programme *The World This Weekend*:

'King asserts that Wilson is unfit to govern the country. How fit is King to be Chairman of the International Publishing Corporation? In 1963 the shares of IPC stood at 16/9d. Now, five years later, they stand at 18/6d. Hardly a very great growth at a time when many shares have doubled and trebled in value. That doesn't look as if Mr King is the brilliant businessman that he tries to make himself out to be . . .

'Well, Mr Cecil Harmsworth King has a curious background. He had seven uncles—tons of uncles. One of them was Lord Northcliffe. He was a megalomaniac. He went mad. His other uncle, the first Viscount Rothermere—he was a megalomaniac and a coward. Mr King is just a megalomaniac.'

Mr Emanuel Shinwell:

'In short, will the Government surrender to public opinion and succumb to the clamorous demand of Cecil King, the top sergeant in one of the largest newspaper corporations? Taking a cool look and practical assessment of the situation, my answer is: THERE WILL BE NO SURRENDER. CECIL KING CAN GO TO BLAZES.'

'Well,' said Cecil, 'nothing surprising in all that nonsense is there?' Such raillery didn't ruffle the Northcliffian quiff on his brow: megalomania was merely a little man's assessment of a big man born to lead, and where one would eventually be going—to blazes or to paradise—was more in the hands of the Almighty than of Manny Shinwell. Nor was the Sabbath calm at *The Pavilion* disturbed by the comment in the *Observer*; David Astor rarely bared his teeth as Editor and even then did not bite deeply, but on this bizarre occasion the editorial declared that the spectacle made Mr Wilson look a straightforward character by the side of 'the devious Mr King'.

It was the financial indiscretion which generated the furore and anger. The *Observer* said:

As for Mr King's specific charge that the reserve figures never fully reveal the actual position, this is a long-standing practice. Mr King himself has admitted this on television . . .

So he has caused a financial panic by giving the impression of saying something new when not doing anything of the kind. And he has done this because he wants to overthrow the present administration.

King recorded in his diary that he had some talk with Denis Hamilton on May 13: he did not mention that the previous day the newspaper of which Hamilton is the Editor-in-Chief, the *Sunday Times*, had some talk about King:

Mr King speaks from a privileged position. There is no question whatever about the right of a newspaper proprietor to call for a Prime Minister's resignation. But an inescapable question is raised by a member of the Court of the Bank of England who chooses, in sinister terms, to imply that a Prime Minister has misrepresented the real economic situation.

Patrick Hutber of the *Sunday Telegraph*, the shrewdest of the City editors, observed that if the foreign holders of sterling didn't get panicky it wouldn't be King's fault.

Wilson, at the centre of the mounting controversy, had returned from Bristol to Chequers and was spending the week-end on routine State papers, hoping for weather fine enough for a round of golf. Politically the forecast was thunderous. The Labour Party's reaction to Cecil's peremptory farewell to Harold was to unite in defence of the Prime Minister and the Government. Ian Mikardo said that owning a newspaper didn't give a man any more political qualifications or knowledge than owning a fish and chip shop; 'He's got the nerve to lecture the Government because some of their mistakes are directly the result of their having taken his advice.' Jennie Lee, Minister of Arts, probed more deftly: 'Mr Wilson has offered Mr King every honour and made every concession to him. What is now plain is that the *Daily Mirror*'s relationship with the Labour Government is that of a Trojan horse–it likes to be within the gates but within the gates to ensure that Socialist principles are not put into practice.' The pro-Wilson chorus was loud and clear.

The test to be applied to 'Enough is Enough' is not what harm or good it did to Wilson but what harm it did to Cecil King. On the eve of the onslaught, May 9, King told his diary:

'Some two or three weeks ago I said to Hugh Cudlipp I thought the time had come to step out and launch an all-out attack on Wilson and that the Labour defeats in the local elections would provide the peg on which to hang the attack. Hugh thought the matter over and agreed. So tomorrow there will be a piece signed by me on the front page.'

It was true that Hugh could postpone the day no longer and concurred, with an adjustment in the timing: the attack had not been discussed merely for weeks or months but for longer than a year. What the diary was not told was that I had stated my views as clearly as the basic English at my command would allow in the letter of March 19 1967 from Madras: 'The most hazardous line to take would be "Wilson Must Go". A frontal all-out attack on Wilson may well pull the whole Party together behind him. Michael Foot would not hesitate to assail the perfidy of the *Mirror*.' In the event, fourteen months later, Foot instantly drafted a motion in the Commons calling for King's removal from his directorship of the Bank. No gift of prescience was needed to know what would happen.

The most prophetic comment came from Colin Valdar in his column 'Dog watches Dog' in the *UK Press Gazette*:

Close readers of 'Enough is Enough' might sense the act of a man clearing up some unfinished business before emptying his desk drawers for his successor . . . In pencil, perhaps, one might mark the file 'Cecil King's Last Stand'.

Valdar was a former Editor of the *Sunday Pictorial*, but he had no inside knowledge.

The King diary for the material days exudes the calm of a man bestride events, quizzically contemplating the battlefield after the first bombardment. He noted that the newspapers were pretty hostile, as were the politicians. Crossman's attack was discarded as very poor stuff; he recorded also that 'Wilson looks pretty bedraggled on TV, as well he may.' Stacks of letters had arrived, mostly hostile, but Lord Robens and for some curious reason Garfield Weston, the Canadian biscuit millionaire, were honourably mentioned as supporters of the piece. The rest was silence.

The languid prose of the diary, and also his public demeanour, concealed what was in fact his intense excitability at this time. I had a front-row seat and shared many a talk and impulsive phone call. He was acting out of character. Cecil King was on the rampage, exhibiting the same boyish ebullience he publicly displayed in the General Election of 1964.

He had sought to be the candid counsellor of Prime Ministers and his advice had been spurned. It was now his intention and expectation that the authority of his pronouncement and its timing would bring Wilson down in ignominy and that in the political chaos there would materialise the moment he had prophesied, the final act when he and those names he had written down on slips of paper, revised, testily removed and occasionally restored, would at last be called upon (or call upon themselves) to exercise direct power or direct influence and save Britain. Without, as he now knew, the titular blessing of Lord Mountbatten.

The King I had known and understood and, I say without hesitation, revered had usually been susceptible to criticism and suggestion from those who dared. This is why the unlikely partnership flourished for so long and so effectively. But 1968 was Man of Destiny Year: he listened to what he wanted to hear and was no longer immune to flattery from people outside the office. Yet it was still essential to conserve some of the china in the shop.

The morning after his statement was published he told me he was irritated by something Anthony Wedgwood Benn had said on television; to correct the fact he would draft a statement to the Press Association at five o'clock and would show it to me later:

'Mr Anthony Wedgwood Benn, the Minister of Technology, inferred on TV last night that my critical attitude to the Govern- *implied!* ment was due to my disappointment at not being given office. To quote his own words, Mr Benn said: "He's annoyed because he hasn't been given a job by Wilson. That's what it boils down to."

'No Government office is in my eyes more influential or more independent than the position I hold as Chairman of the International Publishing Corporation.

'When I had lunch with Mr Callaghan on September 18 he asked me if I would accept a post in the Cabinet—not the Exchequer which he occupied himself: not the Foreign Office

341

occupied by Mr Brown, but anything else? He explained this idea was put forward without the Prime Minister's knowledge. But disclaimers of this kind are not always to be taken seriously particularly in matters of such importance. I replied that I saw no reason to join his sinking ship. He protested that it was not sinking and that Labour would win the next election. Of this I said there was no hope.

'The sinking ship is much lower in the water now.'

By the time the statement reached me Cecil was presiding over a meeting of the Newspaper Publishers Association in Bouverie Street, and I sent him the following note by hand:

'I have been discussing with Pick [Edward Pickering, then Editorial Director of the *Mirror* newspapers] the proposed statement to the PA tonight. It is our joint and considered view that the present statement would be damaging not only from your own point of view but from the newspaper's as well if you betray in public a confidential talk with Callaghan.

'I have been concerned about this for some hours and it is my frank opinion that you should not disclose this dialogue with Callaghan.

'Unless you strongly feel otherwise, I will not issue it to the Press Association.'

He telephoned me immediately. Cecil on the war-path was not an easy man to dissuade, but the statement to the PA appeared with no reference to Mr Callaghan and the confidential talk. The point of concern was that if we were to publish confidential discussions with Ministers when their government was still in power no Minister would talk to King or his principal lieutenants ever again, and the contacts we had assiduously built up over the years would vanish overnight. The complete dialogue between Callaghan and King on September 18 1967 was later disclosed in King's book, one among a host of others.

In a week bereft of gaiety an amusing aspect of the statement was that Wedgwood Benn hadn't made the provocative remark at all. The gibe was attributed to him in an agency transcription of the TV programme, but it was made by Lord Avebury, still more recognisable as Mr Eric Lubbock, the former Liberal MP for Orpington. There had to be a public correction.

One more exercise was necessary to preserve the remaining

china. Cecil had been insistent to me and senior members of the editorial staff that his onslaught should not fade out as a one-day or one-week wonder, that we were conducting a crusade and not merely publishing one controversial article. It seemed prudent to me to leave that battle until a later day, but the day was as soon as Sunday, forty-eight hours after 'Enough is Enough'.

I had hoped that one prominent follow-up article in our Sunday newspaper, entitled 'Why I Spoke Out,' again signed by Cecil H. King but not on this occasion written by him, would fulfil the specification of a 'crusade'. That is why I suggested it—but with no great expectations—and why it appeared.

Cecil phoned me at my home in Sonning to discuss the reactions of the other Sunday papers, inquiring how I proposed to develop the onslaught in Monday's *Daily Mirror*. I had the task of reminding him that, unlike Lord Beaverbrook whom he had publicly criticised for so doing, we did not conduct vendettas against public personalities however righteous or in the public interest our views might be. The result, reached after some painful and prolonged silences and a fresh exhortation from him that we must retract not one word, was an editorial written by me, read over to Cecil, and published on page one:

NO VENDETTAS

The *Daily Mirror* does not conduct personal vendettas against politicians or any other public personage. Never has: never will . . .

Yesterday in the *Sunday Mirror* Mr King explained in detail, and with no retraction whatsoever, why he had spoken out, repeating that he believes it essential in the interests of the nation and of the Labour Party too that the Prime Minister 'should be persuaded or compelled to give up his high office'.

The same issue reported critical replies from five Government Ministers . . .

Mr Wilson's boldness, whenever it is exercised, will continue to be fairly reported—and encouraged and applauded.

Mr Wilson's political weaknesses will also continue to be fairly reported—and exposed.

The choice of leadership lies within the Parliamentary Labour Party and nowhere else.

They should not hesitate too long.

It was left to Mr Jenkins to dispose of the debris in Parliament on May 13, the first occasion the matter was mentioned in the House. His manner was variously described as lofty or faintly disdainful, a stance which in the case of Mr Jenkins did not call for exhausting rehearsal or even a brief course at a drama school. King's letter had said he was resigning from the Bank because he was becoming more and more involved in political controversy—'so I accepted his resignation without hesitation,' said the Chancellor. (*Laughter*.) Would he repudiate categorically the disgraceful and thoroughly unpatriotic remarks made by Mr King about the country's economic position and about its reserves? Mr Dickens (Lab., Lewisham) said many backbenchers felt that the Chancellor and the Government had listened in the past far too readily to Mr King and the *Mirror* newspapers instead of to members on the Government side of the House and the Labour movement in the country. Mr Jenkins replied that he certainly thought the article was irresponsible and he certainly repudiated what was said about the reserves: the practice was exactly the same as that started by Mr Selwyn Lloyd, continued by Mr Maudling and defined by Mr Callaghan in 1966. Mr Callaghan had said that the figures given of the monthly reserves were quite accurate, but the practice had grown up over recent years, and he thought it was a desirable practice, under which the central banks through co-operation offset the flow of short-term movement. Mr Jenkins said this was desirable in the interests of world trade and stability of the exchanges and he saw no reason to discontinue the practice.

Mr Barnett (Lab., Heywood and Royton) suggested that Mr King's statement indicated appalling ignorance and the need for a course for Bank directors. 'Mr King,' replied the Chancellor, 'said frankly on television on Friday night that he spoke with no special banking or economic expertise. I sometimes wish he would show equally becoming modesty about political questions.' (*Laughter*.)

King had been cut down to size in Parliament, a major demolition operation, by ribald laughter, but one nagging side-issue remained. There was the problem of domestic Labour politics and the fragile neighbourliness between Harold and Mary in No. 10 and Roy and Jennifer in No. 11. Harold Wilson's claim that with Roy Jenkins he soon established the closest of relationships was specious; there never has been any *rapport* between them beyond the call of any immediate business in hand.

The fact that Jenkins had not immediately telephoned the Prime

Minister on the night he received Cecil King's letter might have created in Mr Wilson's mind the suspicion that 'Enough is Enough' was a King-Jenkins plot to ease him out of the Party leadership. Hence Mr Jenkins's soothing words in the radio programme 'In the Public Eye' on May 16. King's statement, he said, had led to a determination in the Labour Party to solve the country's problems without outside interference. He rejected the suggestion that Mr Wilson should resign: it was easy in a period of difficulty for a party, a government, or a country to look for a scapegoat.

Jenkins had no knowledge in advance of King's broadside: it was another of those plots that never was.

How was the battle of the gladiators now looking on the other side of the Colosseum? Mr Wilson said of King in his book: 'I alone was in a position to assess the measure, to a person of his calibre, of certain of his personal disappointments.' There is no further clue from Harold Wilson: merely the enigmatic statement that the Prime Minister alone could assess their measure. King publicly disclosed that he was offered a peerage by the Prime Minister in November 1967, adding wearily 'for the fourth or fifth time'. He said: 'I am not interested in such things anyway.' What he did not disclose in his otherwise uninhibited diaries was that he had told the Prime Minister that because other ennobled newspaper proprietors had been made viscounts he could only accept an earldom. Earl King? Wilson pointed out that he had already announced he was not recommending to HM the Queen hereditary peerages. Life barons only. There was no provision for a life earl. Whereupon Cecil King cited a precedent more than a century old; he had researched the prospect, but the glittering prize was not forthcoming.

The solitary public reference made to the request for an earldom– known only at the time to the applicant, the rejector (who received the letter), and myself (who saw the letter), and presumably Dame Ruth–appeared in the *Daily Mail* on May 31 1968, the morning after King was deprived of his own crown:

> Another account: Mr King wished for an earldom.
> But a Labour Government does not give out hereditary
> titles. A life peerage? No thank you. Before long the
> campaigning grew taut and deadly.

The author of the disclosure was Mr Walter Terry, then Political Editor of the *Daily Mail*, later Political Editor of the *Daily Express*:

he was the only journalist, apart from myself, who knew. His implication, if intended, that the campaign grew taut and deadly because of King's 'personal disappointment' is unjustified; no blandishment or patronage, however rarefied, would have deflected King from his course and purpose in 1967, 1968 or at any other time.

The campaign grew taut, but not deadly. Mr Wilson continued in office. Mr Edward Heath, valiantly leading an ungrateful Tory Party, replaced him for a while, but Harold Wilson was still presiding at No. 10 Downing Street for eight years after he was publicly executed and his remains disposed of by Cecil King in 1968. He retired, or voluntarily redeployed his talents, in the spring of this year, 1976.

The King Conspiracy, as it was regarded by the Prime Minister's entourage and by some political commentators, was never a conspiracy in a judicial sense; it was not a combination of persons for an evil or unlawful purpose, or an agreement between two or more to do something criminal or illegal. So far as King was concerned he was conducting a mission with the zeal of a missionary; he wanted the Parliamentary Labour Party to knife its appointed leader, but would have settled for an act of *hara-kiri* by the leader himself.

In *The Labour Government, 1964–1970* Mr Wilson records the devastating rout of the Labour Party in the borough elections, almost as bad as the previous year, 1967, and then turns to the impact of the King attack:

'Yet again we faced a serious problem of morale. There was a further challenge: before the votes were counted, Mr Cecil King, correctly anticipating the results, claimed the boroughs and the parliamentary by-elections as grist to his demand that "enough is enough". Britain needed a new Prime Minister, Labour a new leader. By a strange coincidence this secured a leading place in the journals he then controlled, though I was left in no doubt about the disgust felt by a considerable number of his employees. But it was a lead story, too, in the rest of the press and on the television screens.

'I was not concerned about Mr King's disenchantment . . . [He then referred to "certain of King's personal disappointments".] But his doom-laden forecasts about the economy could be damaging. He was a director of the Bank of England and to the ignorant it might be assumed that part-time members of the Court of the Bank "knew something" of the financial position

Britain was facing. This would have been difficult at any time, but this was a bad week for such behaviour. Whether he had realised it or not, we were but a few days from the date when six-month forward sales of sterling made in the week before devaluation were coming up for settlement. The Bank of England had expressed to the Treasury their concern about monetary movements on that day: Mr King's *démarche* could not have been worse timed. But before the Chancellor could act to remove him from the Court he had the grace to resign . . .'

In Bristol Mr Wilson was 'pursued everywhere for comments on Mr King's statement, which did not seem to me important'. The pugilists in this heavyweight contest, now reaching the last surprising round, affected the same indifference to the rival in the ring. Wilson whimsically referred to his assailant as a member of the professional WMG (Wilson Must Go) group and King observed that Wilson was smaller and more insignificant than ever. Mr King's 'statement' did not seem important to the Prime Minister, but–

' . . his attack of 9th May,[1] however, coming as it did from a Bank of England director, did have some effect on the market. The effect of it, combined with the borough results–hailed as a sign of political disintegration–produced a heavy run on sterling on the Friday. Informing Parliament of his acceptance of Mr King's resignation from the Bank, on 13th May the Chancellor repudiated the scare-mongering.'

On May 30, twenty days after 'Enough is Enough', Cecil King was in the headlines again; this time they were not written by himself.

---

[1] The attack was published in the *Daily Mirror* on May 10 1968, but televised the night before from the early edition.

23

'Regicide in London'

Cecil Harmsworth King said on a public occasion that he could be dismissed by his board of directors at any time; the audience assumed he was joking and so did Cecil. It was an example of his Irish humour, a gentler version of the Tartar sense of irrepressible fun which led Tamerlane the Great to dictate before his death the epitaph inscribed on his nephrite tomb in Samarkand: 'If I were alive today mankind would tremble.'

The news that Cecil had gone overnight as the head of the largest publishing group in the world was received with incredulity. *The Times* called it perhaps the most dramatic coup in newspaper history since Mr King himself ousted Guy Bartholomew from the top job at the old *Daily Mirror* in 1951, and said that Fleet Street was astonished. The *Observer* settled for 'electrifying'. The *Daily Express* said that his position was thought to be unassailable, invincible. In the United States where the news was described as sensational, there were jaunty headings such as 'King Deposed' (*Time*) and 'All the King's Men' (*Newsweek*); when I saw 'Lion of Fleet Street Jungle Felled' it occured to me 'felling' lions was a precarious occupation. *Fortune*, the monthly Bible of the higher echelons of business executives in America, recorded the event in sombre fashion, 'Regicide in London': the murder of a King.

He refused to resign and was therefore dismissed. I will relate why and how the dismissal took place and why it was resolved that only one method could be invoked. The critics of the brutality dwindled when Cecil's Book of Revelations was later published: none knew him except his closest colleagues, and few of them as nakedly as he unveiled himself in his diaries. I met Lord Shawcross, chairman of the second Royal Commission on the Press, in the *White Tower* restaurant by chance a few evenings after the event. 'I don't want to know why,' he said, 'I want to know *how*.'

Three or four months before the decision was formally reached I pointed out to some of my restless colleagues that Cecil was not the sort of man to whom one could casually hand his National Insurance cards and ask to leave by the back door, hinting at the presentation of a gold watch or an acceptable piece of Georgian silver at some later date to suit his and our convenience, the company paying his bus fare. Under the Articles of Association the directors could remove the Chairman as Chairman by a *majority* vote. He could only be removed from the board as a director by a *unanimous* vote. One last-minute vacillator, emotionally overcome by the tension or the personal tragedy of the event, or by remorse or cowardice, or sincerely seeking some more pleasant solution where manifestly in the case of Cecil King there was none, could have reduced the situation by one vote to a farce with no finality except confusion. I was aware of that eventuality: it is usually possible, though not always, to assess how individuals will behave under strain and anxiety. The *Sunday Times* a few days after the climax said that 'the spectacularly brutal nature of King's dismissal is still something of a mystery' and referred to a 'breakfast assassination', but the clue to the mystery was in paragraph 100(g) of the Articles of Association.[1] A King who is no longer king could scarcely be expected to behave as a constructive courtier under a new regime and monarch; the man awaiting a higher call from the State would not conceivably accept a lower level in a commercial company of which he was already head.

The desirability of unanimity was obvious. The probability, in view of all that had been said by directors over the months, was reasonably strong, but it was essential that every director was physically present when the decision, one way or the other, was reached. When I was on a visit to the Scottish office with Edward Pickering on May 16 I telephoned Frank Rogers, who had left London on May 8 on a business tour of Japan and Hong Kong, telling him there was no need to truncate his journey provided he was back in London on the week beginning May 27; we had discussed the situation many times and most recently the day before he set off. I also cabled Arnold Quick in Czechoslovakia and remember his reply: 'Roger. Wilco.' The Corporation's legal adviser was Ellis Birk and the Financial Director Gordon Cartwright. I consulted them about procedures.

Jodi and I had been invited to a buffet supper at Chelsea Park Gardens by Cecil's eldest son Michael and his wife Libby on May 28. Michael had been the Foreign Editor of the *Mirror* but was at that time Public Relations Director of the CBI; he was totally unaware of what was happening at Father's citadel or of what was about

---

[1] 'The office of a director shall *ipso facto* be vacated if he shall be requested in writing by all his co-directors to resign.'

to happen. Cecil might well have been present at the party, but that night was at a gala concert with Dame Ruth celebrating the twentieth anniversary of the State of Israel and listening to Artur Rubinstein. He recorded in his diary that at the reception Tommy Balogh cut him dead and Dick Crossman took one look and fled.

I phoned Cecil on the morning of Wednesday, May 29, to warn him not to be surprised if he bumped into forty or fifty people wearing dog-collars on the ninth floor during lunch-time: they were young parish priests from the diocese of Southwark on their annual post-ordination course, visiting the *Mirror* for us to indoctrinate them or they to indoctrinate us. I talked to them at lunch-time with the *Mirror*'s Editor and top writers, and their leader, Canon Derek Tasker, told me with some pleasure that Mr King had stopped him in the corridor, chatted and shaken him by the hand. The Canon mentioned on a later occasion his surprise to hear the news the next day. 'Sky-pilots,' I said, 'are known to be an ill omen, and there were fifty of you.'

Cecil lunched with Pamela and Michael Hartwell (Chairman of the *Daily Telegraph*), discussing the state of the nation, and that evening he and Dame Ruth were having a quiet supper in his suite at the office before or after some function he had to attend. It was, ironically and sadly, the last supper, but the disciples were not present. They were gathered in Orbit House, part of the *Mirror* complex and at that time the registered offices of the Corporation: it was not a clandestine affair in a secluded hotel room miles away as some supposed.

This was the final unhurried discussion and formal meeting at which every director was invited to say his piece in the presence of every other director and did so. They had their responsibilities to shareholders and staff; it was not a gathering of the flunkeys of a Harmsworth dynasty or of the unquestioning yes-men of an individual, however formidable he might be. 'According to one man who was there,' said *The Times*, 'every director expressed the view that Mr King should go. They made their points, it is said, with dignity, reluctance and a genuine feeling of sorrow for the man who had given so much of his life in the service of the group.' The description is correct. The request for the resignation of the Chairman was signed by every director and it was agreed that a letter I then drafted should be delivered to his home at Hampton Court by the company secretary, John Chandler, the following morning, Thursday:

May 29 1968

Dear Cecil,

I have been instructed to inform you by letter of some decisions which have been reached by all your IPC colleagues.

They were reached with great reluctance, and solely in what all believe to be the long-term interests of the Corporation. It is also fair to you to say that the views increasingly expressed by directors over the past year or so had reached a stage where a discussion among ourselves could no longer be postponed.

The feeling is that your increasing preoccupation and intervention in national affairs in a personal sense rather than in the more objective publishing sense has created a situation between you and your colleagues which is detrimental to the present and future conduct of the business of IPC.

It has been decided that the retirement age for Chairmen of IPC should be sixty-five, in keeping with the rule laid down by you for all other directors; that you should therefore retire immediately as Chairman.

It has also been decided that I should succeed you as IPC Chairman.

The decisions were unanimous on each point, and I enclose the formal request for your resignation signed by all of your co-directors in accordance with the provisions of the Articles of Association of IPC.

It is also the wish of the directors of IPC that you should simultaneously resign as a director of the Reed Paper Group.

It is the desire of every one of us that in any announcement we pay full and very genuine tribute to your tremendous contribution to the expansion of the company during your seventeen years as Chairman.

Our view, again unanimous, is that the best course would be for you to announce your resignation tomorrow, Thursday.

Three of us who have worked with you for many years-myself, Frank Rogers and Don Ryder-will be ready to see you together on Thursday morning at IPC to discuss the appropriate next stage. The decision of your co-directors was that an announcement should be made as early as possible on Thursday.

Sincerely,
Hugh Cudlipp

Cecil phoned me on the internal hot line at 9.35 a.m. when Don Ryder and Frank Rogers were with me in my room. I had suggested that if Cecil phoned either of them separately we should stand by the agreement of the previous night's meeting of directors and insist on seeing him together, but I felt, and said, that if he phoned me with a request to see him personally and alone I would immediately agree: this would indicate that he wanted a private talk and we should not refuse to allow this to happen. A phone call to me of that nature might have suggested a desire to handle the matter in a friendly and co-operative way, and we were determined if possible to soften the inevitable blow to his pride.

On the phone Cecil said, 'I understand you want to see me.' The temperature was zero. I replied, 'Yes. We will come up right away.' It is curious how banal the conversation tends to be on these occasions.

On the way in the directors' private lift from the fifth floor to the ninth I said to my colleagues, 'You can be sure that though three of us are expected there will be only one chair in front of the William Kents as usual. I'll take that, but won't start the proceedings until you have settled in your pews.' I anticipated long pauses from Cecil, designed to promote in the unhappy delegation a sense of discomfort, doubt or guilt, and asked my colleagues not to imagine I had suddenly become inarticulate and rush to my aid if I, too, fell in with the long pause technique.

There was one chair in front of the octagonal desk, and there was a long pause. I felt that Cecil should open the meeting, giving his reaction to the letter. He thought otherwise, but eventually offered, 'Well . . .?'

I said he had received our letter, that it was necessary under the Articles of Association for it to be written stating the vote at the meeting the night before, and I therefore thought he would wish to give his reactions to it. Was he prepared to resign?

There was another long pause, with Cecil's eyes focused firmly and accusingly on me.

Frank Rogers, sitting on my right, broke the silence: 'I would like to say, Cecil, that—' (King's head turned slowly to Frank to give him the benefit of the formidable glare I had received for the previous minute) 'all your colleagues hold you in high esteem and affection. You should not doubt this. We have done what we think is right for the Corporation, and that is our duty as directors. But the affection . . .'

Cecil King: An odd way of showing it.

There was another long pause, and the beam from the lighthouse

352

The night the Queen Mother became the first woman member of the London Press Club. The laugh was raised by my remark as President: 'Of course, we don't really expect that when Her Majesty the Queen telephones you at Clarence House she will often be told that the Queen Mother has nipped out for a quick one with the boys and girls at the Press Club.'

With Sydney Jacobson and Harold Wilson at the Labour Party Conference, 1971.

Two cartoons by Richard
Willson. The first appeared
when Cecil King disturbed the
skeletons in the Harmsworth
family cupboard in his book
Strictly Personal.

'Old King Coalition and his Fiddlers Three'
(The 'fiddlers' depicted are William Rees-Mogg, Editor of
The Times, Lord George-Brown, and myself).

turned again on me. 'Resign? Resign today? Certainly not. It would look as if I had been found with my hand in the till. Certainly not.'

Pause.

Cudlipp: I'm sorry you take that view, Cecil. You leave me with no alternative but to go back and consult the board.

King: You can go and consult anybody you like.

Pause.

It seemed to me, nevertheless, that he had not yet said his ultimate piece and had carefully considered in advance just what he would say and when he would say it. That was his style.

Don Ryder spoke next, as the glare revolved accusingly to him: 'I would like to say something that Hugh will probably not say himself, but I think should be said. You should know that this is in no way, and has not at any time been, a revolt led by Hugh against you.' Don said more on these lines, but the expression on Cecil's face was not encouraging to a dissertation on the subject of loyalty.

'I think,' said King, 'we have had enough insincerity for one morning.'

Cecil then turned to me with the same matchless slow-motion: 'If you wish to say to me that the time has come for me to go, I don't want to outstay my welcome. Far from it. In two or three months' time, or something like that . . .'

Pause.

Cudlipp: I will discuss this suggestion with our colleagues and, of course, will let you know within an hour or so what their reply is. Will you be in the office all day?'

Cecil, opening his arms in a gesture of lofty patience and a hint of resigned boredom, said, 'I am at your disposal.'

Later he was asked by a newspaper whether the meeting was cordial. 'Well,' he said, 'you could hardly say it was riotous.'

Don Ryder, Frank Rogers and I withdrew for a talk in my room. It was obvious to anybody who had worked with Cecil as long as we had, and who knew his methods, that he would employ such a period of respite not to clear up his affairs and gracefully retire, but to conduct a subtle campaign to dominate his colleagues one by one, selecting first the weakest or most emotional or most gullible, and to hold rigidly and triumphantly to his original intention to retire at seventy and not a day, or an hour, or a minute sooner. It would have been impossible for the Corporation to breathe or to conduct an important daily newspaper and publishing enterprise under a patched-up taut regime: under such a truce some members of the board, certainly the three present and Ellis Birk, would themselves have resigned, protecting Cecil's pride but leaving notable gaps in the organisation.

In my room these views were expressed emphatically by Don Ryder and Frank Rogers and by me. I called a meeting of the directors in Orbit House where we had met the night before. I reported what Cecil had suggested and made a point of not calling upon Rogers or Ryder until all had expressed their views, and I also made a point of speaking last. There was no doubt of the reactions to Cecil's idea of an interregnum. Some remembered his decisive handling of Guy Bartholomew's dismissal and his airy reference in public to the affair years later: 'I only had one real battle here and that was when I wanted to get rid of the previous Chairman of the *Mirror*. No one else on the board would support me, but one year later he was in the street and I was Chairman.' There were other dismissals by Cecil, beginning with the disconcerting phrase: 'Your colleagues have lost confidence in you.' I recollect no formal board meeting conducted by him at which the victim was informed of the reason for his ordained execution and amiably invited to parade his views in opposition.

It was unanimously decided by the thirteen directors present that since a resignation that day with an agreed statement was spurned by King, there was no alternative to his dismissal but a degrading retreat by his colleagues. The second letter was signed and delivered to Cecil's room:

May 30 1968

Dear Cecil,

Frank Rogers, Don Ryder and I reported back to all members of the board after our discussion with you this morning. All your remarks were conveyed in full.

The unanimous view of the board is that the decisions which were made last night cannot be revoked or altered in any way.

The letter of request which was delivered to you this morning stands. Accordingly, therefore, you have ceased to be the Chairman and a director of IPC.

An announcement will be made later today.

All the directors regret that the announcement cannot, as things stand, be made in the form of a resignation.

Sincerely,

Hugh Cudlipp

The next decision was that as many as possible of the IPC staff in all divisions–newspapers, magazines, books, printing–should be aware of the change before they heard it on TV or read it in the morning papers; five p.m. was settled as the earliest practical time of the meetings, the public announcement to go to the Press Association simultaneously for distribution to the Press. Arnold Quick had efficiently called a gathering of his Magazine Division executives at five in the *Connaught Rooms*. It would have been risible if the world's largest communications set-up, though distracted by a major internal problem, failed to try to communicate with its own management and employees on a domestic issue of this momentous scale.

One factor we did not reckon with on this occasion was Cecil's unusual but sparkling impetuosity. From the moment he received the second letter he did not sit brooding. He phoned Independent Television News immediately and asked for the News Editor. 'This is Cecil King,' he said, 'I am phoning to tell you I have been dismissed from my position in IPC.' Just that: no further explanation. Peter Cole, on the other end of the line, described it as one of the most astonishing calls he'd ever had, but expressed no surprise and simply asked the great man when he could come over and be interviewed. Was it a hoax? One precaution he did take; he rang me to check the information. A 'no comment' statement would have been asinine, so Tommy Atkins, the board spokesman, confirmed the news before there had been time to tell even the top brass of the staff: down-the-line communication, so noble a concept among middle management at seminars, took another nose-dive.

Cecil also phoned the BBC at 2.20 and they put out a news flash at 3.52 covering the brief facts. An IPC shareholder called the *Financial Times*–that's how *they* heard the news–to say the BBC had interrupted the racing to announce that Mr King was sacked as boss of IPC and then interrupted again to say he was also sacked as a director. 'He wasn't really worried about the horses,' said the FT 'Men and Matters' column, 'he was more than happy with the efforts of the ex-Chairman Mr Cecil King and anything but delighted at the prospect of Mr Hugh Cudlipp as Chairman. For a start, he said, Mr King would be much tougher with the unions than Cudlipp.'

IPC issued a statement at four o'clock saying that Mr King had ceased to be the Chairman and a director of the Corporation, and that Mr Cudlipp had been unanimously elected in his place. It added:

'The whole of the board take this opportunity of placing on

public record their appreciation of Mr Cecil King's tremendous contribution to the expansion of IPC and the *Daily Mirror* Group during his seventeen years of chairmanship.

'He will always be held in great esteem and affection by his colleagues.'

The first succulent interview was on ITN at 5.55 with Cecil King talking to Reginald Bosanquet:

Bosanquet: Why do you think they dismissed you?

King: Oh, I think it is a counter-attack by the Labour Party members of the board on what I said on the front page of the *Daily Mirror* a fortnight ago.

Bosanquet: Now, this really is an important question. Why did you sign it?

King: Because I thought it was important and I shouldn't hide behind the masthead of the paper.

Bosanquet: Did you consult the board about that article?

King: No, we don't ever consult the board, but it had been done by agreement with the Editors, and the Editor-in-Chief, who is Hugh Cudlipp.

Bosanquet: Did Mr Cudlipp ask you to sign it specifically?

King: No.

Bosanquet: When you heard about this, Mr King, did you put up a fight?

King: There is nothing to be done about it. If your colleagues want you to go, you go.

Bosanquet: You once, I think, said in an interview, that you were the sort of person who people tended to come round corners and find you sitting there. Did you come round a corner and find Mr Cudlipp sitting there this morning?

King: It could be. After all, I am sixty-seven.

Bosanquet: One always had the impression that you and Mr Cudlipp were friends. Are you still friends?

King: I should have thought there was a certain chill about our relationship today, wouldn't you think?

Bosanquet: Yes, I would, that's why I asked you.

King: Yes, I think you are right. You know what Fleet Street is. It's a bit of a jungle. I mean, you know, it's not played like an old-fashioned minuet, is it?

Bosanquet: Can you think in your own career of anything parallel, that you might have done to someone else?

King: Well, I removed my predecessor, Mr Bartholomew.

In the ITN interview broadcast at ten o'clock, the same interview, there were additional points:

Bosanquet: Mr King, you mentioned the counter-attack by the Labour members of the board. Who were they?
King: Well, I should think Mr Cudlipp and Mr Ellis Birk would play a leading part in that. Mr Ellis Birk has been a devoted Socialist all his life, his wife was made a life peeress not so long ago. [1] I would have thought those two would be the most politically minded, and would be anxious to turn the paper back to a warmer attitude to the Labour Party than had been apparent lately . . .
Bosanquet: Your company, I think, is publishing its preliminary accounts tomorrow. Will there be anything in that which might indicate why the company is dissatisfied with you, apart from–as you say–the political aspect of your behaviour?
King: Well, the accounts as everybody knows are going to be unsatisfactory. But I have no particular responsibility. There are certain areas of the company doing less well than we hoped earlier in the year. We think that those will be pulled round in the coming year. I have been Chairman for seventeen years, during which time though we have had our ups and downs, it's absolutely enormously outdone the downs (sic) . . .

I just think it is interesting that the *Daily Mirror* and Mr Cudlipp will now presumably switch over to the support of the Labour Party just in time to nail his flag to the mast of the ship as it goes down. I think that a mistake. He evidently thinks different.
Bosanquet: You mentioned the Labour Party hitting back. Do you see the Prime Minister's hand in this particularly?
King: Oh, I should have thought not.
Bosanquet: You don't feel there is any connection or *rapport* between Mr Cudlipp and the Prime Minister?
King: There might be, but I don't think that would motivate Mr Cudlipp.

The transmission ended with a quote from me on King's suggestion that he had been dismissed as a counter-attack by Labour Party members on the IPC board. I had said: 'The most endearing aspect of Cecil's complex character was always his Irish sense of humour.'

---

[1] Baroness (Alma) Birk became a diligent and effective Under Secretary of State in the Department of the Environment.

Those fifteen words were the single statement I made during the fracas: it seemed fairer and wiser to leave the public entertaining to Cecil.

He was in orbit. There was a further appearance on the BBC's *24 Hours* at 9.55 with Michael Barratt:

Barratt: What does it feel like now to be on the receiving end?

King: Well, I hope I have treated the people I have dispensed with with more courtesy than I received in my turn.

Barratt: You have had no feeling of courtesy today? The actual announcement, really, is quite pleasant—it pays tribute to you. Are you suggesting this was done in a rather dirty fashion?

King: Oh no, not dirty fashion, but the first warning I had was when I was shaving this morning . . .

Barratt: Was that article at the time written and published entirely on your own initiative?

King: Oh, Mr Cudlipp approved it, and so did all the Editors involved.

Barratt: Mr Cudlipp, Mr Lee Howard, the Editor of the *Mirror* and *Sun*. So they concurred in its publication?

King: Oh yes.

Barratt: But did they actively support it?

King: They concurred, anyway . . . Fleet Street is a bit of a jungle. I'm not surprised to find once more that that's the nature of the Street.

Barratt: So you seem to be saying there was a bit of dirty work at the crossroads here?

King: Well, obviously this wasn't cooked up after midnight last night, was it? There must have been a background of which I was kept in ignorance.

Barratt: You were highly critical, of course, of Mr Wilson personally. As Mr Cudlipp has been promoted does this mean that he is a Wilson man, a Wilson supporter?

King: Oh, I don't think so, no; for some considerable time he has been a Roy Jenkins supporter.

Barratt: Really? So are we likely now to see a line in the *Mirror* supporting Jenkins, and continuing to criticise Mr Wilson personally?

King: I should have thought not too openly promoting Mr Jenkins—might be damaging to Mr Jenkins—but the underlying idea is certainly that, yes.

Cecil described the letter as 'curt', which it wasn't, and made much of the point in his marathon television appearances that he received it while shaving, as if that denoted some macabre or sinister intent; one has to be doing something or other between eight and nine a.m. The intention was to give him the opportunity to ponder, discuss the situation with his wife, in whose judgement he had abounding faith, and resolve his attitude before he came to the office at, I guessed, the normal scheduled time. It was impossible to forecast Cecil's reaction to the dismissal, but it would be unlikely to upset his programme; nothing ever had. I had long realised that if the end of the world coincided with something he had already planned for that day the world would simply have to make other arrangements. We were fortunate he was not otherwise engaged on this occasion.

There is no authority like Mrs Beeton on cookery, or Emily Post on etiquette, or the Queensberry Rules or Debrett's *Correct Form* which deals with the art or craft or unpleasant duty of giving some-body the sack or push, pronouncing the order of the boot, drumming out, or striking off the rolls. There is no impeccable, time-honoured ritual which will be acknowledged as such by the recipient. The victim who hears by letter accuses his executioners of a lack of mettle, or worse, for not telling him boldly to his face. He who is verbally apprised of the news wails that they told him to his face, just like that, callously and without warning. No doubt Ralegh and Essex in their dying thoughts complained that the axe was blunt, and Cecil on this distressing occasion was as human as any of his own victims: 'They sent a secretary and the secretary delivered the message while I was shaving.'

Yet King's grandeur, or was it regal egotism, was admirable from the moment he received the letter to his impish haste to be first with the news after his talk at the office reached deadlock. ('When I knew I was out I rang the BBC and ITV and told them. That was how the Editor of the *Daily Mirror* heard the news. He has my sympathies.') In private the mood was icy anger, in public buoyant truculence, notably in the television studios. In most of his off-the-cuff reactions he behaved with restraint and disdain, even with wry humour, but not initially with abuse or recrimination: that came later. The philosophical attitude hardened as he built up an impressive indict-ment.

After a few days Cecil was telling the *Sunday Express* he had been stabbed in the back for his views. 'I will not retract a single one.

Harold Wilson is leading this country into a financial crisis and he must go. I was fired because I wrote that, but what I said will come true, mark my words.' His wife, Dame Ruth, was also quoted, proud to stand by such a man, as one would expect from so spirited an ally. 'I think anyone who puts his country and its needs before himself and his office is a man of great courage,' she said. 'He doesn't count the sacrifices he has had to make.'

The *Sunday Express* told its readers, picturesquely, that the interview with Cecil took place on 'the sun-drenched banks of the Thames outside his seventeenth-century home near Hampton Court'. He was photographed on his knees, weeding the garden, now again a humble seeker after knowledge, but he was in defiant form. 'Of course, I didn't know I would be kicked out when I wrote the article for the *Daily Mirror*, but that doesn't make any difference. Even had I known I would still have written it. It had to be said for the sake of the country. I do not lightly put my name to things.'

Within a month Cecil was ruminating that it sounded as if a majority of the board wanted a new chairman but were so scared of confronting him or giving him any opportunity of fighting back that they decided the first he would hear of their plans would be his dismissal; 'If this is really all there was to it, it must be the most badly bungled affair in recent commercial history.' (Spectacularly brutal, necessarily or otherwise, it may have been: badly bungled it was not. Cecil was dismissed and stayed dismissed.)

On May 30 he rejected the loaded invitation by a television interviewer to say that he had been dismissed in a rather dirty fashion: 'Oh no,' he said, 'not dirty fashion.' But a month of meditation, feeding the rooks and weeding in the garden ('The weeds like the poor are always with us'), enlivened the scenario.

There was no personal acerbity between us in the trying month, especially for him, between the noisy farewell and the AGM. The idea that he was turfed out of his ninth-floor suite with a few hours' notice was nonsense; he was told he could keep it for any reasonable period. When Dame Ruth dramatically told the *Guardian* 'He has to have all his things cleared up by today' she was misinformed or misquoted.

During the week after the climax Cecil phoned me in the office: 'I understand you are having some trouble with the shareholders. I think it might be helpful if we discussed this, if you so wish.'

When I joined him in the suite he said, 'I must say the *Daily Mirror* is brilliant this morning. As usual you have beaten the others stone cold.' Bobby Kennedy had been shot just before midnight on June 4 at the *Ambassador's Hotel* in Los Angeles and died of the wounds two days later. I explained that we had been fortunate in having two of our superlative writers, John Pilger and George Gale, staying in the hotel who actually witnessed the assassination. 'That's not luck, that's planning,' said Cecil; 'you only have luck on newspapers if you deserve it.' It was a magnanimous gesture in the circumstances.

We talked about the restless shareholders and I explained that my advice was that nothing more should be said in explanation until the AGM when, of course, it was my intention to make a statement.

'If I am attacked,' he said, 'you can count on me to defend myself.' And then, less abrasively, 'A slanging match between you and me wouldn't help anybody and certainly wouldn't help IPC. We would both be too good at it.' I told him that at no time then or before the meeting, would I say anything in public about him not shown to him in advance; also that I would send him well in advance, certainly with a notice of thirty-six hours, any statement I decided to make. He indicated his approval, but made no similar offer. To describe the atmosphere as affable would be an exaggeration, but he was, as usual, civil. We exchanged letters later to ensure that he would be given the opportunity to speak at the AGM. The excited audience would no doubt have been surprised to know of the courtesies arranged behind the scenes.

Shareholders had been unhappy about their dividends for several years and the current results were dismal. Yet they had little to complain about, at any rate in the dramatic sense, at the AGM of 1968.

The event was planned to take place at a hall in the City, but the seating capacity of 350 for this particular occasion was inappropriate. The address–St Mary Axe, EC 3–was too appropriate. The only place it could be moved to at short notice was the *Café Royal*, poised at the pivot of London and therefore easily accessible to all shareholders. What I was determined to avoid was a last-minute adjournment of an overcrowded meeting to accommodate protesting shareholders who might be unable to hear or see what was going on. I was prepared for the other newspapers to enjoy a feast of words at our discomfort, but not, hopefully, an orgy.

In the financial columns they had been puffing at the embers:

> Considerable disquiet has been aroused. No official ex-
> planation of any sort has been forthcoming from the board.

It is understandable that some of the large shareholders in IPC are restive.

This is yet another case of shareholders, the owners of the business, being treated in a peremptory manner by their directors.

It is up to them to take a stand.

King himself had issued an effective trailer: 'I shall be there and I will make a speech. I shall certainly not be there to talk about the weather. I am not going to talk about the future, am I? The significance of what I say is for my audience to decide.' I felt reasonably assured of a full house. Tommy Atkins, adept at promotions and booking unlikely stadiums at a second's notice for happier occasions, was puzzled as I raised an eyebrow when he announced he had acquired the Napoleon Room (seating capacity 800) with the Marie Antoinette Room (capacity 400) for an overflow. I remembered that Uncle Northcliffe on a visit to Fontainebleau tried on the Emperor's cockaded *chapeau* and found it too small for him.

On the morning of the meeting the three lifts at the *Café Royal* were running hot, conveying seven or eight hundred men and women to the fourth floor; I observed the operation while handing in my coat at the ground-floor cloakroom and walking to the first floor where the directors were gathering for coffee.

In the Napoleon Room, Cecil, flanked by the stalwart Dame Ruth, was already prominently seated in the front row, peering at the ceiling or glancing impassively at the excited people around him, a figure of calculated calm awaiting his moment; 'A distinguished businessman,' said the *Daily Express*, 'who had lost his newspaper empire but not his aplomb.'

Just before twelve o'clock, when the meeting was due to begin, Frank Rogers leaned over to me and said, 'Cecil's here.' I told him I knew, but he repeated 'Cecil is *here*' several times, trying to indicate to me that he was standing in front of me. This was the famous eye-ball to eye ball picture so lavishly displayed in the newspapers, but the dialogue was less dramatic than the photograph.

King: Well, quite a turn-out.
Cudlipp: That is what I was saying to Frank.
King: I will stand up and say my piece and then shut up.
Cudlipp: Fair enough. I will invite you to a microphone on the platform as soon as I have finished my statement.

The first interruption came from a shareholder complaining about the change in the venue of the meeting, adding, 'This meeting is in the Napoleon Room. We all know what happened to Napoleon.' (*Laughter and acclamation.*) I did not know whether he was referring to Napoleon I, II or III.

I read out to the shareholders the letter that dismissed their Chairman. And here, condensed but for the record, are my opening remarks before calling upon Cecil:

'I am happy to see that Mr King is with us here today at the Annual General Meeting. (*Acclamation.*) It is my intention–and I am sure that all shareholders will approve–to afford Mr King an opportunity to speak as soon as I have completed these introductory remarks.

'It was the hope of Mr King's colleagues that when he had considered the position, he would have agreed, without undue publicity and controversy, to offer his resignation as we had suggested. The position was that his colleagues regarded him–and still regard him–with high respect. We, nevertheless, had decided that his long period of service and leadership must now end.

'The suggestion that this was in any sense a political upheaval by any or all of his colleagues as the result of Mr King's article in the *Daily Mirror* of May 10th was fanciful. (*Cries of "Rubbish" and "Nonsense".*)

'So far as I am aware, only one member of the IPC board is a member of the Labour Party. I would not be surprised if most of the others are fully paid-up members of the Tory Party. The suggestion, fostered by some newspapers and television commentators–for discernible reasons of their own–that Mr King was asked to resign by his fellow directors because of the particular political views he expressed in his article in the *Daily Mirror* was quite untrue.

'So far as I am concerned, his personal strictures on Mr Wilson's administration were justified, and I said so to Mr King. I do not recollect, in thirty years of working in close collaboration with Mr King, many divergences in our attitudes to politics or to national affairs.

'His prophecy that "We are now threatened with the greatest financial crisis in our history" was a personal prophecy, and his statement that the crisis was "not to be removed by lies about our reserves" was a personal statement–both made from his own

363

particular knowledge and experience. I was in no position to endorse or refute them: had he made these references in a public speech they would of course have been published by every newspaper in the land, and possibly also in Zurich, Basle and Kuwait.

'It was not the quality or the nature of Mr King's politics that had caused a situation between himself and his colleagues which was detrimental to the present and future business of the Corporation: it was the quantity, the preoccupation, the personal intervention in national affairs.

'I trust that it is understood, and is acceptable now, that the power of Mr King's colleagues to act resided solely in the Articles of Association. Thirteen directors do not lightly embark upon a course which leads them, in complete unanimity, to advance a change in the chairmanship which had already been planned and had indeed been publicly announced by Mr King himself a year or so ago.'

The speeches and the uproar, and the later comparative calm, are too recent to recall in detail, but it would be ungenerous not to give Cecil King credit for his histrionic performance: the mood was Alec Guinness, and the audience were waiting for the seismograph to flutter.

On the day of his departure he had told the Press that if there had been any intrigues he knew nothing of them; there was no indication that 'it was coming'. At the AGM he warmed to the theme. 'On no single occasion has any single director expressed any dissatisfaction with my conduct in the chair, so that anything that happened came to me as a complete surprise and with no background of any kind whatever.' He complained that even the Chairman had the right, the same as other directors, to be given notice of a board meeting; there was no notice of a board meeting and therefore there was no instruction and no board meeting; yet Mr Cudlipp had the effrontery to say the letter was sent on the instructions of the board. (The letter dated May 29 did not use the phrase 'board meeting', but at the AGM I had said erroneously before reading the letter that it had been signed by me 'on the instructions of the board'). Then came the killer punch-line the shareholders and the reporters were waiting for, all the more effective because it was delivered without declamation, with no departure from the traditional Cecilian monotone: 'The thing was just a conspiracy of a particularly squalid kind . . . if they called a board meeting and had said to my face that they wanted a new chairman, there was nothing I could do except accept the position with the best grace I could. But, no–to face me at a board meeting was evidently more than their courage would rise to. So the method they pursued was to send their secretary over there (pointing to John Chandler) to see me trembling one morning at 8.15 to hand me a letter to tell me that I was to be out in three hours' time. I had been a member of the staff for forty-two years, a member of the board for thirty-nine years, Chairman for seventeen years, and I was given three hours to clear out. I was even asked, with a piece of absolute unequalled effrontery, to help them in the manoeuvre by going quietly and not telling people what had happened.'

I was tempted to applaud the performance, but the audience would have been confused and the meeting had a long way to go. I thought the highlight of what he called his swan song was the reference to his erstwhile colleagues: in the circumstances he was handsomely civil to me but the other two directors he mentioned were savaged in varying degrees. The technique he chose was the Slow Burn:

> 'In 1965 I supposed that I had five years before my retirement and I thought it was my duty to arrange for a management set-up to take the place of my own when I retired. Five years, I thought, would give time for the new organisation either to work, in which case I could slide out more or less unnoticed when the time came, or alternatively if it did not work there would be time for me to make any necessary adjustments; and with this in view I persuaded the board to elect Mr Hugh Cudlipp Deputy Chairman–in fact, Chairman-Designate.'

The microscope was now more meticulously adjusted.

> 'Mr Cudlipp is the best popular newspaper editor in the world, and he is not really the conductor of an orchestra, which is what one expects of a chairman–he is more of a first violin, but a very good first violin. I think his colleagues would all say that in the three years that have passed since 1965 he has been a better Chairman than we had even expected . . .
>
> 'The second appointment was of Mr Frank Rogers to be Managing Director. Mr Frank Rogers has been in charge of our printing production labour problems in the *Mirror*. In that position over a period of about four years he has done more to improve the productivity of our Fleet Street business than everybody else put together in twenty-five years.

'He did a magnificent job and set an example to the other papers which they would have been well advised to copy. But, of course, making him Managing Director of IPC, which is a very much larger and more complex job, I think he has been inclined to spend too much money on central services. I think, possibly, that some of his new enterprises show less prospect of profit than one would wish. We decided over a year ago that not enough was being done to enhance the advertising and sales revenue of our company and that a marketing director would be a sound appointment. This was more than a year ago, and Mr Rogers has not submitted a name, or at any rate had not by May 30th. I think this was unduly dilatory on an important point. The point I am trying to make is that I think Mr Frank Rogers has not established himself as Managing Director of the Corporation; I think he may still do so; I think he should be given time . . .

'The third leg on which the future top management was to rest was Mr Gordon Cartwright, the Finance Director, who has the very highest professional qualifications and has been with us for some time. I think from what I have said about the misfortunes of Hamlyn's[1] and the unreliability of the forecasts of profits, and I think the control of expenditure—and I have had complaints from at least two directors about the conduct of negotiations of a financial character—I think I could fairly say that the third leg has not stood up, and had I still been Chairman by now I would have taken steps to strengthen the finance/accounting side of the business.'

Gordon Cartwright's anger was understandable and apparent. He should have exercised his right to reply, or I should have invited him to do so.

Other directors were awaiting their turn in the torture chamber and were disappointed or relieved when their names were not mentioned.

Some shareholders, including Miss Warren, were unconvinced that the decision to ask King to retire was not based on his political statement; 'It was too soon and too impressive to believe that it was not organised,' she said. I replied:

'Well, I did say in my opening statement, and I can only repeat what I said, there was certainly no political feeling on my part.

[1] Mr King had explained earlier in his speech that the accounts of the Paul Hamlyn book division had been switched over to a computer. 'This was done in a way which evidently was not successful,' he said.

As Editorial Director of the company at that time not only did I willingly publish this article but I said to Mr King that I agreed with what he said about the Wilson Administration. I think it is absolutely clear, and I am quite sure Mr King would agree, that it is highly unlikely that I would be a party to any move arising out of that article.'

The majority of shareholders at company annuals can usually be relied upon to shout 'Shut up' or 'Sit down, beaver' or 'Let's get on with the business' to over-persistent or over-truculent questioners or interrupters, and even at the most rowdy and excitable of meetings there are salty or amusing moments. Mr S. Rothstone sought to ask Mr King 'What length of notice he gave to his predecessor in office at the *Daily Mirror* (Mr Bartholomew) and to his predecessor at the Reed Paper Group (Mr Philip Walker) and also to his Managing Director (presumably Mr John Coope), who were most unceremoniously treated and bundled out.'

Mr Wilmott was concerned about the Articles of Association; would the board consider going very carefully through these Articles to see whether they could be amended in some way which would prevent a recurrence of what had happened in the past few months to Mr King? 'Well,' I replied, 'some of you might think I would make that my first task.' (*Laughter.*)

The Man of Destiny was still big news, and this was not the last occasion he would be involved in a raging controversy. The headlines in the newspapers were more or less as he or I would have predicted:

'SQUALID PLOT'–CECIL KING (*Evening Standard*); MR CECIL KING'S BITTER ATTACK ON IPC BOARD (*Financial Times*); MR KING FIRES HIS PARTING SHOTS (*The Times*); CECIL KING SPEAKS OF 'CONSPIRACY' (*Daily Telegraph*); MR KING GROWLS HIS WAY OUT OF THE JUNGLE (*Guardian*), and on another page the *Guardian* headlined its fuller report: CECIL KING'S 'SWAN SONG' OUT OF TUNE WITH IPC'S NEW 'CONDUCTOR'.

Two of the newspaper verdicts on the riotous meeting are amusing enough to resurrect, one pro-Cudlipp the other pro-King. Miscellany in the *Guardian* chuckled over the personality clash:

Hemlock and Molasses came intermingled, naturally. Cecil King felt free to dismiss his successor, Hugh Cudlipp, as a better first violinist than orchestra conductor:

but it was the IPC annual meeting and IPC shareholders could hardly have forgotten how Cecil (pre-chop) had designated Cudlipp as his heir. Therefore the musical barb was followed by an immediate King admission that Hugh 'has been an even better Chairman that we would have expected'. There was no argument about that yesterday . . . Awkward moments were adroitly fudged over . . . By the time Cecil got his say, he'd self-evidently lost. Shareholders afterwards seemed vastly reassured about Cudlipp's tycoon talents. Why push Roy Jenkins for PM? one wondered: Hugh would do it much better himself.

Kenneth Fleet, the City Editor of the *Daily Telegraph*, assumed a graver demeanour:

> It was Cecil King's day. Unlike Caesar, the deposed chairman of International Publishing Corporation was allowed to give his own oration at yesterday's annual meeting. He did not squander the chance.
> The IPC shareholders who had come in their hundreds to see a fight, loved it . . .
> Entertaining as was Mr King's swan song it contained plenty to make IPC shareholders anxious about their investments.

The more perceptive and informed newspapers knew there was more to it than a board revolt over 'Enough is Enough'. Robert Jones wrote in *The Times*:

> In the past year or two that close harmony, in which at times it seemed that the extrovert and articulate Mr Cudlipp and the introspective, moody and shy Mr Cecil King often seemed to act as much in concert as Siamese twins, has been showing signs of strain. And Mr Cudlipp's growing alienation was shared by many other key executives at IPC.

The growing alienation of the 'many key executives' was not with King's political attitudes or messianic crusade as such—most of them were not political animals—but with the amount of time and devotion he assigned to the nation's problems. IPC had problems of its own and had indeed invited McKinsey & Co., the American business-efficiency consultants, to come inside and form a view of part of the empire.

The Economist was less polite.

> So Mr King has gone the same way he came in–by a boardroom putsch . . . Mr Wilson was certainly lucky in that Mr King's attack was launched from a crumbling managerial position. Some IPC managers have long been unhappy about the regime.

Enough was too much. The *Daily Telegraph*'s comment about the disaffection of the group management team was accurate:

> Growing resentment among the technically-minded, research-orientated executives who are led by Mr Rogers, the Managing Director, has resulted from Mr King's reported habit of upturning carefully laid plans for what appeared to be 'unscientific' reasons. IPC is now big business, which means the reign of the rational, sometimes impersonal, executive. That is not a mould into which Mr King fits.

I shall return to the fascinating myths which surrounded what King described as his unexpected dismissal. How did Westminster and Mr Harold Wilson react to the news of May 30? The *Guardian*, in kittenish mood, said that at Westminster 'it was sunshine all the way. Ministers were asked time and time again "Will you recognise the new Republican regime?" The word for it all was glee, unmitigated schoolboyish glee–a giant toppled from his beanstalk.'

Who, in retrospect, could begrudge Wilson the wry comment in his book:

> 'A fortnight later his colleagues on the board of the International Publishing Corporation suddenly realised the meaning of his slogan "enough is enough", and found it had an unintended significance for them. He was sacked while shaving . . . In the event, though no longer a newspaper proprietor, he had no difficulty in finding press space for his views and throughout 1968 and the following year, even when our payments were in strong and growing surplus, he steadfastly maintained his watch for the financial doom which never came.'

In the House of Commons a motion was drafted and signed by Michael Foot, endorsed by Ian Mikardo, Tom Driberg and three other Labour MPs, headed 'For King and Cudlipp'. It wished Mr Cecil Harmsworth King a long retirement uninterrupted by the demands of public service, and urged the Prime Minister not to appoint Mr Hugh Cudlipp to the Court of the Bank of England.

In public Cecil King complained: 'The first warning I had was when shaving this morning . . . This obviously wasn't cooked up after midnight last night, was it? . . . There must have been a background of which I was kept in ignorance.'

In private, to people not engaged in the front line, he said: 'I taught them too well.'

24

Fascinating Myths

There were a number of piquant incidents at a soirée at 11 Downing Street on Thursday, May 23. It was the meat in the sandwich between 'Enough is Enough' and King's own exit. Jennifer Jenkins, the conspicuously intelligent wife of the Chancellor was 'At Home', and Jodi and I had said Yes before King's big blast appeared in the public prints. It occurred to me in the circumstances, still the subject of lively conjecture and political dispute, that my presence might be an embarrassment, but the jocular reply from the Chancellor's secretary was that absence might be more embarrassing than presence. Roy Jenkins possibly considered that a total black-out of anybody in the *Daily Mirror* hierarchy might imply that he knew in advance of Cecil's bombshell: 'a fresh start under a new leader' embraced the possibility of leadership by Jenkins as well as by other contenders who might be on the list of nominations of the Parliamentary Labour Party.

Dick Crossman spotted me first at the reception and with his usual ebullience started to address me while I was still five yards away. He was then Leader of the House and Lord President of the Council, and what he said was audible to more than a dozen people. 'Cecil is a fool,' said Dick; 'a Wykehamist should know better. Doesn't he understand? We'll never get rid of the little man now. Cecil's attack is Harold's insurance policy. He's given him security for life.' I would have preferred to discuss the subject more discreetly.

Mr and Mrs Wilson arrived as I was chatting briefly with the Chancellor. For the one and only time in a long acquaintance Mary gave me a look like the accusing glare from the widow in the 'Keep Death Off The Road' advertisement, though later, in more friendly circumstances, she could not recall the incident.

After the dismissal of Cecil King, the *Sunday Telegraph* published a story on June 2 by Peter Paterson, under the headline 'How Wilson got a hint, and Cudlipp a shock,' referring to events which did or did not occur at the party:

> The Prime Minister was less remote from the manoeuvring than leaked versions of the crisis indicate . . .

While there is no evidence that the Prime Minister actually plotted the downfall of his outspoken critic, it seems clear that he knew in advance that it was going to happen.

... before the IPC board decided that Mr King had to go, the Prime Minister attended a party given by Roy Jenkins, Chancellor of the Exchequer, who was the embarrassingly hot *Mirror* favourite for Premier during Mr King's anti-Wilson campaign. Hugh Cudlipp, regarded by some as the Iago to his old chief's Othello, was among the guests.

The Prime Minister and Mr Cudlipp retired to a nearby settee and spent half an hour in animated conversation. No one overheard them, but in the light of subsequent events no one doubts what they were discussing.

At the same party, when a publisher asked about Mr King's forthcoming book, for which Mr Cudlipp had been acting as middleman, he was told enigmatically, 'Relax'. . .

All the indications are that the skids had already been under Mr King for some time. Timing was, however, vital. Cudlipp showed distinct signs of alarm when, a week ago, a Left-wing journalist friend suggested to him that it was time for IPC to get rid of Mr King. The journalist had no idea, of course, that his suggestion was already about to be acted on.

The *Guardian* also put the pertinent question: 'There remain, of course, innumerable loose ends for the tying. When, for instance, did Harold hear about the plot to oust his persecutor?'

The dialogue between Mr Wilson and myself did not, in fact, include any reference to the announcement to be made the following week about the future of Mr King, nor had the affair been resolved at that time. Harold, in breezy form, was enthralling two women guests with a description of the funeral (Adenauer's) he had attended the year before in Germany. It was 'a working funeral', he said, telling them how he was squeezed into a small car with de Gaulle. The ladies asked him about the arduous responsibilities of Premiership, and in an aside to me he said: 'My problems are only Queen-size. I preferred the literary style of the Monday editorial ("No Vendettas") to the Friday piece ("Enough is Enough").' But Peter Paterson was right about Cudlipp's shock. The Left-wing journalist to whom he referred was Paul Johnson and the dialogue took place at the same party. Paul arrived rather late and said to me at the doorway as I was leaving, 'Hugh, I think it is time you got rid of King. He is turning the *Mirror* into a proprietor's newspaper.' I suppose the remark, made in all innocence, as Paul explained later, was overheard by four or five guests at the sort of political party where all ears were flapping. One year later, to the day, Paul Johnson recalled the incident in his review for the *New Statesman* of Cecil King's first book, *Strictly Personal*:

> Cudlipp looked startled, as well he might; by then the *putsch* must have been in its final stages of preparation, and any leakage could–indeed must–have been fatal. But the secret was kept; King fell; and those who trouble to read this curious volume of memoirs will realise why his fall was inevitable.

Was the Sunday Times *correct in describing the dismissal of King as* '*spectacularly brutal*'? Proprietors like Thomson, Esmond Rothermere or Max Aitken cannot be removed except by the intervention of the Almighty. Northcliffe was still the proprietor of the *Daily Mail* when he was raving mad, and there are cases of newspapers suffering unduly because their proprietors have passed their prime but will not take a sabbatical or graciously retire. Cecil King was an appointed chairman holding a minute proportion of the shares in a public company. It was the duty of his colleagues on the board to decide when the curtain should fall.

The *Sunday Times* is in a like-it-or-lump-it position with Lord Thomson. It happens to be in a like-it position but it would have to lump it anyway: there are no means at all, brutal or spectacularly brutal, by which the Canadian can be obliged to accept a one-way ticket to Toronto. When he was asked whether anything similar could happen at *The Times* Roy was breezily confident. 'We own seventy-eight per cent of our own shares. I think I can walk in in the morning and feel there has been no palace revolution.' He thought Editors were 'more familiar with conditions and had no concept of megalomania which could easily happen with a proprietor who felt he had a lot of power'.

In an interview with William White of the *Evening Standard* after the news was announced, Cecil said: 'Do you expect me to fight this decision, to create a rift, getting support from other directors, splitting the board and leaving the company in tatters?' It was that specific danger which had to be reckoned with and prevented. The man who described Fleet Street as a jungle would know, as I did, that no beast is more dangerous in the jungle than a wounded tiger.

A request to depart in three months' time, or in six months, or even in a year would have been received with amused contempt, and any notion that the matter could be amicably resolved at a board meeting in the presence of the Chairman could only be suggested by Cecil himself or by somebody who had never met him. Nor could I or others accept that a man who unilaterally announced staying on until seventy in spite of his own rule about retirement at sixty-five would be likely to consider a second opinion on the same matter two years later. The end had to be irrevocable.

Was anybody, other than IPC *directors and one company official, aware in advance of 'the conspiracy'?* No. Roy Jenkins did not know in advance of 'Enough is Enough', as Mr Wilson might have suspected, and neither Mr Wilson nor any other politician knew in advance of King's impending departure. The suggestion that the Prime Minister's hand might have played any part in the dismissal was naïve. Nobody on the first rung of journalism or politics could conceivably have thought so and King was big enough, as usual, to knock the myth on the head when it was first put to him by the television interviewers. The Prime Minister's hand? No, he thought not. Any connection or *rapport* between Mr Cudlipp and the Prime Minister? There might be, but he didn't think that would motivate Cudlipp. It was only during the grumbling aftermath that the idea was mischievous enough for him to resurrect and savour. I was surprised and saddened to read the following item, dated February 25 1971, in his diary for 1970–74. It concerned his seventieth birthday celebration at which Edward Heath, then Prime Minister, was a guest.

'Ruth had more confidential talk with Ted than I did. He said his greatest problem just now is the subversive fifth column "reaching right up to the top". He also said he had not yet got to the bottom of the part played by Wilson in my expulsion from the *Mirror*.'

Cecil records the remark was confidential and then quotes it: A's version of what C said to B is inadmissible evidence in a court of law, not only in cases of rape. I apologise to Mr Heath if he was misheard, misunderstood or misquoted.

Was King fired because of 'Enough is Enough'? He made many
references to this ennobling theory: it was a pleasing plinth to ascend.
The letter, written by me, made it crystal clear that it was not the
nature of the politics but preoccupation and personal intervention,
the game of power politics, which had become intolerable. In the
mind of one director 'Enough is Enough' was the last straw; to others
it was of no consequence, a comma in a process then regarded by the
majority though not by all as inevitable. King was not asked to resign
by a unanimous vote because of 'Enough is Enough', but it was the
occasion. Most of the directors were anti-Labour and were no doubt
delighted with King's piece in its political aspects. He had publicly
said the same thing, without the allegations of lack of integrity and
'lies about our reserves', in a television interview with Robin Day on
March 31.

I personally advocated the precise day of the week for the article to
appear–not on the *eve* of the borough elections as he had planned but
on the night when the voting was completed and the results, predictably gloomy, were pouring in. Publication on an earlier day that
week would have exposed the newspaper as well as Cecil King to the
charge of sabotaging Labour's chances deliberately at the polling
booths. Not his intention and not acceptable to me.

'I should think,' said Mr King, 'that Mr Cudlipp and Mr Ellis
Birk would play a leading part in that counter-attack.' Mr Cudlipp
could not lead a counter-attack on the publication of an article he
had not refused to publish: nobody could play a leading part in a
counter-attack which did not take place and was never discussed.
There was an IPC board meeting the Tuesday after King's article
appeared, planned well before the event, and any director (as usual)
was open to say what he thought fit. Only one director expressed
any view at all after Cecil had referred to his Sermon on the Front
Page and the furore it had caused.

King mentioned on television, without naming him, one director
who would be 'highly displeased' by the article; he meant Ellis Birk.
It is true that Birk was highly displeased. It is true that so far as Birk
personally was concerned 'Enough is Enough' was the end of Cecil.
In Ellis Birk's own words, which are also true: 'When I got back to
London we (he and I) talked for several days. You were at first
reluctant to organise Cecil's dismissal but were finally persuaded by
me on the basis that this was the culmination of a series of events
which had taken place over the previous twelve to eighteen months
which had demonstrated that Cecil was no longer fit to be Chairman

of IPC. He was out of tune with the board and had devoted too much of his time to power politics and not paying sufficient attention to the many problems which were developing within IPC. Once you had agreed, we discussed a plan of action and your consultation with other directors on the timing of the dismissal began.'

The drop of £4,000,000 in the company's profits in 1967–68 from £10,500,000 to £6,600,000 also had no relevance to the parting. Chairmen take the beaming bow when things go well and hold the baby in public in sorry times, but the profits or losses are the responsibility of all. King said, and rightly said, that he did not think he had been replaced because of the poor financial figures expected from IPC the next day: he added, untypically, 'A number of other directors are more intimately concerned with the departments which show disappointing profits.'

It was a coincidence that the figures had to be announced the day after the decision: there is always some reason or other available to those who wish to vacillate, but on this occasion there was no resort to an alibi for further delay.

Why not face to face? The insinuation that his colleagues (handpicked by him presumably for their integrity as well as ability or potentiality) were overnight too weak-kneed to meet him face to face was good propaganda on the telly. It was absurd in view of their expressed readiness to meet him face to face within an hour or two of his receipt of the letter, and it was comical since they did not change their minds or budge an inch during or after the confrontation of which he said they were so scared. Cecil was still assuming an omnipotence and omniscience they no longer recognised.

The decision on how and when the news should be conveyed was taken at my instigation. I judged that a letter, giving him time for contemplation before meeting us soon for discussion, was less hurtful than an instant confrontation or a phone call announcing that 'Three of us want to come to see you to tell you we have decided you ought to go.' As it transpired, he was wearing a bullet-proof waistcoat.

The Case of the Trembling Secretary. Cecil created the situation comedy of a rabble of forelock-touching directors, fearful of the wrath or disapproval of a scion of the Harmsworths, guiltily tucking their message of foreboding into the hot hand of a giggling typist and ducking for cover: uncouth minions unworthy of a moment of his time or consideration.

The letter was taken by the Secretary of the Corporation, a barrister and accountant, John Chandler, and the request to him was that it should be delivered not later than eight a.m. Because he had been involved in the late meeting of the board the previous night he was unable to raise any transport other than a local taxi hired in Welwyn Garden City. The postman directed him to *The Pavilion*, and as the driver joggled along the Hampton Court towpath he was pulled up by Cecil's chauffeur who informed him (*a*) that he had a puncture, and (*b*) that Mr King's house was a hundred yards further on. Mr Chandler was met at the door by Mr King's manservant and shown into the drawing-room. Cecil arrived in a long dressing-gown, opened the letter, and moved over to the window to read it in a lighter place. He said that he would be in to see the board that morning. Mr Chandler, no longer worried by the puncture, reported to the office that the mission had been fulfilled.

There was one monstrous fabrication. When the *Daily Mirror* was threatened with suppression during the war because of its critical attitude to the Government's performance, the Cabinet ordered an inquiry into the ownership of the *Mirror*. In a period less excitable and paranoidal one would have assumed that none could have a stronger vested interest in annihilating Hitler and his Nazi thugs than a rich Jew; yet in some overburdened minds at that time some significance was attached to the fact that shares in the *Mirror* were owned by Sir John Ellerman. At the end of the war a mere 150,000 were held by him and his associates out of a total of 5,600,000. The recurring name of Ellerman was mentioned again by William Hardcastle on BBC television when Cecil King was dismissed: 'One of the most interesting aspects is that the largest shareholder of IPC is one of the most mysterious and probably the richest men in Britain. Little is known about him, little is known about his politics, but he is known to want his business to be run for business and not political dabbling, so I imagine the mysterious Sir John Ellerman had an important part to play in this whole thing.'

This was hyperbole, especially the reference to 'his' business. *The Times* also referred to 'Sir John Ellerman, the shipping magnate, who is the biggest individual IPC shareholder,' adding that Mr Ellis Birk, the life-long Fabian and Labour Party supporter, was the representative on the board of the interests of Sir John; the following day *The Times* published Mr Birk's categorical statement that he was not and had never been Ellerman's representative in that group.

There was no representative, at any time. Ellerman played no part in the appointment, elevation or dismissal of Cecil King and King never met him, nor did Ellerman play any part at any time in any decision affecting the newspaper's commercial conduct or editorial policy. In the Ellerman empire it was an investment among thousands, an entry in the portfolio of his financial advisers. Birk in his professional capacity was legal adviser to most of the Ellerman business and at that time had met him on only rare occasions. I was the only *Mirror* or IPC director who had ever met Sir John informally and the meeting, described in Chapter 12, occurred when I was on the staff of Lord Beaverbrook's *Sunday Express*.

The monstrous fabrication was that Cecil King had been kicked off the board because leading British financiers were worried at his criticisms of the British economy and that 'Jewish bankers' had paid out £2,500,000 in bribes, presumably to some or all of the other directors of IPC to get rid of him. I still impatiently await my cut. What was so insane about the suggestion was that nobody I ever met was more pro-Semitic than Cecil. Apart from 'Enough is Enough' for the *Daily Mirror* and a follow-up in the *Sunday Mirror*, the only other article he personally signed in our newspaper extolled the virtues of twelve leaders of industry in this country as the initiators of stimulus, productivity, enterprise and employment. His object was to encourage a more enlightened attitude to immigration: all were Jews.

No newspaper, creditably, reported or commented upon this psychopathic gossip.

Was the formal vote to end the reign of Cecil King a conspiracy of a particularly squalid kind? Cecil was a master of machination who was engaged in a crusade in private to undermine the Prime Minister and in public to denounce his Government as lacking in integrity. The charge therefore merits consideration.

The reason nobody warned Cecil King is that nobody really believed he should continue to rule on the principle of World Without End. There were no suggestions or pledges of secrecy; far from there being a desire or need for conspiracy the prevailing mood was of regret and of not a little anxiety about how and when a change could be brought about. At the AGM King expressed his complete surprise at the whole affair because 'on no single occasion has any single director expressed any dissatisfaction with my conduct in the chair'. But what was apparent was that the only person who would not be a party to peaceful change was Cecil Harmsworth King. An ambitious man engaged in redirecting the affairs of the nation and rearranging the furniture at No. 10 Downing Street and in other departments of the Establishment is in no mind to concede with good humour the sole source of his power. What had to be punctured was the pride of a lonesome intellectual who now regarded himself as beyond the criticism or influence of mortals, or at any rate mortals in the office.

I was reminded that in the problem over King my duty as Deputy Chairman was to find out what other directors thought, and I made these conditions: first, that any director I saw would be seen in the presence of another director and never the same one; second, that during the inquiry the question of succession was not brought up by anyone at any time: third, that any views expressed by any director, before any two other directors—one of whom was me—would have to be repeated before all directors.

The other stipulation I made, when it was reasonably clear that the decision would be unanimous, was that I would be in sole charge of the tactics. Once the decision was made there could be no second thoughts. If this was a conspiracy, or a conspiracy of a particularly squalid kind, I would act in no other way if confronted again by the same combustible situation, the same giant and the same beanstalk.

Cecil King's claim on television that 'I hope I have treated the people with whom I have dispensed with more courtesy than I received in my turn' is not substantiated by a single fact or by a single instance. There was no courtesy except financial to Guy Bartholomew when Cecil King decided the time had come for him to go, and certainly no formal board meeting to which Bartholomew was invited. 'Eventually I collected the votes of my colleagues, who said I would never succeed in shifting Bart but that I had their vote. Then early one morning I told him he had lost the confidence of his board and must vacate the chair. He rang one of the other directors, Bolam, the Editor, and found he was supporting me, so his reign was over.' The circumstances were, of course, vastly different.

Cecil harboured the delusion, and still does, that Don Ryder was in an opposing role to his dismissal, or reluctantly acquiesced, or was abroad, or was too busy to attend the decisive meetings. Don was the only IPC and Reed director invited to Cecil's seventieth birthday party, two years after the event, and they continued to lunch together. Cecil's notion was nonsense. Lord Ryder was among the boldest— quite certain, however regretfully, that the time had come for Cecil to cease to be Chairman. He did not dodge the question in any way when it was put to him in *The Money Programme* on BBC 2 on November 5 1971.

The reluctant David was Paul Hamlyn. Tommy Atkins had introduced Paul to the firm and Cecil had immediately offered him a directorship in IPC as the head man of the Corporation's book-publishing activities. King had a regard for individualists, self-made men, and people who enjoyed the talents he lacked himself. Paul passed the three tests, abundantly. And when King acquired the Hamlyn Publishing Group Paul himself acquired a fourth dimension, the easy independence of the millionaire. His world was Books for Pleasure, Prints for Pleasure, Records for Pleasure, Golden Pleasure Books and Music for Pleasure. He was not a writer or a painter or a musician himself, but he was and is a brilliant, original marketer, an entrepreneur in cut-price culture, serving a hungry and grateful public. Paul, for his part, was impressed by the size of Cecil King and of everything with which he was associated. The son of the late Professor Hamburger found a new father figure. The ambience of the William Kent writing tables in the office, and the mahogany Chippendale armchairs was attractive, tasteful and pleasing, a hint of Disraelian flamboyance. A close and genuine relationship was quickly established.

Paul had been a director of IPC for only three years when the notion that the time had come for Cecil to go was generally accepted. It was a shock to Paul, but he did not exercise his right to refuse to vote for King's dismissal.

Was I another of the myths in orbit on this auspicious occasion? The unanimous decision of the IPC directors was to anoint me as Cecil's successor in the commercial and financial sense as well as in my existing role in the editorially creative sphere; they were unanimously misguided.

Books with an autobiographical flavour tend to share a common blemish, self-glory and self-justification, especially when they are written by politicians or publishers, or Scottish engineers who find themselves creating and ruling the BBC. Critics are demolished in a rhetorical flourish and half-truths are deployed as semi-colons. The familiar theme is that in the struggle against the ineptitude and indecision of one's fellow men, who are merely doing their diminutive best, Our Hero emerges accompanied by a suitable Wagnerian *leitmotiv*, watchful, unerring, sagacious, imperturbable, omnipotent. The classic example of this brand of self-deluding prose is Lord

Reith's *Into the Wind*. Even the grandiloquence of the title, with its instant vision of the indomitable captain on the bridge in the midst of typhoon and terror, spurs one to reach for the spittoon or pull the chain. If the same fault is apparent in *Walking on the Water*, it is due to inadvertence.

In a Granada television performance in January 1967 Cecil said: 'One has to provide for one's succession, which I have done. If I fell under a bus this afternoon Mr Hugh Cudlipp will take my place.' He hadn't consulted his colleagues or mentioned the matter to Cudlipp. In May 1968, discussing his dismissal that day, he said: 'Obviously Cudlipp wanted my job. He and Birk were the prime movers in the matter.' When, after the decision at the meeting on the night of May 29, my name was mentioned as Cecil's successor I offered to absent myself accompanied by any others whose names might be considered. I was told, I believe by Arnold Quick, that was unnecessary; nobody expressed a contrary view and I was enthroned. There might have been discussions in my absence on this important matter but none in my presence.

What was needed was a new mind uncommitted about past events and utterly unsentimental, a ruthless pruner, a cold diagnostician, a steely administrator. Cecil King had built up a publishing empire mighty in size but had failed to reorganise and rationalise it with sufficient speed and was now himself absorbed by the self-imposed chore of running Great Britain Ltd as well. By moving me to a different sphere we transformed a competent Editor into an uninspired example of the sort of Chairman who was really needed at that juncture to embrace the activities of the whole group. What was required was not a good first violinist or even a conductor but a ruthless surgeon who would cut and cut deep. In the writhing disarray which was still then IPC the need was not for an evangelist but a new Moses descending from Mount Sinai with Ten New Commandments proclaiming 'Thou Shalt Not', and then more saying 'Thou Shalt'. Instead, we called down the man on the flying trapeze to check and double-check the cash-flow at the box office half-way through his act and to ensure by fair means or foul that the rival circuses were not allowed to do too well at our expense.

The successes in newspaper publishing have been achieved by a combination of talents at the top, working in reasonable harmony or even disciplined friction. Northcliffe wailed prophetically on his death-bed that, 'Harold will ruin my paper, he will think too much of the money,' yet the Harmsworth empire was founded by the

editorial genius of Northcliffe and the financial genius of his unattractive brother Harold, the first Lord Rothermere. That was the prime
example, but there were others. The restless, rampaging Max Beaverbrook, a great inventive journalist in the middle-class arena, harnessed
himself with the penny-pinching administrator E. J. Robertson. Roy
Thomson, making no secret of his money-mania, attracted by all that
glittered, elevating the status of a magpie to a bird of prey, yet leaving
his Editors to edit their own newspapers. King and I. ('Northcliffe
was good as a journalist and bad as an administrator,' said King. 'I'm
not a journalist, just a good administrator.') The idea of two for the
price of one doesn't work in publishing on an immense scale.

25

The Tall Leprechaun

Cecil Harmsworth King was a squatter on a commanding peak from which he observed and deprecated the follies of the rest of humanity. On his daily professional rounds he wore a veneer of super-eminence and stately confidence with the effortless comfort of a bespoke suit of armour. When the sun went down and he was alone in his domestic hideaway at the top of his Georgian house in Chelsea, overlooking the Thames, he luxuriated in self-pity and self-abnegation, pondering whether he might bring it all to an end.

The solitary confinement was self-imposed. He published his nocturnal soliloquies so that the world could witness, with more distaste than sympathy, his inner agonies and vanities.

He assessed himself, in Lord Reith's pretentious phrase, as 'never fully stretched', and harboured a grudge against the age in which he was born because mankind hesitated to surrender to him unconditionally. King complained, 'Life has always been difficult for me because this is not my world.' It wasn't his century or country: it wasn't seventeenth-century England and he wasn't Oliver Cromwell, and it wasn't twentieth-century France and he wasn't General de Gaulle. He stood impetuously in the wings of history, with mounting expectation as he aged that the call would come in time. He was numbed by the thought that wars could be won and crises overcome (or swept under the carpet), and that the human race could reproduce its kind without his personal intervention or guidance.

He confessed his disillusion and disappointment when he quoted Herbert Asquith's letter of 1892 to Mrs Horner as the colophon to the book *Strictly Personal*, published in 1969:

'Do you remember the Theban, somewhere in Herodotus, who says—that of all human troubles the most hateful is to feel that you have the capacity for power and yet you have no field to exercise it? That was for years my case, and no one who has not been through it can know the chilling paralysing deadening depression of hope deferred and energy wasted and vitality run to seed. I sometimes think it is the most tragic thing in life.'

Cecil King also thought it was the most tragic thing in life. At the age of sixty-eight he was intoning blank despondency: 'It is said that to love other people you must first love yourself. I don't know whether this is true, but it is certainly a fact that at least until recently I have hated myself and have always wanted to commit suicide. I haven't desisted because I regard it as a sin, but because it is finally to throw one's hand in, and I am not going to run away. The unusually big part sleep plays in my life may be due to a death-wish. I resign myself easily and completely to sleep, and should not be put off if I knew I should not wake up.'

The death-wish was recurrent throughout Cecil's adult life, and it was an aspect of the inner conflict of which I alone of his colleagues was aware. Over dinner together at *Au Jardin des Gourmets* in Greek Street he had told me one evening that thoughts of suicide frequently entered his mind during periods of frustration and un-happiness. Was it a self-dramatising fantasy, exhibiting self-pity and seeking sympathy and concern from others? Not, I thought, in a man of his age, position, pride and intellect. He would not wish gratuitously to display to me a lack of moral fibre. It was not a grotesque mental image to be dismissed as a passing caprice; judging from the earnestness of his conversation it was a proposition he occasionally considered, still on the agenda.

I suppose it was the one and only talk of a truly intimate nature between us during an association of thirty-five years. He told me, the same evening, of new plans in his personal life which for a while he did not want to be publicly announced or known in the office.

The first of these confidences weighed deeply with me on the night we were deciding in Orbit House just how Cecil's dismissal should be imparted to him. A letter affording him the opportunity for discussion with Dame Ruth would be less 'spectacularly brutal' than a sudden announcement on the ninth floor of a building towering over Holborn Circus.

The three most impressive men I have met in my life are David Lloyd George, Winston Churchill and Cecil King, in that order; I do not say *greatest* men because the third had the essence of great-ness but did not and could not achieve it.

The missing factors in his character put the ultimate influence or power he sought in national affairs beyond his reach: neither Gaitskell nor Wilson, nor indeed Heath, was enamoured of the notion of a boa constrictor as his mentor. Ted Heath planted a

The eyeball-to-eyeball picture lavishly displayed in the national Press after Cecil King's dismissal in 1968 as Chairman of the International Publishing Corporation. It was taken at the beginning of the lively annual general meeting of the company in the Napoleon Room of the Café Royal, London, where King trounced his former colleagues.

The Mirror Group team covering the Labour Party Conference at Blackpool, 1973. *Front row:* Political Editor, John
Beyan; Matthew Coady, political columnist, *Sunday People*;
Hugh Cudlipp with Jodi Cudlipp; Sydney Jacobson. *Back
row:* Pat Morphew, secretary; Terry Lancaster, *Mirror*
political columnist; Geoffrey Goodman, Industrial Editor.

At the Foyles literary luncheon to launch King's book *Strictly
Personal*–one year after the noisy parting: myself, then
Chairman of IPC, Lord Thomson of Fleet, and Cecil King.

flowering chestnut tree in the garden of *The Pavilion* at Hampton Court to celebrate Cecil's seventieth birthday, but he didn't invite King to plant a laburnum in *his* back garden.

His family intended him for the Foreign Office or the Army, but he would not have reached the top in either. His outspokenness, non-conformism and wilful indiscretion would have resulted in diagonal rather than vertical promotion in the diplomatic service. On his foreign journeys as a publisher he indulged, in the noble cause of unvarnished truth, in disparaging his country rather than in extolling its virtues. He would have excelled in theory at general-ship, but before you can play chess with armies you have to lead and inspire by example a platoon of disgruntled and licentious soldiery and be regarded by your superiors as a pleasant fellow in the officers' mess. He certainly did not lack personal courage, but the spur of pugnacious leadership in the field is abounding optimism. In the role of Baden-Powell he would have regarded the relief of the Mafeking siege as an unlikely event, and would have dismissed as certifiable wishful thinking the notion that 335,000 British and French troops, defeated and demoralised, could be lifted from the Dunkirk beaches by British motor-boats and warships under heavy bombardment and return to fight again to bring the Germans to their knees. Once Rommel had reached Alamein he would have written off Egypt as forever lost. On December 26 1940 he wrote in his war diary: 'Of recent months my real thoughts have been turned to what will happen after our defeat, rather than to what can be done to avert it.'

He would probably have achieved a measure of renown if he had chosen science. His patience would have been an asset. One can study and research and contemplate in solitude without being on social terms with what is wriggling or fermenting or transmogrifying at the other end of the microscope. His significant acquaintances in that realm included Sir Peter Medawar, Lord (Professor Patrick) Blackett and Sir George Thomson, from whom he heard in casual dinner-table conversation in 1939 of the discovery of nuclear fission which could be developed into a super-bomb. He knew about it long before Downing Street or the White House.

His capacity for greatness was generated by three attributes–his prodigious knowledge, for it was in books that he found the communion that eluded him with people; his grasp of world events, acquired from extensive travel and pow-wows with the people who mattered in most countries; and his foresight, not always vindicated but more often than not. He did not lack vanity and ruthlessness, but I do not recall that many of the Greats had a craving for solitude, or brooded over their personal 'unattractiveness' to others, or practised the art of invisibility.

The most significant blemish of all, of which he was frequently told but would never acknowledge, was his hyper-depressive attitude to men and events; what he regarded as his zest for realism and truth was usually pathological pessimism. He said that his favourite last words were *nil desperandum*, but he devoted his life to despair. He told me several times that what he heard as a director of the Bank of England fortified his gloom. The Achilles' heel was his proven melancholia, not his suspected megalomania.

The anatomy of leadership obsessed him, and he would discourse on the subject at an instant's notice as if one were merely intruding upon his thoughts. He was constantly bemoaning the lack of it, not only in politics but in the Church and in business, professional and academic spheres; he despised conformity and compromise and rejected rule by consensus as the ultimate full stop to human progress or even survival. ('Imagine a picture painted by a committee.') The root of the problem in the twentieth century lay in modern concepts of education. The trend of Government education was egalitarian, mixing the wheat with the chaff, retarding the clever for the benefit of the stupid. It was, unashamedly, the doctrine of the elite. King was anti-Tory and once fleetingly described himself as a Liberal, but he had no regard for the pious simplicities of orthodox Socialism. Leaders must look like leaders and behave like leaders. He deplored as wholly destructive the notion that the President of the United States, the most powerful man in the world, should look and behave like everyone else. 'Denunciation of the personality cult and applause for collective leadership merely make the ruler's task more difficult.'[1] Britain's need was for geniuses. The authentic thoughts of the humble seeker after knowledge are manifestly not the thoughts or aspirations of the humble seeker after Socialism.

Great publisher he was, acknowledged everywhere, and his influence on the newspaper industry was exercised through his

[1] The thoughts are from an article by Cecil King, which few will have seen, in ARK, printed and published at the Royal College of Art in spring 1971.

chairmanship of the Newspaper Publishers' Association, urging a fresh approach to hoary problems, stimulating a training scheme for journalists, master-minding a Press Council in which the Government and the public might have some faith, creating a Joint Board for unions and management to face the economic malaise of the Press. In his own organisation the influence was more personal, despatching his principal lieutenants and Editors and writers and night editorial executives to the established and the emerging countries (it was his concept, nobody else's) so that they might know instead of imagining the world. We brought the leading Editors of all Western and Eastern European countries, and of the USSR, to London to discuss the political future of the Continent and the Western World. He was a powerful activist in averting a third world war, prophesying and encouraging *détente*, visiting and being visited by Jean Monnet, the father of the European Community. He made our newspapers European-conscious, pioneers in campaigning for entry into the Common Market. He perceived the Wind of Change in Africa long before Harold Macmillan and encouraged the young African independence leaders while the Tories were still putting them into gaol.

So it should have ended and would have ended, but he emerged from the safer shadows of the *éminence grise* and, like a reckless impresario, cast himself in the leading role of his own production. It was now his patriotic duty, as he saw it, to offer himself with swiftly diminishing reluctance as the saviour of his country.

The major tragedy of his life was self-induced, an act of self-immolation. When he had achieved the eminence of Great Publisher he sought to use it as a lever for power in a wider field and consumed himself with a new ambition for which the Almighty, in whom he believed, had mischievously not equipped him. Cecil King, the student of history, marinated in political and constitutional biography, forgot the recent history of his own ubiquitous dynasty, the Harmsworths, the Royal Family of Fleet Street, and sought to emulate Northcliffe and the first Lord Rothermere in the sphere where they had notoriously failed and made asses of themselves and their newspapers. With all his knowledge and foresight he had not comprehended that the Fourth Estate cannot absorb the preceding three. He had often talked to me about the political uncertainty of Uncle Alfred and the political ineptitude of Uncle Harold, but now, with far greater political insight, was driven by an atavistic urge to crown their grander follies and become the puppeteer of Prime

387

Ministers and Cabinets. He dented the accepted modern image of
Fleet Street and in 328 words, 331 including his own headline
'Enough is Enough', revived the odious legend of the power-drunk
Press Barons of the first half of the century. It was not his intention
but it was his achievement. An intellectual weariness with the
trend of events in his time became a social duty to propagate re-
trenchment and reform. The sense of duty became a mission, the
mission a crusade, the crusade an obsessional presumption that he
and he alone, with or without the assistance of others, could persuade
mankind to retrace its steps. The queasiness of Cudlipp about a
'Wilson Must Go' campaign, the anxieties of Ryder at Reed International, the doubts of Ellis Birk, the concern of the Editors, were
not scripted in the final act when Cecil was on the stage alone.

It's debatable, but I would say that the true character of a man or
woman emerges with the starkest clarity under the stress of an
unexpected crisis. There was no reason on God's earth why King
need retain any sort of relationship with me after the palace
revolution. He was aware there could not have been a revolution
without my name on the death warrant; I could, for an appreciable
time, but not for ever or possibly not for very long, have snuffed
out the insurrection. Yet our relationship remained forgivingly
cordial with an absence of rancour in the chance meeting at some
function or other, and the exchange of pleasant letters.

'I have a great deal to attend to,' he told the viewers, 'I'm not dead
yet, you know. I don't intend to retire into a bathchair with my bread
and milk. Anyway, other things . . .'. 'I do not propose to go on
hawking my grievances around,' he told the people in the Napoleon
Room.

It was not long, in our correspondence, before 'Yours sincerely'
became 'Yours very sincerely' and was restored to 'Yours ever',
'Yours always' and 'Yours as always'. I wrote to Graham Sutherland
so that I could report progress on the portrait. Cecil told me he was
much impressed by a television documentary I did on the more
unfortunate citizens. He thought the 'propaganda' for the Welsh
miners was excessive; 'Their productivity was abysmally low and
has fallen since their pay went up, but then you are Welsh and
anyway Wales is much better TV than Nottingham. The Salford
part I thought excellent.' He wrote to me also with a cutting from
his local paper about a young and aspiring cartoonist: 'The cartoons
are of course imitative, but seem to me to show remarkable promise

for a boy of eleven. It occurs to me it might be an idea for one of your chaps to keep an eye on him. Political cartoonists, as we have reason to know, do not grow on trees.'

I was invited, with his knowledge and approval, to two functions to launch his books. One of them was on May 30 1969, one year to the day after his dismissal, at the Foyles Literary Luncheon for *Strictly Personal*, at which I was asked to say a few words:

'I believe that I have one–and only one–special qualification for saying a word of thanks to our chairman and to Mr Cecil King at this splendid luncheon today. I am one of the few people mentioned in *Strictly Personal* who escapes the Cecilian lash–I, who more than anybody else, might have expected nine or ten strokes of the best!

'I am not denounced as are the other victims of his frank pen, as a humbug, a nonentity, mean, penny-pinching, dishonest, illiterate, or buttoned-up. Nor even as a compulsive or crude womaniser. Nor even as a high-grade mental defective. Nor am I accused of the problem–at any rate in the serialised version– which, it is alleged, afflicted Mr Jinnah.

'After thirty years of working with Cecil King, and enjoying working for him, and learning almost all I know from him, I regard this as no mean achievement. In *Strictly Personal* Cecil bares not only his own soul without mercy but also the soul of anybody who happens to be passing by! It may be safely prophesied that autographed copies of this book will not be found upon the shelves of any of his living relatives. Nor are copies likely to be deposited reverentially in the tombs of his ancestors. Nor will this book be treasured by politicians, with few exceptions, of any colour, race or creed. They are all weighed in the balance and they are all found wanting.'

Over the succeeding years he could not resist, understandably, the occasional splenetic reference to me or IPC in the diary, but almost invariably it came from the luncheon guest who did not know or care if he was quoted, or did not trouble to deny it if he was quoted unfairly or out of context.

June 19 1968: 'Malcolm Muggeridge had known Hugh Cudlipp for a great many years and likes him, but thinks him a weak man, quite incapable of holding his job as Chairman of IPC, from which Muggeridge expects him to be ousted within a year.'

July 2 1968: 'Paul Hamlyn looked in this afternoon to my office at Reed's. He was in a very emotional state, but evidently regards me with affection, and wants to see me from time to time. He said very little about my dismissal but said that if he hadn't signed the document he would himself have had to go.' (This was the first and exclusive news of a threat or suggestion or hint that nobody ever made.)

July 22 1968: 'Lunch with Paul Hamlyn at his invitation. He wanted to tell me he planned to leave IPC, a move which caused me no surprise ... He thought Hugh's idea was that Aubrey Jones (then about to become Deputy Chairman of IPC) should do the chores of chairmanship while Hugh flitted around the world.'

February 27 1970: 'Both at dinner last night and at lunch today when I ran into Norman Collins as well as lunching with Denis [Sir Denis Hamilton, Chairman and Editor-in-Chief of *The Times*], the big job is the plight of IPC. What deep trouble they fell into–and how soon!'

He did not mention that on the day after his departure the directors had no alternative but to reduce the final dividend to ordinary shareholders from thirteen to ten per cent, bringing the total payment for his final year as Chairman down from twenty-one per cent to eighteen per cent, and dipping into the reserve funds for £1,308,000 in order to meet the dividend payment. What trouble they fell into, and how soon.

Had I been in Cecil's position, and I was in that position on more occasions than one, I am sure I would have dispensed more invective or anger; he was, indisputably, a big man.

There is an essentially human side of Cecil King that was as much a part of the whole as his external coldness and infuriating superiority. He would stop to listen patiently to mental defectives or reeling drunks who importuned him on the rare occasions when he was walking in the streets.

The death of Bernard Gray, our war correspondent, in a submarine in the Mediterranean was not a matter for a note of condolence to his widow. Cecil visited the family and advised on the education of the children for more than twenty years, and I was unaware of it until Mrs Gray told me.

When John Falls and his wife were killed in an air crash in 1950, Cecil–who had already brought up with his first wife Margot their own family of four–took on the responsibility of rearing his great-niece Sheila Falls, then six months old, together with her brothers as wards of court. 'I am devoted to her and I wish her every happiness,' he said when he gave away the bride at her marriage in 1973 in the Chapel Royal at Hampton Court Palace.

I knew of many kindnesses he extended, surreptitiously, to the most unlikely of people. 'He was a beast,' said Cassandra with a twinkle in his eye, 'but a just beast.'

Cecil King's reputation survived his dismissal. He continued to publicise his forebodings in *The Times* and other newspapers, warning the human race and especially the British against the errors of their ways. He found time, too, to entrance the Royal Institution with an account of the remarkable feats of his wife in extra-sensory perception. He explained that he was not himself a 'sensitive', but Dame Ruth was, and he had been a witness over the years of various phenomena.

She woke up after a vivid dream of a fire in a wooden hotel in Ireland where they had stayed at Rosapenna in Co. Donegal. The hotel was burnt to the ground three weeks later.

On a flight to Manchester she was not feeling very well, and when the air hostess asked her if she was feeling better after a cup of tea, she heard herself say, 'I should be quite all right now if we hadn't burst a tyre.' Emergency instructions were given to the passengers and a very bumpy landing was achieved on one good tyre. The pilot drew Dame Ruth aside and asked, 'How did you know I had burst a tyre on take-off?' She replied, 'I don't know how I knew.'

She delayed the departure of a flight from London to Paris until they were both able to board the plane. 'My wife's comment was that as a child she could always stop a train.' I have selected only a few of the phenomena among the many for which Dame Ruth was responsible. It is a good thing, from the nation's point of view, that her gifts are not widely known to the unions: Dame Ruth, in a mood of petulance, could bring the nation's transport to a standstill.

The goodwill and sympathy Cecil enjoyed during and after 'the palace revolution' were wantonly dissipated by the man himself in 1972. I have yet to meet the articulate apologist, except King, who will attempt to explain away, or excuse, or rationalise the outrageous disclosure, without the permission or knowledge of his guests, of the private talks that took place in good faith over the dining-table with an educated and trusted host. The fabric of the British Press and any other democratic Press is based upon the exchange of confidences, and reporters have risked and will continue to risk imprisonment to preserve the anonymity of their sources of information. King, a publisher of world-wide repute who employed reporters and was briefly, by the grace of Lord Northcliffe, a reporter himself on the *Daily Record* in Glasgow, pitifully dishonoured the traditional code. Not for money which he did not need, or for notoriety which he had already achieved, or for any ideological purpose, which is customarily the defence of a spy. The decision was simply *To hell, I'll tell*, a defection which would torment the soul of a Catholic priest in a wood-wormed confession box for the rest of his days on earth. King told *all* in his diaries.

The names of the top civil servants who accepted the hospitality of a man they respected and of a newspaper whose influence impressed them were camouflaged with asterisks or hyphens or fabricated with initials such as A.B. and C.D., but it did not need an identity parade or an Identikit picture to establish who they were: all else was laid bare.

Cecil's own explanations of his conduct were blandly indifferent or breath-takingly bombastic, unbelievable if they had come from any other public figure:

'If I don't want something quoted I wouldn't say it.'

'Political commentators are so mealy-mouthed. They proceed on the well-established principle that if you scratch my back I will scratch yours.'

'In some quarters it seems to be thought immoral to take down and publish remarks made in the course of a friendly lunch. These conversations were at no time supposed to be secret.'

'How can one make a breach of confidence three or four years after the event? If I'd published the conversations the next day it would have been a different matter.'

If Cecil had decorated the façade of *The Pavilion* with newspaper notices in the tradition of the theatres in Shaftesbury Avenue the towpath strollers would have enjoyed themselves hugely:

'Petty. Snobbish. Sanctimonious. Arrogant'–*Sunday Express*
'Born Sneak and Breaker of Confidences'–*H. B. Boyne, Daily Telegraph*
'Nauseating end to many a meal'–*Economist*
'Monumental Gnat'–*George Gale*

'Epitome of Upper-middle-class Aridity'–*Tribune*
'Who Does This Chump Think He Is?'–*Clive Irving*

Bernard Levin said, 'It *is* enjoyable–oh, my paws and whiskers, it is enjoyable,' but he had some social hints for King's future guests:

> The first thing I did after finishing this astounding and devastating book was to make a note that, should I ever be invited to lunch by its author, I would listen much and say nothing... So outrageous, unlimited and appalling is his indiscretion, which makes Lord Butler seem a Trappist and Mr Crossman a deaf-mute, that he really ought, for decency's sake, to have his invitation-cards embossed RSVP in one corner and 'You are not obliged to say anything, but it is my duty to warn you that anything you say will be taken down and may be given in evidence' in the other.

'It is only the unique vanity of character which he displays in his own book that will save relations between politicians and the Press from being permanently poisoned,' said the *Evening Standard*. And Mr Boyne had a telling point in the *Daily Telegraph*: 'Mr King has the effrontery to observe, apropos secret information about the state of the reserves which he gained as a Bank of England director, that Ministers were not informed of the true situation "owing to their inability to keep their mouths shut".'

King said in an interview that it would not have happened had he remained at the *Mirror*. That was of some consolation to his colleagues but of none to his victims.

Something else happened after he left the *Mirror* that, I trust, would not have happened had he remained. For a reason incomprehensible to me King conceived the notion that Sir Oswald Mosley had some relevance in the late 1960s and early 1970s. The Mosley File was familiar to anybody with a memory. Between 1918 and 1930 he had been successively a Conservative, then Independent, and then Labour Member of Parliament, moving to the Left at subsonic speed. In 1930 he founded the New Party, annihilated in the 1931 election. Then, moving at supersonic speed to the Right, he formed and led the British Union of Fascists, aping the Italian Blackshirts. During the war he was arrested under Defence

Regulations and resided at Brixton and Holloway Prison until 1943 when he was released because of ill health.

Mosley was a magnificent orator, a Wykehamist and a Sandhurst officer of personal courage who survived many a Parliamentary brickbat and bravely faced many Left-wing bricks at his riotous meetings. Politically he was an ugly episode in the pre-war history of Britain, the leader of a movement which attracted thugs and anti-Semites. In the post-war period he lived, and still lives, at 1, Rue des Lacs, Orsay 91, Essonne, France, twenty miles south-west of Paris, conveniently forgotten by the British nation he had hoped, in his misguided way, to save.

Early in 1968 Cecil King told me that Mosley had written *My Life*. The suggestion had been made that our newspapers might be interested in serialising the book and that Cecil might be interested in meeting Sir Oswald Mosley in London. To my astonishment Cecil *was* interested. I expressed my view rather explosively. The idea of Mosley lunching at the *Mirror* offices as the guest of the Chairman was abhorrent, and no meeting took place at that time.

After the parting between King and the *Mirror* there were a series of meetings. He met the author of *My Life* at a press conference to launch the book. He lunched with Mosley in his sitting-room at the *Ritz* on November 14. In 1969 he lunched with him again on March 20, dined with him 'at his charming little house at Orsay'–the *Temple of Glory*–on April 24, and invited him back for dinner at *The Pavilion* on September 17. The Oswald Mosleys dined again at *The Pavilion* on Sunday, November 9.

Cecil King was not totally starry-eyed over the aged man, seventy-one in 1968, who planned to be Britain's dictator in the 1930s. He recognised Mosley was at pains now to convince everybody he was never anti-Jewish, never pro-German, and never favoured violence at his meetings. 'Surely he protests too much,' was King's comment. He thought Mosley was still hoping to play some political part in Britain. 'He thinks we must all be ready–but ready to do what?' After their meeting on March 20 King thought that Mosley saw himself in charge at last, which seemed to King 'quite fantastic'. On April 24 he recorded that Lady Mosley was a very nice woman and that she and R. (Dame Ruth) got on immediately and well. Mosley was presented as a fanatical European who thought the whole of Britain's future turned on that subject alone, and that a world economic crisis was inevitable. At their final 1969 meeting in November, pixilated but not dominated by the phantom of thirty years ago, King records that Sir Oswald seemed to be in touch with various personages on the Continent and here, was certain a major crash was coming, and was concerned to organise appropriate steps to contain the consequences. 'He is confident he still has a part to play. *Can* this be so?'

No. It demonstrably wasn't so.

They held another summit in France in March 1972 when Mosley was seventy-five and King seventy-one, an elite Dad's Army of lost leaders mustering a total strength of two. Sir Oswald, for his part, said he admired King as 'a great publicist–someone who knows what the country is thinking'. What was the mutual attraction? Their frequent meetings cannot be airily dismissed as an Old Boys' Reunion: Mosley had left Winchester before Cecil had arrived, and Cecil would not wish to be reminded of the most miserable years of his life at that public school. Mosley in his Blackshirt days had been eulogised in 1934 by King's Uncle Rothermere in the *Daily Mirror* when he owned it, but surely to King's disgust?

There is, perhaps, a magnetic force that draws together in the barren twilight of their lives, in their loneliness and their final rejection, the Men of Destiny upon whom inadvertently or wisely destiny did not call.

A. G. Bather, King's housemaster at Winchester, was right in his final report on 'Chaste Minerva'. He discerned that there was still 'much of the child' about him. Even in the most solemn years of his adulthood there were occasional glimpses of the boyish streak of mischief and flamboyance in spite of the basic social shyness. The publication of diaries never intended for publication was one example.

He was reared in an atmosphere of emotional hypothermia from which his heart never fully thawed out. His be-knighted father's family was socially and financially overshadowed by his mother's millionaire brothers, and was partially dependent upon Northcliffe's largesse. His reserved nature and ineptitude at games made his schooldays unhappy, even nightmarish. In his own self-portrait he is the shy, shrinking violet, brilliant but liable to be overlooked by the undiscerning: in reality he is a tall, egregious Narcissus–hating himself, he says, but also admiring himself more than any man he has ever met. There are the thoughts of suicide, but he could always be relied upon to put plenty of other personalities higher on the list for liquidation.

Did the *éminence grise* become the *éminence verte*? No, because there was no man he envied. He felt capably a King among pygmies, but in his ultimate ambition he was frustratingly doomed to be only a Pretender. The boundless ambition was never quenched, but inwardly he remained insecure and immature, an untrusting loner longing to be loved, an ageing *enfant terrible* in reluctant retirement, his ego massaged by his adoring second wife.

Revelations The publication of his two Books of Relevations, *The Cecil King Diary 1965–1970* and *The Cecil King Diary 1970–1974*, are not wholly explained by the boyish streak of exhibitionism. This time the sense of mischief was callous rather than impish. The contents read singularly like the compensating maliciousness of a man who, having achieved power but never greatness, feels the need to sustain his shrinking Kingly self-image by disparaging and discomfiting others, especially those in public life still enjoying more active prominence.

In a brief interview with a German magazine, *Jasmin*, he said, two years after his departure: 'Power is what I miss most. The feeling that millions listen to me. That I can give orders to thousands.' (The translation into German and back into English may not do him justice, but the thoughts have the ring of authenticity.) He was described as a white-haired gent in Harris tweed. He was photographed in the uncertain winter sunshine strolling with his hands in his pockets along the towpath outside Hampton Court with the River Thames faintly etched in the background. The last of the autumn leaves were on the ground and there were pools of rainwater, and he was wearing an Armistice poppy in his lapel.

He retired in 1975 to a modest bungalow in the Dublin suburb of Donnybrook; the name is proverbial because of its boisterous annual summer fair, held until 1855, an event notorious for its drunken rioting and bacchanalian orgies.

One of his hobbies with Dame Ruth was to restore a dilapidated cemetery near their home in the hope of turning it into a public garden, and their gesture aroused some curiosity among the neighbours. The identity of the distinguished recluse was spotted by *Hibernia*, the Irish magazine, and Cecil jumped at the chance to poke a finger in the Irish political pie and publish in a Catholic country a eulogy of the Protestant Dr Ian Paisley: Paisley is 'a *good* man', in force of personality in a different class altogether from 'the ministerial puppetry of British politics'. King thought it important to point out that the prevailing view of Paisley was wrong. In his first reference to the Moderator of the Free Presbyterian Church in his book *On Ireland,* King wrote, 'As Dr Paisley says, Irish troubles are all the fault of the Pope: it was he who gave Ireland to Henry II. It has to be said that the Pope was Adrian IV, the only Englishman ever to become Pope.'

The Man of Destiny is a tall leprechaun. In Paul Hamlyn's *Encyclopaedic World Dictionary* the character in Irish folk-lore is lightly dismissed as a pygmy, sprite or goblin, but the description is inadequate. A leprechaun has supernatural qualities and a puckish sense of humour.

VI
END
STORY

26

'The Unpardonable Vanity'

God, it was fun. So far as journalism was concerned I didn't do a stroke of work in my life. It was a pleasurable mental exercise. I was paid frugally at first and sumptuously later on, but was always surprised I was paid at all for the editorial side of my activities: what for—enjoying myself and informing and entertaining others? Who would mind working around the clock if every day is punctuated by the impulse of events, when the only routine is the exceptional and the unexpected, when the norm is the abnormal?

Knowing what is going on is the lure of journalism. *Explaining* to vast audiences what is going on is the art. *Influencing*, or trying to influence, what is going on is the self-imposed mission. According, at any rate, to my creed.

Battling over the politics of their newspapers is by no means a common interest among all Editors. Most of them are content to obey His Master's Voice and express their own views with a cross on a secret ballot paper. Arthur Christiansen, Editor of the *Daily Express* for nearly twenty-five years, did not care what was said about this or that public issue but was deeply concerned with how it was said and with how it 'looked'. Percy Cudlipp, as Editor of Beaverbrook's *Evening Standard*, did not personally endorse many of the paper's policies: 'That is not the point,' he said to me. 'I am an advocate, like a lawyer in court, rewarded for my skill in putting my client's case.' It was not an attitude I could assume with the same bland professional aplomb. I was always in the propaganda business myself so far as a newspaper's opinions were concerned.

Political opinion is a small proportion of a newspaper's activities and is never the major factor in the success of the product. The broader the policy, the less partisan, the greater the acceptance by a wider audience.

The *Mirrors* are first and foremost popular newspapers, delivering their news with a terseness that the masses can comprehend, stating their views in a forthright manner with no if's or but's or maybe's, and packed with entertainment. They are *fun* newspapers, serious only on

serious matters of national importance, and then serious indeed. It is
their 'bloody impertinence', as somebody said, that hooks the readers.
At their gayest they specialise in original ideas and my special
function was as a merchant of ideas whether I was trading under the
title of Features Editor, Editor, Editorial Director, Joint Managing
Director, Deputy Chairman or Chairman. To Cecil King our newspapers were in the short term a political hand grenade, and in the long
term hopefully an atom bomb. To me they were principally a fascinating operation in mass communication in dozens of different spheres.
We barked for the under-dog when he wasn't getting a square deal,
but we also groomed him, threw sticks, gave him bones, took him
'walkies', and kept him happy with a variety of diets.

It was the stunts that made the paper talked about. They were
stunts with a meaningful angle.

When Lady Docker invited forty Yorkshire miners as guests
aboard her yacht *Shemara*, the wives were peeved they had been left
out of the beano. I promptly brought the ladies to London for a day
and night out as the guests of the *Mirror*. One of them asked Noel
Whitcomb, 'Shall we see the Bloody Tower, luv?' 'You shall see the
whole bl-blooming town,' said Noel. The programme was lunch at
the *Dorchester*, sight-seeing, cocktails and champagne dinner at the
Savoy, boxes at the Theatre Royal, Drury Lane, then back to the
Yorkshire mining villages, each with four cigars for the men who that
day stayed at home.

Rab Butler, as Chancellor of the Exchequer, solemnly warned the
nation that 'We must not drop back into easy evenings with port
wine and overripe pheasant.' Irresistible: I did not recall being reared
on the diet in Cardiff. I phoned Donald Zec that wet Saturday
morning and asked him to preside over a no-expense-spared feast
that night in a private room at the *Savoy* with port and overripe
pheasant for a dozen typical citizens of London Town. He managed
to round up a charlady, a bus driver, a fishmonger, a hall porter, a
secretary, a hairdresser and a dentist's assistant.

The workers' verdict? Mrs Mary Corbin, a char from Peckham:
'Well, now I've had it I don't want it.' Bus driver Stanley Lack:
'Very nice change, but I'm a bread-and-cheese man myself.' Dentist's assistant Vivien Hammond: 'I can't face it. Do you happen to
have any stew?' And this was Zec's verdict for the Chancellor: 'Port
and pheasant? They can take it. They can leave it. They're hardly
likely to get it. I don't think they want your port and pheasant, Mr B.'

Andy Capp, a workshy, beer-swilling, rent-dodging, wife-bashing, pigeon-fancying, soccer-playing, uncouth cadger, setting an appalling example to the youth of Britain, was created by Reggie Smythe who was born in Newcastle. My idea was merely to produce a cartoon of earthy Northern flavour solely for the Northern edition and Bill Herbert set about finding the right artist. Andy Capp became, and remains, world famous. The Germans know him as Willi Wacker, the Italians as Carlo, the Portuguese as Ze Do Bone, the Danes as Kasket Karl, the Finns as Lasta, the Austrians as Charlie Kappl, and the Dutch as Jan Met De Pet. Andy Capp isn't only a Geordie, he's universal.

The fun was a two-way service. Gaiety attracts gaiety. In 1965 I received a note from the man who, as Lord Hailsham, became Lord Chancellor:

> House of Commons,
> London S W 1.
> 18 November '65
>
> My dear Hugh,
>   In celebration of the defence by the *Mirror* of the principles of purity and good taste
>
> this humble
offering
from
Quintin Hogg
>
> In *A Midsummer Night*, playing 'Puck',
> A Shakespearian actress got stuck
> But, as she'd never heard
> Of that four-letter word,
> She merely observed: 'What bad luck.'

I had not bought poetry before, but Quintin was happy to settle for £5 a line.

There were, of course, the occasional grim interludes. One morning in the office Tom Tullett, a former policeman who became head of the *Mirror*'s Crime Bureau, was handed a visitor's slip from a gentleman from Gravesend:

Person you wish to see: Mr Tullett.
Business: Confidential.

'Good morning,' said Mr Tullett, 'what can I do for you?'

'I want to confess to a double murder,' said the visitor.

'Who have you killed?'

'A man and a woman, on the marshes at Gravesend. Teenagers, I think. I had a shot gun and two knives but I strangled them. I wanted to get it off my chest. I wanted to tell someone.' He pointed to a parcel with newspaper wrapping on the table. 'It contains parts of their bodies,' he said. 'I removed skin.'

He was a grossly perverted sexual psychopath, found guilty of manslaughter 'by reason of diminished responsibility' and sentenced to twenty-one years' imprisonment. He was one of a number of major criminals who dropped into our massive Confession Box in Holborn Circus to tell us of their misdeeds. At one time I contemplated installing a closed circuit television link with Scotland Yard.

Shortly after this macabre episode the Goya portrait of the Duke of Wellington was removed from the Tate Gallery by a man wishing to make a protest. It was deposited in a railway cloakroom in the Midlands and the thief was good enough to send the cloakroom ticket to the *Mirror*.

Instead of 'World's Greatest Sale', the words which usually appeared at that time under the title of the newspaper, I changed the legend to:

NATIONAL ART TREASURES RECOVERED AND MURDERERS' CONFESSIONS RECEIVED

I changed the legend on one other occasion when we were able to be of some small service to the Duke of Edinburgh. This time it announced: 'RECOVERER OF ROYAL SHIRTS'. Don Coolican told the *Mirror* in October, 1972:

YOUR ROYAL HIGHNESS— YOUR SHIRT!

The *Mirror* to the rescue—of Prince Philip's Wardrobe

The *Daily Mirror*, fearless fighter for the truth, friend of the people and now . . . recoverer of Royal shirts.

As our changed title-head above acknowledges, we achieved this new accolade yesterday when we got back one of Prince Philip's shirts after it had been . . . ahem . . . er . . . 'nicked'.

This one, size fifteen collar, blue striped cotton, button

cuffs and with the tiniest of tails, was among four stolen on
Monday.

It was being delivered to the Royal shirt-dealers, Harrods, from the makers when a gang collared the lot as the
van made deliveries elsewhere in the West End.

Since then Scotland Yard has been trying to hunt down
the Royal shirt thieves, put them in cuffs and button them
up behind bars. But without any success . . .

Until the *Mirror* had a brown-paper parcel dropped in
their front office by a young, fair-haired man who made a
quick exit.

He didn't stop to talk but left behind a letter which he
asked us to pass on to the Duke of Edinburgh. In the parcel
was a new shirt with the Royal name sewn inside.

The letter was signed 'The Diehards' and said:

'Your Royal Highness, somewhere between the vicinity
of Harrods and Buckingham Palace, we "hijacked" four of
your Highness' shirts. We have sent one of said shirts to
the Editor of this paper as proof of our sincerity.

'We will return the other three to Your Highness in
"mint condition" if you will have your "Good Lady" use
her Royal Decree to meet our demands, which are as
follows:

'Firstly, that she compel Edward Heath to apply for the
Chiltern Hundreds and then make him Assistant Master
of the Queen's Music, which will give him more time to go
"Morning Clouding" . . .'

There were three other demands from the Diehards, all of a
diehard nature. And a PS about the Royal shirts: 'We admire your
taste, sir.'

Scotland Yard sent Detective Inspector Joe Blakeny, of West End
Central Police Station, who was leading the hunt for the thieves, to
collect the shirt and the letter from me at the *Mirror* building. I was
chairman that evening, as President of the Press Club, at a dinner in
honour of Prince Philip, an honorary member of the Club, and was
able to reassure His Royal Highness that he was no longer a member
of the Shirtless Ones.

There was another ingredient in the *Daily Mirror* besides fun and
provocative politics–a sense of social justice over and above Party

considerations, a third dimension that made the newspaper of some major significance in the land. It was not, like the *Daily Express*, a pedlar of dreams, forever gospelling the joy of materialistic possessions and of nostalgic faith in our imperialist past. It was critically patriotic, often to a strident degree:

Wake up, Britain!
WE'RE LIVING IN
THE PAST
WE'RE TOO SLOW
TOO SLEEPY
TOO DAMN
SMUG!

The *Mirror* did not accept the concept that the good things in life should remain the monopoly of those Upstairs, or that the right or ability to govern resided in a privileged clique of aristocrats and their expensively educated relatives and friends. It challenged elitism, but also challenged the threat of the big battalions in the trade unions whenever they set their sights to upstage Parliament.

These qualities remain and I hope will endure. This is the policy that attracts the good writers. With the notable exception of Bernard Levin, I know of no regular Fleet Street writers to equal Keith Waterhouse, John Pilger, Terry Lancaster and the late but legendary Cassandra. Richard Crossman wrote for the Group for twelve years, and Woodrow Wyatt, a major middle-of-the-road commentator, still does. Geoffrey Goodman, the best-informed industrial editor of the 1960s and 1970s, described the insurgence on the factory floor as he saw it, and was never pruned or discouraged because his view of this or that industrial Bill opposed the paper's view. Ralph Champion in the United States, and Peter Stephens on the Continent were high-grade individuals who reported and interpreted events with a freedom which is regrettably not enjoyed by the foreign correspondents of all newspapers. In different spheres, where freedom was also desirable, Peter Wilson wrote about sport and Donald Zec about the illusory world of entertainment with a freshness and outspokenness rarely achieved in the rivals. Marjorie Proops, whose stock-in-trade is her warmth, common sense and sincerity, became the best-known journalist in the country, explaining and not condemning the new uninhibited attitude to sex and the sexes. The women executives in my time–Ailsa Garland, Felicity Green– were recognised and upgraded long before an Act of Parliament declared sex discrimination illegal. Felicity Green succeeded Tommy Atkins as the head of Promotions and Publicity and became the first working woman journalist to join the board of a national newspaper.

They were all, at some time or another, sought by other papers and offered tempting bribes, but the *Mirror* suited them and they suited the *Mirror*. The bond was stronger than a salary cheque or a better car. The atmosphere in the newspapers that matter for any considerable period of time is like that.

The editorial directors—the men between the Editors and the management—who worked with me when I moved on from editing a specific newspaper were Edward Pickering and Sydney Jacobson. The Editors of the *Daily Mirror* were Jack Nener (1953–1961), Lee Howard (a decade in the chair, 1961–1971), and Anthony Miles, now Editorial Director of the Group. The Editors of the *Sunday Pictorial*, later the *Sunday Mirror*, were Colin Valdar (1953–1959), Lee Howard (1959–1961), Reg Payne (1961–1964), Michael Christiansen (1964–1972), Robert Edwards (1972–). *The People* was edited successively by Stuart Campbell, until his death in 1966, Robert Edwards and then Geoffrey Pinnington.

I do not think they found my overlordship of their activities excessive because there was a strong similarity in our attitudes to life in general. And it was always known by Editors of the *Daily Mirror* that if deep trouble arose as the result of words written by me I would be at their side at the bar in the House of Commons or in the dock in the Royal Courts of Justice.

Who dominates the policies of newspapers? The answer is, which newspaper?

In the world of publishing, notably of newspapers, the delusion of grandeur is the vocational hazard, fermented in the case of vain proprietors by their professional entourage who have nothing to lose except their integrity. Why tell the Old Man he's not the Almighty and lose your job? Why disillusion the deluded? Let nature take its course.

Call it walking on the water. It is better not to try because of the considerable risk of drowning. Yet there are many who have not been deterred by the risk.

Northcliffe died insane. His brother Harold, who succeeded him as proprietor of the *Daily Mail*, sought to turn the world's most stable democracy into a Fascist state. One of Beaverbrook's encyclicals to his Managing Editor Charles Wintour proclaimed: I'll tell you one thing about leader writing. The voice of the *Express*: the voice of God. It's the voice of God. You know what I mean by that. Speak out, fearlessly.' William Randolph Hearst decided to remove Britain from the map of the world; he also escalated a Cuban insurrection into the Spanish-American War. John Norton, the Australian liar who owned *Truth* in Australia, was a power-drunk megalomaniac.

Some have succeeded in *appearing* to walk on the water for short distances without apparent mishap, no doubt suspended on wires from a helicopter or standing on the conning tower of a submerged submarine.

Beaverbrook self-mockingly described himself as the chief shareholder, but he was actively the Editor-in-Chief of all his newspapers, better at the job even than the able Editors he employed. Roy Thomson rigorously edits the balance sheet of the *Sunday Times* and *The Times* and publicly acknowledges that he leaves the journalism to the journalists. The man in overall charge of editorial policy at Thomson House and New Printing House Square is unquestionably Denis Hamilton, shrewd enough to allow immense freedom to the Editors, Harold Evans and William Rees-Mogg. The Chairman and Editor-in-Chief of the daily and Sunday *Telegraph* have never been known to differ; they are one and the same man, Lord Hartwell. Nor was there any noticeable strife between the Honourable David Astor, who is financially committed to the *Observer* as a commercial product, and the Honourable David Astor who edited the *Observer* with marked individualism for twenty-seven years until 1975. It is too early to know whether he will be in such blissful concord with his successor in the editorial chair. The management of the *Guardian* mind their own business and the Editor traditionally minds his.

Viscount (Esmond) Rothermere had a much tighter grip on the major editorial policies of the *Daily Mail* and London *Evening News* than was known outside the office until his son Vere Harmsworth took over the day-to-day running of the business. The first sign of editorial schizophrenia appeared during the second election of 1974 when the *Daily Mail* traditionally supported the Conservatives and the *Evening News* (same management) opted for Labour. I suspect that in the next election the *News* will return to the fold.

It is nonsense to expect any proprietor to say to his Editor: 'Here it is. I will take all the financial risks in this precarious industry, but you can say what the hell you want to say in my newspaper any time you like.' It is manifestly greater nonsense to accept the current notions of the militants who advocate that the editorial staff, and maybe the compositors and doormen, should decide the policy of the newspaper and hire and fire (but not pay) the Editor. I have yet to meet an Editor who would be sufficiently servile to be a puppet on a union string. With a single proprietor he can manoeuvre, cajole, persuade or dissuade, threaten to resign and state publicly why. What goes into a newspaper, and when, and with what force, is in practice the result of a battle of wits, and if the advocacy and the conviction are strong enough the proprietor does not necessarily win all the battles.

The notion that a newspaper office is a Tower of Babel with a multiplicity of views on policy is a myth. I could not pick up a copy of Crockford's *Guide to the Clergy*, or the ABC *Railway Guide*, or Sutton's seed catalogue, without instantly thinking of a highly opinionated editorial. But, however facile he may be with his pen, however ferocious and compelling his advocacy, if you ask the average newspaper leader writer, 'What are we going to say today?' he will look at you as if he has never seen you before.

In the Mirror Group the Chairman is never the controlling share-holder because there isn't a controlling shareholder. Like any other director, the Chairman is elected and can therefore be dethroned. Of the last three chairmen I was the only one to give up the throne peacefully, at the time I said I would, and of my own volition. But the dismissal of two chairmen over a considerable period of time was not a sign of instability in one publishing house which did not exist in others. You can't fire the proprietor but you can ask an elected chairman to retire. Other publishing houses occasionally envied this unique facility.

I did not seek, in any permanent sense, to be a resident in Valhalla, and the sniping was as much fun as the support and the occasional applause. It is never displeasing to read the view which Alan Watkins attributes to Iain Macleod:

'His view, which he expounded to me several times, was that in any country, certainly in Britain, there was only a small number capable of assuming the highest responsibilities. He generally cited Lord Cudlipp (as he now is), Lord Beeching and himself . . . What counted was "ability", which remained undefined. Macleod's view was that, as with the elephant, you could recognise it when you saw it.'[1]

[1] *Politicians and the Press* by Alan Watkins, to be published by Jonathan Cape, 1977.

But there were less flattering, perhaps more realistic, views. Among my favourites was the remark by Clive James, reviewing in the *Observer* a BBC TV documentary entitled 'Cudlipp and Be Damned':

'A lawyer, Mr Ellis Birk, set the general tone of the programme . . . by leading off with the ringing assertion that Cudlipp was "the greatest tabloid journalist of all time". It was hard to still a wicked interior voice which insisted on pointing out that this was tantamount to calling a man the greatest manufacturer of potato-pistols who had ever lived, or the greatest salesman of sticky sweets in the history of dentistry. Nevertheless such a naughty itch required ruthlessly to be suppressed.'

How powerful is the Press? I see no reason to change in 1976, after two more decades of experience and observation, the view I held in 1953:

'The assumption that newspapers form and control public opinion cannot be substantiated: newspapers sell in spite of their policies as much as because of them. However brilliantly or subtly it may be conducted, a Press campaign will fail

if it flies in the face of public opinion;

if it advocates a course of action which the average reader instinctively rejects as unfair or imprudent; or

if it deals with an aspect of life beyond the readers' daily experience or interest.

'The newspaper with integrity and a ripened sense of responsibility may advocate lines of national action whether its public are interested or not. But a campaign will flourish only

if it is in tune with public opinion which already exists;

if it stimulates with new ideas and information a process of thought already formed in the minds of the masses;

if it advocates a solution to a problem or scandal already angering the average reader.

'A newspaper may successfully accelerate but never reverse the popular attitude which common sense has commended to the public. Where there is evidence of public wrath over a political or social issue it may effectively direct that feeling against an individual, but the newspaper which lightly or wrongfully apportions blame will find that public contempt will boomerang against itself.'

With few exceptions in my time the British public exhibited more sense, and sense of history-instinctively, not intellectually–than most of the politicians and the Press. The people were uneasily aware of the Hitler menace in 1933 when Stanley Baldwin was cynically concealing the need for rearmament so that he could win the election of 1935. There was no response to Winston Churchill's idiotic campaign against independence for India because it was unreal and unjust, it tried to halt human progress, it defied the thoughts of the untutored about what was right and wrong. Beaverbrook's puerile assurance, in ever bigger type, that 'There Will be No War' was a device designed to reassure his advertisers but it didn't delude his readers. Neville Chamberlain's egocentric notion that he, of all men, could chat up the dictators and maintain peace in Europe on honourable terms was a confidence trick which diverted public attention from the real issue, but only fleetingly. *They* turned to Churchill as the wartime supremo but *they* rejected him as peacetime leader as soon as the war was over: the public has a memory, and its instinct was sound on both occasions. In his first speech in the first post-war election Churchill said that the Socialist system could not be established without a political police, a Gestapo. The Beaverbrook Press proclaimed: 'Gestapo in Britain if Socialists Win'. But the Socialists won and there was no Gestapo. Churchill and Beaverbrook didn't know, or affected not to know, the difference between National Socialism (German) and Socialism (British). The public has a basic common sense. Cecil King's curt dismissal of Harold Wilson in 1968 merely strengthened his position in the Labour Party. When the Labour Party was tearing itself to shreds over the issue of the Common Market, the referendum among the people was decisive.

No. I do not overrate the power of the Press or the oratory of the politicians. The *Mirror* 'Vote for Him' campaign in the post-war election of 1945 turned what would have been a very comfortable Labour victory into a Labour landslide. The minuscule Labour majority of 1964 would have been a minority if the *Mirror* had not run its ear-splitting pro-Labour campaign, and there were other elections in the post-war years in which the *Mirror* exerted some small influence. But the power of the Press is no greater than it should be.

Newspapers, like any other business, have to make money for their proprietors or shareholders and feed and clothe their staff. Newcomers to the industry, a few of whom–notably Alex Jarratt– have made a great contribution, at first find themselves wondering,

'What is the difference between publishing news and canning beans or making motor cars?'

There are differences. News is more perishable than fresh strawberries or cream. Nothing is staler than yesterday's except the day's before. You can't pop it in the fridge until the demarcation or redundancy dispute, or bloody-minded go-slow, is settled even on dishonourable terms. Hot information has the life span of an ephemera, the insect which lives only for a day. Even Leyland or Chrysler can still flog their end-product, however delayed, when the shop stewards are gracious enough to allow production to proceed.

The mayfly transience of news, and the betrayal of the advertiser who often provides a newspaper's principal revenue, inevitably lead to capitulation by management and shameful exploitation by the unions. Another factor which does make newspapers different from the canning of beans is the traditional sense of public service among the best elements in the industry.

Somebody, not I, will one day write a book about the finance of the British Press, but it will be no more or less interesting than the finance of any other industry.

The Mirror Group was in an enviable position during its growth period because of the high profitability of its central product. In the Cowley and Bartholomew years the *Mirror* board was protected by the *Pictorial* board, and *vice versa*, from a take-over bid from outside. When, during the exciting Cecil King expansionist period the business grew into the International Publishing Corporation, the result of our own marauding, the sheer size of the mammoth enterprise was, hopefully, its own protection. But there were other equally big or bigger fish in the sea as the industry faced its troika of problems–the phenomenal rise in the cost of the basic raw material, newsprint, over-manning, and the high cost in redundancy payments for the overdue technological change.

Covetous eyes were studying the IPC balance sheets to assess the possibilities of splitting the Corporation into parts, selling the divisions to the highest bidders, or absorbing one or some of them, and exploiting the property amassed when IPC itself was on the rampage in the take-over business. The Odhams buildings in Covent Garden were a succulent bait. Lord Kearton of Courtaulds had ideas, and visited my office to propound them. Robin Gill, formerly Lord Grade's deputy at Associated Television, was engaged in talks with Rothschild and Lazard. Samuel Newhouse, the American publisher, was pondering a deal with Bowater to make a bid for IPC.

The choice for IPC was not whether to remain independent or merge with Reed, with whom it had been in harness for many years (with the whip cracked by IPC), but whether to negotiate a merger with Reed (with the whip cracked by Reed) or continue to risk a take-over bid by outsiders. The birds of prey who were circling around had powerful resources.

IPC lost its freedom to act with complete commercial independence and became a division of Reed. What it gained was the greater financial strength of the new larger structure at a time when mounting problems were facing the whole of the publishing industry and some publishers were seeking Government aid to finance the new technological revolution in production. Don Ryder, now Lord Ryder, Chairman of the National Enterprise Board, then Chairman and Chief Executive of Reed, became the head man of the combination. One of the agreements of the merger was that IPC would continue to exercise the complete editorial freedom of all its publications. This was essential to the newspapers and on no single occasion did Ryder deviate from that agreement.

I had decided, as my friends knew many years in advance, to call it a day in the newspaper business when I reached sixty. I had been running newspapers in one capacity or other since I was an Editor at twenty-four. Old men are tiresome in journalism, and I did not want to be a tiresome old man like Bartholomew, jealously and cantankerously bullying instead of gently persuading younger performers with new approaches. My principal assets as a communicator were that I knew what the 'ordinary people' were thinking, understood their fears and aspirations, and was sympathetic to the ever-changing outlook on life of the younger generation. Anyone attempting to substantiate such claims after the age of sixty would in my view be a charlatan.

In October 1972, fifteen months ahead of my departing date, I repeated my belief that people in the top creative jobs in journalism should be eager and happy at a certain time to hand over to younger men. 'I shall be sixty next year. Our newspapers especially appeal to the younger generations, and I feel it would be an unpardonable vanity for a man of over sixty to have the final word on editorial plans and policies.'

There were useful by-products in making the announcement well in advance. There could be no rumours, damaging to the company, of internal dissensions following the Reed take-over two and a half years before. It demonstrated that it was possible to relinquish the chair-

413

manship of IPC of one's own volition and in one's own time, without palace revolutions and television appearances on the theme of 'I wuz robbed'. There was a new scene in Fleet Street, and the new editorial cast at the head of the Mirror Group newspapers would know, at more than a second's notice, the roles they would be likely to be called upon to play. They would not be trammelled, in a new situation, with the standards and philosophy I had favoured in the past but were possibly less sacrosanct than I had imagined.

For me, personally, there were other by-products. I demonstrated that I did not delude myself with the self-satisfying megalomania of editorial indispensability, that I had no pretension to water-walking. At sixty you can do other worthwhile things that can't be embarked upon at sixty-five or seventy.

My brother Percy, Herbert Gunn (Editor of the *Evening Standard*, the *Sunday Dispatch*, and then the *Daily Sketch*), Percy Elland (*Evening Standard*) and, of course, Arthur Christiansen (Editor of the *Daily Express*)–they all died at the job years before they were sixty. I was one who got away.

I decided that the Prime Minister, the Archbishop of Canterbury, the Pope and various other functionaries, the Soho vice vendors, the BBC, the trade unions, Scotland Yard and the bolshie undergraduates would have to carry on in future without my advice or admonition. The younger generation would have to fend for itself. So far as I was concerned the same went for the soccer hooligans, gabby coroners, defaulting insurance companies and the MCC. I was happy to see that on March 16 this year the Rt. Hon. Harold Wilson followed my example and said good-bye to Downing Street at three score years, to be 're-deployed' as Sir Harold.

The House of Lords is full of the re-deployed, for the most part distinguished or significant men and women I have encountered, usually in combat, in public life.

Lord Home over there: when he became Prime Minister in 1963 I described him as a nice chap and a polite peer, Alec (not Smart Alec–just Alec), and wrote an editorial called 'Brand X is the Boss'. Lord Shinwell, now ninety-two, a little peeved with me when I invited him at seventy to write an article under the headline 'By An Angry Old Man'. Lord Gardiner, our leading counsel in the Liberace case, and Lord Salmon, the judge who presided over the hearing. Lord Goodman, to whom I sent a cheque for £40,000 for his client Lord Boothby after a defamatory article in one of our newspapers when I was painting my boat in Honfleur. Bob sits not far from him on the Cross Benches. Lord George-Brown, with whom I occasionally have a glass of wine in the Bishops' Bar. I wrote an editorial about him during the Labour Party Conference at Scarborough in 1967 when George was Foreign Secretary. It extolled his brilliant speeches, his many qualities, his courage, but he cannot have relished the opening sentences:

> The trouble about Mr George Brown is not that he drinks too much, but that he shouldn't drink at all.
> His best friends know it, but his enemies won't tell him.
> Genial George was born with so much natural ebullience that all it needs is a splash of soda . . .

Lord Hailsham is pleasantly and brilliantly prominent on the Tory Front Bench; the former Lord Chancellor who, as an MP in 1940, was wondering why I hadn't been called up. Lord Avon is there occasionally, vociferously opposed by the *Mirror* when he embarked upon the Suez campaign as Prime Minister, but deeply touched when the same newspaper wrote gratefully of his career as a whole during one of his wretched illnesses. So is Lord Wigg, who described me rather rudely as 'a Fleet Street hack' when Duncan Sandys appointed me a member of the Grigg Commission into pay and conditions in the Services. George Wigg publicly praised the report when it was published, and I reminded him on a later occasion that Randolph Churchill was awarded £5,000 in damages when *The People* had called *him* 'a Fleet Street hack'. Lord Sandys also appears in the Upper House. And Baroness Summerskill, who wrote progressive articles for me in 1935 when I was Features Editor of the *Mirror*; and most of the union leaders who liked to chide me at annual TUC conferences on the iniquities of the *Mirror*. And, recently, Selwyn Lloyd, the retired Commons Speaker who said to Jodi, 'How do you like being married to Danger Man?'

I don't know whether old men forget. They certainly forgive.

ACKNOWLEDGMENTS

C & T Publications Ltd for the Winston Churchill letters in Chapters 8 and 9; MacGibbon & Kee for extracts from *Aneurin Bevan* by Michael Foot in Chapter 14; Hamish Hamilton for *The Mirror: A Political History* by Maurice Edelman in Chapter 3; the BBC, ITN, Fleet Street friends and their publishers, notably the *Guardian*, for quotations from their interviews and comments which play an essential part in the narrative. I thank Sir Max Aitken for his permission to publish a letter he wrote to Cecil King concerning Lord Beaverbrook.

The following have supplied photographic material; Saidman Brothers (*facing page* 64, *bottom*); War Office (*facing page* 161, *top*); *Punch* (*facing page* 193, *top and bottom*); Planet News (*facing page* 320, *top*); the BBC (*facing page* 320, *bottom*); Press Association-Reuter (*facing page* 321, *top*); Keystone Press Agency (*facing page* 352, *top*); the *Observer* and Richard Willson (*facing page* 353, *top and bottom*); and Central Press Photos (*facing page* 385, *bottom*).

INDEX

INDEX

Adam, General Sir Ronald, 153
Adamson, Iain, 238
Age, Melbourne, 196, 199
Aitken, Sir Max, 186, 286, 313, 373
Alexander of Tunis, Earl, 161–5,
  167, 222
Amery, Leo, 117
Anderson, Sir John, 123, 125, 127,
  132
Answers, 37
Ardwick, Lord, (*see* John Beavan)
Argus, Melbourne, 199, 200, 205
Ascroft, Eileen, 64, 99, 187, 188,
  214, 230, 257, 258, 302
Astor, Hon. David, 408
Atkins, H. W. 'Tommy', 244, 311,
  362, 380, 406
Attlee, Earl, 63, 67, 99, 127, 129–31,
  175–7, 192, 210, 212, 220, 223
Avebury, Lord (Eric Lubbock), 342
Avon, Earl of (Anthony Eden), 72,
  89, 91–3, 104, 120, 132, 145, 206,
  209, 211, 213, 226, 228, 229, 230,
  415

Baldwin, Earl, 32, 63, 64, 70, 72,
  73, 75, 80, 91, 92, 101, 102, 104,
  106, 108, 318, 331, 411
Balogh, Lord, 350
Barbados Advocate, 230, 282
Barkworth, Harold, 183
Barnes, Dr Alfred, Bishop of
  Birmingham, 20, 177, 178, 179
Bartholomew, Harry Guy, 9, 51–6,
  59–72, 75, 79, 83–6, 89, 129, 130,
  135, 171–3, 182–5, 193–6, 198–
  200, 203, 205, 206, 243, 259, 260,
  270, 277, 281, 286, 307, 354, 367,
  379, 412
Baxter, Sir Beverley, 278

Beavan, John (Lord Ardwick), 213,
  218, 220, 247, 248, 313, 320, 321,
  322, 329
Beaverbrook, Lord, 8, 13, 29, 49, 70,
  74–6, 83, 100, 120, 126, 128–30,
  148, 157, 172, 186–94, 285–90,
  311, 331, 342, 382, 401, 407, 408,
  411
Beecham, Sir Thomas, 272
Beeching, Lord, 321, 409
Benn, Anthony Wedgwood, 341,
  342
Berry, Michael (*see* Lord Hartwell)
Berry, Pamela (*see* Lady Hartwell)
Bevan, Aneurin, 31, 34, 42, 188,
  206, 212, 214, 215, 222, 223, 289
Beveridge, Lord, 122, 285
Bevin, Ernest, 26, 120, 123, 130, 141
Beyfus, Gilbert, 231–8
Birk, Baroness (Alma), 357
Birk, Ellis, 66, 247, 331, 335, 349,
  357, 375, 377, 378, 381, 388, 416
Black, Sheila, 279
Blackett, Lord (Professor Patrick),
  285, 385
Blunt, Dr Alfred, Bishop of
  Bradford, 179, 180
Bolam, Silvester, 174, 193, 194
Booth, Nathaniel, 44
Boothby, Lord, 100, 220, 414
Bosanquet, Reginald, 356, 357
Bottomley, Arthur, 292
Bottomley, Horatio, 65, 96, 200, 315
Boyd, Francis, 312
Boyne, H. B., 392, 393
Bracken, Lord (Brendan), 100
British Army Newspaper Unit,
  153–5, 159
British Gazette, 32
British Worker, 32

Brooke, Rupert, 143
Brownlee, L. D., 52
Budd, Major Edward, 152
Butler, D. E., 218
Butler, Lord (Rab), 122, 132, 133, 211, 214, 218, 222, 393, 402

Caldecote, Viscount (Sir Thomas Inskip), 120
Callaghan, James, 295, 315, 319, 331, 333, 341, 342, 344
Campbell, Stuart, 86, 87, 143, 171, 173, 407
Camrose, Lord, 83, 129
Capp, Andy, 403
Cartwright, Gordon, 349, 366
Cassandra (Sir William Connor), 50, 57, 60, 64, 65, 72, 73, 75, 77, 80, 83, 89, 129, 132, 133, 135, 144, 145, 158, 159, 198, 222, 225, 231–8, 321, 330, 405
Castle, Barbara, 292, 319
Castlerosse, Lord, 290
Chamberlain, Joseph, 288
Chamberlain, Neville, 76, 91–5, 97, 98, 100–6, 108, 110, 114, 116–20, 123, 124, 130, 143, 183, 328, 411
Champion, Ralph, 38, 406
Chancellor, Sir Christopher, 247
Chandler, John, 350, 377
Charles, H R H Prince of Wales, 208
Charlton, Warwick, 152
Chichester, Sir Francis, 244
Christiansen, Arthur, 172–4, 186, 187, 289, 401
Christiansen, Michael, 407
Churchill, Randolph, 29, 338, 415
Churchill, Sir Winston, 32, 33, 56, 63, 70, 78, 80, 94, 99, 100, 104, 106, 108–10, 114, 116–23, 127, 128, 130–4, 136, 144, 145, 147, 150, 152, 157, 161, 192, 206–11, 219, 230, 232, 235, 282, 283, 288, 311, 328, 384, 411
Clark, General Mark, 159, 162–7

Clausewitz, Karl von, 147
Coleman, Terry, 253
Collins, Norman, 390
Cook, A. J., 26, 27, 31, 34
Cooke, James, 69, 195
Coolican, Don, 404
Coope, John, 367
Cooper, Duff, 105, 121
Country Life, 273
Cowley, John, 51, 53, 55, 56, 60, 61, 71, 81, 84, 89, 115, 129, 136, 171, 412
Cripps, Sir Stafford, 173, 285, 288, 289
Cromer, Earl of, 331
Crossman, Richard, 156, 222–4, 265, 271, 308, 309, 319, 337, 340, 350, 371, 393, 405
Crusader, 158, 177
Cudlipp, Percy, 13, 16, 23–5, 28–30, 49, 99, 187, 248, 259, 289, 401, 414
Cudlipp, Reginald, 13, 16, 17, 30, 35, 38, 39, 259
Cummings, A. J., 180

Daily Express, 65, 70, 76, 172, 174, 186–94, 248, 250, 274, 285, 286, 309, 345, 348, 362, 401, 405, 407, 414
Daily Herald, 13, 16, 99, 129, 212, 213, 224, 246–51, 307
Daily Mail, 32, 35, 51, 52, 54, 61, 63, 65, 70, 76, 78, 158, 172, 199, 250, 251, 345, 373, 407, 408
Daily Mirror (Sydney), 195
Daily News (New York), 49, 54
Daily Record (Glasgow), 60, 307, 329, 392
Daily Sketch, 49, 50, 242, 414
Daily Telegraph, 49, 78, 129, 209, 231, 243, 293, 307, 309, 313, 350, 367–9, 392, 393
Daily Telegraph (Sydney), 195, 201
Daily Times (Nigeria), 182

Daily Worker, 134, 135
Davenport, Keith, 335
Davidson, Reverend Harold (Rector of Stiffkey), 45
Davis, William, 252
Dawson, Geoffrey, 74, 76, 77, 79
Day, Robin, 322
de Gaulle, General, 154, 315, 372
de Launay, Basil, 249, 302
Dépêche de Constantine, 155, 156
Dinsdale, Dick, 248, 250
Docker, Lady Norah, 402
Drawbell, James Wedgwood, 49, 50, 259
Driberg, Tom (Lord Bradwell), 369

Economist, The, 210, 285, 369, 392
Edelman, Maurice, 64–6, 75, 79
Eden, Anthony (*see* Lord Avon)
Edinburgh, HRH Duke of, 180, 181, 325, 326, 404, 405
Edward VIII (Duke of Windsor), 70–6, 179
Edwards, Robert, 252, 321, 407
Eighth Army News, 152, 158
Eisenhower, General Dwight D., 152, 161, 162, 209
Elizabeth II, HM the Queen, 180, 181, 325, 326, 345
Ellerman, Sir John Reeves, 188–91, 288, 377, 378
Ellerman, Lady, 188, 189
Elliott, Sydney, 248
Elwyn-Jones, Lord, 309
Evans, Harold, 408
Evening Chronicle (Manchester), 43,
Evening Express (Cardiff), 31   [44
Evening News (London), 408
Evening Standard (London), 13, 29, 30, 49, 70, 128, 187, 252, 259, 289, 315, 367, 373, 393, 401, 414

Fairclough, Alan, 218
Falkender, Baroness (Marcia), 291, 298, 331

Ferris, Paul, 263
Fleet, Kenneth, 368
Field, Xenia, 239
Financial Times, 33, 279, 310, 355, 367
Foot, Michael, 223, 289, 336, 369
Foster, J. Kemp, 35–42
France Soir, 226
Fraser of Lonsdale, Lord (Sir Ian), 189, 190
Fuller, General J. F. C. ('Boney'), 99, 143, 144
Fyfe, Hamilton, 50

Gaitskell, Hugh, 32, 206, 212–15, 222, 227, 247, 249, 265, 316
Gale, George, 321, 322, 361, 392
Gallico, Paul, 87
Gardiner, Lord (Gerald), 214, 231, 232, 309, 414
Garland, Ailsa, 406
Garvin, J. L., 102
George-Brown, Lord, 249, 296, 315, 342, 414, 415
Gill, Robin, 412
Goebbels, Dr Joseph, 79, 102, 115, 135
Goering, Hermann, 115, 175, 176
Goodman, Lord (Arnold), 414
Goodman, Geoffrey, 406
Goodman, Mark, 238
Gordon, John, 57, 66, 187, 192, 193,
Gourlay, Logan, 192   [273
Grade, Lord (Lew), 202, 307, 412
Grant, David, 84
Gray, Bernard, 97, 390
Green, Felicity, 301, 406
Greene, Graham, 13
Greenwood, Walter, 270
Grigg, Sir James, 157
Grimond, Jo, 214, 304, 314
Guardian, 33, 156, 180, 211, 225, 231, 253, 279, 300, 310, 313, 314, 316, 317, 332, 360, 367, 369, 372, 408

Gubbins, Nathaniel, 193
Gunn, Herbert, 414

Hailsham, Lord (Quintin Hogg),
   141, 214, 217–20, 122, 403, 415
Hair, Gilbert, 239
Halifax, Lord, 99, 120, 221
Hamilton, Sir Denis, 339
Hamlyn, Paul, 366, 380, 390, 397
Hardcastle, William, 192, 330, 377
Harding, Field-Marshal Lord, 151,
   155
Harmsworth, Alfred (see Lord
   Northcliffe)
Harmsworth, Cecil, 263
Harmsworth, Esmond (see Lord
   Rothermere)
Harmsworth, Geoffrey, 263
Harmsworth, Harold (see Lord
   Rothermere)
Harmsworth, Vere, 408
Harris, Bernard, 189, 191
Hartwell, Lord (Michael Berry),
   246, 313, 350, 408
Hartwell, Lady (Pamela Berry), 309,
   350
Healey, Denis, 294
Hearst, William Randolph, 281,
   407
Heath, Edward, 216–18, 220, 298,
   300, 312, 314, 327, 331, 346, 374,
   384, 405
Henderson, Rupert, 196, 205
Herbert, Sir Alan (A.P.), 29
Hirshfield, Lord (Desmond), 298
Hoare, Sir Samuel, 120, 283
Hogg, Quintin (see Lord Hailsham)
Home, Lord, 206, 215–19, 294, 414
Hope, Bob, 192
Horniblow, Bill, 199
Howard, Anthony, 273
Howard, Lee, 320, 358, 407
Howard, Peter, 289
Hulton, Sir Edward, 213
Hutber, Patrick, 334, 339

Hyland, Jodi, 230, 296, 302, 349,
   371, 415
Hyman, Joe, 304

Innes, Ralph Hammond, 163
Irving, Clive, 393

Jacobson, Lord (Sydney), 212, 213,
   218, 225–8, 248, 250, 295, 318,
   322, 335, 407
James, Clive, 409
Jane, 65, 237
Jarratt, Alex, 411
Jay, Douglas, 265, 292, 314
Jenkins, Clive, 35
Jenkins, Jennifer, 344, 371
Jenkins, Peter, 300, 316, 317
Jenkins, Roy, 294, 317, 319, 333,
   334, 336, 337, 344, 345, 358, 368,
   371, 372, 374
Jennings, Richard, 56, 60, 75–80, 89
Johnson, Paul, 373
Jon, 158
Jones, Aubrey, 390
Jones, Jack, 35
Jones, Kennedy, 50
Jones, Robert, 368
Jones, Thomas, 106, 107
Juda, Elsbeth, 310
Juda, Hans, 310
Junor, John, 215

Kaye, Danny, 192
Kearton, Lord, 412
Kemsley, Lord, 43, 44, 49, 311
Kennedy, Joseph, 285
Kennedy, Robert, 361
Keynes, Lord (Maynard), 285
Khrushchev, Nikita, 30, 33
King, Cecil Harmsworth, 9, 10, 30,
   32, 52–4, 60–4, 66–8, 73, 74, 77,
   79, 81–9, 92, 93, 96, 99, 104, 107,
   114, 116–18, 125, 127, 129–34,
   141, 145, 171, 172, 182–4, 193,

194, 199–201, 203, 204, 206, 221,
222, 224–7, 235, 237, 242, 246–9,
253, A Man of Destiny, 255–397,
402, 411, 412
King, Colin, 278
King, Francis, 278
King, Lady (Geraldine Harms-
worth), 261–4, 274
King, Sir Lucas White, 261, 264,
296
King, 'Margot' (Agnes Margaret),
262, 270, 390
King, Michael, 278, 349
King, Dame Ruth (Dr Ruth
Railton), 293, 307, 345, 350, 360,
362, 374, 384, 391, 394, 396

Lancaster, Terry, 406
Lanchester, Elsa, 56
Lang, Archbishop, 74
Laughton, Charles, 56
Lee, Baroness (Jennie), 339
Levin, Bernard, 393
Levy, Phillip, 222
Liberace, 220, 231–8
Liddell Hart, Basil, 99, 111, 112,
143, 144, 285
Lloyd George, David, 8, 13, 14, 28,
33, 42, 99, 105–12, 118, 194, 262,
313, 318, 384
Lloyd-Hughes, Sir Trevor, 298
Low, David, 102, 198

Machray, Douglas, 248
McKay, Alex, 199
Macleod, Iain, 216, 218, 295, 409
Macmillan, Harold, 67, 91, 118, 151,
155, 161, 206, 211, 213–17, 219,
295, 387
Mahood, 316
Margach, James, 334
Margaret, HRH Princess, 182
Martin, Kingsley, 210
Massingham, Hugh, 206

Matthews, Tom, 225
Maudling, Reginald, 218, 344
Maxwell, Robert, 252
Mayhew, Christopher, 210, 279
Medawar, Sir Peter, 385
Mee, Arthur, 28
Melbourne Herald, 200, 202
Mellor, William, 248
Menon, Krishna, 228
Mikardo, Ian, 336, 339, 369
Miles, Anthony, 10, 407
Mirror Magazine, 253
Molloy, Mike, 82
Monckton, Lord (Sir Walter),
229, 230, 285
Montgomery, Field-Marshal
Viscount, 152, 157, 222
Moran, Lord, 207, 208
Morning Star, 243
Morrison of Lambeth, Lord
(Herbert), 32, 120, 123, 126, 131
131–6, 284
Mosley, Sir Oswald, 62, 63, 265,
322, 393–5
Mountbatten, Countess, 188
Mountbatten of Burma, Earl, 188,
193, 288, 303, 304, 324–7, 341
Muggeridge, Malcolm, 28, 29, 213,
389
Murdoch, Sir Keith, 199, 202, 203
Murdoch, Rupert, 203, 205, 246,
249, 252, 302

Nelson, Bob, 199
Nener, Jack, 407
News Chronicle, 163, 180, 207, 231,
251
New Scientist, 13
News of the World, 13, 16, 17, 30,
196, 246, 252, 259
New Statesman, 67, 129, 210, 213,
222, 373
Newspaper Proprietors' (later
Publishers') Association, 70, 126,
128, 129, 342

Newton, Sir Gordon, 279
Nicholson, Basil D., 49, 50, 55, 56, 59, 259
North, Rex, 173
Northcliffe, Lord (Alfred Harmsworth), 9, 50–4, 65, 76, 83, 257, 261–6, 274, 281, 283, 288, 299, 311, 313, 316–8, 338, 362, 373, 381, 382, 387, 392, 395, 407
Northcliffe, Lady (Molly), 274
Norton, Ezra, 195, 198, 200, 201, 205
Norton, John, 200, 201, 407

O'Brien, Lord (Leslie), 332
Observer, 33, 102, 206, 322, 338, 348, 408, 409
Ocean News, 149, 150
Olivier, Lord (Laurence), 193
Owen, Frank, 128, 289

Packer, Sir Frank, 195, 201, 202
Paisley, Dr Ian, 396
Parker, Bryan, 333
Parnell, Bunny, 37, 42
Paterson, Peter, 371, 372
Patience, John, 199, 200
Payne, Reg, 290, 407
Pearl, Cyril, 200
Penarth News, 34, 35, 37, 39, 41, 270
Penarth Times, 38
People, The, 87, 129, 252, 318, 321, 407, 415
Pétain, Marshal, 107, 113
Pickering, Edward, 60, 289, 325, 329, 342, 349, 407
Picture Post, 213
Pilger, John, 361, 406
Pinnington, Geoffrey, 252, 407
Powell, Enoch, 323
Profumo, John, 217, 219, 220
Proops, Marjorie, 406
Punch, 147, 252

Quick, Arnold, 349, 355, 381

Railton, Dr Ruth (see Dame Ruth King)
Randall, Michael, 252
Reed International, 203, 412
Ress-Mogg, William, 408
Reith, Lord, 177, 380, 383
Ribbentrop, Joachim von, 102, 106, 115, 175
Rigby, 198
Robb, 158
Robens, Lord (Alfred), 304, 308, 312, 315, 321, 324, 340
Robertson of Oakridge, Lord (General Sir Brian), 162–6
Robertson, E. J., 192, 311, 382
Robinson, John (Bishop of Woolwich, 1959–69), 20
Rochez, Harry, 249
Rogers, Frank, 250, 305, 306, 349, 351–4, 362, 365, 366, 369
Rommel, Field-Marshal Erwin, 150–1
Roome, Wallace, 51, 84, 86, 129
Roosevelt, President Franklin Delano, 136, 150, 152, 162
Rose, Sir Alec, 245
Rothermere, Lord (Esmond), 70, 73, 74, 129, 172, 263, 373, 408
Rothermere, Lord (Harold), 51, 53, 61–3, 66, 67, 77, 78, 96, 237, 266, 278, 297, 317, 318, 331, 338, 381, 387, 407
Rubinstein, Artur, 350
Runyon, Damon, 87
Russo, Peter, 200
Ryder, Lord ('Don'), 351–4, 379, 388, 413

Sainsbury, Lord, 315
Salmon, Lord (Cyril), 231–8, 414
Sandys, Lord (Duncan), 216, 415
Sapt, Arkas, 51

Scott, Laurence, 279
Selwyn-Lloyd, Lord, 215, 217, 344, 415
Shawcross, Lord (Hartley), 224, 304, 308, 348
Sherren, Veere, 306
Shinwell, Lord (Emanuel), 285, 338, 414
Short, Edward, 337
Smuts, Field-Marshal Jan, 109
Smythe, Reggie, 403
Soames, Sir Christopher, 217, 219
South Wales Echo, 28, 29
Southwood, Lord, 129, 282
Spectator, 253, 321
Springer, Axel, 259, 266
Stephens, Peter, 311, 406
Stevens, Jocelyn, 281
Stewart, Michael, 292
Suffern, Roy Thistle, 56, 60, 72
Summerskill, Baroness (Edith), 415
Sun, 213, 242, 246–53, 302, 318, 329
Sunday Chronicle, 49, 50
Sunday Express, 57, 76, 115, 186–95, 215, 285, 286, 309, 359, 360, 378, 392
Sunday Telegraph, 158, 309, 339, 371, 408
Sunday Times, 252, 309, 311, 322, 339, 349, 373, 408
Sutherland, Graham, 310–12, 315, 388
Sutherland, Kathleen, 311
Sydney Morning Herald, 196

Taylor, A. J. P., 65
Terry, Walter, 345
Thackeray, Ralph S., 156, 158, 171
Thatcher, Margaret, 147
Thomas, Cecil, 53, 59, 74, 81, 83, 135, 184, 185
Thompson, J. Walter, 49, 50, 54
Thomson, George Malcolm, 29, 187, 289

Thomson, Lord (Roy), 246–8, 280, 307, 311, 373, 382, 408
Thorneycroft, Lord (Peter), 216
Times, The, 33, 51, 70, 74, 76, 77, 92, 111, 243, 279, 309, 313, 316, 348, 350, 367, 368, 377, 391, 408
Tribune, 393
Truth (Australian), 195, 196, 198, 200, 201, 408
Tullett, Tom, 403, 404
Turnbull, Clive, 199

UK Press Gazette, 340
Union Jack, 152, 156–8, 160–5, 177

Valdar, Colin, 340, 407
Vansittart, Lord (Robert), 99
Vansittart, Lady (Sarita), 99
Vicky, 207, 222

Waite, Keith, 198
Walker, Philip, 367
Wallace, Edgar, 51
Waller, Ian, 334
Walters, John, 69
Ward, Baroness (Barbara), 285
Wardell, Brigadier Mike, 148
Waterhouse, Keith, 405
Waterlow, Sir James, 258
Watkins, Alan, 409
Watts, David, 310
Waugh, Evelyn, 49
Week, The, 134
Weinstock, Sir Arnold, 304
Wells, H. G., 125
Western Mail, 31, 34
Weston, Garfield, 340
Whitcomb, Noel, 402
Whitlam, Gough, 203
Wigg, Lord (George), 65, 415
Wilberforce, Charles, 94–6, 98, 101, 102
Williams, Bob, 19
Williams, Francis, 248
Williams, Sir John, 199

Williams, Mrs Marcia (*see* Baroness Falkender)
Williams, Sir Owen, 272
Wilson, Sir Harold, 9, 32, 202, 210, 218, 221, 244, 258, 259, 282, 284, 291–300, 307, 309, 310, 312–16, 318, 319, 322–31, 334, 335, 337–340, 342–7, 358, 359, 363, 369, 371, 372, 374, 384, 411, 414
Wilson, Lady (Mary), 331, 344, 371
Wilson, Peter, 40, 86, 142, 158, 406
Windsor, Duchess of, 70–4, 179
Winn, Godfrey, 57, 144, 193

Winterton, Deryck, 218
Wintour, Charles, 407
Woman, 246, 248, 307
Woman's Mirror, 230
Woman's Own, 246, 307
Woman's Weekly (Australia), 196
Wyatt, Woodrow, 210, 405

Zec, Donald, 402, 405
Zec, Philip, 60, 66, 134–6, 185, 193
'Zeno', 239, 240
Zuckerman, Lord (Solly), 326, 327